Contents

Series Preface

J. Kevin Nugent

*Univ. of Massachusetts at Amherst
and Children's Hospital
Harvard Medical School*

In the year 1626, Thomas Nugent, a farmer living at Coolamber in the county of Westmeath in Ireland was cutting turf when he came upon a pair of giant antlers. "They were the only wonder of those halcyon days because of their prodigious largeness", wrote Sir William Piers in 1682. When they were cleaned and erected on Mr. Nugent's wall "they were no less than twelve feet in length and the palms out of which the smallest horns branched, were as broad as the targets, which in those days men of the blade used to wear" (Piers, p. 52). In fact, the Giant Irish Elk was the largest deer that ever lived and his antlers have never been exceeded. Their size seem all the more impressive as paleontologist Stephen J. Gould points out, when we recognize they were grown and re-grown annually (Gould, 1977).

The giant deer evolved during the glacial period of the last few million years but became extinct in Ireland about 11,000 years ago. The question that has engaged scientists ever since has been why the giant deer became extinct. The most popular explanation has been that the giant antlers were an example of overspecialization and that the Elk, weighed down by the excessive weight, became defenseless and died out. However, recent studies have shown that in fact there is a strong positive correlation between antler size and body size in the Irish Elk, so that the original overspecialization argument for its extinction must be rejected. Why then did the giant deer become extinct? The consensus among paleontologists today is that the Irish Elk flourished in Ireland for only a brief warm period of 1000 years, but was unable to adapt to the cold epoch that followed (Gould, 1977). Extinction became the fate of the giant deer because they were unable to adapt to the changing conditions of climate. For man on the other hand, it is his biological plasticity and his capacity for adaptation over a wide range of environments that has constituted his success as a species. Unlike the ill-fated Irish Elk who was locked into his environment, man has been able to transform his environment in order to meet his survival needs. In the end it is his capacity for material culture that has enabled the human species to forge new and unique adaptations in every corner of the globe.

The range and variety of the different expressions of adaptation is nowhere more evident than in the diverse ways in which societies protect, nurture, and educate their young. Although parenthood is a universal phenomenon, patterns of child-rearing are highly variable across the human species. Over the last fifty years, anthropologists have documented the diversity of child-rearing practices in different cultures and have consistently demonstrated the degree to which the environments of infancy and early childhood are shaped by cultural values and practices (e.g., LeVine, 1980; Whiting & Whiting, 1975; and Whiting & Edwards, 1988). In a parallel but complementary tradition, cross-cultural studies in psychology have shown that differences exist in newborn behavior among cultural groups around the world. While the basic organizational processes in infancy are universal, it is argued, the range and form of these adaptations are shaped by the demands of each particular culture (Lester & Brazelton, 1982).

However, despite this growing comparative tradition, it must be acknowledged that much of our contemporary knowledge of child development is the product of Western cultural history (Bronfenbrenner, Kessel, Kessen, & White, 1986). Kessen and Cahan (1986) in their review of the history of psychology also conclude that child development as a scientific endeavor has been a predominately North-American-European enterprise and as such could be characterized as a narrow and essentially local tradition. Given the narrow database, there is a growing awareness that the empirical findings of child development cannot be generalized to most of the world's children today.

The overarching goal of this series therefore is to add to the database of research in infant development by describing the developmental processes of infancy over a wide range of cultural and social environments. By presenting multiple alternative examples of the context of infant development, our goal is to stimulate continued discussion on the ways in which biological, social, and cultural factors influence the course of human development from the beginning. Specifically, the goals of the series are: (1) to assemble reports of original empirical research on infancy from different countries around the world, (2) to present this material from a variety of disciplinary perspectives, (3) to document the use of the Neonatal Behavioral Assessment Scale (NBAS) as a research tool in different cultural settings, and (4) to ultimately examine the relationship between biology, culture, and infant development by documenting different neonatal environments and child-care practices in different cultures. Finally, we hope that these studies will not only extend the depth and richness of the existing canon of infancy research but because of the diversity of settings will challenge our core assumptions about infancy on the one hand and our beliefs about the nature of child development itself on the other.

References

Bronfenbrenner, U., Kessel, F., Kessen, F., & White, S. (1986). Toward a critical social history of developmental psychology. *American Psychologist, 41* (11), 1218–1230.

Gould, S. J. (1977). *Ever since Darwin.* New York: Norton.

Kessen, W., & Cahan, E. (1986). A century of psychology: From subject to object to agent. *American Scientist, 74,* 640–650.

Lester, B. M., & Brazelton, T. B. (1982). Cross-cultural assessment of neonatal behaviors. In D. Wagner & H. Stevenson (Eds.), *Cultural perspectives on child development.* San Francisco: Freeman and Co.

LeVine, R. A. (1980). A cross-cultural perspective on parenting. In M. Fantini & R. Cardenas (Eds.), *Parenting in a multicultural society.* New York: Longman.

Piers, Sir W. (1981). *A chronological description of the county of Westmeath, 1682.* Naas: Meath Archeological and Historical Publications.

Whiting, B. W., & Edwards, C. P. (1988). *Children of different worlds: The formation of social behavior.* Cambridge, MA: Harvard University Press.

Whiting, B. B., & Whiting, J. W. M. (1975). *Children of six cultures: A psychocultural analysis.* Cambridge, MA: Harvard University Press.

Acknowledgments

We would like to offer our sincere thanks to Marie Donovan, Harvard University, who contributed so much to the preparation of this first volume; to Patricia Scott, Harvard University and Belfast, Northern Ireland; to Carmen Peralta, Brown University; to John Hendler, University of Massachusetts at Amherst and to Kate Neff, Child Development Unit, Children's Hospital, Boston. Above all, we offer our sincere thanks to Barbara Bernstein and Walter Johnson who have unflinchingly supported this enterprise from the beginning. We would also like to thank the Ablex staff, in particular Patricia Higgins, Production Coordinator, and Carol Davidson, Production Manager.

Foreword

Lewis P. Lipsitt

Brown University

From the earliest days of work in the child development field, interest has centered on two major domains of inquiry. The first has to do with the generality of the laws of human behavior and development. In this domain, we are interested in knowing what kinds of regularities exist in the universe of development. Questions asked are of the type, At what age do most children first smile, crawl, walk, speak in three-word sentences, and use logical principles in reasoning? G. Stanley Hall's 1891 work on "The Contents of Children's Minds" addressed the question of whether children of different ages think differently and hold in memory different constellations of ideas. This piece of Hall's work was mostly about developmental, maturational, or "age-determined" differences in human attributes.

Another fascination that child developmentalists have had from the start has been with individual differences. Not all children of age 8 have, to borrow further from Hall, precisely the same "mental contents." Indeed it is virtually impossible to study generalities in behavior and development without exploring and documenting somehow the variety of ways in which one can be 8 years of age. The very presence of variation in characteristics that exist in the generality commands attention to variation. It is this variation, combined with measures of central tendencies for any groups studied, that permits discovery of statistically reliable group differences—as between 4-year-old children and 6-year-olds, or between British and American children, or between those who speak one language and those who speak another.

It is extraordinarily important that we become knowledgable not only about general laws of early development and behavior, but about group and individual differences as well. Verities relating to the human condition and the diversity of life conditions go hand in hand, sharing equal status in a world of inquiry that seeks to understand everything. Indeed, if we are to understand the origins of human behavior and the full range of determinants of human development, it is imperative that once we have first grasped the presence of differences we address the fact that different life "conditions" and destinies are the result of different histories. Ideally, at any given point in a person's life, it would be possible to study where the person's current status (conditions or attributes) came from, and what the developmental consequences are likely to be. Access to the infant enables at once the study of the consequences of fetal and birth antecedents and the relevance of these early characteristics for subsequent life trajectories. Cross-cultural studies of infants and infancy also show the great impact of environmentally arranged conditions in our pursuit of knowledge about outcomes. They especially illuminate the presence of individual differences at birth, the products of hereditary factors and the intrauterine milieu, and the plethora of early developmental outcomes that are possible.

Individual differences in humans are dictated in part, of course, by chromosomal variations. While hereditary factors as determinants of life destinies are well acknowledged in the scientific literature and in public conceptions of how people get to be the way they are, not enough attention has yet been paid to such early developmental antecedents as the moment and intent of conception, the quality of the fetal environment, delivery maneuvers, style of neonatal care, and attitudes of the caretakers toward babies. Some of these differences are clearly culturally linked, varying from one social group to another; others are familial, and others are idiosyncratic. In any event, newborn babies, and humans in the first years of life, are different from one another, both within and between cultures. A full understanding of the human condition must take great care to honor those differences and explore their origins. Studying infants cross-culturally, moreover, permits exploration of a wider range of relevant parameters than is available in any one culture, and thus allows examination of a greater breadth of potential within the species. It would be impossible, for example, to study in humans the effects of bottle versus breast feeding, or protracted versus short-term breast feeding, if the culture under study forbids or constrains certain feeding practices; where no mother in the culture breast-feeds beyond the child's sixth month, it is impossible to know the consequences of longer-term breast feeding. Thus, through exploring a larger range of human conditions, cross-cultural studies serve the overarching goal of understanding humankind in general, while revealing the uniqueness of specific cultures and their practices. Such studies especially illuminate the consequences for a culture of specific social limitations and permissions, as well as the impact on individuals of the rules of the culture, particularly non-normative, outlying, or "deviant" individuals. For example, a long-term breast-feeding mother in North America is regarded very differently from a mother engaging in the same practice in Kenya.

This volume is a veritable cornucopia of information about infancy the world over, about the vast variety of conditions under which children are conceived and raised, and about the characteristics of the infants themselves. Questions addressed here relate to such issues as:

1.   what childbirth and infants are like in a culture where teenage pregnancy is normative rather than scorned.

2. the effects on neonatal behavior and development of intrauterine nutritional deprivation.

3. the conditions of recovery, and the recovery phenomenon itself, of infants born under or enduring perinatal distress.

4. the effect of altitude of birth location (an interesting "cross-cultural/geographic" variable) on the size and morbidity of infants.

5. the influence of smoking, drug intake, and other teratological factors in a large group, in this case, Swiss women.

6. the behavioral characteristics of neonates in Nepal, one of the least-developed countries of the world.

7. the neonatal condition and development of Efe pygmies in Zaire, in which culture the common practice is to pass new babies around frequently from one adult to another.

8. the superior motor competence in American black neonates (with no differences due to socioeconomic level), in comparison with American Caucasians.

9. infant behavior in a very poor culture where undernourishment is typical, but in which massage, oil rubs, and motor exercise are frequently given.

10. the effects of extended contact by rooming-in practices in the neonatal period on the behavior of Portuguese mothers and their infants.

11. effects of enhanced mother-infant contact in the special care nursery on performance of the baby, satisfaction of the mother, and nursery personnel.

12. the differences in behavior of neonates and their mothers from varying social groups and geographic/ethnic origins in Israel.

13. a comparison of Chinese, Malay, and Tamil newborns, all of them born in Malaysia.

14. a study of a displaced Laotian culture, the Hmongs, to the United States, in which the babies were studied five times from birth to 18 days of age.

15. temperamental factors in a study of American Indian babies.

The studies are "wrapped up" in an Afterword by one of the co-editors of the volume, pediatrician/researcher T. Berry Brazelton, whose Neonatal Behavior Assessment Scale (NBAS) is the glue that holds the studies together. In this final chapter, in which he summarizes all the chapters and provides a critical commentary on some, Dr. Brazelton emphasizes the importance of the neonatal period for understanding both babies and their mothers. As in many of the chapters, he alludes to contemporary ways of looking at infants, not merely as responders to the environmental stimulation in their midst, but as self-regulating and stimulating creatures in their own right. The NBAS is used widely today not only as a research and clinical tool for assessing the capabilities of infants in the first 30 days of life, but also for instructing parents about the full range of behavioral capabilities of infants. Indeed, the baby's own characteristics can and do generate responses from the caretakers. Both baby and mother are learning about each other, and from each other, from the very beginning.

This volume is a valuable research resource, representing significant advances in the cross-cultural and developmental understanding of the period of infancy and of babies themselves—and of the many different ways of being an infant, and being a parent.

PART I
BIOSOCIAL INFLUENCES ON NEWBORN BEHAVIOR

Chapter 1

Ecocultural Context and Developmental Risk: Birth in the High Altitudes (Peru)*

Carmen Saco-Pollitt

Department of Psychology
University of California
Davis, CA

Introduction

Life in high altitudes, whether in Ethiopia, Peru, Bolivia, or Nepal, is life under some degree of physical and biological stress (Little & Baker, 1976; Pawson, 1976). Above approximately 3,000 m (10,000 ft) there are particular biophysical environmental characteristics, such as low oxygen and barometric pressure, reduced relative humidity, reduced gravitational force, increased radiation, and marked variation of temperature in relatively short periods of time, which create an ecological context significantly different from any other in the world. In this context the growth and development of children is shaped to reach a level of biological adaptation that does not affect either reproductive competence or energy balance. Otherwise, survival would be endangered. The effects of high altitude on the physiological adaptations of children and adults have been well documented. There is a scarcity of information, however, on the effects of high altitude on the psychobiological and social development of children.

In 1973 it was estimated that about 30 million people in the world lived at or above 3,000 m, and a high proportion of them lived in the Andes. In Peru, specifically, it was estimated on the basis of census data that in 1970, 100,000 infants were born at altitudes above 3,000 m (Sobrevilla, 1973).

* Portions of this chapter have been previously published as "Birth in the Peruvian Andes: Physical and Behavioral Consequences in the Neonate." *Child Development, 52*(1981), 839–846. The research for the experimental portion of this chapter was supported in part by National Science Foundation Grant BNS-76-21603.

The study outlined herein assesses the newborn behavior of native Peruvian Andean children born at approximately 4,300 m above sea level in a mining center in the central Andes, Cerro de Pasco. A comparison is made of their performance on the Brazelton Neonatal Behavioral Assessment Scale (hereafter, BNBAS; see Brazelton, 1973) at two points in time during the first 60 hours of life, with that of infants born in Lima, at 150 m (490 ft) above sea level. A secondary purpose of this study is to compare body size measurements of both groups of infants.

In addition to the contribution of these data to the understanding of the growth and development of infants living in high altitudes, the findings have theoretical relevance to cross-cultural research. These data illustrate how the ecological context may adversely influence a child's growth and development, and they raise questions regarding the biological and cultural mechanisms that may enter into play to protect the developmental course of the young organism.

The Broad Ecological and Cultural Context: The Andean Region

The Andean *altiplano* ("high plateau") is a large section of the South American Andes, rising above 2,500–3,000 m. It stretches from Colombia in the north to Chile in the south. The most significant environmental stress at this altitude is hypoxia, a reduction of the amount of oxygen reaching body tissues. Other stresses are cold, humidity, high solar radiation, high winds, rugged topography, and poorly developed soils, with marginal availability of certain nutrients (P. T. Baker, 1969; Dollfus, 1976; Frisancho, 1975; Petropoulous & Timiras, 1974; Thomas & Winterhalder, 1976).

Native and traditional agricultural products are quinua, oca, maize, barley, and potatoes. Nutritional surveys in Nuñoa, in the southern Andes, show that these are still the basic constituents of the staple diet, with little consumption of animal protein (Picon Reategui, 1976). Traditional livestock include members of the camel family: the llama, guanaco, alpaca, and vicuña.

The Inca empire had its center in the Andean altiplano. The core ethnic groups of the native Andean population, the Quechuas and the Aymaras, originally were agricultural people. These peoples underwent significant cultural changes following the arrival of the Spaniards. The *conquistadores* arriving in Peru in the 15th and 16th centuries left reports on the stressful effects of high altitude. During Francisco Pizarro's campaign in the highlands, for example, soldiers suffered from mountain sickness and horses collapsed from exertion. It was also reported that in the highlands "the production of a live child by Spanish parents was a rare, almost unique phenomenon" (Monge, 1948). Such observations most likely encouraged the Spaniards to move their capital from the highlands to the coast, where most Europeans settled.

Social and Demographic Characteristics

People living in the Andes—particularly in the rural areas—have an extremely low admixture of genes from Europeans, and virtually none from African peoples (Baker, 1969). Differences exist between regions, however, with the most populated areas having a larger proportion of admixture. The few cities in the altiplano have been made primarily Hispanic, whereas the rural areas retain, to a large extent, the cultural patterns prevalent before the arrival of the Spaniards (Baker, 1969).

The social structure in the high Andes can be characterized, in gross terms, as being related to race as well as to degree of Westernization and wealth. The terms used for class designation are related to race: *mestizos* (of mixed Indian and European blood); *cholos* (acculturated Indians); and *indígenas,* or indigenous Indians (Quechua and Aymara). The criterion in making social distinctions uses both ethnic and economic characteristics, as well as signs of modernization, such as wearing Westernized clothing and speaking Spanish, the official language of Peru. A substantial number of Indians speak exclusively Quechua or Aymara. In certain regions the category of *blanco* is used for those who claim pure European descent.

Photo 1.   Peruvian Andean mother and children near high-altitude study site.

Biological Adaptation to High Altitude

Upon abruptly rising into altitudes above 2,500 m, lowlanders generally suffer respiratory distress, shortness of breath, fatigue, dizziness, vomiting, headache, and an increased, rapid pulse rate. This symptomatology subsides as transport of oxygen adapts to the low pressure of the oxygen in the ambient air (Frisancho, 1975). Adaptation represents a mechanism of compensation, through changes in the cardiovascular, hematologic, and respiratory systems, for the reduction of oxygen in the tissues to increase oxygen volume (Lenfant & Sullivan, 1971). A highland native, conversely, uses a greater amount of oxygen per unit of body weight than does the recent migrant (Baker, 1969). Among natives there is an increment in the total lung capacity and an absolute and relative increase of residual air. There is a positive correlation between altitude and transverse thoracic diameter of natives (Monge, 1968).

In contrast to this comparatively large lateral growth, the linear growth of the Andean native tends to be smaller than that of the lowlander of the same genetic stock (Haas, 1983). A critical question in connection with this finding is whether the small size is an adaptation to high-altitude conditions, or whether it is the result of a deficient diet. Growth assessments of middle- and upper-class children, as well as studies of migrants from low-to-high and from high-to-low altitudes, suggest that the growth retardation observed in the Andean native is generally due secondarily to the ecology of the high altitude, rather than a deficient diet (Haas, 1983). Moreover, the results of animal experimentation controlling for dietary intake concur with the findings of studies on humans (Petropolous & Timiras, 1974). In summary, the adaptive value of small stature in the highlands has not yet been conclusively determined (Frisancho, 1977; Haas, 1983), though small stature in the Andean native has not been associated with any particular symptomatology indicative of a pathological process.

Compared to populations living close to sea level, the probabilities of infant mortality and low birthweight are increased at altitudes past 2,500–3,000 m above sea level (Grahn & Kratchman, 1963; Haas, Baker, & Hunt, 1977; Mc-Clung, 1969). Mazzes (1965) assessed the relationship between infant mortality and altitude among the 24 departments (the largest administrative units in the country) of Peru. A correlation of .70 and .73 for 1958 and 1959, respectively, were found between the altitude of the capitals of the departments and the respective neonatal mortality. Mazess controlled for total death rate and post-neonatal death rate to obtain a more accurate estimate of the relationship between neonatal mortality and altitude. The lowest partial correlation obtained was .53, which was still highly statistically significant.

McCullough, Reeves, and Liljegren (1977) assessed the relationships between gestational age, birthweight, and infant mortality between 1960 and 1973 in the state of Colorado in the United States. A significantly higher infant morality rate was observed in the high-altitude area (above 2,749 m as compared to lower-altitude areas (below 2,130 m), although medical facilities were either similar or better in the high-altitude region. These differences were primarily determined by a much greater neonatal mortality rate in the high-altitude as compared to the lower-altitude areas. Moreover, the deaths occurred primarily among preterm infants (gestational age < 38 weeks).

Dutt (1974) compared the infant mortality of children at three altitude levels (< 500; 2,500; > 3,700 m). The socioeconomic and educational level of the mothers was controlled by rigorous selection of the samples, and all had similar access to medical facilities. As expected, there was a linear relationship between infant mortality and altitude. These differences, however, were explained solely by differences in neonatal mortality. These findings concur with those from McCullough et al. (1977).

Nelson (1984) recently completed an analysis of the relationship between infant mortality and altitude in Peru, restricting the sample to 98 provinces (out of 146) lying over 1,500 m above sea level. In contrast to previous studies, Nelson also had (for each province) aggregate data on maternal illiteracy and educational level, minimum monthly wages, services (e.g., water, electricity), and percent of economically active men in agriculture. To estimate the portion of the infant mortality variance that could be accounted for by altitude, Nelson used a regression analysis and entered the altitude variable as the last predictor variable in the equation. Illiteracy was the most potent predictor variable, but altitude still accounted for a large and statistically significant portion (22%) of the variance. The available evidence suggests that the association between altitude and birthweight is due to slow intrauterine growth and is not the result of a short gestational period (McCullough et al., 1977). Experimental laboratory work also shows a DNA and lipid content reduction and delayed myelinogenesis in rodents exposed to high-altitude conditions (Cheek, Grayston, & Rowe, 1969; Petropoulous, Vernadakis, & Timiras, 1969). The functional integration of the central nervous system is also affected in these conditions, as indicated by immature response of young rodents to electroshock treatment (Timiras & Wooley, 1966).

The form and shape of the placenta have distinctive features in pregnant women in the Andean region. In high altitudes the placentas are heavier and have a higher volume and a larger total area of the villous and capillary surface than do placentas at sea level (Kadar & Saldana, 1971; Kruger & Arias Stella, 1979). There also is a higher ratio between the weight of the placenta and that of the newborn infant (Sobrevilla, 1971). These morphological and morphometric traits may be protective of the fetus, but this contention has not yet been documented.

Whether the delay in fetal development observed in high altitudes also affects the central nervous system remains unknown. Metcoff, Novy, and Petterson (1967) have suggested that the intrauterine environment of the pregnant mother protects the fetus from the adverse biophysical characteristics of the high-altitude environment. The available evidence on the atypical growth of the fetus at high altitude does not support this hypothesis. In addition, the effects of undernutrition of pregnant women on the growth of their fetuses suggest that the offspring are not necessarily protected by the intrauterine environment. Newborn infants of malnourished women have shown important behavioral differences as compared to appropriate controls (Brazelton, Tronick, Lechtig, Lasky, & Klein, 1977).

The present study was undertaken to assess the behavior of infants born in high altitudes. The rationale behind it lies in the epidemiological concepts of web of causality and web of effects. The epidemiological approach to causality postulates that generally there is no single agent that causes one specific effect; rather, there are a series of contributory or antagonistic factors that determine the final outcome. Likewise, it assumes that one specific etiological factor may have an array of effects as a function of the contextual setting (Stallone, 1972). In connection with high altitude, it is assumed here that the stress factors associated with neonatal and infant mortality, as well as with intrauterine growth retardation and low birthweight, may also have effects on the early development of the central nervous system.

Child-Rearing Practices in the High Altitudes

A critical question in connection with the biophysical stress to which newborns are exposed in the high altitudes is: What caretaking practices have been adopted by the natives to protect the survival and development of their young in such an environment? What has been the cultural response to the ecological pressure?

LeVine (1969), among others, postulates that a sociocultural system selectively implements child-rearing practices that have been functional in a given context. This selectivity does not mean an explicit decision was made by the members of the system; choices can be made without awareness of the selection process or of the adaptive functions that a particular caretaking practice may fulfill. Therefore it may be inferred that the predominant child-rearing practices used by cultural groups have been selected and maintained to a large extent because they protect the organism against environmental pressures. For example, Whiting (1981) has shown that climate is an environmental determinant of the ways in which infants are carried by caretakers and of the frequency of physical contact between mothers and infants. He shows that the colder the winter temperature, the higher the frequency of cradles being used to carry infants.

The low oxygen pressure, the cold environment, the abrupt changes in temperature, the topological and climatic limitations on agriculture and, therefore, on the availability of nutrients, are some of the stressors that affect the growth and development of infants in high altitudes. Child-rearing practices directed to the regulation of body temperature, to the protection against upper respiratory infections, and to meeting nutrient requirements are therefore particularly important.

It must be noted that there is hardly any information on the anthropological and psychosocial aspects of infant development in the Andean region. There are some ethnographic reports from different regions of the altiplano, but most of these reports do not provide substantive information on sampling. The observations presented here must therefore be taken cautiously.

Throughout the rural districts and in some urban areas of the altiplano the delivery of infants is generally attended by the *comadrona* (midwife), who bathes the baby immediately after birth. In some areas (e.g., Andahuaylas) the objective of this bath is to prevent "rotting of the body" (Castillo Rios, 1975). This bath may be in cold water, and it may be a week before the baby is bathed again. Among natives there is the strong belief that frequent baths could affect an infant's lungs, resulting in pneumonia (Castillo Rios, 1975).

T. S. Baker (1976) points out that clothing with insulating qualities and the use of solar radiation to raise body temperature are cultural responses to reduce the stress from cold. In Nuñoa, for example, infants are dressed from birth in at least three layers of homespun clothing: diapers and undershirt; a tunic and sometimes leggings and socks; one or more sweaters; and a knitted hat. This clothing, combined with infrequent diaper changes, provides a warm, humid envelope that protects the infant against low temperature and low humidity at the same time. There are reports from both the central and the southern Andean region (Kardonsky-Titelman, 1982) that clothing may not be changed for periods of about 15 days because of fear that the child may catch cold. At home, during the day, the child is placed in the sunniest area adjacent to the house. When the child is being nursed the mother usually sits near the fire (T. S. Baker, 1976). In certain Andean regions, during the first months of life, the baby sleeps close to the mother (Kardonsky-Titelman, 1982), and with siblings in other regions (Baker, 1976). When the mother leaves the home she usually carries the infant tight against her back; often infants are placed in such a way that they cannot move either arms or legs (Haboud de Ortega, 1980; Kardonsky-Titelman, 1982; Zamalloa Gonzales, 1976).

In some parts of Cuzco the constant proximity of the mother and infant is explained by the people's belief that the spirits of their ancestors and the high mountains represent aggressive forces which are constantly on the watch for new young souls whom they can take away. The people believe that the spirits of their ancestors have the power to make the infants feeble and ill. This belief is the explanation often given by some women in Cuzco as to why they carry their very young babies on their backs when they go to work in heavy agricultural activities (Haboud de Ortega, 1980; Zamalloa Gonzales, 1976).

Throughout the rural Andean region, over 90% of infants are breast-fed, and this generally lasts up to about the 2nd year of life (T. S. Baker, 1976; CEPAL, 1983; Cornejo Muñoz, 1972). By about 4 months of age some additional form of feeding is introduced, generally light soups. According to Zamalloa Gonzales (1976), there is a different treatment in the feeding of boys and girls. The former receive complementary feeding earlier but are breast-fed for a longer period of time. Gonzales also claims that there is a difference in the quality of the foods given. Boys are more likely to receive animal protein at an earlier period. Greater attention to males is related to a belief that males are expected to be stronger and should be protected during the first years of life. There is a clear understanding that infancy and early childhood are the dangerous years, when the risk of death is high.

High infant mortality probably determines the formation of realistic expectations regarding the likelihood of survival among infants. Castillo Rios (1975) notes that parents in the Andes generally do not take an infant's death as a tragic event. It is generally assumed that this has been "God's decision" and as such must be accepted and respected.

The Ecological and Cultural Context of the Study: Cerro de Pasco

Cerro de Pasco, the site of the present study, is located in the central portion of the Andean altiplano, 300 km northeast of Lima. Its altitude is 4,300 m (about 14,200 ft) above sea level; the oxygen pressure is estimated at 82 mm of mercury (mmHg), and the barometric pressure is about 750 mmHg. With about 34,000 people, it has the largest population at this altitude in the world (Del Valle & Sobrevilla, 1973).

Cerro de Pasco is an important mining center, producing mostly copper, but also vanadium, silver, gold, zinc, and bismuth. It is built practically on top of the mine beds and in an uneven terrain. The physical environment is far from hospitable, being extremely cold and arid. During the day, temperatures oscillate between 10 and 13 °C; night temperatures go down to 8 °C from July to December and below 0 °C from December to may. In the latter months there is abundant rain, hail, or snow, with frequent and violent storms in the early hours of the afternoon.

There is scarcely any vegetation in Cerro de Pasco, except for the *ichu* (natural pasture). As it is a relatively large and active city compared to other urban centers in the Andes, the availability of imported food has increased. The market is more active than in most cities in the Peruvian sierra. The industrial development related to mining exploitation there is also atypical for the region.

The mines in Cerro de Pasco, discovered in 1630, were exploited by Spaniards and mestizos during the 17th and 18th centuries. In 1902 a North American company, the Cerro de Pasco Copper Corporation, negotiated an agreement to take possession of a major portion of these and other mines in the Andes and established a financial center of enormous influence in the Peruvian sierra, and in the rest of the country as well. In 1973 the Peruvian government recovered control of the total operation, which is today run by Centromin Peru, the government mining industry. This was the administrative and political situation when the data for this study were collected from June to December 1976.

Cerro de Pasco does not have a stable population. As a mining center it attracts people from near and faraway towns and villages, and the in-and-out migration must affect the gene pool of the population. This remains an uncontrolled variable in studies of adaption to high altitudes in the region. High-altitude adaptations that may evolve over generations may not be present among migrants.

Cerro de Pasco was selected as the site of the study for two reasons: (a) The Hospital La Esperanza, where the sample of babies was obtained, provides probably the best medical care in the Peruvian Andean region; and (b) the Institute of High Altitude Studies from the Cayetano Heredia school of medicine provided access to its laboratory in Cerro de Pasco, contacts with the community, and lodging facilities.

Demographic and fertility data on Cerro de Pasco are available from a carefully conducted survey sponsored by the Institute of High Altitude Studies (Del Valle & Sobrevilla, 1973). Two probability samples were used, one from households and the other from women attending a family planning program that had been in operation for 4 years. From the total population (about 34,000 inhabitants), 47% were under the age of 15. Only 28% of the inhabitants were natives of the area. Marital unions were formed at a young age for women; slightly less than 25% of the women 15–19 years old were already part of a conjugal union, including both consensually and officially married women.

Photo 2.   Mother and child of Cerro de Pasco.

Half of the housing consisted of only one room. The average number of people per household was 5.1. Over 90% of the households had electricity, 39% were connected to the potable water system, and 20% had indoor bathroom. The mining corporation provided communal showers, toilets, sinks and outdoor faucets in the housing of mining workers; 87% of the households had a radio.

Of the population over 5 years of age, 28% had no schooling (8% of those had had some type of day care or preschool experience), 46% had from 1 to 5 years of elementary education, and 22% and 4% had some secondary and college education, respectively. A larger number of women (31%) than men (10%) had never attended school. The situation is changing rapidly in Cerro de Pasco, however, as children who are 7 to 14 years of age have rates of school attendance of over 90%.

The household survey indicated that in 4 years there had been a decline in infant mortality rates, from 100 per 1,000 to 70 per 1,000 live births. This rate is substantially lower than the 190 per 1,000 live births reported for the province of Pasco, where Cerro de Pasco is located (Amat y Leon, 1981). The incidence of childhood mortality rates varies sharply with socioeconomic status: 61% of women in the lowest status group have had at least one child die, while only 30% among the highest status group have had a child die.

The mean desired number of children for women 15–49 years old in a conjugal union was 4.4; the mean for women who had attended the family planning clinic was lower, 3.9 (or half a child less). The mean number of children desired by the women varies inversely with socioeconomic status, from 5.0 to 3.8 from the lowest to highest classes, after standardization for age.

The sample for the present study was obtained from the mining industry hospital and is restricted to families with one member working in this industry. It is important to note that mining workers—skilled and semiskilled—have substantially higher salaries than other workers in Cerro de Pasco. They also have better health care available. Their hospital is known to provide good medical care to pregnant women and newborn infants. The standard quality of medical care in the altitude samples provided a way to control the possibility that differences between the samples were related to factors other than altitude.

Methods

Sites. The high-altitude sample was obtained from the Hospital La Esperanza in Cerro de Pasco (4,300 m). The low-altitude sample was obtained in Lima (150 m), where the newborns were selected from the Hospital del Rimac (associated with one of the two leading medical schools in Peru) and from the Hospital Central No. 2, which provides services to public and private employees.

Subjects. The two altitude samples were composed of 20 female and 20 male newborns in each. Entry criteria included: length of gestation estimated to be between 38 and 41 weeks, using Usher's procedure (Usher, McLean, & Scott, 1966); Apgar score of 7 or more at 1–5 min; full gestation and birth occurred in the respective altitude sites; mothers in the two samples living in low- and high-altitude regions, respectively, for a period of no less than 5 years immediately prior to the conduct of the study; maternal age between 16 and 39 years; exclusion of multiple births; the first stage of labor not longer than 24 hr, second stage not longer than six hr, ruptured membranes not longer than 24 hr, and no hemorrhaging or shock; normal delivery; no evidence of congenital abnormalities, cephalohematoma, or bruising; no clinical evidence of sepsis, icterus above 14 mg, seizures, or hemorrhage. In addition, birthweights had to fall within the 10th and 90th percentiles of the birthweight distributions for the respective altitude populations.

In the absence of regional standards, the following descriptive statistics were calculated from medical record data: In Lima, 2,648 records from a 12-month period from the Hospital del Rimac were reviewed, and 25% of them were randomly selected. The 10th and 90th percentiles were calculated to be 2,701 and 3,890 g, respectively. In the Hospital La Esperanza in Cerro de Pasco all, or 427, records for a similar time period were reviewed; the 10th percentile was at 2,240 g and the 90th percentile at 3,370 g.

Both samples were matched for father's and mother's education and for father's occupation. For statistical control of confounding covariate effects, data also were collected on gestational age, age of mother, mother's height, parity, gravity, last interbirth spacing (see Table 1), and prenatal care.

None of the variables on the mothers' reproductive histories showed statistically significant differences between samples. Maternal height discriminated between samples at a statistically significant level. Also, a comparison of the timing of prenatal care showed that, while in the high altitude 26% of the women made their first prenatal checkup visit in their third trimester, all women in Lima had their first prenatal checkup in the first 6 months of pregnancy ($\chi^2 = 11.21$; $p = .003$). Subsequently, the correlations were calculated between these confounding variables and all the dependent variables. Maternal height was the only variable that correlated with some of the anthropometric variables. Accordingly, its effects were controlled through covariance analysis.

In 10% of the Lima sample, both the patronym and mastronym were

Table 1. Biomedical and Prenatal Variables: _t_-Test Comparisons between High-Altitude and Low-Altitude Samples

	High Altitude			Low Altitude				
	N	M	SD	N	M	SD	t	p
Gestational age (months)	40	39.15	0.86	40	39.35	1.09	0.90	n.s.
Age of mother (years)	40	26.65	5.54	40	25.75	5.83	0.71	n.s.
Mother's height (cm)	38	146.28	5.37	31	154.00	6.12	5.50	.0001
Parity	40	3.42	2.39	39	3.15	2.27	0.52	n.s.
Gravity	40	3.77	2.60	39	3.38	2.38	0.70	n.s.
Last interbirth spacing (years)	32	2.40	1.26	26	2.38	2.08	0.05	n.s.

Quechua; in 30%, one of the two was Quechua. In Cerro de Pasco these distributions were 7% and 27%, respectively. Based on these indicators it can be assumed that the ethnic composition of the two samples was not significantly different.

Measurements

Anthropometry

Following the recommendations by Weiner and Lourie (1969), the body size measurements were obtained when the infants were between 24 and 36 hr old.

Body weight. In each of the two hospitals in Lima and in Cerro de Pasco a scale suitable for infants was used. All scaled were accurate to 5–10 g and were calibrated daily with 1 kg lead weight. Infants were measured without clothing, lying on a diaper or on sterilized paper similar to the one used for calibration.

Recumbent length. Crown-to-heel length was measured with infants in the supine position on an infantometer with a fixed headboard and adjustable footboard. A nurse held the infant's head to the headboard, while slight traction was applied to the legs. Two independent measures to the nearest millimeter were taken for each baby, and an average was calculated.

Head circumference. The maximum circumference of the head on a horizontal plane was obtained using a cloth tape. Measurements were recorded to the nearest millimeter.

Arm circumference. This measure was taken in the left arm midway between the acromion and the olecranon, with the baby in prone position. It was recorded to the nearest millimeter, with a cloth tape.

Triceps skinfold. A Harpenden caliper was used over the left tricep midway between the acromion and the olecranon. The measurement was recorded 60 s after the application of the caliper, when the readings tend to stabilize with newborn infants (Brans, Sumners, Dweck, & Cassidy, 1974).

Subscapular skinfold. A Harpenden caliper was used just below the angle of the left scapula, the fold being picked up parallel to the natural cleavage of the skin.

Correlation coefficients for weight, recumbent length, and head circumference were calculated between the measurements obtained by the investigator (when the infants were between 24 and 36 hr old), and the measurements recorded in the medical records. For the high-altitude sample the correlations for weight, recumbent length, and head circumference were .97, .82, and .85, respectively. These same correlations for the low-altitude sample were .97, .71, and .51. All correlations were highly statistically significant.

Behavior

The BNBAS (1973) was used to evaluate all infants. A first evaluation was carried out when the infants were 24–36 hr old, and a second one was conducted when they were 48–60 hr old. Of the 80 infants, 6 in each altitude sample were evaluated only once because they left the hospital early. The infants were consistently examined halfway between feedings.

The investigator had been trained in the use of the scale in the Boston Hospital for Women under the guidance of a graduate student who had worked with Brazelton's research team. She also completed a reliability check with one of Brazelton's research colleagues at the Child Development Unit at Children's Hospital, Boston.

An advanced psychology student in Lima was trained in the administration of the Brazelton scale to establish a reliability check. The student observed the investigator in the evaluation of 18 infants from the Lima sample. Subsequently, both scored the scale. Intertester reliability was estimated for 10 randomly selected items of the scale with 10 subjects per item. There was an average agreement of 80%. The procedure was not carried out in Cerro de Pasco because of lack of available personnel.

In the two hospitals in Lima, the infants' cribs were wheeled by the investigator to a separate room where she was alone with each baby, except for the 10 cases of reliability check. In Cerro de Pasco all evaluations were made in the nursery where, after the early morning hours, there was little movement of personnel. The age of the infants at both evaluations, as well as the intervals after feeding, are presented in Table 2. The infants in Lima were younger than the infants in Cerro de Pasco in the second evaluation.

Results

Statistical comparisons between samples showed that the infants in Lima, on the average, were heavier and longer and had a larger arm circumference than the infants in Cerro de Pasco (see Table 3). Conversely, the groups did not differ substantially in head circumference and subscapular and triceps skinfolds. Within each altitude group, the male infants were longer and had a larger head circumference than the females.

Table 2. Infants' Chronological Age and Feeding Conditions at Both Behavioral Evaluations

	High Altitude			Low Altitude				
	N	M	SD	N	M	SD	t	p
Age (hrs):								
First evaluation	40	30.1	4.7	40	30.6	4.5	.45	n.s.
Second evaluation	34	54.1	5.2	34	51.4	2.5	2.50	.015
Time after feeding (min):								
First evaluation	40	91.8	34.2	38	102.4	41.2	1.24	n.s.
Second evaluation	32	88.7	32.3	28	106.0	44.4	1.71	n.s.

Table 3.   Mean Values For Anthropometric Measures of Infants in Lima (LA) and Cerro de Pasco (HA)

		LA	HA	M
Birthweight (g)	Boys	3,200.8	2,884.8	3,042.8
	Girls	3,050.0	2,764.8	2,907.4
	Total	3,125.4*	2,824.7*	
Crown-to-heel length (cm)	Boys	49.4	48.1	48.7*
	Girls	48.8	47.3	48.0*
	Total	49.1*	47.7*	
Head circumference (cm)	Boys	34.8	34.6	34.7*
	Girls	34.3	33.8	34.1*
	Total	34.6	34.2	
Subscapular skinfold (mm)	Boys	3.49	3.43	3.46
	Girls	3.63	3.57	3.59
	Total	3.56	3.50	
Tricep skinfold (mm)	Boys	3.41	3.12	3.27
	Girls	3.48	3.22	3.35
	Total	3.44*	3.17*	
Arm circumference (cm)	Boys	10.35	9.77	10.06
	Girls	20.28	9.65	9.97
	Total	10.31*	9.70*	

Note. Analysis of variance was used for subscapular skinfold, while all other anthropometric comparisons were done using covariance analyses. These latter analyses were required to control for the confounding effects of maternal height and weeks of gestation.
$* = p < .05$.

For the analyses of the behavioral data, the Brazelton Scale items were classified into four clusters or dimensions, following the Adamson, Als, Tronick, and Brazelton (1975) conceptual classification of the items in the scale. These analyses were restricted to the 20 of the 26 items that yielded a statistically significant ($p < .05$) reliability coefficient from the correlations of the test-retest scores on the 68 subjects evaluated twice. In the first evaluation 9 (45%) out of the 20 reliable items discriminated between altitude groups at a statistically significant level (see Table 4).

The differences on the Interactive Processes items (Dimension I) indicate that in comparison with the infants born in Lima, the infants in Cerro de Pasco were less likely to be attentive to environmental stimuli in general and less likely to be oriented to the purposely presented visual and auditory stimuli. A similar directional difference was observed in the degree of the infants' responsiveness to being held by the examiner.

The data on Motoric Processes (Dimension II) demonstrate that in comparison with the low-altitude newborns, the high-altitude infants were less active and more hypotonic; their movements were more jerky and they were less likely to keep their heads up when they were moved from a lying to a sitting position. The remaining discriminatory item—Organizational Processes: State Control (Di-

Table 4. High-Altitude and Low-Altitude Samples: Means of Discriminatory Items in the Brazelton Scale, and Summary of Two-Way ANOVA Results

Dimensions	First Evaluation				
	HA	LA	F	df	p
I.					
Orientation inanimate visual	3.91	5.24	4.98	1/62	.029
Orientation inanimate auditory	4.96	5.67	6.02	1/69	.017
Alertness	3.33	4.72	10.20	1/75	.002
Cuddliness	3.80	4.67	5.96	1/75	.017
II.					
General tonus	4.45	5.10	4.29	1/76	.042
Motor maturity	3.84	4.64	7.93	1/74	.006
Pull-to-sit	5.61	6.68	7.37	1/73	.008
Activity	3.50	4.57	16.30	1/76	.0001
III.					
Self-quieting activity	3.70	5.63	13.64	1/73	.0001
Startles					

Dimensions	Second Evaluation				
	HA	LA	F	df	p
I.					
Orientation inanimate visual					
Orientation inanimate auditory					
Alertness					
Cuddliness	4.39	5.29	5.15	1/63	.027
II.					
General tonus					
Motor maturity	4.32	5.35	13.19	1/64	.001
Pull-to-sit	5.18	6.97	15.23	1/63	.0001
Activity	3.70	5.06	22.23	1/63	.0001
III.					
Self-quieting activity	4.09	5.45	8.34	1/62	.005
Startles	3.17	2.44	6.00	1/64	.017

Note 1. Dimension I = Interactive Processes; Dimension II = Motoric Processes; Dimension III = Organizational Processes: State Control; Dimension IV = Organizational Processes: Physiological Response to Stress.

Note 2. Because not all subjects gave scorable responses to all scale items and the number of subjects was reduced from first to second evaluation, the results from each evaluation were analyzed separately instead of using a repeated measure design.

mension III)—suggests that the infants in Lima were more successful than those in Cerro de Pasco in quieting down by themselves.

The only items that discriminated between males and females were part of Dimension IV—Organizational Processes: Physiological Response to Stress—which includes three items. The mean for males (5.16) in the case of Tremulousness was larger at a statistically significant level, $F = 5.22, p = .025$, than the mean for females (4.10). Further, the F value for Startles also showed a clear trend toward statistical significance (M for males $= 3.03$, M for females $= 2.45$), $F = 3.68, p = .059$. These two items indicated that as compared with the female infants, the males tended to show more frequent tremors in the extremities while awake, or sometimes while asleep, and more frequent startles. Difference in sex also determined a significant difference in Lability of Skin Color ($F = 4.56, p = .036$), but in this case there was a trend toward an altitude-by-sex interaction, $F = 3.61, p = .061$. In the high-altitude sample, the male infants had a smaller mean (4.43) than the females (6.37), but in the low-altitude sample the mean for the male newborns (5.35) was slightly larger than that of the females (5.0). These data suggest that in Cerro de Pasco the male infants were more likely to show a more stable and healthy skin color than the female infants. In summary, whereas the items on Tremulousness and Startles suggest a more mature neuromotor behavior on the part of the female infants, in the case of the high-altitude infants the item on skin color suggests the converse.

In the second evaluation, 6 (30%) of the items discriminated between the low- and high-altitude groups. Of these 6 items, 5 were included among the 9 discriminating items of the first evaluation. A notable change between the first and second evaluation is that the discriminating strength of Dimension I is apparently lost. In this classifying group, the number of statistically significant differences dropped from 4 in the first evaluation to 1 in the second evaluation. The only new discriminatory item was Startles, indicating a more mature behavior in the infants in Lima.

Analyses of the main effects of sex, and of sex-by-altitude interactions, showed that the discriminating finding on Dimension IV (Physiological Response to Stress) items of the first evaluation were no longer sustained. In this second evaluation, Self-Quieting was the only item that discriminated between males (4.20) and females (5.32), $F = 5.88, p = .015$. The only analysis of variance that gave a significant treatment by sex interaction was Irritability ($F = 5.48, p = .022$). In this case the means for the male and female subjects in the high-altitude sample were 5.0 and 5.18, respectively, and 6.35 and 4.94, respectively, in the low-altitude sample.

To estimate whether changes that had taken place between evaluations in Dimension I were time dependent, analyses of variance with repeated measures were caluculated on the three items that discriminated between altitude groups in the first but not the second evaluation. None of these statistics showed time effect. There was a statistically significant effect ($F = 5.11, p = .027$), however, for altitude across evaluations in the case of Orientation Inanimate Auditory. In Alertness there was a clear statistical trend toward an altitude effect ($F = 3.35, p = .072$). Accordingly, although there was a decrement of effects from the first to the second evaluation for Dimension I, some of the altitude effects were still observed over some specific interactive processes when the first and second evaluations were combined.

In summary, 9 out of the 26 items in the Brazelton Scale discriminated between the high- and low-altitude samples in the first evaluation. Of these 9 items, 4 are part of Dimension I; another 4 are included in Dimension II; and the remaining item belongs to Dimension IV. In the second evaluation 8 out of the 26 Brazelton items showed statistical differences between groups. Of these 8, 5 were included among the 9 items that discriminated between groups in the first evaluation. Of these 5 items, 3 were part of Dimension II, 1 from Dimension I, and the remaining item from Dimension III. Accordingly, 4 discriminating items in the first evaluation lost their statistical significance in the second evaluation; 3 of these 4 items are included in Dimension I.

Finally, out of 23 between-group comparisons across evalutions using ANOVA for repeated measures, there were 9 that discriminated between groups at a statistically significant level. Of these 9 comparisons, 4 were in Interactive Processes (Orientation Inanimate Auditory; Orientation Animate Auditory; Cuddliness; Consolability); 3 were in Motoric Processes (Motor Maturity; Pull-to-Sit; Activity); 1 in State Control (Self-Quieting Activity); and 1 in Physiological Response to Stress (Startles).

The four a priori dimensions developed by Adamson, et al. (1975) enabled this study to organize conceptually the information collected. As it turned out, the items that discriminated between the high- and low-altitude groups belong to all four conceptual dimensions. To determine whether these differences reflect a set of processes similar to or different from the conceptual categories proposed by Adamson et al. (1975), a principal component analysis with varimax rotation was calculated.

This analysis is restricted to the items that discriminated between groups in the first evaluation. In this analysis, 10 rather than 9 items were included. Response Decrement to Light (from Dimension III) discriminated at a statistically significant level between groups in the first evaluation. The correlation between the first and second evaluation on this item was not statistically significant, however, either in the low-altitude sample or when both high- and low-altitude samples were combined. Thus this item was excluded in the report of the between-group differences for the first evaluation.

As observed in Table 5, the principal component analysis yielded three factors, which in sum accounted for 61% of the total variance. The first factor, which accounted for 33% of variance, included three items from Dimension I (Orientation Inanimate Visual; Alertness; Orientation Inanimate Auditory) and one item from Dimension II (Motor Maturity). Factor II explained 15% of variance and included three items from Dimension II (General Tonus; Pull-to-Sit; Activity) and one from Dimension I (Cuddliness). Finally, the last factor (13%) included two items from Dimension III (Response Decrement to Light; Self-

**Table 5.   Principal Component Analysis for Brazelton Scale Items
That Discriminated Between Groups in the First Evaluation**

Factor 1	Loading	Factor 2	Loading	Factor 3	Loading
Orientation inanimate visual (I)*	.82	General tonus (II)	.87	Response decrement to light (III)	.87
Alertness (I)	.80	Pull-to-sit (II)	.75	Self-quieting activity (III)	.80
Orientation inanimate auditory (I)	.74	Activity (II)	.67		
Motor maturity (II)	.50	Cuddliness (I)	.38		
Variance explained	33%		15%		13%

*Roman numerals in parentheses refer to the dimension to which a particular item belongs according to the conceptual classification by Adamson et al. (1975).

Quieting Activity). The correspondence between the factors of the principal component analysis and the factors proposed by Adamson et al. (1975) is striking.

Discussion

The results of the anthropometric comparisons between the infants in Lima and Cerro de Pasco are in agreement with previous reports from newborn studies in Peru (Haas et al., 1977). There is a difference of 436 g between the mean birthweights of the Cerro de Pasco ($M = 2,824$ g) and the sample ($M = 3,260$ g) studied by Haas et al. (1977) in Puno. There is no substantive difference in altitude between these two locations, however; Puno is 3,780 m above sea level. This difference between samples from the southern and the central Andes has already been noted by Haas et al. (1977) and was attributed to socioeconomic differences.

A comparison of the socioeconomic characteristics of the samples from Cerro de Pasco and Puno does not support this contention. In fact, the data suggest that the people in the Cerro de Pasco sample were probably better off than those in the Puno sample. For example, the mean years of father's education in Puno and Cerro de Pasco were 7.8 ($SD = 3.6$) and 9.7 ($SD = 3.6$), respectively; and of mother's education, 4.5 ($SD = 3.2$) and 6.95 ($SD = 4.2$), respectively. More relevant data are necessary before this developmental intrauterine difference between infants born in the southern Andes and those born in the central Andes is explained.

In addition to the limitations imposed by the high-altitude environment over physical growth, the data from this study show that high altitude also delays the neuromotor development of the fetus. Therefore, the hypothesis (Metcoffd et al.,

1967) that the intrauterine environment of the pregnant mother protects the fetus from the adverse high-altitude environment is not tenable. Specifically, interactive and motoric skills included in the behavioral repertoire of newborn infants are partly affected. This contention is strongly supported by the results of the principal component analysis. The first two factors, which together accounted for almost 50% of the total variance, were formed primarily by items in Dimensions I (Interactive Process) and II (Motoric Processes). It is therefore justified to assumed that the newborns in the high altitude are not as successful in adapting to their environment, at least during the first days of life, as the infants born close to sea level.

Differences between the first and second behavioral evaluations in the number of items that discriminated between the high- and low-altitude samples are apparent in Dimension I (Interactive Processes). In this Dimension, only 1 (Cuddliness) of the 4 items that discriminated between altitude groups in the first evaluation also discriminated between groups in the second evaluation. Note, however, that in the analysis of variance with repeated measures for Orientation Inanimate Visual, Orientation Inanimate Auditory, and Alertness, the time-of-evaluation effects and the time-by-altitude interactions were not statistically significant.

In the case of Orientation Inanimate Auditory there was a statistically significant altitude effect across time, $F = 5.11, p = .027$; and the F value for altitude effect on Alertness was 3.55, $p < .07$. Thus the direction of the differences between the high- and low-altitude samples was the same in 3 out of the 4 items in Dimension I from the first to the second evaluation. Despite the fact that the magnitude of the difference decreased, this consistency must be underscored.

The results of the behavioral observations on the infants in Cerro de Pasco agree with those reported for full-term underweight infants (Als, Tronick, Adamson, & Brazelton, 1976), infants of toxemic mothers (Schulte, Schrempf, & Hinze, 1971), and undernourished newborns in populations having endemic malnutrition (Brazelton et al., 1977). There is a consistent pattern of maturational delay in interactive and motoric processes. Whereas the subjects of those studies represent a clinical population, the subjects in this report represent what is taken as the norm for high-altitude populations. In Peru, well over 100,000 infants are born every year in high-altitude regions.

There is a higher than expected prevalence of minimal cerebral dysfunction among preschool or school-age children diagnosed as full-term, underweight infants at birth (Fitzhardinge & Steven, 1973). This datum and the similarities between the developmental signs of the clinical sample noted above and of the high-altitude infants suggests that the latter group may be at risk for later developmental deficits.

As pointed out in the introduction to this chapter, culture responds to pressures from the ecological context through the selection of child-rearing practices that function as protective or compensatory mechanisms to protect the development of the young child. If high altitude does indeed represent a potent stressful ecological factor, then the Quechua and Aymara cultures must have, over generations, selected child-rearing practices that prevent developmental deficits in the native high-altitude child. There are also biological mechanisms that may enter into play which, along with cultural practices, tend to direct the developmental path of infants and young children toward a normal course.

Recent thinking in developmental psychobiology (Bateson, 1976; McCall, 1981; Scarr-Salaptek, 1976) postulates that humans, like any other animal species, follow a species-typical path (or creod) along which nearly all members of the species tend to develop. This is a self-correcting feature of the developmental process, which canalizes the organism to maintain the species-specific developmental path even under conditions of stress. In the Andean context, this reorienting biological force may, in conjunction with the cultural system, protect the young child from the stress associated with high-altitude hypoxia. In this connection it is important to note that Haas (1976) did not find significant altitude-related differences in the motor development, measured with the Bayley Scale, of 2-month-old to 2-year-old Peruvian infants. After a few months of life, at least, neuromotor development was not affected by high altitude.

Haas and collaborators (1982) also have reported that a longitudinal analysis of physical growth velocity in the first year of life shows that the differences observed between high- and low-altitude infants in Bolivia could be explained by the initial differences in birth size. In that study, the increments of growth in weight and recumbent length suggest very little difference in growth rate. Much of the variation in size throughout the first year of life was related to size at birth. Although birth size is a strong influence in later growth, in this study there is no evidence of further altitude effects. This is also likely to happen in the area of behavioral development; in this case the effects of the birth differences would gradually disappear.

Another illustration of possible adaptive mechanisms in the realm of physical growth and development is the well-documented finding (Frisancho, 1976) that the high-altitude native has a larger lung volume than the lowlander. This enlarged lung volume is possibly the result of adaptations to high-altitude hypoxia during the developmental period (Frisancho, Martinez, Velasquez, Sanchez, & Montoya, 1973).

Cerro de Pasco is located at an unusually high altitude (4,3000 m) and as a mining center it has high influxes as well as migrations of people. The findings of this study could well be restricted to populations living in similar geographical conditions and with similar demographic characteristics.

References

Adamson, L., Als, H., Tronick, E., & Brazelton, T. B. (1975). *A priori profiles for the Brazelton neonatal assessment.* Manuscript available from Children's Hospital Medical Center, Child Development Unit, Boston, MA.

Als, H., Tronick, E., Adamson, L., & Brazelton, T. B. (1976). The behavior of the full-term but underweight newborn infant. *Developmental Medicine and Child Neurology 18*, 590–602.

Amat y Leon, C. (1981). *Desigualdad interior en el Perú*. Lima, Perú: Centro de Investigaciones de la Universidad del Pacífico.

Baker, P. T. (1969). Human adaptation to high altitude. *Science 163*, 1149–1156.

Baker, T. S. (1976). Child care, child training and environment. In P. T. Baker & M. A. Little (Eds.), *Man in the Andes. A multidisciplinary study of high-altitude Quechua*. Stroudsburg, PA: Dowden, Hutchinson & Ross.

Bateson, P. P. G. (1976). Rules and reciprocity in behavioral development. In P. P. G. Bateson & R. A. Hinde (Eds.), *Growing points in ethology*. London: Cambridge University Press.

Brans, Y. W. Sumners, J. E., Dweck, H. S., & Cassidy, G. (1974). A non-invasive approach to body composition: Dynamic skinfold measurements. *Pediatric Research, 8*, 215–222.

Brazelton, T. B. (1973). *Neonatal Behavioral Assessment Scale*. London: Spastics International Medical Publications/Heinemann Medical Books.

Brazelton, T. B., Tronick, E., Lechtig, A., Lasky, R. E., & Klein, R. E. (1977). The behavior of nutritionally deprived Guatemalan infants. *Developmental Medicine and Child Neurology, 19*, 364–372.

Castillo Rios, C. (1975). *Los niños del Perú. Clases sociales, ideología y política*. Lima, Perú: Editorial Universo.

CEPAL. (1983). *Five studies on the situation of women in Latin America*. Santiago, Chile: United Nations.

Cheek, D. B., Graystone, J. E., & Rowe, R. D. (1969). Hypoxia and malnutrition in newborn rats: Effects on RNA, DNA, and protein in tissues. *American Journal of Physiology, 217*, 642–645.

Cornejo Muñoz, R. (1972). *La mujer de Chakan: participación en la vida familiar*. Tesis para optar al título de antropólogo, Universidad de San Antonio Abad del Cuzco.

Del Valle, D., & Sorevilla. (1973). *Cambios de la fecundidad en Cerro de Pasco*. Lima, Perú: Instituto de Investigaciones de la Altura.

Dollfus, O. (1976). Classification and structure of Andean geosystems. In J. Ruffie, J. C. Quilici, & M. C. Lacoste (Eds.), *Anthropology of Andean populations*. Paris: Iserm.

Dutt, J. S. (1974). Altitude, fertility and early childhood mortality: The Bolivian example. *American Journal of Physical Anthropology, 44*, 175.

Fitzhardinge, P. M., & Steven, E. M. (1973). The small-for-date infant, II: Neurological and intellectual sequelae. *Pediatrics, 50*, 50–57.

Frisancho, A. R. (1975). Functional adaptation to high altitude hypoxia. *Science, 187*, 313–319.

Frisancho, A. R. (1976). Growth and morphology at high altitude. In P. T. Baker & M. A. Little (Eds.), *Man in the Andes. A multidisciplinary study of high-altitude Quechua*. Stroudsburg, PA: Dowden, Hutchinson & Ross.

Frisancho, A. R. (1977). Developmental adaptation to high altitude hypoxia. *International Journal of Biometeorology, 21*, 135–146.

Frisancho, A. R., Martinez, C., Velasquex, T., Sanchez, J., & Montoya, H. (1973). Influence of developmental adaptation on aerobic capacity at high altitude. *Journal of Applied Physiology, 34*, 176–180.

Grahn, D., & Kratchman, J. Variations in neonatal death rate and birthweight in the United States and possible relations to environmetal radiation, geology and altitude. *American Journal of Human Genetics, 15,* 329–352.

Haas, J. D. (1976). Prenatal and infant growth and development. In P. T. Baker & M. A. Little (Eds.), *Man in the Andes. A multidisciplinary study of high-altitude Quechua.* Stroudsburg, PA: Dowden, Hutchinson & Ross.

Haas, J. D. (1983). Nutrition and high altitude adaptation: An example of human adaptability in a multistress environment. In R. Djson-Hudson & M. A. Little (Eds.), *Rethinking human adaptation: Social and biological models.* Boulder, CO: Westview.

Haas, J. D., Baker, P. T., & Hunt, E. E. (1977). The effects of high altitude on body size and composition of the newborn infant in Southern Peru. *Human Biology, 49,* 611–628.

Haas, J. D., Moreno-Black, G., Frongillo, E. A., Jr., Pabon, J., Pareja, G., Ybarnegaray, J., & Hurtado, L. (1982). Altitude and infant growth in Bolivia: A longitudinal study. *American Journal of Physical Anthropology, 59,* 251–262.

Haboud de Ortega, M. (1980). *Educación: Un doble proceso. El caso de San Pedro de Casta.* Tesis de grado, Pontificia Universidad Católica del Perú.

Kadar, K., & Saldana, M. (1971). La placenta en la altura I. Características macroscópicas y morfometría. In R. Guerra García (Ed.), *Estudios sobre la gestación y el recién nacido en la altura.* Lima, Perú: Universidad Peruana Cayetano Heredia.

Kardonsky-Titelman, V. (1982). *La crianza y la socialización del niño en Latinoamerica. Estudio de casos: Colombia y Perú.* Bogotá, Colombia: Informe para la Fundación Ford.

Kruger, H., & Arias Stella, J. (1979). The placenta and the newborn infant at high altitudes. *American Journal of Obstetrics and Gynecology, 164,* 586–591.

Lenfant, C., & Sullivan, K. (1971). Adaptation to high altitude. *The New England Journal of Medicine, 284,* 1298–1309.

LeVine, R. A. (1969). Culture, personality and socialization. In D. A. Goslin (Ed.), *Handbook of socialization theory and research.* Chicago: Rand McNally.

Little, M. A., & Baker, P. T. (1976). Environmental adaptations and perspectives. In P. T. Baker & M. A. Little (Eds.), *Man in the Andes. A multidisciplinary study of high-altitude Quechua.* Stroudburg, PA: Dowden, Hutchinson & Ross.

Mazzes, R. B. (1965). Neonatal mortality and altitude in Peru. *American Journal of Physical Anthropology, 23,* 209–214

McCall, R. B. (1981). Nature-nurture and the two realms of development: A proposed integration with respect to mental development. *Child Development, 52,* 1–12.

McClung, J. (1969). *Effects of high altitude on human birth.* Cambridge, England: Cambridge University Press.

McCullough, R. E., Reeves, J. T., & Liljegren, R. L. (1977). Fetal growth retardation and increased infant mortality at high altitude. *Archives of Environmental Health,* 36–39.

Metcoff, J., Novy, M. J., & Petterson, E. N. (1967). Reproduction at high altitude. In K. Benirshke (Ed.), *Comparative aspects of reproductive failure.* New York: Springer-Verlag.

Monge, C. M. (1948). *Acclimatization in the Andes: Historical confirmation of climatic aggression in the development of Andean man.* Baltimore, MD: Johns Hopkins University Press.

Monge, C. M. (1968). Man, climate and changes of altitude. In Y. A. Cohen (Ed.), *Man in adaptation. The biosocial background.* Chicago: Aldine.

Nelson, M. *Infant mortality in Perú.* (1984). Unpublished master's thesis, School of Public Health, University of Texas.

Pawson, I. G. (1976). Growth and development in high altitude populations: A review of Ethiopian, Peruvian and Nepalese studies. *Proceedings of the Royal Society of London, 194*, 83–98.

Petropoulos, E. A., & Timiras, P. S.   974). Biological effects of high altitude as related to increased solar radiation, temperature fluctuations and reduced partial pressure of oxygen. In *Progress in human biometeriology: The effect of weather and climate on man and his environment.* Amsterdam: Swets & Zeitlinger.

Petropoulos, E. A., Vernadakis, A., & Timiras, P. S. (1969). Nucleic acid content in developing rat brain after prenatal and/or neonatal exposure to high altitude. *Federation Proceedings, 28*, 1001–1005.

Picón Reátegui, E. Nutrition. In P. T. Baker & M. A. Little (Eds.), *Man in the Andes. A multidisciplinary study of high-altitude Quechua.* Stroudburg, PA: Dowden, Hutchinson & Ross.

Scarr-Salapatek, S. (1976). An evolutionary perspective on infant intelligence. In M. Lewis (Ed.), *Origins of intelligence: Infancy and early childhood.* New York: Plenum.

Schulte, F. J., Schrempf, G. & Hinze, G. (1971). Maternal toxemia, fetal malnutrition and motor behavior of the newborn. *Pediatrics, 48*, 871–882.

Sobrevilla, L. A. (1971). Análisis matemático de la relación ponderal placenta; recién nacido en la altura. In R. Guerra García (Ed.), *Estudios sobre la gestación y el recién nacido en la altura.* Lima, Perú: Universidad Peruana Cayetano Heredia.

Sobrevilla, L. A. (1973). Embarazo y parto en los Andes, cambios fisiológicos y alteraciones de la reprodución humana. In L. A. Sobrevilla (Ed.), *Fisiología de la reproducción y atención integral de la madre.* Lima, Perú: Universidad Peruana Cayetano Heredia.

Stallone, R. (1972). Environment, ecology and epidemiology. *World Health Organization Chronicle, 26*, 294.

Thomas, R. B., & Winterhalder, B. P. (1976). Physical and biotic environment of Southern highland Peru. In P. T. Baker & M. A. Little (Eds.), *Man in the Andes. A multidisciplinary study of high-altitude Quechua.* Stroudsburg, PA: Dowden, Hutchinson & Ross.

Timiras, P. S., & Wooley, D. E. (1966). Functional and morphological development of brain and other organs at high altitude. *Federation Proceedings, 25*, 1312–1320.

Usher, R., McLean, F., & Scott, K. (1966). Judgement of fetal age: II. Clinical significance of gestational age and an objective method for its assessment. *Pediatric Clinics of North America, 13*, 835–848.

Weiner, J. S., & Lourie, J. A. (1969). *Human biology: A guide to field methods* (IPB Handbook No. 9). Philadelphia: F. A. Davis.

Whiting, J. W. M. (1981). Environmental constraints on infant care practices. In R. H. Munroe, R. L. Munroe, & B. Whiting (Eds), *The handbook of cross-cultural human development.* New York: Garland.

Zamalloa Gonzales. (1976). Ciclo vital en Sayllapata. Estudio de la cultura compesina del distrito de Saypata, provincia de Paucartambo, Cuzco. *Revista Alpanchis Phutufinga, 4.*

Chapter 2

The Aarau Study on Pregnancy and the Newborn*
An Epidemiologic Investigation of the Course of Pregnancy in 996 Swiss Women, and Its Influence on Newborn Behavior Using the Brazelton Scale

H.S. Fricker
R. Hindermann

*Department of Pediatrics and Obstetrics
and the Clinical Laboratories,
Cantonal Hospital, Aarau*

R. Bruppacher

*Department of Social and Preventive Medicine,
Faculty of Medicine,
University of Basel*

* Supported by Grant No. 846 of the Research Foundation (W + W), Cantonal Hospital, Aarau. The authors acknowledge with gratitude the highly valued support and assistance of the following: The research fund of the Aarau Kantonsspital; Drs. F. Cottier, H, Kipfer and F. Baltzer for carrying out many of the Brazelton examinations and interviews with the mothers; Dr A. Bubenhofer for help in the analysis of the data; Prof. E. Gugler and Prof. W. Stoll, who made it possible for us to conduct the entire study at the Women's Hospital and the Aarau Children's Hospital; the nurses and midwives of the delivery room, the maternity ward, the out-patients' department, and the neonatal ward, for their interest and good will; Prof. W. Burgi and the laboratory technicians of the Central Laboratory for the blood and urine tests; the dataprocessing department, Hoffmann-La Roche, in particular Dr. F. Bovey, for help in evaluating and processing the data; Ms. B. Leishman for help in translation and preparation of the manuscript; and in particular the study secretary, Ms. A. Greber, for her untiring efforts in support of the study.

27

Introduction

Medical science was for a long time influenced by the belief that the unborn child is, to a great extent, protected from harmful outside influences. Until well into the present century it was thought that possible damage to the fetus was overshadowed by the devastating effects of the infectious diseases of early childhood such as diphtheria, whooping cough, and scarlet fever. Congenital syphilis and toxoplasmosis were, until as recently as 50 years ago, the best known fetal diseases. Later, the importance of viral infections, particularly rubella, was recognized and made the subject of intensive study. In the 1960s, the thalidomide tragedy directed attention toward drug-induced prenatal injury.

In addition to the teratological effects occurring mainly in the first trimester, effects in the second and third trimesters, such as chronic fetal illness and postpartum withdrawal symptoms, have gained recognition in recent years. Psychotropic agents, which act by a direct pharmacological influence on cerebral metabolism, can cause lasting effects on the developing brain that will become manifest after birth in subtle disturbances of central nervous system (CNS) function. In addition to medication, smoking and alcohol use have been recognized as important influences. Some researchers view physical and emotional stress as additional causes of disturbed fetal development.

In Switzerland there are as yet no epidemiological data available on the use of coffee, alcohol, tobacco, and medication, and on other possibly important events during pregnancy. Also there has been virtually no prospective research into the discrete effects of events on newborn behavior during pregnancy. These two aspects thus were the focus of interest of the Aarau study on pregnancy and the newborn. The study was designed to provide an overview of the type and frequency of influences during pregnancy, and to relate these to the characteristics of the newborn. One of the most important instruments, the Neonatal Behavioral Assessment Scale (hereafter, BNBAS; see Brazelton, 1973), was expected to provide early indications of subtle disturbances of higher brain functions.

Population and Methods

The Aarau Women's Hospital forms part of the cantonal hospital of the canton of Aargau, Switzerland. It is the tertiary-care center of a large district and also serves as the only maternity unit for the surrounding area, covering almost all deliveries in the region. The demographic and socioeconomic features of this region are representative of the entire canton of Aargau, regarded as the "typical" Swiss canton. The population studied can therefore be regarded as representative of German-speaking Switzerland.

The study included 996 Swiss mothers with single births and 20 with twin births, as well as 85 Italian mothers with single births and one who gave birth to twins. In total, we studied 1123 children from 1102 pregnancies. The Italian mothers and infants were included for a cross-cultural comparison to be published elsewhere. Because of the study conditions, that is, the number of investigators and availability of examination rooms, only the first 6 consecutive admissions for delivery were included on any given day during the 11-month study period (January to November 1981). Therefore 185 mother-child pairs could not be included during this time period. Furthermore, only babies that could be examined were admitted to the final study population; consequently, 4 stillbirths and 2 neonatal deaths were excluded. The following report is based on the results of the 996 Swiss single pregnancies.

Collection of Pregnancy Data

Women admitted to the clinic for childbirth were asked by the midwife before delivery about any complaints or illnesses and about the use of medication, coffee, tea, cigarettes, alcohol, or illicit drugs during pregnancy. Additional information concerning social background, family relationships, the course of previous pregnancies, physical activity during pregnancy, and prenatal classes, as well as physical or emotional stress during pregnancy, was obtained during the mother's subsequent stay in the maternity ward. Further information on the course of pregnancy and delivery, as well as each infant's neonatal course, was taken from the pertinent hospital records.

Thin-layer chromatographic assays (Michaud & Jones, 1980) for drugs and their metabolites in the urine and for thiocyanate, and gamma-glutamyltransferase blood tests were carried out upon admission of the women to the delivery ward. About a third of the pregnant women had been under the care of the Women's Hospital prenatal clinic. It was possible, therefore, to obtain information from these women during pregnancy and to validate it with laboratory tests.

Measurement of the Effects on the Newborn

Each newborn was assessed at birth using these 3 measures: Apgar score, umbilical cord pH, and anthropometric data. Between days 3–5 of life a pediatric examination along with the behavioral assessment (i.e., the BNBAS) were carried out. The latter two examinations were conducted by a physician who was unaware of the mother's history. Each child was examined once. The 90 children who, because of birth defects or illness, had been transferred to the neonatal ward of the pediatric department, included 55 premature infants who were assessed upon attaining a gestational age of 38 weeks or more. "Normal, healthy" children and those moved to the children's hospital will be discussed, in part, separately in a later section (see "Circumstances of the BNBAS Examination" and "Newborn").

We selected the Brazelton Neonatal Behavioral Assessment Scale (Brazelton,

1973) in order to record not only gross neurological abnormalities but also subtle differences in CNS function during the first week of life and to determine possible effects of the surveyed influence factors (Tronick et al., 1976). In addition to the individual development of the newborn, we looked for possible systematic differences that might be statistically correlated with the factors named.

At the Aarau Women's Hospital, the newborn child stays in the mother's room during the day. The mother usually remains in the maternity ward from 7 to 10 days after birth. The BNBAS examination was carried out in the appropriate department of the hospital in a dimly lit, quiet room, with a temperature of 25°C. The nurses laid the prepared baby to sleep in his bassinet after a feeding. During the examination, the mother usually was present as a nonintrusive observer. Babies transferred to the pediatric department were examined there under the same conditions. The BNBAS was applied as part of the routine neonatal examination from January to November 1981. Given the large number of examinations, we often were unable to wait until the baby was asleep. Because the BNBAS was applied as part of the routine neonatal examination, 88 children were included who were not in initial states 1–3; 62 were awake (initial state 4), and 26 were active or crying (initial states 5 and 6). This will be considered in the analysis of methodological influences.

Behavior observations were carried out by five examiners: One man (H.F.), who was the study leader (1), and four women (R.H., (2), F.C., (3), H.K., (4), F.B., (5)). Examiners 1–3 had been trained by Barry Lester and Kevin Nugent of Children's Hospital, Boston. Examiners 4 and 5 were instructed by the other three. Examiners 1 and 2 participated throughout the entire duration of the study. Examiners 3, 4, and 5 participated only for a few months. With the exception of the initial introductory phase, each was forced to work alone by the pressure of work. Special care was taken to ensure that the examining physician was not aware of the case history of the mother concerned.

Description of Study Population

Circumstances of and care in pregnancy vary widely around the world. Before addressing the results of the BNBAS we will describe the specific situation of our study population, their living conditions, behavior, and course of pregnancy.

Sociodemographic background

Table 1 gives the composition of the study population, with respect to age and parity. The youngest mother was 18, the oldest 42; the mean age was 27.6 years. About half the mothers were primiparae; on average, each multipara already had

Table 1.   Age and Parity of Mother at Delivery ($N = 996$)

Parity	Age groups (in years)					All ages
	≤22	23–25	26–28	29–31	≥32	
1	80	142	126	91	42	481
2	30	74	105	88	65	362
3	1	10	30	38	48	127
4	—	—	4	7	10	21
5	—	—	1	1	3	5

1.3 children. Less than one-sixth had already had more than 2 children. Teenage pregnancies are a rare occurrence in Switzerland. Women tend to have their first child in their late twenties.

In the study population, the size of the family (including the newborn) was on average 3.8 persons. Of the mothers, 95.8% were married; 2.5% were living with a partner; and 1.7% were single. These figures correspond closely to those given for the entire Aargau canton (4.4% unwed mothers) and for Switzerland as a whole (5.4% unwed mothers). Only 1 family in 100 counted an adult of retirement age among the family members. In only 2 cases was the partner unemployed, a figure reflecting the favorable employment situation in the region at that time. Of the women, 83% managed the household alone with only occasional help from the husband; in 12.5% of the cases the husband or partner helped regularly; 2.5% of the women did not keep house at all.

Of the families, 30.3% lived in their own houses; 25.4% lived in town houses or small apartment buildings; 37.3% lived in large apartment buildings; and 7.0% lived in farmhouses. The mean number of rooms available, including living room and bedrooms, was 4.2. The households that had hot water, bathroom, and use of a washing machine totaled 98.1%. A separate room had already been reserved for the newborn by 76.5% of the families. The great majority of the mothers (63.5%) were from villages with a population of between 1000 and 10,000; 17.2% lived in small- or medium-sized towns with more than 10,000 inhabitants; 14.7% lived in villages with fewer than 1,000 inhabitants; and 4.6% were living on farms or in small rural settlements.

Some of the women (27.1%) had received training as secretaries or clerical assistants; 15.6% were trained in nursing or other health care professions; 11.9% were trained as sales clerks; 10.9% had learned a trade or were running their own small businesses; 5.7% were unskilled workers; 9.7% were teachers; and 7.2% were employed in housekeeping services or in hotels. Civil servants constituted 3.1%; 2.8% worked on farms; and 1.5% were in the liberal professions.

At the beginning of the pregnancy, 42.1% were working in their own households and had no outside employment. Figure 1 shows how the proportion of

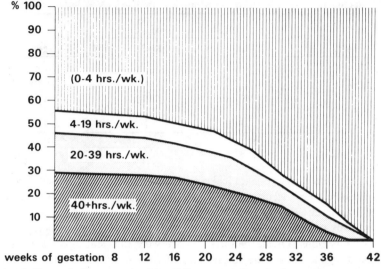

Figure 1. Percent of women working full- or part-time during pregnancy

mothers working full-time, half-time, or part-time changed with the progress of pregnancy. When interviewed in the postpartum period, 45.9% of the women stated that they did not plan to take up employment again (full or part-time); 20.3% wished to start work again after 1–2 years; 10.5% mentioned some kind of home work; and 23.3% had no definite plans for subsequent employment.

Life-style During Pregnancy

The mothers were interviewed by a doctor in the postpartum period and asked about physical stress during pregnancy: 9.0% did most of their daily work in a sitting position and 9.6% spent most of their working time standing, whereas 81.3% stated that their working position varied. On average, they had 9.4 hours of rest (including sleep) daily. Nearly 62% said they had not felt physically overtaxed at any time during their pregnancies, 32% reported occasional physical strain, 6.2% reported frequent strain, and only 0.3% (i.e., 3 women) reported constant physical strain. In 63.8% of the women, the stress-load level remained constant throughout pregnancy, while in 15.7% it decreased and in 20.1% it increased.

It also is interesting to note the extent of elective physical stress. In sporting activities, 20.8% of the women were members of a sport club. Before pregnancy, 5.5% of the women had engaged in a sporting activity daily, 41.3% at least once a week, and 53.2% rarely or never. During pregnancy, 38% reported some modified sporting activity. The interview in the postnatal ward also covered

emotional stress. Chronic emotional strain, for the most part due to problems
with the marital partner, was cited by 16% of the women. In 22%, brief bouts of
emotional stress were reported; 62% of the mothers reported no negative emotional stress during the pregnancy.

Smoking before pregnancy was reported by 29.5% of the women. After the
onset of pregnancy, this figure dropped to 21%, and in the last trimester to 18%.
The average daily tobacco consumption among smokers was 17.3 cigarettes
before pregnancy, and 10 in the last trimester. This finding corresponds to those
in other studies reporting 40–50% smokers among working women, and 10–
15% among housewives (Abelin & Müller, 1983; Biener, 1981).

During the interview in the maternity ward, the women were asked whether,
in their opinion, smoking has an influence on the unborn child. Sixty-three
percent stated that smoking results in lower birthweight, 13% claimed that it
could cause birth defects, 10% suspected other effects, and 13% were unable to
give an answer.

When asked by the midwife about alcohol use during pregnancy, 46% of the
mothers reported complete abstention, 51% occasional alcohol use, and 3% daily
use, usually 1–2 glasses of wine. Fewer than 1% took beer or liqueurs during
pregnancy. In none of the women reporting daily alcohol consumption was the
level of gamma-glutamyltransferase elevated.

Before pregnancy 78% of the women drank coffee daily, with an average of
3.2 cups per day. During pregnancy, this figure dropped slightly to 73%, with a
daily average of 2.5 cups. Tea drinking did not decrease during pregnancy; about
20% of the mothers reported drinking 2 cups daily. Screening of the urine
showed traces of caffeine in 65% of the women on admission to the delivery
room.

Only 3 women reported using marijuana. In all cases, the use of hard drugs
was denied. Although it is difficult to verify the responses in this respect, the
Toxilab screening disclosed no signs of drug abuse. This most probably is
attributed to the fact that in Switzerland drug addicts are unlikely to bring a
pregnancy to term, and the few exceptions would prefer the anonymity of a large
city hospital.

Table 2. Smoking Before and During Pregnancy ($N = 996$)

	Nonsmokers %	All smokers %	Smokers % (>10 cigarettes/day)	Number of cigarettes smoked daily by smokers
Before pregnancy	70.5	29.5	19	17.3
First trimester	79	21	7	11.4
Second trimester	80.5	19.5	5.5	10
Third trimester	82.0	18	5	9.8

Pregnancy Care

The following information was obtained by the doctor in the postnatal interview. Of the primiparae 68% and of the multiparae 26% had attended childbirth education classes, on average for 8 hours. One-third of the primiparae had attended a 6-hour instruction course on baby care. One-third reported having gained experience while caring for other people's babies, and one-third awaited the birth of the child without any special preparations. In 20% of the cases, husbands of the primiparae had attended a baby-care course. Almost all mothers intended to breast-feed. Only 4% stated that they were not in the position to do so and 1% said they did not wish to breast-feed.

The women reported an average of 8 prenatal visits: 4% had 2 or less, 29% had 3–6, 58% had 7–10, and 9% had more than 10 checkups during pregnancy. There was no difference between primiparae and multiparae in this regard. One third of the women entrusted their family doctor with the surveillance of their pregnancies, one third went to a gynecologist, and one third attended the outpatient clinic at the Women's Hospital. About 20% visited a doctor for illness unrelated to pregnancy, with an average of two consultations.

Course of Pregnancy

The women's complaints and illnesses were reported by the midwife. Approximately 17% of the pregnant women reported no illnesses or other complaints, while 54.5% mentioned one or more somatic illnesses, for the most part viral infections (41%), allergies (10%), and urinary tract infections (7.4%). One or more psychosomatic complaints were mentioned by 47%: insomnia (29%), or headache or pain of other origin (21%). Problems associated with pregnancy were outlined by 43%, most often morning sickness (26%). Obstetric complications occurred in 36%; varicose veins and other problems of the lower limbs in 23%; premature labor in 9%; and vaginal bleeding in 9%.

The medication taken by the women during their pregnancies is listed in Table 3. Some 33% of the women indicated they had not used any systemic medication (mostly taken by peroral route). The most frequently used drugs were analgesics; vasoactive drugs, antibiotics, and psychosedatives, most prominent among them being the benzodiazepines. These often were prescribed to counteract the expected nervousness when tocolytics were given. There were astonishingly small differences in occurrence between primiparae and multiparae.

Course of Delivery

The data on the course of labor were taken from the obstetrical case record. These are summarized in Table 4. Of note is the very low rate of cesarean sections for the Swiss mothers, which was even lower for the multiparae.

Table 3.   Drug Intake During Pregnancy (Entries: Percentage of women taking the corresponding preparations at least once during pregnancy)

Medication group	Primiparae % (N = 481)	Multiparae % (N = 515)	Total % (N = 996)
Analgesics	17.5	17.9	17.7
Antiemetics	12.5	14.6	13.4
Psychotropics, including seda- tives and hypnotics	12.1	14.6	13.4
Of which benzodiazepines	10.4	12.6	11.5
Expectorants	12.5	12.2	12.3
Antacids	12.9	12.6	12.8
Laxatives	13.1	11.5	12.2
Other GI drugs	1.5	1.4	1.4
Spasmolytics	1.2	1.9	1.6
Tocolytics	7.9	10.5	9.2
Vasoactive drugs	14.8	18.4	16.7
Diuretics	4.6	2.5	3.5
Gestagens	4.2	5.0	4.6
Other hormones	1.2	1.6	1.4
Antibiotics	14.1	15.1	14.7
Other systemic medications	2.3	1.9	2.1
Any systemic medication	64.2	69.3	66.9
Topical medications	6.0	7.0	6.5
Multivitamin preparations	31.4	29.1	30.2
Iron preparations	79.8	83.9	81.9

Table 5 lists the most important medication groups used during labor. Only 7.1% of the women had general anesthesia, most of them for cesarean section. The most frequently used types of drugs were opiate and nonopiate spasmolytics. Multiparae received significantly fewer drugs than did primiparae; 37.5% went

Table 4.   Summary of Obstetric Data

	Primiparae % (N = 481)	Multiparae % (N = 515)	Total % (N = 996)
Spontaneous birth	74.2	85.6	80.1
Cesarean section	7.3	6.4	6.8
Vacuum extraction	12.9	4.3	8.4
Forceps delivery	3.5	1.4	2.4
Partial extraction	1.7	2.1	1.9
Extraction	0.4	—	0.2
Vertex presentation	92.7	95.7	94.3
Deflexion presentation	1.7	0.2	0.9
Breech presentation	5.2	3.5	4.3
Gestational age ≤37 weeks	4.4	2.9	3.6

Table 5.   Medication During Labor (Entries: Percentage of mothers receiving at least one corresponding preparation between admission and delivery)

Medication group	Primiparae % (N = 481)	Muliparae % (N = 515)	Total % (N = 996)
CNS active drugs	77.3	40.8	58.4
Of CNS active drugs:			
General anesthesia	7.7	6.6	7.1
Benzodiazepines	22.2	10.9	16.4
Spasmolytics	77.5	50.1	63.3
Tocolytics	10.2	4.1	7.0
Any systemic medication	89.0	62.5	76.2

through labor without medications. Only 11.0% of the women giving birth to their first child went through labor and delivery without medication.

Newborn

Data for the newborn were taken from the hospital records. As already stated, the study included only children who survived the first week. Table 6 gives 5-minute APGAR scores and the corresponding umbilical arterial pH.

Table 7 gives the anthropometric data. Considering the gestational age, the data correspond well to the normal intrauterine growth curves for Swiss children (Largo, Walli, Duc, Fanconi, & Prader, 1980).

The 90 Swiss singleton newborns transferred to the pediatric department within the same hospital complex remained hospitalized for between 2 and 114 days. Of these, 26 were suffering from respiratory distress syndrome, 10 of them requiring respiratory assistance. A total of 11 demonstrated a transient cardiorespiratory adaption disorder. In 47 cases infants developed hyperbilirubinemia, in 8 cases as a result of blood group incompatibility. Two were treated with an exchange transfusion, and the others with phototherapy. Anemia

Table 6.   Apgar Scores and pH of Umbilical Arterial Blood (Values expressed as absolute number and mean ± SD of score in each scoring range)

Sex	5-minute Apgar score			
	0–4	5–7	8–10	Total
Male	—	10	463	473[a]
		7.15 ± 0.13	7.30 ± 0.07	7.29 ± 0.08
Females	4	16	492	512[a]
	7.19 ± 0.03	7.22 ± 0.11	7.30 ± 0.07	7.30± 0.07

[a]Results are incomplete for 7 males and 4 females.

Table 7.   Anthropometric Data of the Newborn (M and SD)

Item	Males ($N = 480$)	Females ($N = 516$)	Both Sexes ($N = 996$)
Birthweight (g)	3,456 ± 506	3,281 ± 450	3,365 ± 485
Birth length (cm)	50.0 ± 1.1	49.2 ± 2.1	49.6 ± 2.3
Head circumference (cm)	34.8 ± 1.4	34.2 ± 1.2	34.5 ± 1.3
Ponderal index (g/cm³ %)	2.75 ± 0.22	2.74 ± 0.21	2.74 ± 0.22

was present in 3 children, polycythemia in 8 infants. Hypoglycemic blood sugar values were found in 13 neonates, although only 4 had clinical symptoms. Other reasons for transfer to the pediatric department were septicemia (6 cases), amniotic infection (4 cases), and mild infections (11 cases). Severe neurological abnormalities were manifested in 3 children, 2 had seizures, 1 had ileus, and 1 necrotising enterocolitis.

Deaths occurred in 2 cases soon after birth because of severe congenital malformations (Potter syndrome and complex cardiac abnormality). At the pediatric examinations, 5 infants showed major congenital defects; 1 had trisomy 21, 2 had congenital dislocation of the hip, and 2 had a cheilognathopalatoschisis (cleft palate). In addition, 18 cases of minor malformations were identified, including 2 cases of syndactyly or hexadactyly, and 4 infants had heart murmurs consistent with a small ventricular septal defect (VSD). In total, the malformation rate was 2.4%, which corresponds to the average observed in larger comparable cohorts.

Contextual Variables of the BNBAS Examination

Presentation of the Results and Statistical Analysis

The results of the BNBAS examination were transformed and aggregated into the "seven clusters score" (Lester, Als, & Brazelton, 1982). As did Kaye (1978) and Leijon and Finnstrom (1981), we found it difficult to standardize the scoring of the items within the seventh cluster (Reflexes) and, therefore, confined ourselves to the first 6 clusters described by Lester et al.

We limit ourselves to the presentation of the mean (M), standard deviation (SD), and number of cases analyzed (n) for the cluster scores. As this study was observational in nature and dealt with varied and rather general hypotheses, the statistical analysis was intended more as an aid in assessing the differences found than as an actual test of specific hypotheses. We were unable to find a statistical procedure that would be satisfactory in all respects. As mean scores of generally large groups were to be compared, we decided on parametric tests, despite our doubts about normal distribution of the scores for individual items. Nonparametric methods were applied in some univariate analyses and gave virtually identical results. To provide a consistent overview, as far as possible all scores were tested in the same way. The general linear models procedure (GLM) of the Statistical Analysis System (General Linear Models Procedures, 1982) was found to be the most feasible, as it allowed assessment of both classification and continuous variables in a variety of ways, as well as to make multiple comparisons. This also allowed for control of influences recognized as important in later statistical analysis, with the GLM analysis used to correct for interfering variables.

We shall use the probabilities of the type I hypothesis as our main criterion because it is more sensitive to the effects of variables under investigation. Significance is defined as a probability of the null hypothesis below .05. Significance results, however, must be interpreted with caution as they also could result from interdependence between the variables in the model.

Circumstances of the BNBAS Examination

The cross-sectional study of a large population allows examination of the influence of the circumstances on the BNBAS score. We shall discuss the importance of initial state, time of day, amount of last feeding, time elapsed since last feeding, and influence of the examiner.

We are aware that here we do not cover all possibly important, subtle influences of the examination conditions (De Vries & Super, 1978), for example, the presence of the mother, which might have influenced the examiners during administration of the adversive stimuli (e.g., pinprick, pull-to-sit, and Moro reflex). Furthermore, in rooming-in, mothers, each in their own way devoted a differing amount of time to interaction with the baby, resulting in a different amount of stimulation for each child in the early days of life. The examiners were disturbed to different degrees by interfering variables, possibly resulting in a subtle influence on perception and examination style. For this chapter, the previously mentioned influence variables were selected after a preliminary review of the results had shown them to be those of greatest importance for our analysis.

To exclude as many of the possible potentially interfering infant variables, we refer in this paragraph to a collective of normal healthy children to demonstrate any methodological influences. We define a normal, healthy child as follows:

birth at term, 38th–42nd week of gestation
birthweight above the 10th percentile of the Winterthur intrauterine growth
    curves (Largo et al., 1980).
absence of congenital malformations
absence of perinatal asphyxia, no birth trauma (e.g., plexus paresis)
no illness during neonatal period (infections, respiratory or metabolic disturbances, gastrointestinal disorders, CNS disorders)

Of the 516 girls, 418 (81%) fulfilled these requirements, as did 370 (77%) of the 480 boys. For the analysis of the examining conditions, our collective was thus reduced in size from 996 to 788 (79.1%).

Completeness of scores. We first compared the cluster scores of the children in whom not all, but more than half of the corresponding items could be collected, with those in whom all items within a cluster were available. We thus established that the means of the scores for Habituation, Orientation, Regulation of State, and Range of State differed to a statistically significant degree ($p \leq$ 0.02 to 0.0001 in the t-test). They were markedly lower for Habituation and Orientation, and markedly higher for Regulation of State and Range of State when not all items could be collected. We thus decided to use only the results from those children for whom all items within a cluster were available. This meant that many children were excluded, particularly in the clusters Regulation of State (121) and Habituation (89). This loss, however, appeared justified in view of the possible systematic errors that would have entered the analysis as a result of an incomplete assessment.

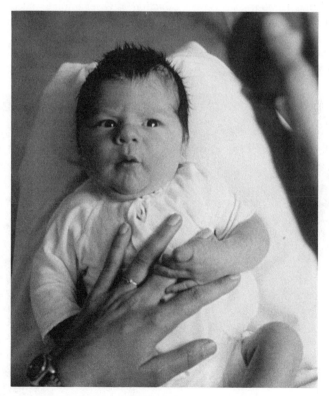

Photo 1.   Orientation Cluster: Vertical following of ball.

Sex and initial state. Because we could not exclude systematic differences between boys and girls, the scores in Table 8 are broken down not only according to the different initial states, but also according to sex. Surprising differences were found between the initial states, but the pattern proved to be practically identical in boys and girls.

In Table 8 it is clear that the instruction that the child should be in state 1–3 at the start of the BNBAS examination is a wise one (Brazelton, 1973).

The comparison of states 1–3 with states 4–6 shows significant differences between the mean scores for the clusters Orientation and Motor Performance, both in the t-test and the Wilcoxon two-sample test ($p < .0001$ and $p = .02$, respectively). For the scores Regulation of State and Range of State, the variances differed significantly (F test; $p = .02$ for each). The cluster Autonomic Regulation showed no differences.

As expected, the babies with initial state 4 achieved the best scores in the Orientation cluster. This corresponds to the observation of Sameroff (1978) that children who were awake during habituation assessment were more aroused during the rest of the examination. As the BNBAS assessment systematically seeks the "best performance," the evaluation of Orientation as such would be better applied in children who are not asleep initially. This, however, would conflict with the collection of the items for Habituation.

In view of the observed differences, in the following group comparisons we

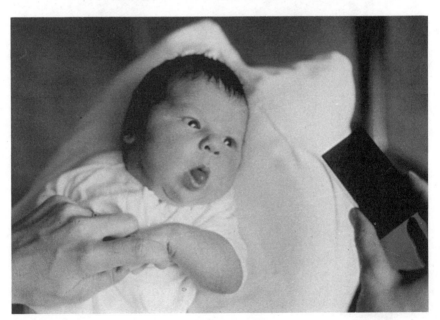

Photo 2.   **Orientation Cluster: Responding to inanimate auditory stimulus.**

Table 8. Cluster Scores Versus Initial State and Sex of Baby (Entries: $M \pm SD$ (n))

	Initial State						
	1	2	3	4	5	6	All
Male							
Habituation	7.34 ± 0.95 (83)	6.11 ± 1.27 (154)	6.83 ± 0.29 (3)	—	—	—	6.54 ± 1.30 (240)
Orientation	4.97 ± 1.38 (83)	5.30 ± 1.53 (199)	5.31 ± 1.63 (12)	6.37 ± 1.32 (24)	5.42 ± 1.77 (2)	6.23 ± 1.70 (10)	5.33 ± 1.52 (330)
Regulation of State	4.77 ± 1.06 (78)	4.93 ± 1.20 (155)	4.69 ± 1.11 (12)	5.34 ± 1.23 (14)	3.75 (1)	4.75 ± 1.58 (10)	4.88 ± 1.17 (270)
Motor Performance	4.97 ± 0.75 (96)	4.99 ± 0.74 (223)	5.08 ± 0.51 (13)	5.20 ± 0.75 (24)	5.70 ± 0.71 (2)	5.20 ± 0.66 (9)	5.01 ± 0.74 (367)
Range of State	3.47 ± 0.54 (96)	3.54 ± 0.62 (224)	3.58 ± 0.92 (13)	3.54 ± 0.68 (21)	3.75 (1)	3.56 ± 0.63 (9)	3.53 ± 0.61 (364)
Autonomic Regulation	6.47 ± 1.00 (89)	6.60 ± 1.02 (205)	6.87 ± 0.67 (10)	6.96 ± 0.84 (16)	6.83 ± 0.71 (2)	6.63 ± 1.28 (10)	6.57 ± 1.01 (332)
Female							
Habituation	7.34 ± 1.00 (105)	6.05 ± 1.23 (194)	5.88 ± 2.30 (2)	—	—	—	6.50 ± 1.31 (301)
Orientation	4.75 ± 1.67 (99)	5.43 ± 1.54 (218)	5.20 ± 1.70 (20)	6.40 ± 0.85 (22)	5.33 ± 0.47 (2)	5.05 ± 1.89 (6)	5.29 ± 1.60 (367)
Regulation of State	4.83 ± 1.13 (85)	5.13 ± 1.16 (161)	4.37 ± 1.03 (15)	5.81 ± 0.90 (17)	—	4.04 ± 2.10 (6)	5.01 ± 1.19 (284)
Motor Performance	4.84 ± 0.79 (111)	5.06 ± 0.72 (246)	4.93 ± 0.98 (22)	5.41 ± 0.61 (22)	5.40 ± 1.41 (2)	4.80 ± 0.88 (7)	5.01 ± 0.76 (410)
Range of State	3.46 ± 0.61 (112)	3.55 ± 0.61 (252)	3.83 ± 0.63 (22)	3.87 ± 0.55 (21)	3.75 ± 0.35 (2)	2.44 ± 0.38 (4)	3.55 ± 0.62 (413)
Autonomic Regulation	6.67 ± 0.91 (102)	6.84 ± 0.80 (231)	7.12 ± 0.79 (14)	7.06 ± 1.00 (22)	7.00 ± 1.41 (2)	7.16 ± 0.59 (6)	6.82 ± 0.85 (377)

(*continued*)

Table 8. (*Continued*)

	Initial State						
	1	2	3	4	5	6	All
	Both Sexes						
Habituation	7.34 ± 0.97 (188)	6.08 ± 1.25 (348)	6.45 ± 1.28 (5)	—	—	—	6.52 ± 1.30 (541)
Orientation	4.85 ± 1.54 (182)	5.37 ± 1.54 (417)	5.24 ± 1.65 (32)	6.38 ± 1.11 (46)	5.38 ± 1.06 (4)	5.79 ± 1.81 (16)	5.30 ± 1.56 (697)
Regulation of State	4.80 ± 1.10 (163)	5.03 ± 1.18 (316)	4.51 ± 1.06 (27)	5.60 ± 1.07 (31)	3.75 (1)	4.48 ± 1.76 (16)	4.95 ± 1.18 (554)
Motor Performance	4.90 ± 0.77 (207)	5.02 ± 0.73 (469)	4.98 ± 0.83 (35)	5.30 ± 0.69 (46)	5.55 ± 0.93 (4)	5.02 ± 0.77 (16)	5.01 ± 0.75 (777)
Range of State	3.46 ± 0.58 (208)	3.55 ± 0.61 (476)	3.74 ± 0.74 (35)	3.70 ± 0.63 (42)	3.75 ± 0.25 (3)	3.21 ± 0.77 (13)	3.54 ± 0.62 (777)
Autonomic Regulation	6.58 ± 0.96 (191)	6.73 ± 0.92 (436)	6.72 ± 0.87 (24)	7.02 ± 0.93 (38)	6.91 ± 0.92 (4)	6.83 ± 1.08 (16)	6.71 ± 0.93 (709)

included only newborns in whom the examination began in initial states 1–3. Even between these states, surprisingly large, statistically significant differences could be observed (Table 8). For example, Habituation scores were significantly better when the baby was in state 1 at the start of the BNBAS examination. This applies to both boys and girls. In contrast, the scores for Orientation were better when the examination began in state 2 or 3. The cluster score for Regulation of State was markedly better with initial state 2 than with initial state 1. For babies in initial state 3 the cluster score for Habituation included only a few children, as most awoke before all items had been tested and were, as mentioned earlier, excluded from the analysis.

Linear model analysis of the influence of sex and initial state, taken together, showed that the initial state had a highly significant influence on Habituation and Orientation ($p < .0001$ and $p = .001$, respectively), but was only of moderate significance for Regulation of State ($p = .016$) and Range of State ($p = .0033$), and of no influence on Motor Performance and Autonomic Regulation. Only in the cluster Autonomic Regulation did sex have a statistically highly significant influence ($p = .0006$), the girls having a demonstrably higher score than boys.

Time of day. Given the many human biological and physiological processes that are subject to a distinct periodicity, the time of day also could be regarded as an important influence in the assessment of the BNBAS scores. The time intervals given in Table 9 relate to the last feeding before the examination, that is, the first, second, or third feeding. For administration reasons, practically no examinations were carried out after the fourth and fifth feedings.

In the cluster score Orientation, the time of day had a strong influence: The mean values improved gradually from early morning to afternoon. The cluster score Range of State also showed a systematic relationship to the time of day, although in this case the mean scores continuously deteriorated with time. These

Table 9.   Cluster Scores Versus Time of Examination (Entries $M \pm SD$ (n))

	06.00–10.00	10.00–14.00	14.00–18.00	All times
Habituation	6.42 ± 1.42 (133)	6.59 ± 1.25 (245)	6.51 ± 1.29 (160)	6.52 ± 1.30 (541)
Orientation	4.92 ± 1.77 (147)	5.23 ± 1.53 (292)	5.39 ± 1.40 (184)	5.21 ± 1.56 (631)
Regulation of State	5.08 ± 1.15 (128)	4.88 ± 1.15 (233)	4.19 ± 1.15 (140)	4.93 ± 1.15 (506)
Motor Performance	4.99 ± 0.74 (167)	5.00 ± 0.76 (331)	4.94 ± 0.73 (205)	4.98 ± 0.75 (711)
Range of State	3.62 ± 0.61 (169)	3.55 ± 0.58 (336)	3.44 ± 0.65 (206)	3.53 ± 0.61 (719)
Autonomic Regulation	6.74 ± 0.83 (149)	6.72 ± 0.98 (301)	6.58 ± 0.92 (194)	6.68 ± 0.93 (651)

differences were statistically significant ($p = .009$ and $.056$, respectively) in the general linear models (GLM) analysis which controlled for initial state and sex.

This analysis also showed a significant interaction between initial state and time of day for the cluster score Motor Performance ($p = .0026$). The cluster scores Habituation, Regulation of State, and Autonomic Regulation, however, would not appear to be influenced systematically by the time of examination. This still applies when the analysis corrects for sex. To our knowledge no investigator has systematically studied the influence of the time of day. Some authors report that, in the two comparative groups, all children were examined at the same time of day (Saxton, 1978).

Amount of last feeding and time interval. In the Aarau Women's Hospital, the children are fed (by breast or bottle) at approximately 4-hour intervals, or at least 5 times daily, starting at 6 a.m. As we examined several babies each day, it was not always possible to time the BNBAS examination exactly halfway between feedings. The only clusters to show an influence of the time interval since the last feeding were Regulation of State and Motor Performance. Both revealed a slight improvement in mean scores with increasing time since feeding.

These relationships, however, did not reach statistical significance when initial state, examiner, sex, and amount of feeding also were controlled. There was a significant influence in the cluster Autonomic Regulation ($p = .0008$), with a marked decrease of the scores for the boys, and a slight improvement for the girls with growing time interval.

We also assumed a relationship with the amount consumed at the last feeding, as related to body weight on the examination day. The average consumption per feeding on the corresponding day of life was around 3% of the body weight. Despite a broad distribution around this mean, no significant relationship to the cluster scores could be demonstrated.

Sex of baby and examiner. A preliminary analysis of the results suggested that different examiners assessed boys and girls differently. Thus, in analysis of the influence variable "examiner," the findings again were initially broken down according to sex (see Table 10).

If a comparison is made of the individual examiners' cluster scores listed in Table 10, differences emerge in the assessment of boys and girls. These often are contradictory and cancel one another out in the total. The differing assessments of boys and girls were not related to the sex of the examiner. In purely numerical terms, the most clear-cut differences between the mean cluster scores of the individual examiners were in the cluster Orientation. Between examiners 2 and 3, there was a difference of 1.6 points in evaluating girls. Despite this, multivariate analysis disclosed no relationship between an infant's sex and the observer for the cluster score Orientation. Only in the cluster score Autonomic Regulation did all examiners rate the girls better than the boys.

GLM analysis, correcting for initial state, again showed a significant influence of sex only for the cluster Autonomic Regulation ($p = .0002$), the girls'

Table 10. Cluster Scores Versus Examiner and Sex of Baby (Entries: $M \pm SD$ (n)

	H.F. (♂)	R.H. (♀)	F.C. (♀)	H.K. (♀)	F.B. (♀)
			Male		
Habituation	6.46 ± 1.32 (79)	6.41 ± 1.63 (54)	6.69 ± 1.04 (45)	6.39 ± 1.15 (24)	6.82 ± 1.05 (38)
Orientation	5.28 ± 1.40 (92)	4.73 ± 1.91 (78)	5.39 ± 1.35 (68)	5.77 ± 1.22 (35)	5.22 ± 1.02 (50)
Regulation of State	4.83 ± 0.79 (69)	4.15 ± 1.36 (54)	5.01 ± 1.16 (52)	5.12 ± 0.88 (31)	5.51 ± 1.09 (39)
Motor Performance	4.90 ± 0.63 (93)	4.95 ± 0.87 (77)	5.14 ± 0.75 (73)	5.11 ± 0.69 (38)	4.89 ± 0.68 (51)
Range of State	3.40 ± 0.58 (93)	3.68 ± 0.77 (78)	3.66 ± 0.43 (72)	3.66 ± 0.50 (39)	3.23 ± 0.51 (51)
Autonomic Regulation	6.13 ± 0.96 (91)	6.41 ± 1.15 (64)	6.90 ± 0.97 (59)	6.94 ± 0.79 (39)	6.78 ± 0.77 (51)
			Female		
Habituation	6.22 ± 1.22 (110)	6.62 ± 1.57 (64)	6.81 ± 1.25 (43)	6.33 ± 1.02 (40)	6.89 ± 1.32 (44)
Orientation	5.45 ± 1.26 (129)	4.17 ± 2.05 (82)	5.71 ± 1.42 (65)	5.51 ± 1.35 (44)	5.62 ± 1.14 (44)
Regulation of State	4.82 ± 0.87 (86)	4.52 ± 1.42 (54)	5.30 ± 1.23 (47)	5.08 ± 0.90 (37)	5.56 ± 1.12 (37)
Motor Performance	4.87 ± 0.73 (131)	4.75 ± 0.89 (84)	5.16 ± 0.71 (66)	5.36 ± 0.59 (49)	5.08 ± 0.65 (49)
Range of State	3.43 ± 0.57 (130)	3.70 ± 0.84 (85)	3.66 ± 0.50 (69)	3.59 ± 0.47 (51)	3.34 ± 0.45 (51)
Autonomic Regulation	6.53 ± 0.86 (128)	6.65 ± 0.91 (62)	7.23 ± 0.69 (56)	7.13 ± 0.73 (50)	6.88 ± 0.63 (51)
			Both Sexes		
Habituation	6.32 ± 1.27 (189)	6.52 ± 1.59 (118)	6.75 ± 1.14 (88)	6.35 ± 1.06 (64)	6.85 ± 1.18 (82)
Orientation	5.38 ± 1.32 (215)	4.44 ± 2.00 (153)	5.55 ± 1.39 (117)	5.63 ± 1.29 (67)	5.40 ± 1.09 (79)
Regulation of State	4.82 ± 0.84 (155)	4.34 ± 1.40 (108)	5.15 ± 1.20 (99)	5.10 ± 0.88 (68)	5.54 ± 1.09 (76)
Motor Performance	4.88 ± 0.69 (224)	4.84 ± 0.88 (161)	5.15 ± 0.73 (139)	5.25 ± 0.64 (87)	4.98 ± 0.67 (100)
Range of State	3.42 ± 0.58 (223)	3.69 ± 0.81 (163)	3.66 ± 0.46 (141)	3.62 ± 0.48 (90)	3.28 ± 0.48 (102)
Autonomic Regulation	6.36 ± 0.92 (219)	6.53 ± 1.04 (126)	7.06 ± 0.86 (115)	7.05 ± 0.76 (89)	6.83 ± 0.70 (102)

scores being significantly better. The interaction between examiner and sex of baby proved not to be significant. A complex interaction between initial state, examiner, and child's sex, however, was slightly significant for Autonomic Regulation ($p = .049$).

To date, the only study we know of which addressed itself to the question of interaction between examiner and the baby's sex was conducted by Kaye (1978). No relation with actual or assumed sex of the child was found for either the individual items or the factor scores. A study by Horowitz et al. (1977) of 65 Israeli newborns showed that the sex of the children as a factor was controlled for by analysis of variance. This showed significant sex-related differences for only two items (Orientation Inanimate Visual and Cuddliness), with higher scores for girls. The study did not break down the results according to examiners (two women and two men).

Leijon and Finnstrom (1981) analyzed their results for sex differences, using the same subscales or cluster scores that we have used. In their analysis, as in ours, the boys scored significantly lower than the girls for the cluster Autonomic Regulation. Multiple regression analysis also demonstrated significantly lower values for the boys in the cluster Habituation. Leijon and Finnstrom, too, did not separate the values for the different examiners, and thus it is not clear whether the identified sex differences were the same for both examiners. Lester, Emory, & Hoffman (1976) found a significant sex difference for an attention orientation factor in favor of the girls when the findings in newborns aged 12–36 hr were subjected to multiple linear regression analysis.

Interexaminer differences. GLM analysis, controlling for initial state and child's sex, yielded high significances for interexaminer differences ($p < .0001$) for all six cluster scores. In the clusters Habituation, Orientation, and Autonomic Regulation, the interaction between initial state and examiner significantly influenced the mean scores ($p = .034, .045,$ and $.013$, respectively).

An item-by-item comparison of the results of individual examiners, excluded for reasons of space, showed that the scores of examiner 2 were usually broadly distributed over the full range of values 1-9, which was reflected in a higher standard deviation, while examiner 1 gave more medium scores. We had the impression that the nature of the assessment was related to the personality profile of the observer. For example, the scoring range of examiner 4, a young pediatrician of optimistic nature, who had great difficulty in giving a child a poor score, was in general clearly higher than that of examiner 2, an experienced child psychiatrist.

Studies published to date in which the BNBAS was used have often involved several examiners. In most cases, it was mentioned that the interobserver reliability had a correlation coefficient of .85 to .9. The usual procedure (Horowitz & Brazelton, 1973) in testing interobserver reliability consists of having one person conduct the examination in the presence of another, who acts as an observer. The two participants subsequently make their evaluations independently of each other. In this case, however, the interobserver reliability relates only to the allocation of scores, not to the examination technique (Sameroff, Krafchuk, & Bakow, 1978b).

The particular feature of the BNBAS in seeking out the best behavior in the newborn gives the examination technique special importance. In this connection, it might be expected that people with very different personality structures will behave differently in the role of caretaker and thus will elicit differing behaviors from the newborn. It is very doubtful whether even careful training and reliability testing would be able to eliminate these differences (Rosenblith, 1961; Sameroff et al., 1978b). We know of only one systematic study of this examiner effect, carried out by Mitchell in Seattle. These results, however, are as yet unpublished.

Although the fact is not mentioned in the methods section of most papers using the BNBAS, it is usual practice to check the interobserver uniformity of assessment frequently. The reliability of examiners has been reported to remain stable for a period of 12 months (Als, Tronick, Lester, & Brazelton, 1979).

Leijon and Finnstrom (1981) arranged for the same examiners to assess the same child on two consecutive days. This demonstrated a marked day-to-day instability, which they considered to be an inherent characteristic of the newborn. Similar findings have been reported by Sameroff (1978a) and Tronick et al. (1976). This might be due in part to the methodological influences described earlier and not least to the very different initial states. Leijon and Finnstrom (1981) and Sameroff (1978) have even found an influence of the predominant state on the results of the BNBAS.

Summarized assessment of examination conditions. In view of the marked influence of the examiner on the results, it seemed necessary to reassess the significance of all the investigation factors, using again the GLM procedure. This showed quite clearly that the influence variable examiner contributed most to the variance in results in our study. For all six cluster scores, this influence was highly significant. Only for the cluster Habituation was the initial state variable of even greater significance (F value, type I = 77.8 vs. 8.56, both $\rho <$ .0001). The initial state was also highly significant for the cluster Orientation (ρ = .0006) and Regulation of State (ρ = .028). Occasionally other variables had an influence—for example, the sex of the child and the time elapsed since the last feeding on Autonomic Regulation (ρ = .003 and .0008, respectively), and the time of day on Regulation of State (ρ = .026). In Habituation and Autonomic Regulation there was an interaction between initial state and examiner (ρ = .034 and .017, respectively). In Motor Performance there was a marked, significant interaction between initial state and time of day (ρ = .003). These influences, however, appear to be sporadic in comparison with those of initial state and examiner and, therefore, in the following analyses of other influence variables, only the latter two will be taken systematically into consideration.

Characteristics of the Newborn

Age at time of the examination. The BNBAS examination was planned for day 4 or 5 of life, and most of the examinations were, in fact, made at this time. For practical reasons, however, some examinations had to be conducted on day 3 or day 6 of life as, throughout the study, only two or three examiners were involved at any one time, sharing the work of examining babies and interviewing mothers in the maternity ward. Some redistribution of examining times was unavoidable.

Table 11 shows that the babies were divided into groups according to hours between delivery and examination: up to (and including) 72 hours, 73–96 hours, 97–120 hours, and over 120 hours. There is no systematic and clear increase in scores from day 3 to day 6 for any of the clusters, not even for Orientation, where we expected a likely increase in scores. The score for Regulation of State even gradually decreased with increasing age. When initial state and observer are corrected for, however, the cluster scores for Habituation, Regulation of State, Motor Performance, and Autonomic Regulation show statistically significant differences between the means, which are difficult to interpret.

Horowitz et al. (1977) has conducted a detailed assessment of the stability of scores in the course of the first days and weeks of life, in longitudinal studies. Their research also mentioned that the day-to-day variability is more apparent for the individual items, and less so for the cluster sum scores. While Tronick et al. (1976) found a gradual increase in the scores of 54 newborns between days 1 and 10 of life, Ferrari and Pinelli (1980) found no improvement between days 3 and 5 in the 20 healthy, full-term babies they studied. In fact, they noted a slight deterioration in the Orientation score. In addition to medication during labor there were, however, other notable differences between the Tronick et al. and our own study population. In the Tronick et al. study, 25% of the newborns had a ponderal index of less than 2.2; among our newborns, this was the case in less than 5%.

Table 11.   Cluster Scores Versus Age of Baby (Entries: $M \pm SD$ (n))

	≤ 72 hr	73–96 hr	97–120 hr	≥ 120 hr
Habituation	6.37 ± 1.24 (33)	6.54 ± 1.27 (313)	6.56 ± 1.35 (278)	6.32 ± 1.21 (52)
Orientation	5.50 ± 1.72 (45)	5.14 ± 1.57 (352)	5.19 ± 1.53 (337)	5.45 ± 1.58 (67)
Regulation of State	5.43 ± 1.18 (42)	4.96 ± 1.12 (269)	4.76 ± 1.16 (277)	4.49 ± 1.41 (47)
Motor Performance	4.96 ± 0.66 (55)	4.95 ± 0.79 (388)	4.98 ± 0.75 (378)	4.57 ± 0.84 (74)
Range of State	3.62 ± 0.70 (55)	3.52 ± 0.65 (393)	3.54 ± 0.59 (385)	3.37 ± 0.55 (77)
Autonomic Regulation	6.54 ± 0.99 (53)	6.65 ± 0.93 (353)	6.70 ± 0.98 (347)	6.42 ± 1.20 (69)

In a study conducted in Kansas (Aleksandrowicz & Aleksandrowicz, 1974), more marked changes in the first days of life were found than in the Israeli study (Horowitz et al., 1977). The greater stability of the Israeli newborns was attributed to the smaller amount of medication used to assist delivery. In our study population, 25% of the mothers received no medication during labor, and the others mostly received only relatively low doses of opiate-spasmolytics.

Gestational age. We were interested to learn whether the exclusion of babies with gestational age less than 38 weeks or more than 42 weeks would affect the scores of the clusters. In Table 12 the children studied are divided into three groups: premature births examined on reaching the 38th week of gestation; full-term deliveries (38th–42nd week); and postmature births (over 42 weeks). The gestational age of the children in our study was determined on the basis of the obstetrical history, and in any unclear or doubtful cases an additional assessment was made by the Dubowitz method (Dubowitz, Dubowitz, & Goldberg, 1970).

Even when we corrected for initial state and examiner, the gestational age had a significant effect on all cluster scores, all of them improving with increasing age, with the exception of Orientation. This was most pronounced for Habituation, Motor performance, and Autonomic Regulation (ρ = .006, < .0001, and < .0001, respectively) and was least marked for Range of State (ρ = 0.04). For the cluster score Orientation, we expected better results for the premature infants, as they were older at the time of examination and had been exposed to intensive acoustic and visual stimuli for a substantially longer period before the BNBAS examination. The greater frequency of neonatal complications in this group, however, obviously had a counteractive effect. A certain improvement in mean scores with increasing gestational age is to be expected. We were surprised, however, that postmature children (> 42 weeks) scored markedly better than full-term babies for all clusters, except for Orientation and Range of State.

The BNBAS has been validated for the examination in full-term babies (Brazelton, 1973). It also has been used for premature infants with assessment dates

Table 12.   Cluster Scores Versus Gestational Age (Entries: $M \pm SD$ (n)

	<38 weeks	38–42 weeks	>42 weeks	All ages
Habituation	5.97 ± 1.40 (18)	6.50 ± 1.28 (623)	7.21 ± 1.22 (35)	6.52 ± 1.29 (676)
Orientation	4.89 ± 1.70 (29)	5.22 ± 1.55 (730)	5.24 ± 1.78 (42)	5.21 ± 1.56 (801)
Regulation of State	4.33 ± 1.16 (16)	4.87 ± 1.16 (584)	5.03 ± 1.34 (35)	4.87 ± 1.18 (635)
Motor Performance	4.09 ± 0.91 (34)	4.96 ± 0.75 (816)	5.07 ± 0.76 (45)	4.93 ± 0.78 (895)
Range of State	3.26 ± 0.60 (34)	3.54 ± 0.62 (829)	3.49 ± 0.69 (47)	3.52 ± 0.62 (910)
Autonomic Regulation	6.02 ± 1.41 (31)	6.65 ± 0.95 (748)	6.96 ± 0.97 (43)	6.64 ± 0.98 (822)

adjusted according to the mother's due date (Field et al., 1978). In another study, Field, Dabiri, Hallock, and Shuman (1977) found that postmature neonates had lower scores in all areas, which were reflected at follow-up with a poorer assessment for motor function at 4 months, and in the mental scores on the Bayley scale at 8 months. The infants studied were born to older mothers who had an unusually high number of obstetric complications. At the Women's Hospital in Aarau, induction of labor is used conservatively. Instead, the pregnancy is monitored carefully by repeated amnioscopy and cardiotocography. The favorable results in postmature infants may be due to this careful, conservative approach.

Parity. The duration of labor and the stress to the child during delivery differ greatly in primiparae and multiparae. We therefore also carried out a multivariate analysis to assess the differences in cluster scores in relation to parity, but found none.

Summarized assessment of all contextual variables. The analysis of contextual variables and of the other influence variables directly affecting infants of primiparae and multiparae in a common linear model confirmed that in addition to initial state and the examiner, the time of day and the gestational age can influence findings. The amount taken at the last feeding, the time elasped since the last feeding, and parity can be ignored. The baby's age, in this more general model, had a significant influence only on the clusters Regulation of State ($\rho =$ .0002) and Motor Performance ($\rho =$ .015), both improving with increasing age. Again, marked sex differences are limited to the cluster score Autonomic Regulation.

Strauss and Rourke (1978) and Kaye (1978) developed very complex statistical calculations to demonstrate the stability and reproducibility of the BNBAS results in the individual child. In our investigation, we found that the behavior of the child is to some extent dependent on external conditions and that factors independent of the BNBAS may play an important role. Thus it would appear that, in future scientific investigation, an attempt must be made to attain the greatest possible standardization of potentially influential context variables. The child's inner condition, as expressed by initial state, must also be carefully respected. The influence on the child from each examiner's different personality should also be subjected to further research.

Influence of Events During Pregnancy on BNBAS Assessment

Definition of the Examined Population

The relationship between various influences during pregnancy and the BNBAS cluster scores was analyzed on the basis of findings in pregnancies that culminated in the birth of singleton infants in states 1–3 at the start of the examination.

As Table 10 shows, 910 infants could be analyzed. As in the earlier sections, we pooled findings in the analyzed collective for initial states 1–3 and the five examiners but took these important context variables into consideration in the statistical analysis, using the general linear models (GLM) procedure.

The objective of our study made it necessary to examine as complete a collective as possible. Therefore, we also examined the newborns who were transferred to the children's hospital, including premature and postmature children. We had to take into account also that, for some children, hyperbilirubinemia or other neonatal illnesses, as well as separation from the mother, can act as further interfering variables (Telzrow, Snyder, Tronick, Als, & Brazelton, 1980).

The analysis involved only results for which a score was available for *all* items within a cluster. We were aware that children who were excluded because of missing individual items were possibly located in some of the examined subgroups, particularly in the clusters Habituation, Orientation, and Regulation of State. The inclusion of incomplete cluster scores might have caused an even stronger systematic error.

Smoking Before and During Pregnancy

Table 13 shows the influence of smoking habits both before and during pregnancy. The smoking habits before pregnancy would probably have exercised an effect well into the first trimester. The corresponding first part of the table thus might provide an indication of organic impairment in the mother or a global effect in early pregnancy during the implantation phase and organogenesis. From the second part of Table 13, presenting smoking habits in the third trimester, it should be possible to identify more of a direct pharmacological effect of possible withdrawal symptoms in the child. The relevant group, however, included only a few smokers of over 20 cigarettes daily.

From the table it can be seen that there are practically no differences in the means of the cluster scores between light or moderately heavy smokers. The impression of the midwives and pediatric nurses involved, that children of those who smoked were more lively and irritable and cry more often, was not confirmed. The group of children born to those who smoked over 20 cigarettes daily, however, shows markedly lower mean scores for the cluster Habituation and Orientation. GLM analysis confirms a significant, negative effect on the cluster score Orientation when the mother smoked before the pregnancy ($p = .031$), and a significant effect on the cluster score Habituation when the mother smoked in the third trimester ($p = .032$). Conversely, it was surprising to note that the mean score for the cluster Autonomic Regulation improved with increasing cigarette consumption, although the difference was not statistically significant.

The influence of smoking during pregnancy on neonatal behavior has been studied by Saxton (1978). He compared 15 children of mothers who smoked over

Table 13.   Maternal Smoking Habits and Brazelton Cluster Scores
(Entries: $M \pm SD$ (n))

	Nonsmokers	Smokers: number of cigarettes daily		
		1–10	11–20	>20
		Before Pregnancy		
Habituation	6.41 ± 1.43	6.47 ± 1.42	6.57 ± 1.38	6.41 ± 1.44
	(616)	(88)	(115)	(44)
Orientation	5.14 ± 1.68	5.19 ± 1.68	5.14 ± 1.70	4.40 ± 1.55
	(698)	(105)	(138)	(49)
Regulation of State	4.96 ± 1.25	5.02 ± 1.38	4.91 ± 1.37	5.10 ± 1.18
	(704)	(105)	(138)	(49)
Motor Performance	4.94 ± 0.78	5.02 ± 0.71	4.96 ± 0.78	4.82 ± 0.94
	(704)	(105)	(138)	(49)
Range of State	3.53 ± 0.62	3.51 ± 0.70	3.52 ± 0.71	3.58 ± 0.53
	(704)	(105)	(138)	(49)
Autonomic Regulation	6.63 ± 1.02	6.76 ± 0.99	6.58 ± 0.98	7.00 ± 0.98
	(704)	(105)	(138)	(49)
		Third Trimester		
Habituation	6.41 ± 1.44	6.71 ± 1.28	6.40 ± 1.49	5.73 ± 1.49
	(713)	(110)	(35)	(5)
Orientation	5.13 ± 1.67	5.14 ± 1.74	4.75 ± 1.72	4.67 ± 1.71
	(813)	(127)	(44)	(6)
Regulation of State	4.95 ± 1.26	5.06 ± 1.42	4.96 ± 1.16	5.50 ± 1.15
	(819)	(127)	(44)	(6)
Motor Performance	4.95 ± 0.78	4.91 ± 0.84	5.03 ± 0.73	5.27 ± 0.43
	(819)	(127)	(44)	(6)
Range of State	3.53 ± 0.65	3.51 ± 0.63	3.49 ± 0.50	4.00 ± 0.35
	(819)	(127)	(44)	(6)
Autonomic Regulation	6.64 ± 1.02	6.62 ± 1.03	6.99 ± 0.78	7.39 ± 0.61
	(819)	(127)	(44)	(6)

15 cigarettes daily during pregnancy, and 17 children of nonsmoking mothers, using the Brazelton assessment, conducted on days 4–6 of life. He found significant differences for the reaction to auditory stimuli in two items. In our study, the corresponding items showed no significant deterioration. The lack of relation between smoking and the other cluster scores raises the question as to the reliability of the data recorded by the midwife during labor. A comparison with the prospective data obtained during the prenatal check-ups yielded a good agreement between the two sets of findings. Thiocyanate determination in serum and the screening for nicotine in the urine on admission did not indicate secret nicotine abuse by the avowed nonsmokers.

Experience shows that pregnant women tend to underestimate the number of cigarettes they smoke. Thus the lack of precision of these data is unlikely to have influenced the findings to any appreciable extent. In our study, a relationship of the data on smoking with the gestational age at birth was absent, but other clinical findings in the newborns showed marked differences between the children of smokers and nonsmokers: for example, lower birthweight, shown in many other studies as well (American Academy of Pediatrics, 1976; Meredith, 1975; Naeye, 1981), and also a significantly lower percentage of babies satisfying the "normal baby" criteria as maternal nicotine consumption increased (Meyer, Jonas, & Tonascia, 1976).

Alcohol Consumption During Pregnancy

In the interview with the midwife, the women indicated their alcohol use during pregnancy in terms of "never," "sometimes," "daily." The average intake of the few daily consumers was about 15 gm of pure alcohol and had no effect on the BNBAS or on birthweight and other pediatric variables. Again, there is the possibility of concealment. The testing of gamma-glutamyltransferase values showed no differences between alcohol users and abstainers, and also no indication of alcoholism. In Switzerland, the corresponding age group of the total female population has an alcohol dependence rate of 0.7% (Muster, 1983; Wüthrich, Hausherr, & Müller, 1977). We found no clinical signs of the fetal alcohol syndrome as described, for example, by Streissguth, Landesman-Dwyer, Martin, and Smith (1980) in any of the infants that we examined.

Coffee Consumption During Pregnancy

Table 14 lists the means of the individual clusters as related to maternal coffee consumption. For Orientation and Motor Performance, there was a decrease in scores as coffee consumption increased, which attained significance ($p = .024$

Table 14. Coffee Consumption by Mother in Third Trimester and Brazelton Cluster Scores (Entries: $M \pm SD$ (n)

	Number of cups daily				
	0	1	2	3	≥4
Habituation	6.62 ± 1.28 (162)	6.35 ± 1.33 (150)	6.57 ± 1.27 (166)	6.53 ± 1.27 (107)	6.52 ± 1.33 (91)
Orientation	5.29 ± 1.48 (198)	5.30 ± 1.63 (171)	5.31 ± 1.59 (191)	5.20 ± 1.31 (124)	4.77 ± 1.74 (117)
Regulation of State	5.05 ± 1.10 (158)	4.82 ± 1.15 (133)	4.79 ± 1.19 (148)	4.72 ± 1.14 (102)	4.92 ± 1.32 (94)
Motor Performance	4.94 ± 0.82 (223)	5.03 ± 0.75 (188)	4.96 ± 0.75 (214)	4.88 ± 0.74 (143)	4.79 ± 0.80 (127)
Range of State	3.52 ± 0.62 (225)	3.55 ± 0.65 (192)	3.52 ± 0.65 (220)	3.46 ± 0.59 (145)	3.57 ± 0.58 (128)
Autonomic Regulation	6.69 ± 0.95 (196)	6.55 ± 0.99 (177)	6.60 ± 1.03 (198)	6.83 ± 0.91 (135)	6.56 ± 0.99 (116)

and .048, respectively) when initial state and the influence of the examiner were controlled; in the other cluster scores, there was no significant correlation with coffee consumption during pregnancy.

Studies by other authors have shown no clear, predictable effects on the child because of coffee consumption during pregnancy (Linn et al., 1982). In our study, traces of caffeine in the urine were found in two-thirds of the women on arrival at the delivery room. The child therefore was frequently exposed to caffeine until shortly before birth. In view of the longer half-life caffeine has in the newborn (Parsons & Heims, 1981), it might be asked whether the relationship with the Brazelton cluster scores in our study might not be due to a direct pharmacological effect of caffeine, or even possibly to a type of withdrawal syndrome.

Illnesses and Complaints During Pregnancy

The means for the six cluster scores were also calculated for the groups of mothers who complained of headache, insomnia, morning sickness, or premature labor during pregnancy. With the exception of morning sickness, the majority of these complaints were reported as occurring during the third trimester. The mean scores were compared with those of the group reporting no illness or other complaints during pregnancy. Multivariate analysis, again controlling for initial state and examiner, showed no statistically significant correspondences.

Stress During Pregnancy

We also looked for possible consequences of emotional stress. According to the postnatal interview in the maternity ward, four groups describing emotional stress can be formed: none; single acute; repeated acute; and chronic. There were virtually no differences between the means of the cluster scores, and multivariate analysis showed no statistically significant relationships. This would support the view of many prenatal psychologists that emotional stress of the mother during pregnancy in itself does not have a negative effect on the baby; the attitude of the mother toward her unborn child is much more important (Verny & Kelly, 1981). The same negative results were obtained for physical stress (sports activities) as for emotional stress.

Medication During Pregnancy

Table 15 presents the interesting part of the data recorded during each mother's interview with the midwife about the use of medication: Of the mothers, 300 denied any use of medication; 610 reported the use of one or more medications. The table shows that differences between the means of the different groups were minimal. Multivariate analysis controlling for examiner and initial state showed

Table 15. Medication Used by the Mother During Pregnancy and Brazelton Cluster Scores (Entries: $M \pm SD$ (n))

					Medication				
	No medication	Total medication users	Psychotropics	Benzodiazepines	Antiemetics	Analgesics	Tocolytics	Antibiotics	Diuretics
Habituation	6.59 ± 1.29 (205)	6.49 ± 1.30 (471)	6.33 ± 1.32 (95)	6.43 ± 1.34 (82)	6.50 ± 1.37 (104)	6.57 ± 1.34 (126)	6.19 ± 1.37 (69)	6.74 ± 1.23 (100)	6.47 ± 1.52 (23)
Orientation	5.15 ± 1.51 (259)	5.23 ± 1.59 (542)	5.53 ± 1.62 (113)	5.52 ± 1.62 (97)	5.06 ± 1.71 (110)	5.12 ± 1.71 (142)	5.39 ± 1.54 (79)	5.18 ± 1.67 (122)	5.45 ± 1.59 (31)
Regulation of State	4.92 ± 1.15 (213)	4.82 ± 1.19 (422)	4.77 ± 1.11 (84)	4.69 ± 1.09 (72)	4.84 ± 1.14 (82)	4.77 ± 1.17 (103)	4.80 ± 1.18 (60)	4.61 ± 1.19 (92)	4.69 ± 1.24 (25)
Motor Performance	4.98 ± 0.80 (296)	4.91 ± 0.76 (599)	4.86 ± 0.85 (123)	4.83 ± 0.87 (106)	4.73 ± 0.83 (124)	4.86 ± 0.73 (158)	4.82 ± 0.84 (85)	4.88 ± 0.81 (132)	4.93 ± 0.68 (33)
Range of State	3.50 ± 0.61 (300)	3.54 ± 0.63 (610)	3.51 ± 0.66 (125)	3.47 ± 0.64 (108)	3.51 ± 0.63 (127)	3.54 ± 0.63 (162)	3.48 ± 0.70 (89)	3.42 ± 0.66 (136)	3.67 ± 0.67 (33)
Autonomic Regulation	6.73 ± 0.87 (264)	6.60 ± 1.03 (558)	6.42 ± 0.98 (114)	6.35 ± 1.13 (100)	6.73 ± 0.97 (120)	6.63 ± 1.06 (141)	6.39 ± 1.19 (82)	6.66 ± 1.00 (123)	6.51 ± 0.88 (29)

the following significant relationships: For the cluster Autonomic Regulation, lower scores were found in children exposed to psychotropic agents or tocolytics during pregnancy, the differences being slightly significant (ρ = .043 and .048, respectively). Taking the benzodiazepines alone, the statistical association is somewhat more marked (ρ = .007). As mentioned earlier, tocolytics and benzodiazepines are frequently prescribed together. We thus examined the influence of benzodiazepines and tocolytics in the same linear model in which we included the occurrence of premature labor. Here, only the benzodiazepines were shown to be a significant influential factor (ρ = .025). When analysis was limited to the most frequently used benzodiazepine, diazepam, this significance disappeared (ρ = .061). The model described here explained about 10% of the variance of the respective cluster score.

For the cluster Range of State, there was a significantly lower mean score in the group taking antibiotics during pregnancy (ρ = .047), as there was for the cluster Motor Performance in the group taking antiemetics (ρ = .007). Significant associations were observed in 5 of 48 tested relationships. Comparison with the no-medication group does not indicate a substantial, systematic effect of the medication.

Medication During Labor

In the 910 mother-child pairs in this group, 223 mothers (24.5%) received no medication during labor. The others received mainly analgesics and spasmolytics in various combinations. The group of psychotropic drugs consisted mainly of low doses of opiates, and Butylscopolamine was the most frequently administered spasmolytic. We were also interested in the children whose mothers received tocolytics or antibiotics. Table 16 shows that the differences between groups in the means of individual clusters are small. The scores of children whose mothers received no medication scarcely differed from those of children whose mothers were exposed to medication. Multivariate analysis controlling for examiner and initial state, however, yielded the following statistically significant relationships: In the benzodiazepine group, scores for Motor Performance were significantly lower (ρ = .018) and in the cluster Range of State there was an interactive effect of initial state and benzodiazepines (ρ = .038).

There also was an interactive effect on the cluster Regulation of State between initial state and spasmolytics (ρ = .0003). This could be interpreted as an influence of the medication either on the initial state itself, or on the waking up process during the BNBAS examination. In the group of children whose mothers received antibiotics during labor, the scores for Range of State and Autonomic Regulation were significantly lower (ρ = .041 and .029, respectively). Overall, the relationships were sporadic and may have been due to pharmacological effects or to the underlying condition. It is nevertheless interesting to note that the significant differences were detected mainly in the two clusters not influ-

Table 16. Medication Administered to the Mother During Labor and Brazelton Cluster Scores (Entries: $M \pm SD$ (n))

	No medication	Total receiving medication	Medication					
			Pychotropic medication			Spasmolytics	Tocolytics	Antibiotics
			Total	Anesthetic	Benzodiazepines			
Habituation	6.50 ± 1.26 (155)	6.53 ± 1.30 (521)	6.52 ± 1.29 (405)	6.68 ± 1.18 (54)	6.49 ± 1.24 (109)	6.54 ± 1.31 (440)	6.53 ± 1.35 (50)	6.31 ± 1.43 (20)
Orientation	5.25 ± 1.58 (195)	5.19 ± 1.56 (606)	5.17 ± 1.55 (469)	4.97 ± 1.57 (65)	5.13 ± 1.70 (135)	5.20 ± 1.58 (505)	5.21 ± 1.53 (66)	4.90 ± 1.84 (27)
Regulation of State	4.77 ± 1.23 (149)	4.90 ± 1.16 (484)	4.88 ± 1.16 (371)	4.70 ± 1.08 (41)	4.84 ± 1.09 (103)	4.92 ± 1.15 (412)	4.96 ± 1.04 (39)	4.59 ± 1.03 (19)
Motor Performance	4.97 ± 0.78 (220)	4.92 ± 0.77 (675)	4.90 ± 0.79 (522)	4.79 ± 0.81 (68)	4.77 ± 0.86 (150)	4.93 ± 0.78 (568)	4.73 ± 0.87 (67)	4.67 ± 0.98 (29)
Range of State	3.48 ± 0.64 (223)	3.54 ± 0.62 (687)	3.54 ± 0.62 (531)	3.41 ± 0.52 (69)	3.45 ± 0.63 (151)	3.55 ± 0.61 (576)	3.44 ± 0.59 (69)	3.28 ± 0.70 (29)
Autonomic Regulation	6.64 ± 0.96 (193)	6.64 ± 0.99 (629)	6.63 ± 0.98 (484)	6.51 ± 1.00 (60)	6.49 ± 1.12 (135)	6.67 ± 0.99 (531)	6.49 ± 1.24 (59)	6.13 ± 1.29 (26)

enced by the Initial State. In the other clusters a pharmacological effect may be hidden behind the effect attributed to the initial state as contextual variable.

The effect of different medications used to assist labor on the newborn has already been studied in detail by many authors and, among other methods, the BNBAS has been used (Aleksandrowicz & Aleksandrowicz, 1974; Brackbill, Kane, Manniello, & Abramson, 1974; Horowitz et al., 1977). Influences on newborn behavior were found to persist for several days but these effects were usually small (Als et al., 1979). In most of the studies, as in ours, however, it was difficult to differentiate reliably between the effects of the individual drugs (Rosenblatt, Redshaw, & Notariani, 1980). The children whose mothers received no medication scored much the same as those whose mothers received medication during labor. This could indicate that the anxiety and psychological stress during childbirth might affect the child as much as medication. We agree, therefore, with the opinion of Rosenblatt et al. (1980) that drugs given during labor should not be judged a priori to be detrimental.

Discussion

By studying a large number of newborns, we hoped to demonstrate some relevant differences in neonatal behavior patterns corresponding to particular influences during pregnancy. Findings of studies on animals on the effect of medication ingested during pregnancy on fetal brain development and later behavior have been shown to be difficult to prove in humans (Coyle, Wagner, & Singer, 1980; Leonard, 1981; Schlumpf & Lichtensteiger, 1982). The examination of the human newborn is an extraordinarily complex endeavor. Changes in behavior or in higher brain functions resulting from influences on the fetus are, in general, (at least for the present) rather difficult to demonstrate. And even if behavioral correlates of events and conditions during pregnancy can be detected in the human newborn, their meaning for further development remains unclear. Currently available neurological assessment (e.g., Prechtl & Beintema, 1964) and behavioral observation methods (e.g., BNBAS) are capable of predicting only gross neurological abnormalities in later life, and no clear-cut relationship with minor CNS dysfunction on follow-up has been described (Dubowitz & Dubowitz, 1981). Nonetheless, the findings in the newborn phase are relevant, since impairment of neonatal behavior will directly affect the mother-child relationship and thus might influence the further development of the infant.

Our cross-sectional study of almost 1,000 newborns yielded far more clearcut and significant differences in the mean cluster scores of the BNBAS for influences of the circumstances of examination (particularly for initial state and interaction with the examiner) than for the large number of influences during pregnancy that we examined. Statistically significant relationships with tobacco and coffee consumption and with use of certain medications could be demonstrated, however. These relationships are consistent with suspected mechanisms, even if coincidental associations can be expected in such a large number of tested hypotheses.

The importance of describing examination conditions is not surprising, given the complexity of the processes being assessed. This points to the necessity of greater standardization if the BNBAS is to be used for epidemiological purposes. In particular, the number of permitted initial states should be reduced, while gestational age at birth, age in days, and time of examination must be taken into consideration. The differences between examiners probably reflected more on interaction with the newborn than different rating of the observed behavior. This has not been observed to any similar extent by other authors. An analysis of the influence of the personality profile of the examiner and its consideration in the BNBAS seems highly desirable.

It is possible that there are other reasons for the fact that few influences of pregnancy factors were demonstrable despite the large number of children examined, and despite statistical correction for external circumstances, using multivariate analysis. This might be related to the fact that our population was rather homogeneous and extreme cases were generally lacking in our collective—for example, an actual lower social class was not represented. With very few exceptions, the mothers were living in settled conditions, had a sufficient diet of adequate standards, and as a rule received good medical care. These factors are reflected also in other indicators of a favorable course of pregnancy (e.g., in contrast to other studies in the literature, the number of premature births to mothers who had smoked did not increase).

Because of limitations of space we have not discussed the problems inherent in obtaining reliable and concise data in an epidemiological survey such as ours. For example, the history of pregnancy and of coffee, nicotine, alcohol, and drug use could be taken only on admission to the labor ward for more than half our sample. Although every effort was undertaken to validate the information given, the time factor could not be taken into account. A more detailed analysis, therefore, of the time allocation of the different influences, such as medication, might have resulted in more significant relationships.

Lester et al. (1982), for example, have pointed out that different factors of pregnancy and labor have an appreciable influence on the Brazelton scores only when acting together with other factors. In that study, each child was given the Brazelton examination seven times. It also was possible to detect effects on the longitudinal development in the first 10 days of life. This raises the question of how suitable the Brazelton Scale is in its present form for cross-sectional studies of the type described here, using only one examination. Subtle effects of various influences during pregnancy—use of medication, illness, or emotional stress—will emerge more clearly when the behavioral pattern is assessed not by means of a point-by-point analysis, but by dynamic observation and recording of the progressive physiological, motor, and growth development of the child. In more longitudinal studies, according to the Brazelton model (1978), the contribution of the caretaker also must be taken into account.

The absence of a greater number of statistically significant relationships with influences during pregnancy might, of course, also be due to our evaluation of the data. The analysis of a study examining 27 different items is extremely demanding and complex. We thought that the seven cluster scores (here, as mentioned before, reduced to six) offered a rational method of reducing and organizing the data in a manner appropriate to the study concept. This approach simplified the evaluation and presentation of the results, but it also introduced the risk of obscuring effects by summarizing possibly contradictory changes in individual scores. Furthermore, the fact that the analysis concentrates on comparison of means and parametric statistics, although ordinal number series and not interval scales are presented, is hardly likely to have influenced the results in view of the large number of evaluated examinations. We would suggest that the Brazelton results, when used as outcome variables, should not be divided into groups as attempted, for example, in the a priori cluster scores (Als, 1978).

These objectives, however, cannot distract from the fact that the behavior and capability for interaction of the newborn, as expressed by the Brazelton scores, appears remarkably robust in the face of the different influences during pregnancy. The same influences are clearly manifest in the somatic domain (e.g., in anthropometric data and the "normal baby" criteria).

Summary

A broad observational study on the effects of influences on the neonate during pregnancy involved 996 singleton live births to Swiss mothers in a regional obstetric clinic in Aarau. The Brazelton Neonatal Behavioral Assessment Scale (BNBAS; Brazelton, 1973) was applied on days 4 to 6 of life to detect possible relationships between pregnancy events and newborns' behavior.

Several contextual variables were analyzed using a restricted collective of 788 healthy, normal children. Statistical analysis (GLM) of six of the seven Brazelton cluster scores demonstrated a marked influence of initial state and examiner. Female newborns scored consistently better on Autonomic Regulation. Time of day, age (in days) at examination, and gestational age at birth had an influence on some of the cluster scores, while amount of feeding (in percent bodyweight) and parity could not be correlated with them.

Initial state and examiner influence, and mothers' smoking more than 20 cigarettes a day before and during pregnancy were related to lower cluster scores in Orientation and Habituation, respectively. Daily alcohol consumption (reported by only 3% of the women) did not show an effect on BNBAS scores, though coffee consumption during the third trimester was associated with decreased scores for Orientation and Motor Performance. According to our data, no influence of illness and other complaints on the part of the mothers, or of emotional and physical stress on newborn behavior could be demonstrated in this medically and socially well supported population. Of medication used during pregnancy and labor, psychotropic agents, antiemetics, and antibiotics were associated with lower scores for the clusters Motor Performance, Range of State, and Autonomic Regulation.

This study demonstrates the problems in assessing neonatal behavior, but at the same time it confirms the potential of the BNBAS to disclose subtle effects. In view of the many complex methodological issues still confronting behavioral teratogenesis in the human neonate, the results presented should not therefore be regarded as definite proof of the presence or absence of certain effects, but rather as a basis for further, strictly controlled investigations.

References

Abelin, T., & Müller, R. (1983). Trend der Rauchgewohnheiten in der Schweiz 1976–1981. *Soz. Praev. Med.*, *28*, 185–194.

Aleksandrowicz, M. K., & Aleksandrowicz, D. R. (1974). Obstetrical pain-relieving drugs as predictors of infant behavior variability. *Child Development*, *45*, 935–945.

Als, H. (1978). Assessing an assessment: Conceptual considerations, methodological issues and a perspective on the future of the Brazelton Neonatal Behavioral Assessment Scale. In A. J. Sameroff (Ed.), Organization and stability of newborn behavior: A commentary on the Brazelton Neonatal Behavioral Assessment Scale. *Monographs Soc. Res. Child Dev.*, *43* (5–6, Serial No. 177), 14–28.

Als, H., Tronick, E., Lester, B. M., & Brazelton,T. B. (1979). Specific neonatal measures: The Brazelton Neonatal Behavioral Assessment Scale. In J.D. Osofsky (Ed.), *The handbook of infant development.* New York: Wiley.

American Academy of Pediatrics (1976). Effects of cigarette-smoking on the fetus and child. *Pediatrics, 57,* 411–413.

Biener, K. (1981). Tabak-, Alkohol- und Tablettenkonsum berufstätiger Frauen- Repräsentativstudie in der Schweiz. *Schweiz. Aerzteztg., 62,*2861–2865.

Brackbill, Y., Kane, J., Manniello, R. L., & Abramson, D. (1974). Obstetric premedication and infant outcome. *Amer. J. Obstet. Gynec., 118,* 377–384.

Brazelton, T. B. (1973). *Neonatal Behavioral Assessment Scale.* London: Spastics International Medical Publications/W. Heinemann Medical Books Ltd.

Brazelton, T. B. (1978). Introduction. In A. J. Sameroff (Ed.), Organization and Stability of Newborn Behavior: A commentary on the Brazelton Neonatal Behavioral Assessment Scale. *Monographs Soc. Res. Child Dev., 43* (5–6, Serial No. 177), 1–13.

Coyle, I., Wagner, M. J., & Singer, G. (1980). Behavioral teratogenesis: A critical evaluation. Neural and Behavioral Teratology In T. V. N. Persaud (Ed.), *Advances in the study of birth defects* (Vol. 4, pp. 111–133). Baltimore, MD: University Park Press.

De Vries, M., & Super, C. M. (1978). Contextual influences on the Neonatal Behavioral

Assessment Scale and implications for its cross-cultural use. In A. J. Sameroff (Ed.), Organization and stability of newborn behavior: A commentary on the Brazelton Neonatal Behavioral Assessment Scale. *Monographs of the Society for Research in Child Development, 43*, (5–6, Serial No. 177), 92–101.

Dubowitz, L. M. S., & Dubowitz, V. (1981). *The neurological assessment of the preterm and full-term newborn infant.* London: Spastics International Medical Publications/ Heinemann Medical Books.

Dubowitz, L. M. S., Dubowitz, V., & Goldberg, C. (1970). Clinical assessment of gestational age in the newborn infant. *J. Pediat., 77*, 1–10.

Ferrari, F., & Pinelli, M. (1980). Studio del comportamento neonatale: Sperimentazione della scala di Brazelton. *Ped. Med. Chir., 2*, 785–790.

Field, T. M., Dabiri, C., Hallock, N., & Shuman, H. H. (1977). Developmental effects of prolonged pregnancy and the postmaturity syndrome. *J. Pediat., 90*, 836–839.

Field, T. M., Hallock, N., Ting,, G., Dempsey, J., Dabiri, C., & Shuman, H. H. (1978). A first year follow-up of high-risk infants: Formulating a cumulative risk index. *Child Develop., 49*, 119–131.

General linear models procedures (GLM) (1982). In *SAS users guide* (pp. 237–263). Cary, NC: SAS Institute.

Horowitz, F., Ashton, L., Culp, R., Gaddis, E., Levin, S., & Reichman, B. (1977). The effects of obstetrical medication on the behavior of Israeli newborn infants and some comparisons with Uruguayan and American infants. *Child Develop., 48*, 1607–1623.

Horowitz, F. D., Brazelton, T. B. (1973). *Research with the Brazelton Neonatal Behavioral Assessment Scale.* London: Heinemann Medical Books.

Kaye, K. (1978). Discriminating among normal infants by multivariate analysis of Brazelton scores: Lumping and smoothing. In A. J. Sameroff (Ed.), Organization and stability of newborn behavior. *Monographs Soc. Res. Child Dev., 43*, (5–6, Serial No. 177), 60–80.

Largo, R. H., Walli, R., Duc, G., Fanconi, A., & Prader, A. (1980). Evaluation of perinatal growth. *Helv. paediat. Acta, 35*, 419–436.

Leijon, I., & Finnstrom, O. (1981). Studies on the Brazelton Neonatal Behavioral Assessment Scale. *Neuropediatrics, 12*, 242–253.

Leonard, B. E. (1981). Effect of psychotropic drugs administered to pregnant rats on the behavior of the offspring. *Neuropharmacology, 20*, 1237–1242.

Lester, B. M., Als, H., & Brazelton, T. B. (1982). Regional obstetric anesthesia and newborn behavior: A reanalysis toward synergistic effects. *Child Develop., 53*, 687–692.

Lester, B. M., Emory, E. K., & Hoffman, S. L. (1976). A multivariate study of the effects of high-risk factors on performance on the Brazelton Neonatal Assessment Scale. *Child Develop., 47*, 515–517.

Linn, S., Schonbaum, S. C., Monson, R. R., Rosner, B., Stubblefield, P. G., & Rian, K. J. (1982). No association between coffee consumption and adverse outcomes of pregnancy. *The New Engl. J. Med., 306*, 141–145.

Meredith, H. V. (1975). Relation between tobacco smoking of pregnant women and body size of their progeny: A compilation and synthesis of published studies. *Hum. Biol., 47*, 451–472.

Meyer, M. B., Jonas, B. S., & Tonascia, J. A. (1976). Perinatal events associated with maternal smoking during pregnancy. *Amer. J. Epidem., 103*, 464–476.

Michaud, J. D., & Jones, D. W. (1980). Thin-layer chromatography for broad spectrum drug detection. *Amer. Lab.*, *12*, 104–107.

Muster, E. (Ed.) (1983). *Zahlen und Fakten zu Alkohol—und Drogenproblemen.* Lausanne, Switzerland: SFA [Schweizerische Fachstelle für Alkoholprobleme].

Naeye, R. L. (1981). Influence of maternal cigarette smoking during pregnancy and fetal and childhood growth. *Obstetrics & Gynecology*, *57*, 18–21.

Parsons, W. D., & Heims, A. H. (1981). Prolonged half-life of caffeine in healthy term newborn infants. *J. Pediat.*, *98*, 640–641.

Prechtl, H., & Beintema, D. (1964). *The neurological examination of the full-term newborn infant.* London: Heinemann Medical Books.

Rosenblatt, D. B., Redshaw, M. E., & Notariani, L. J. (1980). Pain relief in childbirth and its consequences for the infant. *Trends in Pharmacological Sciences, 1,* 365–369.

Rosenblith, J. F. (1961). The modified Graham behavior test for neonates: Test-retest reliability, normative data and hypothesis for future work. *Biol. Neonate, 3,* 174.

Sameroff, A. J. (1978). Summary and conclusions: The future of newborn assessment. In A. J. Sameroff (Ed.), Organization and stability of newborn behavior: A commentary on the Brazelton Neonatal Behavior Assessment Scale. *Monographs Soc. Res. Child Dev., 43* (5–6, Serial No. 177), 102–117.

Sameroff, A. J., Krafchuk, E. E., & Bakow, H. A. (1978). Issues in grouping items from the Neonatal Behavioral Assessment Scale. In A. J. Sameroff (Ed.), Organization and stability of newborn behavior: A commentary on the Brazelton Neonatal Behavior Assessment Scale. *Monographs Soc. Res. Child Dev., 43,* (5–6, Serial No. 177), 46–59.

Saxton, D. W. (1978). The behavior of infants whose mothers smoke in pregnancy. *Early Human Development, 2* (4), 363–369.

Schlumpf, M., & Lichtensteiger, W. (Eds.) (1982). Drugs and hormones in brain development. *Monographs in Neural Sciences, 9.* Basel, Switzerland: Karger.

Strauss, M. E., & Rourke, D. L. (1978). A multivariate analysis of the Neonatal Behavioral Assessment Scale in several samples. In A. J. Sameroff (Ed.), Organization and stability of newborn behavior: A commentary on the Brazelton Neonatal Behavioral Assessment Scale. *Monographs of the Society for Research in Child Development, 43,* (5–6, Serial No. 177), 81–91.

Streissguth, A. P., Landesman-Dwyer, S., Martin, J. C., & Smith, D. W. (1980). Teratogenic effects of alcohol in humans and laboratory animals. *Science, 209,* 353–361.

Telzrow, R. H., Snyder, D. M., Tronick, E., Als, H., & Brazelton, T. B. (1980). The behavior of jaundiced infants undergoing phototherapy. *Developmental Medicine & Child Neurology, 22,* 317–326.

Tronick, E., Wise, S., Als, H., Adamson, L., Scanlon, J., & Brazelton, T. B. (1976). Regional obstetric anesthesia and newborn behavior: Effect over the first ten days of life. *Pediatrics, 58,* 94–100.

Verny, T., & Kelly, J. (1981). *The secret life of the unborn child.* New York: Summit Books.

Wüthrich, P., Hausherr, H. U., & Müller, R. (1977). Der schweizerische Alkoholkosum. (Arbeitsbericht der Forschungsabteilung No. 1.) Lausanne: Schweiz. Fachstelle für Alkoholprobleme.

Chapter 3

A Cross-Cultural Study of Nepalese Neonatal Behavior*

M. Eileen Walsh Escarce

*Pediatric Gastroenterology Clinical Nurse Specialist,
Departments of Pediatrics, Gastroenterology, and Nursing,
Stanford University Medical Center, Stanford, CA*

A human baby's behavior powerfully influences the caretaking he or she receives (Bell, 1971; Field, 1977; Osofsky, 1976). It is expected that babies who are labeled "full-term and healthy" will have a specific repertoire of behaviors (Brazelton, 1973). Babies who are full-term and healthy but malnourished do not meet these expectations and have shown behaviors significantly different from those of full-term, healthy, and well-nourished babies.

Fetal malnutrition is usually inferred indirectly by relying on a low birthweight for gestational age (Lubchenco, Searles, & Brazie, 1972). Babies whose birthweight is either below the 10th percentile or below two standard deviations from the mean for the week of gestation are called small-for-date or small-for-gestational-age (SGA). The birthweight and adaptive status of human newborns is strongly related to maternal nutrition and health before conception (Barrett, 1982) and during gestation. Thus, birthweight is highly influenced by the mother's pre-pregnancy height and weight, which in turn partly reflect her nutrition throughout her own development—a mother malnourished during her own childhood tends to have smaller offspring. In addition, most babies who are SGA do not have congenital anomalies or intrauterine infections (Lubchenco, 1976) and

*The investigator was partially supported by Professional Nurse Traineeship No.2-A-11-NU 00240, No.2-A-11-NU 00240-05, and a Yale University School of Medicine International Health Fellowship during the conduct of this study. The author wishes to acknowledge Barry Lester, Ph.D. and Joel Hoffman, Ph.D. for their assistance with statistical analyses, and Debra Vollmer, M.A. for her skilled typing of this manuscript.

the most likely cause of their smallness is a reduced supply of nutrients while in utero (Behrman, 1973).

The Rohrer Ponderal Index (PI) has been used in recent years as a more sensitive measure to identify infants suffering from fetal malnutrition. The PI is a weight-length ratio that is a direct measure of body mass (birthweight in grams × 100 divided by the cube of crown-to-heel length in centimeters). A low value indicates thinness, and a high value, obesity. For American infants of gestational age of at least 38 weeks, the 10th percentile of PI is 2.30 and the third percentile is 2.20. Because the ponderal index measures body mass, it controls for skeletal size. In contrast, the small-for-gestational-age category includes infants who are not malnourished but are light because they are short, and excludes infants who are malnourished but are heavy because they are long. Moreover, again in contrast to birthweight, the PI is not related to sex, fetal age, or parity, according to one study (Miller & Hassanein, 1973).

Several studies have shown that even slight differences in nutritional status at birth have significant effects on a baby's behavior in the newborn period. Two American studies (Als, Tronick, Adamson, & Brazelton, 1976; Lester, 1979) found that American full-term infants who are underweight for length (PI < 2.30) show poorer scores on the Brazelton Neonatal Behavioral Assessment Scale (hereafter, BNBAS; Brazelton, 1973) than full-weight controls, and that their poorer scores are correlated with cry patterns associated with central nervous system (CNS) stress (Lester 1979; Lester & Zeskind, 1978). These babies often were described by their parents as undemanding (as they rarely cried), and they seemed not to want to be played with or fed and appeared happiest if left alone. Their poor motor performance and general lack of vigor puzzled some mothers and made them feel uneasy with their babies. On follow-up, which took place between 6 weeks and 9 months, the majority of parents described their babies as "difficult to live with"—they now were easily overstimulated, continously on the go, unpredictable in their sleeping and eating patterns, and generally highly reactive (Als et al., 1976).

Other researchers have shown that American full-term underweight (FTUW) infants are more prone than their full-weight counterparts to later suffer from nonorganic failure to thrive (Rosenn, Stein, & Bates, 1976) or be put up for adoption (Miller & Hassanein, 1973). A cross-cultural study in Guatemala (Brazelton, Tronick, Lechtig, Laskey, & Klein, 1977) has shown effects of intrauterine protein malnutrition on neonates' motor and interactive behaviors similar to those shown in studies on infants in the U.S. Guatemalan FTUW infants were also characterized as underdemanding and poor elicitors of caretaker responses.

Hypothetically, a seemingly apathetic, undernourished baby might have little hope of receiving optimal nurturing from his parents. An unattractive, largely unresponsive, fragile baby who gives the message of wanting to be left alone might cause a parent to feel anxious, frustrated, or inadequate. Such feelings could increase the normal tension accompanying child care, and add to the poor organization of state by the child (Als et al., 1976). In developing countries such an undemanding infant could interact synergistically with a nutritionally depressed caretaker in a stressful environment, failing to elicit the sensorimotor stimulation necessary for catch-up, and making chronic malnutrition an almost certain outcome (Klein & Stern, 1971; Miller & Hassanein, 1973; Rosenn et al., 1976). Thus, a self-perpetuating cycle might emerge in populations where maternal malnutrition results in FTUW infants: The infants' latter behaviors would make them susceptible to continued nutritional and sensorimotor deprivation during early infancy, which in turn has far-reaching effects on their later development.

Nepal, designated by the United Nations as one of the least developed countries in the world, is a nation where 200 of every 1,000 newborns die before they have reached 1 year of age, and 40–50% of children die before age 5 (Acharya, 1977). Low birthweight, resulting from widespread maternal undernutrition (HMG/Nepal, 1979) and lack of antenatal care (Acharya, 1977), is the primary cause of early neonatal mortality and morbidity. The goal of this study was to discover whether Nepalese newborns would display behaviors typical of other FTUW babies.

Description of the Cultural Setting: Nepal

Landlocked between India and China, Nepal is a sovereign, independent Hindu kingdom set among the highest mountain range on Earth, the Himalayas. Modern Nepal was founded in the late 18th century when Pritvi Narayan Shah forged a unified country from a number of independent mountain states by conquest and treaty. After 1800, his descendants were unable to keep political control over Nepal and a period of internal turmoil ensued which resulted in the Rana family gaining power.

Under the Ranas, Nepal became closed to outside influence. This preserved its independence during the colonial rule in India, but contributed to its complete lack of economic development during the period. The political movements toward independence in India had their impact on Nepal, and opposition to the Rana rule grew during the 1930s and 1940s. By 1950, a revolution toppled the Rana regime and restored the Shah dynasty to power. It was then that Nepal's borders were opened to foreigners and Nepal's contact with the outside world was initiated. Since then, contact has increased dramatically with economic assistance programs from various countries and the influx of numerous mountaineers and tourists.

Nepal's geographic variety—high mountains and low valleys—effectively isolates settlements from one another and contributes to the persistence of more than 75 different ethnic groups and 50 different spoken languages (Taylor & Thapa, 1972) within a population of 14 million. The country can be divided into three roughly parallel strips running east to west: the southernmost flat Terai, a central strip composed of hills varying from 3,000 to 12,000 ft above sea level, and the northernmost area encompassing Himalayan peaks ranging in elevation from 12,000 to 29,000 ft. Sixty percent of the population lives in the central hills and represents numerous castes and tribal groups of mixed ancestry (e.g., Mongol, Tibetan, Indian, Burmese, and Newar) who have inhabited the main settlement in the Kathmandu Valley from ancient times.

Over the past two decades, the Kathmandu Valley has gained one-half million people in its population growth. The three main ethnic groups living in the Kathmandu Valley are the Newars, Brahmins, and Chettris. The Brahmins, a high-caste Hindu people from northern India, invaded the western hill area of Nepal in the 12th century. Living in the area at the time were the Khas, a people of Aryan stock racially akin to the Brahmins, but Buddhist. Progeny of mixed Kha–Brahmin parentage converted to Hinduism and became known as Chettris. The Chettri House of Gurkha conquered the Newars of the Kathmandu Valley in the 18th century and the unification of the country followed soon thereafter, with the Chettris and Brahmins becoming the ruling group. Their language, Nepali, became and continues to be the official language of Nepal.

Nepal's designation as one of the least developed countries in the world is reflected by the annual per capita income of 1,000 rupees (U.S. $120). Approximately 94% of the economically active population works on the land in agriculture, herding, forestry, and fishing; 1% works in business, another 1% in industry, and 3% in service occupations. Until recently Nepal's agricultural resources sufficed to support its population at a subsistence level. Only 12–14% of the total land is arable (*Nepal Manual for Health Workers*, 1979), however, and there is no means of agricultural expansion. Therefore, the future maintenance of this tenuous balance is constantly threatened.

Data on Nepal are uniformly weak for the following reasons: Collection procedures are recent and still being refined, resources are scare, and the extreme geography hinders data gathering (Taylor & Thapa, 1972). In the absence of a registration system, fertility and mortality rates are estimated from census and national sample surveys. The Nepal Fertility Survey of 1976 estimated a crude birth rate of 43.6/1,000; in contrast, the crude death rate was only 19.5/1,000 in 1974–1975 (HMG/Nepal, 1979). High fertility in Nepal has been attributed to early and almost universal marriage, the high infant mortality, and a high preference for sons. The infant mortality rate was last reported in 1976 as 152 per 1,000 live births, and between 40% and 50% of children died before they reached the age of 5 years.

Although there are no national data on specific causes of infant and child mortality, nutritional deficiences and communicable diseases have been implicated (Health Service Organization, 1979). Other factors cited are ignorance, poverty, illiteracy, low socioeconomic status, lack of awareness regarding health, and social taboos and practices which lead to the avoidance of the available suboptimal health facilities (Acharya, 1977).

The annual government health budget (based on 1978–1979 figures) amounts to approximately 13 rupees (U.S. $.40) per capita, with less than a third of this amount going to direct services. The 1976 Health Manpower Developmental Research Project reported that government health care services reach only 3% of the persons in need, and as of 1978 there was only one doctor per 30,000 population. The remainder of health services is provided by traditional practitioners, ayurvedic clinics, and private practitioners. A 10-year report on self-care practices in Nepal and India (Parker, 1979) found that self-care or care by relatives and friends was the predominant source of maternity care in Nepal during 1976–1977. Government facilities, traditional healers, and midwives played a minor role. Acharya (1977) reported that only 2% of births occur in Nepal's 33 hospitals, demonstrating the community's lack of access to a hospital or its tendency to choose delivering at home.

Nepali Childbearing and Child-rearing Practices

There is a paucity of literature on motherhood beliefs and practices in Nepal. Nevertheless, the following descriptions are derived from reviews of contemporary Newari, Brahmin, and Chettri practices in the Kathmandu Valley.

Attitudes Toward Fertility

In Hindu religious belief the need for offspring (preferably male) is the only legitimate reason for marriage and sex. Hindu descent is strongly patrilineal. Not only do the lineage name and family lands pass through males, but certain important rituals connected with the continuity of the family and the spiritual peace of the forefathers can be performed only by sons. It is a source of pride to be pregnant and a source of shame to go too many years after marriage without conceiving. Having children, especially sons, is politically important to a woman in a large extended family.

A woman's role in the joint family evolves through three overlapping stages, each stage defined by the "power" with which she must seek to ally herself. While her husband is subordinate to his father and mother (*sasura* and *sasu*), she must please them. During this period any open support or affection that her husband may show is considered disrespectful of the parents. After the *sasura* and *sasu* have died and their sons have set up separate households, a woman's power comes more directly from her relationship with her husband. The third stage occurs when her sons become old enough to marry and bring in daughters-in-law for her to command. If she outlives her husband, she may ultimately exert considerable influence through her sons, who have become the senior males but who nevertheless owe paramount respect to her. Obviously, a woman who has been unable to have children can never attain the power and security of this third stage. If a woman has had no children after 6 or 7 years of marriage, or if she has produced only daughters, the man has the right—even the duty—to bring in another wife. The fact that recent laws demand the first wife's permission (*manjuri*) for a second marriage is sometimes ignored in the village setting, and tradition prevails.

For a woman, then, personal fulfillment within the family and social identity depend upon being a mother. Yet despite this positive attitude toward birth and fertility there remains in the Hindu world view a strong ambivalence about their ultimate value. The ambivalence is part of a deeper religious and philosophical question: Does man achieve spiritual salvation through participation in and contribution to the ongoing organic process of life, or through control of and withdrawal from them? Hinduism views both options as being worthwhile. The "worldly" path followed by most villagers is the ancient Vedic tradition—being a householder, honoring the gods daily, sustaining ancestors with ritual feasts year after year, and producing offspring who will in turn provide ritual sustenance after one's own death. The villager is always aware that there is another, probably ultimate, path—that chosen by the ascetic *sadhus*, who give up caste rank, family, and wealth and seek control of the bodily senses and emotions (eating, elimination, copulation, birth, and death)—to attain release from the very world of organic change and decay in which the villager is immersed. Although the villager and *sadhu* choose different paths, they share a common value system and their common ambivalence toward bodily processes is expressed in terms of purity and pollution. Examples of these attitudes will become clearer in the following discussions of menstruation, conception, pregnancy, labor and delivery, and the naming ceremony.

Menstruation

For Nepali Hindus, not only is *na chune* (menstruation—literally "not touching") connected with fertility and female sexuality, it is also highly taboo. Contact with menstruating women and menstrual blood cause a high-caste Hindu to fall into a state of ritual impurity. For 3 days out of every month, every woman between menarche and menopause becomes polluted and like a female member of the untouchable caste. She must not enter the kitchen or touch food or water that others will eat or drink, and she sleeps in a room apart from others. Bennett (1976) reports that women themselves, while acknowledging menstruation as the source of their much-wanted children (see below), connect it with sin. The most important occasion of the year for childbearing women is the combined festival of Tij and Rishi Panchami, which focuses on purification from the possible sin of having touched a man while menstruating. The *puja* (a purifying bathing ritual) symbolizes the festival's meaning:

> In the privacy of predawn darkness . . . every woman must rub *rato mato* (red mud) on her genitals 360 times and then wash herself with clean water 360 times. (Bennett, 1974, p.9)

The paradox of strong negative feelings toward menstruation and the equally strong rule enforcing coitus on the 4th day (see below) exemplify the pervasive Hindu ambivalence toward sex and fertility.

Conception

Nepali explanations of conception (*garbha basne*) vary from the poetic and religious to the more practical. Bennett (1976) describes several views:

> The seed (*bij*) is the man's and the woman's blood. [It] goes into the seed and forms the baby. A child is found of god, gives the seed and that is a matter of karma.
> Both men and women have seed which is liquid . . . during intercourse the seed mixes in the woman's vagina to form the child whose sex is determined by 'whichever partner's seed was stronger.' There is a strong idea that the woman has a fertile period connected with her menstrual cycle . . . a man has a religious duty to sleep with his wife on the fourth day of her menstrual cycle; if he does not, he commits the sin of a murderer, because it is believed that at that time there is a child in the womb—a little blood is still coming . . . the fifth and the seventh through the fourteenth days are also considered as the woman's fertile period. On the sixth day and after the fifteenth day after menstruation a woman supposedly cannot conceive, and sleeping with her husband then is considered as only for pleasure.
> The number of children a woman will have and even their sex is determined by her own moral history: her *karma*. Although women know that coitus during the specified fertile periods is necessary for conception, her ultimate fertility rests on the spiritual merit that she has accrued in preceding lives. A large number of healthy children, as long as they are not all girls, is not only proof of, but reward for her past virtue.

Despite these many versions of how the child is conceived, it is commonly believed that it is from the blood that would have been lost in menstruation that the child grows. Paradoxically, the infant is not considered impure.

Pregnancy

There are many terms for pregnancy in the Nepali language: *dui-jiu ko hunne* ("being with two bodies"), *bhuri ma bokne* ("carrying in the belly"), and *nani bokne* ("carrying a baby"). A description of Nepali women's concept of fetal development exhibits the clarity of their understanding:

> 'First a seed like that of *til* (sesame) falls and then it grows as big as the *dhal* (rice). Then it becomes as big as the *makai* (corn) and then as the *lapsi seed* (Spondias acuminata) and then as the blood congeals and it grows as big as this (showing a fist) by the third month. Sometimes between the fifth and sixth month the *sas* or life breath enters the child's body. From that point on, the mother will feel the infant kick and it is considered a human being.'—An old woman's description. (Bennett, 1976, p. 21)

There is a common belief that female children develop faster and are stronger and more difficult to deliver than male children. The female's life breath is thought to enter at 5 months, but the male's only after 6 months.

The whole development and delivery of a child is thought of as a heating process of the women's body. After the 8th month of pregnancy the entire body is believed to be heated.

> 'The whole body becomes weary. You don't feel like eating anything and there is a fever within you. From the eighth month there is *atma joro* (fever which is not apparent physically, nevertheless still present within) and you are unable to do heavy work.'—One woman's description. (Bennett, 1976, p. 22)

It is said that village women know that labor is always accompanied by a fever, and experienced women can judge the amount of time left before a woman will deliver by feeling how hot her forehead is.

The pregnant woman's face is said to get thinner (sometimes during the last 2 months) and her eyes to become sunken because the unborn child's appetite is growing and it is eating more of its mother's food. Usually, special efforts are made to feed the woman well during this time. The woman typically continues to do much the same work in the fields and around the house, with the exception of carrying heavy loads. There are certain ritual restrictions on the activities of a pregnant woman as well. After the 5th month she is not allowed to participate in *puja* or to go to a temple. After the 8th month, she may not cook *dhal bhat* (lentils and rice) for her elders or touch water they are to drink.

Labor and delivery

It is considered very important that the mother be kept warm during labor and after delivery. Ghee (yak butter) or oil is heated and rubbed (*seknu*) on the mother's back, rectal area, and stomach. This massage is thought to ease the pains and to speed the passage of the child. Throughout labor the woman wears a waist cloth which is never removed; it is tied high above the stomach "to prevent the child from going up to the mother's mouth." If she is hungry, she will be fed foods such as hot milk, ghee, and rice, or *misri pani* (a heated sugar water), which are thought to be internally warming. The laboring woman is expected to run some fever and to perspire, because the whole process of labor is conceived of as an internal heating of the body which must be aided by warm foods, warm oil rubs, and so forth.

Men, children, and all nulliparous women are excluded from the delivery area. Some say their presence may make the woman's labor longer and more painful. Men are not even supposed to hear the woman's cries during labor, and the shame of letting men hear can be a strong incentive for stoicism on the woman's part. Women also are discouraged from calling the name of their mother during labor, for it is said that three mothers will then bear the burden of labor pain—the delivering woman, her mother, and mother Earth.

The breaking of the waters is called *sano sutak*, after which labor becomes more intense (*kanne betha*). During labor and delivery, women assume either a squatting or a kneeling position. At the time of delivery, the helper gets behind the mother and with her knee or hands presses against the mother's rectum. If this is not done, it is said that the child may come out "where we defecate" and the mother will die (Bennett, 1976).

Women try to face either east or west so the child will be born facing an auspicious direction (i.e., in astrologically good order) (Fleming & Fleming, 1978) rather than toward the north or south, which are associated with death. When the child is born, it may be shown to the mother. It can never be shown to the father until a *jyotish* (astrologer) has been consulted to determine whether the child has been born under a *mulh* (an unlucky astrological sign), which is dangerous to its father. In such cases the child may have to be concealed for a few days from the father, or it may have to be removed from its parents' house altogether and raised by others until the dangerous period has passed.

Sutak (from the Sanskrit *sutaka–birth*) refers to the specific 10-day ritual pollution that is attached to a woman, her husband, and her relatives after she has given birth. It stems from the belief that since the menstrual blood that has not appeared for 10 months now comes with the baby, it is as though all those months of *nachune* are compressed into 10 days (Bennett 1974, p. 28). The *sutkeri* (new mother) is untouchable to all, and especially to men, during this period. Other women can touch her when they come to massage her with oil. Afterward, these women helpers must wash their bodies and hair and change into clean clothes before eating food or touching a man. Since the infant itself is not polluted, he or she may be handled by both men and women.

The *sutkeri* washes her breasts soon after delivery because that is believed to start the milk flowing. Rich food and *juwano ko jhol* (soup made from a medicinal herb) are said to be effective in making milk come. Bennett reports that while some women begin nursing immediately after birth, others whose milk is delayed must wait until the 3rd day. Until the milk has come, the infant may be fed ghee with or without sugar, cow's milk, or *litho* (rice flour and ghee paste mixed with hot water or milk). Once the infant commences nursing, he or she is usually given no supplementary foods until *pasne*, a ceremony during which the infant is fed its first rice meal.

The newborn is bathed soon after birth. During the remainder of the *sutak* and until the *pasne* ceremony, the child is oiled daily. This is believed to mold the infant's shape physically and to convey love and affection (Note 1). In addition, the child should be given no stitched clothes to wear during the first 10 days, and is covered instead with pieces of old saris. A *damai* (member of the tailor caste) meanwhile fashions the clothes that will dress the child after the naming ceremony on the 11th day. These are *bhotos* (sleeveless shirts with strings to tie at the shoulders) and at least one cap with a tiny cape down the back to keep drafts off the child's neck. It is considered bad luck to make clothes from new cloth until a child has had *pasne, so household members and neighbors are expected to contribute cast-off clothing for the infant's tal* (diapers).

The Naming Ceremony

On the morning of the 11th day the *sutkeri* can finally bathe herself, her clothes, and her bedding, to prepare herself for the *nuharan* ceremony. During this, her baby will be named and she and the household will be purified. The rituals vary among the castes, but the idea is essentially the same. After this day, both *sutkeri* and child spend many hours *gam thapne* ("soaking up the sun"), covered with oil. It is believed that the infant needs to be dried and warmed after many months in the watery womb.

Just as female infants are believed to move during the 5th month of pregnancy rather than the 6th, so girl babies are ready for their pasne in their 5th month, one month earlier than boys. This is said to be because girls develop faster, but it may also be due to the fact that females are usually connected with odd numbers and males with even numbers in Hindu symbology. Prior to the *pasne*, the nursing infant and mother are considered an organic and ritual unit. With the first rice eating, the nursing link begins to weaken and the child begins to be perceived as a separate ritual entity.

The Study of Newborn Behavior

Background

Nepali concepts of child development. Nepali adults have a very relaxed attitude toward child development and especially toward their role in it as adults and parents (Bennett, 1976). It is a common belief that all normal children will pass at their own speed through several stages. The first stage, *thangne ko baccha*, is said to last 5–6 months. This refers literally to the "diaper" or "lap" baby. The *kakhe baccha* moves around very little and is content to stay in a basket or a crib suspended from the porch, but should eventually be able to smile, recognize close family members, and grab objects. The *bameh sarne* or crawling stage follows, and overlaps the *tuku tuku hirne* or toddler stage, which may begin anywhere from 10 months to 2 years of age. During this stage, *boli phutiyo* (imitative sounds) and then *tote boli* (baby talk) begin. *Hurrinu* or *kudhne* is used to describe the child who can walk with some assurance. Finally, sometime between the ages of 5 and 6, the child should achieve the *prasasta bolne* stage, now able to converse freely and be understood.

By American standards this timetable is very flexible. The Nepalese view growing up as a natural process proceeding at its own pace, more or less irrespective of any parental influence. This is not to imply that Nepali parents take no interest in their developing offspring. Bennett (1976) contends that although it is true that young fathers in a joint household tend to be detached from the child in public situations, out of respect for their own father who, as head of the household, is still the categorical "father" of the child, the grandfather, grandmother, and mother will spend hours playing "give and take" and later teaching the child to say *namaste* (a respectful greeting). This interaction with the child is seen less as a conscious effort to teach and develop the child than as a pleasurable family pastime. The nature of the role the child plays in these interactions has not been defined previously. The purpose of this study was to explore the characteristics that Nepalese neonates might bring to these exchanges.

Methods

Study design. This exploratory study took place in July 1980 and focused on assessing the behavioral characteristics of urban Nepalese newborns. Two groups of full-term, normal newborns were examined twice during the early postpartum period. Postpartum practices which may have influenced the newborn behaviors were documented.

Setting

Since only 2% of Nepalese babies are delivered in hospitals, this study of hospital-born neonates represents a select group of urban Nepalis. The two hospitals chosen for this study—Shanta Bhawan Mission Hospital and Prasuli Grihi Maternity Hospital—are both located on the outskirts of Kathmandu. Kathmandu is the largest village and the capital city of Nepal, although it is surrounded by six smaller towns with populations ranging from 10,000 to 45,000. The majority of the population in these towns is Newari, and the remainder is either Chettri or Brahmin.

The hospitals Shanta Bhawan and Prasuli Griha. In 1952, Shanta Bhawan Mission Hospital was founded by the United Mission of Nepal as the first

Photo 1.   Nepalese mother and baby in bed at Prasuli Griha Maternity Hospital.
(*Photo by author*)

hospital in the country (Health Service Organization, 1979). It is the best-equipped general hospital in Nepal. The number of births in 1977 was 682; during July 1980, 2–5 babies were born there each week. Prasuli Griha is the public maternity hospital. In 1977, the annual birth rate was 4,024 (Acharya, 1977), representing over a third of the total number (11,973) of hospital births in the country. During July 1980, 20–25 babies were born there each week. Shanta Bhawan reputedly provided a higher standard of care than did Prasuli Griha.

At both hospitals, both the mother's and the baby's length of stay depended on parity: primiparae stayed 3–4 days; multiparae, 1–3 days. From the time of delivery, the babies usually slept cuddled alongside their mothers. Occasionally a crib was set at the end of the mother's bed, but it would be used rarely. The mother was the newborn's primary caregiver throughout the hospital stay. All babies were examined in their own cribs or on a hospital bed. The exams took place amid roosters crowing, birds chirping and flying past, dogs barking while meandering through the wards, the sounds of other babies being born, physicians' rounds, and onlookers entering the exam area to observe.

Subjects

From July 1 to July 23, 1980, a convenience sample of 23 normal full-term newborns—12 from Prasuli Griha Maternity Hospital and 11 from Shanta Bhawan Mission Hospital—was chosen according to the following criteria:

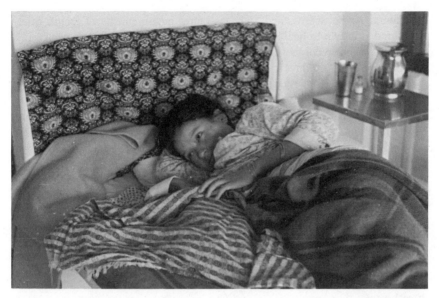

Photo 2.   Nepalese mother and baby *en face* position, in Prasuli Griha Maternity Hospital. (*Photo by author*)

Clinically healthy as defined by physical exam performed and recorded by the hospital pediatrician;

Full-term (38–42 weeks gestation) both by the hospital pediatrician's assessment and by the examiner's Newborn Maturity Rating Classification (Ballard, Kazmaier, & Driver, 1977);

Birth by vaginal delivery, including spontaneous, low-forceps, and vacuum extraction deliveries;

One-minute or 5-minute Apgar scores ≤ 7;

Medications during labor limited to a maximum dose of Phenergan 25 mg/Pethedine 25 mg I.M. given prior to 1 hour before delivery.

Data Collection

Data collection included the following:

Results of a demographic and obstetrical information survey devised by the researcher and completed by interviews with the mother or by hospital chart reviews (information was elicited concerning the parents' ages, father's occupation, family's caste and religion, mother's parity and degree of antenatal care, length of labor in hours, and type, amount, and timing of medication administered during labor or delivery);

Information pertaining to the infant, including its date of birth, sex, age in hours, Apgar scores, and anthropometric measurements of length (measured as crown-to-heel length with the infant placed in the tonic neck reflex position and recorded to the nearest centimeter), weight (measured on a balance scale on days 1 and 3 of life and recorded in grams), and head circumference (recorded to 0.5 cm);

Results of the Newborn Maturity Rating and Classification Scale;

Results of the BNBAS, administered on days 1 and 3 to enhance validity (Brazelton, 1973). The Rohrer Ponderal Index was calculated from the anthropometric measurements on day 1.

Data were interpreted by reduction of performance on all BNBAS items to the following summary cluster scores:

1. A Habituation cluster combining the response decrements to light, rattle, bell, and pinprick;
2. An Orientation cluster including the infant's alertness and orientation to inanimate visual, inanimate auditory, animate visual, and animate visual and auditory stimuli;
3. A Motor Performance cluster based on general tonus, motor maturity, pull-to-sit response, defensive reactions, and activity level in alert states;
4. A Range of State cluster based on the infant's peak of excitement, rapidity of buildup to a crying state, irritability, and lability of states;
5. A Regulation of State cluster including cuddliness, consolability with intervention, self-quieting activity, and hand-to mouth facility;
6. An Autonomic Regulation cluster which includes tremulousness, amount of startle, and skin color lability;
7. A Reflexes score, which is a count of the infant's total number of abnormal reflexes;
8. An Organization for Arousal Level score rating the baby's accessibility for interaction during the exam.

The first six cluster scores are mean scores that range from 1 to 9, with higher scores representing better performance. The score on the Reflexes cluster can vary from 0 to 20, although in this case a lower score is better. The score for the Organization for Arousal Level cluster ranges between 1 and 5. A score of 1 indicates a calm and alert baby throughout the examination, while a score of 5 reflects an infant who more than three fourths of the time is fussy, difficult to console, and difficult to bring back to an alert state to interact with the examiner. Gradations in behavior are assigned intermediate scores and, again, lower scores are better (Lester, Als, & Brazelton, 1978).

Statistical Methods

Score data analysis were performed on the summary cluster scores. Because of the demographic differences between two hospitals (see below), and because the

BNBAS was administered twice to each subject, a repeated measure ANOVA with hospital (Shanta Bhawan vs. Prasuli Griha) and day (day 1 vs. day 3) as the independent variables and day as the repeated measure was first run. The samples from the two hospitals were combined for the purpose of further analysis.

Next, the hypothesis was tested that high- and low-PI infants within the combined Nepalese sample differ. Groups were formed by median split on PI = 2.22, and repeated measure ANOVA with PI (high vs. low) and Day as the independent variables and day as the repeated measure was performed. And last, the hypothesis was tested that Nepalese infants perform better than American infants of equal PI. The combined Nepalese sample, PI = 2.23, was matched with a sample of 23 American newborns with PI = 2.24 ± 0.02. The groups were compared by MANOVA, and univariate repeated-measure analyses were used to determine the sources of any differences. Differences between groups were considered significant with $p < .05$.

Results

Demographic and obstetric data. The total Nepalese sample of 23 babies included 10 males and 13 females. Shanta Bhawan was understood and confirmed by Nepalese nurses to be attended by the "higher class" population. Hospital fees were higher (1–125 rupees, or U.S. $.08–10.00) and fathers' occupations (e.g., law professor, lama, diplomat, engineer, businessman) reflected higher education and a prestigious position in the Nepali community. The diversity of Shanta Bhawan infants' Hindu castes (Brahmin, Chettri, Newar, Rai, Bist, and unknown) represented the transient heterogeneous population of urban Kathmandu.

In contrast, Prasuli Griha hospital was used by "low middle-class" mothers. Hospital fees (0–10 rupees, or U.S. $.00–.80) were minimal, and fathers' occupations (e.g., mechanic, serviceman, student, businessman, technician) reflected a minimal education and low prestige. Moreover, the Prasuli Griha infants came from only two Hindu castes (Chettri and Newar) and probably were more representative of the overall population of the Kathmandu valley.

The mothers' age range (18–35 years, mean 23) was the same at both hospitals. Most (81%) Shanta Bhawan mothers received antenatal care, while only 1 Prasuli Griha mother did. Half of all mothers were primiparae, but only 2 of 23 received medication during labor. The duration of labor varied from 2 to 27.5 hr, and the majority (83%) of births were by normal spontaneous vaginal delivery. Although 4 deliveries (17%) were by forceps or vacuum extraction, all infants were in good condition at birth. All mothers had breast-fed their babies one or more times before the first exam.

Infant data. All babies were clinically healthy, with mean Apgar scores of 7.2 at 1 min and 8.5 at 5 min, mean gestational age 39.7 weeks by Newborn Maturity Rating and Classification Scale, and mean birthweight 2,735 g. This mean birthweight was appropriate for gestational age (AGA), but 3 individual infants were SGA. All head circumferences and lengths were AGA. The mean calculated PI was 2.23 (< 10th percentile), indicating that the average Nepali infant was undernourished (see Table 1).

Group comparisons. Statistically significant differences were found according to hospital for the Range of State cluster ($F(1,45) = 5.73$, $p < .05$) and according to day for the Regulation of State cluster ($F(1,45) = 4.62$, $p < .05$). There were no significant interactions. A combined Nepali group was considered for all further analyses.

Next we tested the hypothesis that high- and low-PI Nepalese infants differ. Groups were formed by median split (PI > 2.22 and PI < 2.22, respectively), and ANOVA, as previously explained, revealed no differences in the summary cluster scores between high- and low-PI groups.

The last analysis tested the hypothesis that Nepalese infants perform better than American infants of equal PI. The Nepalese sample and a matched sample of 23 American infants, as previously described, were found to be significantly different on the BNBAS as shown by MANOVA. Univariate repeated-measures analysis used to determine the sources of the difference showed that the Nepalese

Table 1.   Individual Data on Infants of Total Nepalese Sample

Infant	Sex	Gestational age (weeks)	Birthweight (g)	Crown-to-heel length (cm)	Ponderal Index
1	F	39	2,160	48	1.95
2	M	41	3,250	52	2.31
3	M	41	3,120	52	2.22
4	M	40	3,200	49	2.72
5	F	39	2,650	50	2.12
6	F	41	3,520	53	2.36
7	M	39	2,590	49	2.20
8	F	41	2,500	51	1.88
9	F	39	2,590	49	2.20
10	M	39	2,760	49	2.35
11	M	40	3,220	52	2.29
12	F	41	2,410	49	2.05
13	F	41	2,670	48	2.41
14	F	38	2,640	48	2.39
15	M	39	2,410	49	2.05
16	M	39	2,500	48	2.26
17	F	40	2,600	49	2.18
18	F	39	2,160	45	2.37
19	F	39	2,270	48	2.05
20	F	41	2,720	51	2.05
21	M	38	2,720	50	2.18
22	F	39	2,720	49	2.38
23	M	41	3,520	52	2.50
$M \pm SD$		3.97 ± 1.1	$2,735 \pm 392$	49.6 ± 1.9	2.23 ± 0.19

infants performed significantly better on the Motor Performance cluster (Nepalese M = 5.5; American M = 4.69, $F(1,44)$= 13.08, p < .001) and on the Autonomic Regulation cluster (Nepalese M = 7.14; American M = 5.10, $F(1,44)$ = 65.18, p < .0001).

Additional Observations

A few postpartum practices in both Nepal hospitals deserve comment. Immediately after birth, Nepali mothers lay on their sides in their own beds with their swaddled infants lying alongside in an en-face position. Since the mother was the primary caregiver, mother-infant interactions were interrupted rarely, although the maternal grandmother or other female family members occasionally assisted. Finally, the daily ritual of oil massage, during which the mother rubbed the baby's entire body, was performed in an effort to mold the infant physically and, more important, to convey the mother's love and affection to the child.

Discussion

The absence of a significant difference between BNBAS scores of high- and low-PI Nepalese infants was surprising, as the mean PIs of the comparison groups were markedly different (2.38 vs. 2.08). Two previous investigations have

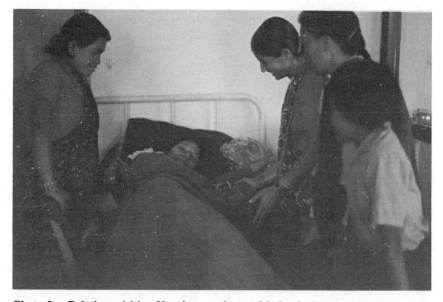

Photo 3.   Relatives visiting Nepalese mother and baby during postpartum period. (*Photo by author*)

shown a strong dependence of BNBAS scores on PI, and in both studies the difference between the mean PIs of the high- and low-PI groups was similar to the above (2.30 vs. 2.15; 2.49 vs. 2.09) (Als et al., 1976; Lester, 1979). One possible reason for the result here is the small sample size; other explanations, however, also must be considered.

For example, if certain behavioral features of Nepalese infants were primarily characteristics of their genetic endowment, a minor dependence on size might be difficult to detect. Alternatively, and more likely, the neonates in this study may not have been "undernourished." The PI was standardized in the U.S., and it need not be an accurate measure of nutritional status in all cultures and ethnic groups. If this sample of Nepalese babies is composed mainly of full-size, well-nourished individuals from a genetically small race, then any deterioration in BNBAS performance dependent on increasing undernutrition would not occur. Further investigations are needed in this important area. It is likely that accurate standardization in other cultures and ethnic groups will become essential for correct interpretation of increasing numbers of cross-cultural studies.

Previous studies of FTUW infants have described their generally poor performance on the BNBAS. Brazelton, Robey, and Collier first described the slow liquid movements and quiet alert states of low-birthweight (mean BW approximately 2.3 kg) Zinacanteco Indians in Southern Mexico in 1969. Subsequently, Als et al. (1976) found the FTUW American babies (mean PI = 2.15) performed significantly more poorly on motor behaviors and interactive processes than their full-weight peers (mean PI > 2.30). Specifically, the former tended to have poor tone, very low activity levels, poor hand-to-mouth coordination, jerky limb movements, and aberrant reflexes. When they came to an alert state, their responsiveness was poor.

These findings were replicated by Brazelton et al. (1977), who discovered that FTUW Guatemalans (mean BW = 2,778 g) also had poor motor and interactive behaviors. The Guatemalan infants demonstrated poor muscle tone and limited spontaneous movements which were jerky and tremulous. They, too, were slow to come to an alert state and when alert were not vigorous. Lester (1979) studied another group of underweight American newborns (mean PI = 2.09) and found that they scored significantly lower on all dimensions of the BNBAS than did their full-weight peers (mean PI= 2.49).

In contrast, Nepalese infants excelled in the areas where other FTUW babies have consistently been weakest. They performed significantly better on the Motor Performance and Autonomic Regulation clusters of the BNBAS than did an American sample of presumably equal nutritional status (mean PI = 2.24). In addition, the Nepalese babies' mean score on the Orientation cluster, which combines alertness and orientation to a variety of animate and inanimate stimuli (i.e., responsiveness), cannot be classified as "poor" (see Table 2).

Explanations for these results must remain speculative at this time One possibility is that the effect of undernutrition on BNBAS scores occurs only at the

Table 2.   Means of BNBAS Summary Cluster Scores
of American and Nepalese Samples by Day of Life

	American		Nepalese	
	Day 1	Day 3	Day 1	Day 3
Habituation	6.2	5.6	6.4	6.4
Orientation	5.7	5.4	5.6	5.3
Motor Performance	4.5	4.8	5.6	5.5
Range of State	3.7	3.8	4.1	3.9
Regulation of State	5.4	5.4	5.3	4.6
Autonomic Regulation	5.2	4.9	7.1	7.2
Reflexes	1.9	2.0	1.9	2.9
Organization for Arousal Level	—	—	2.3	2.2

extreme of low PI. The mean PIs of the FTUW groups in the studies of Als et al. (1976) and Lester (1979) were both less than the 3rd percentile (i.e., 2.20), while the Nepalese sample had a mean PI between the 3rd and 10th percentiles. Further studies are needed in this area, but the previously mentioned lack of difference between high- and low-PI Nepalese previously mentioned argues against this suggestion. A second explanation arises if the Nepalese infants were, in fact, not undernourished, as mentioned previously. In this case, any comparison to an undernourished American sample would be inappropriate and any conclusion invalid.

Superior and unique motor performance in well-nourished African newborns has been described before (Geber & Dean, 1959; Keefer, Tronick, Dixon, & Brazelton, 1982) and attributed to the interaction of genetic and environmental influences. If correct, this interpretation also could apply to Nepalese neonates. Finally, the possibility of systematic error introduced by the examiner during the scoring of BNBAS items must be considered. Although an effort has been made to minimize the source of error by requiring that all persons administering the BNBAS undergo an intensive training course and subsequent reliability assessment; this explanation can never be fully discounted in this type of study.

This study suggests that a low PI, and hence presumed undernutrition, does not alter the behavior of either participant in the mother-infant relationship in Nepal. The importance and prestige afforded motherhood in this society are expected to enhance a woman's desire for and interest in a child. Thus, Nepalese attitudes are reflected by the postpartum practices previously described, whereby mother and offspring interact intensely and may develop close attachment.

A Nepalese mother provides her infant with frequent stimulation in the form of facial confrontation and daily oil massage, and with immediate need gratification in the form of liberal demand breast-feeding. In turn, the Nepalese baby brings to this exchange high motoric competence, mature physiological organization, and high responsiveness, all of which are expected to reinforce the mother's doting.

Whether the high level of attention provided by Nepalese mothers to low-PI babies depends solely on the infant's well-developed behaviors cannot be determined in this study. A possible answer, however, is provided by Graves's (1978) cross-cultural comparison of behavioral observations made in the Kathmandu Valley of well-nourished and undernourished (by anthropometric measurements) children aged 7 to 19 months and their mothers, with an earlier study done in West Bengal. Undernourished children in both cultures exhibited lowered levels of exploratory activity and attachment behavior than did the well-nourished. In contrast, Nepalese mothers showed no differential behavior, while West Bengali mothers were generally less responsive to the undernourished infants. The implication is that, at least through 18 months of age, maternal behavior in Nepal is influenced more by cultural expectations and attitudes than by the child's capacities. A study in the U.S. suggests that the Nepalese culture may be rare in this regard (Als et al., 1976).

In conclusion, this study of Nepalese newborn behavioral characteristics raises some important questions. It must be determined whether a Rohrer's Ponderal Index standardized in the U.S. can be applied cross-culturally without modification. If not, standards for other populations must be established, and a number of intriguing and complex issues regarding cross-cultural studies must be systematically approached. In particular, there is a need to investigate the role of genetic and intrauterine environmental influences on newborn behavior. These factors might differ greatly among different cultures and may explain findings such as our own and those of, for example, African studies. In addition, a possible need to modify the BNBAS in a culture-specific way has previously been discussed (Keefer et al., 1982). The findings concerning the lack of dependence of the mother-infant interaction in Nepal on the child's nutritional status also suggest avenues for further research. Specific cultural expectations and attitudes responsible for this phenomenon need to be investigated more fully, and their possible use to enhance the care of malnourished children need to be explored in other cultures.

Note

1. F. Britto, personal communication, July 18, 1980.

References

Acharya, S. (1977). Care of newborn—Priority in basic health services. *Journal Nepal Med. Assoc., 15*(2), 8–24.

Als, H., Tronick, E., Adamson, L., & Brazelton, T. (1976). The behavior of the full-term but underweight newborn infant. *Developmental Medicine and Child Neurology, 18*, 590–602.

Ballard, G., Kazmaier, K., & Driver, M. (1977). A simplified assessment of gestational age. *Ped. Res.*, *11*, 374.

Barrett, J. (1982). Prenatal influences on adaption in the newborn. In Stratton, P. (Ed.), *Psychobiology of the Human Newborn*. Chichester, England:Wiley.

Behrman, R. (1973). *Neonatology*. St. Louis, MO:C.V. Mosby.

Bell, R. Q. (1971). Stimulus control of parent or caretaker behavior by offspring. *Dev. Psych.*, *4*, 63–72.

Bennett, L. (1976). Sex and motherhood among the Brahmins and Chettris of east-central Nepal [Special issue]. *Contributions to Nepalese Studies*, *3*,1–52.

Brazelton, T. B. (1973). *Neonatal Behavioral Assessment Scale*. London: Spastics International Medical Publications/Heinemann Medical Books.

Brazelton, T. B., Robey, J., & Collier, G. (1969). Infant development in the Zinacanteco Indians of Southern Mexico. *Pediatrics*, *44*, 274–290.

Brazelton, T. B., Tronick, E., Lechtig, A., Lasky, R., & Klein, R. (1977). The behavior of nutritionally deprived Guatemalan infants. *Developmental Medicine and Child Neurology*, *19*, 364–372.

Field, T. (1977). Effects of early separation, interactive deficits, and experimental manipulations on infant motor face-to-face interaction. *Child Development*, *48*, 763–771.

Fleming, R., & Fleming, Z. (1978). *Kathmandu Valley*. Bombay: Kodonsha International.

Geber, M., & Dean, R. (1959). The state of development of newborn African children. *Lancet*, *1*, 1216.

Graves, P. (1978). Nutrition and infant behavior: A replication study in the Kathmandu Valley, Nepal. *American Journal Clin. Nutr.*, *31*(3), 541–551.

Health Service Organization (1979). *Excerpts from country profile–Nepal*, 293–296.

HMG/Nepal: Ministry of Health Department of Health Services (1979). *Annual Report of the Community Health and Integration Project*, 1–52.

Keefer, C., Tronick, E., Dixon, S., & Brazelton, T. B. (1982). Specific differences in motor performance between Gusii and American newborns and a modification of the Neonatal Behavioral Assessment Scale. *Child Development*, *53*(3), 754–759.

Klein, M., & Stern, L. (1971). Low birthweight and the battered child syndrome. *American Journal of Diseases in Childhood*, *122*, 15–18.

Lester, B. (1979). A synergistic process approach to study of the prenatal malnutrition. *Inter. J. Behav. Dev.*, *2*, 377–393.

Lester, B., Als, H., & Brazelton, T. B. (1978). Scoring criteria for the seven clusters of the Brazelton scale. Unpublished manuscript, Children's Hospital Medical Center, Child Development Unit, Boston.

Lester, B., & Zeskind, P. (1978). Brazelton scale and physical size correlates of neonatal cry features. *Infant Beh. and Dev.*, *4*, 393–402.

Lubchenco, L. (1976). *The high risk infant*. Philadelphia, PA:Saunders.

Lubchenco, L., Searles, D., & Brazie, J. (1972). Neonatal Mortality rate: Relationships to birthweight and gestational age. *Journal of Pediatrics*, *81*, 814.

Miller, H., & Hassanein, K. (1973). Fetal malnutrition in white newborn infants: Maternal factors. *Pediatrics*, *52*, 504–512.

Nepal manual for health workers (1979). Kathmandu, Nepal: Tribhuvan University Medical School.

Osofsky, J. D. (1976). Neonatal characteristics and mother-infant interaction in two observational studies. *Child Development*, *47*, 1138–1147.

Parker, R. (1979). Self-care in rural areas of India and Nepal. *Culture, Medicine and Psychiatry, 3*, 3–28.

Rosenn, D., Stein, L., & Bates, M. (1976). The differentiation of organic from environmental failure-to-thrive. Paper presented at American Pediatric Society meetings, Denver, CO, 1975. In Als et al., The behavior of the full-term but underweight newborn infant. *Developmental Medicine and Child Neurology, 18*, 590–602.

Taylor, D., & Thapa, R. (1972). *Nepal.* Kathmandu, Nepal: Population Council, 41–48.

CHAPTER 4

The Infant and the Group: A Look at Efe Caretaking Practices in Zaire*

Steve Winn
Edward Z. Tronick

Department of Psychology
University of Massachusetts
Amherst, Massachusetts

Gilda A. Morelli

University of Utah
Salt Lake City, Utah

As part of our goal of understanding the nature of human caretaking practices and the factors which influence them, we have been studying the Efe. The Efe live in the Ituri Forest of Zaire and are traditionally classified as hunters and gatherers. The caretaking practices and life-style of these technologically simple people differs greatly from what is observed in Western industrial and Third World agricultural societies. The Efe use a system of multiple caretaking of their infants and young children, rather than one in which the primary caretaker of the infant is its mother. This system is not, however, stereotypic or rigid; it contains a good

---

* This research was supported by two grants from the National Science Foundation (People of the Ituri Forest and Children of the Ituri Forest), and funds from the Swann Foundation, the Sigma Xi Society, the National Institutes of Health Small Grants Program, and faculty research funds from the University of Massachusetts.

We would like to thank Robert Bailey, Nadine Peacock, and Barbara de Zalduondo for their invaluable assistance and friendship in the field; Elizabeth Shea-Clement for her assistance in ranking newborn reactivity; and Andy Gianino, Ted Plimpton, and Betsy Adams for their comments on the manuscript.

deal of individual variation. For example, 3-week-old Efe infants are transferred on average 3.7 times per hour and encounter an average of 5.3 different caretakers. But whereas one infant was passed 18 times, encountering 11 different caretakers in less than 2 hours, another infant was not passed at all. Our question, then, was: What factors accounted for this individual variability? We saw this question as one of a set of questions about the relationship between cultural practices and infant behavior, and their relationship to other factors such as social ecology, infant health status, and phylogenetic constraints. A variety of positions exist concerning these relationships.

Brazelton and his colleagues have contributed significantly to the development of one—rather radical—view. Brazelton's research in cross-cultural psychology grew out of his clinical experience with mothers and infants. He was impressed by the individual characteristics of infants and the effects that these characteristics had on the behavior of mothers and others. This view of the infant's abilities was broadened in Brazelton's classic study of the Zinacanteco Indians of Mexico (Brazelton, 1972). He observed that the Zinacanteco infant was quiet and well organized and experienced long periods of alertness. He also observed that elements of these characteristics were present in the adults' personalities as well and were valued by the culture. On the basis of these findings, Brazelton argued that a culture's practices and beliefs were shaped by the behavior of its infants.

This view gained support from the work of Freedman (1974; Freedman & Freedman 1969), who showed that behavioral differences exist among infants of different ethnic groups. But while Brazelton argued that behavioral differences were the result of both genetic and nongenetic inherited factors (e.g., maternal nutrition, perinatal conditions), Freedman believed that these differences were predominately determined by genetic factors. His research findings in and of themselves, however, were insufficient to support his argument. But whatever the determinants of behavioral differences, the demonstration that these differences exist among infants of different cultures is strong supportive evidence for the possibility that infant behavior shapes cultural practices.

In contrast, traditional anthropological research on the relationship between infant behavior and culture generally gives little acknowledgement to the infant's contribution. The Whitings (1975) maintain that the key process underlying the differences consistently observed among people of different cultures is learning. An individual's learning experience is thought to be strongly affected by the ecological and social setting, the tasks assigned, and the people with whom the child interacts. These experiences produce a learned behavioral style that is specific to the culture and which eventually affects its projective system. Initial behavioral differences among infants in different cultures that may influence this behavioral style tend not to be considered.

Mead (1953) and Benedict (1949) theorize that culture defines the meaning of practices. The meaning of a practice and its effects on the lives of people vary among different cultures. Presumably this argument can be extended to include behavior. The meaning of a behavior and its effects on social discourse, then, would also be culturally determined. Caudill's research on Japanese infants (Caudill & Weinstein, 1969) supports Mead and Benedict's position.

Caudill found that by 3–4 months of age, Japanese infants behaved in ways that reflected adult characteristics (Caudill & Weinstein, 1969). He entertained but rejected the hypothesis that infant behavior modified the type of care the infant received. Instead, Caudill argued that Japanese child-care practices, and the meaning adults assigned to these practices, were responsible for shaping the infant's behavior.

Variations of the positions advanced by Brazelton, Mead, and Benedict exist. These variations are more limited in scope because they do not consider the relationship between infant behavior or adult expectations, and cultural practices. For example, a culture-free model based on Brazelton's position maintains that the infant's behavior modifies the behavior of the caregiver (Campbell & Taylor, 1980; Goldberg, 1977; Osofsky & Danzger, 1974). A crying infant may elicit a particular form of caregiving different from that elicited by an alert infant. But the relationship between this modification and cultural practices is not specified. Similarly, a modified version of Mead and Benedict's position sees an individual's expectations about an infant's behavior as influencing the way in which that individual interacts with the infant. For example, parental expectations regarding the care of male and female infants modify the type of care the infant receives (Rubin, Provenzano, & Luria, 1974). But how adjustments in child-care practices, made in response to these parental expectations, actually affect cultural practices and beliefs remains unspecified.

A more biologically oriented position relating newborn behavior to caretaking practices is exemplified in the works of Bowlby (1969) and Schwartz and Rosenblum (1983). Their basic premise is that the immaturity and dependency of the neonate require a particular form of caregiving that can compensate for this immaturity. These researchers, who are considered proponents of what has been referred to as the continuous care and constant contact model (see Tronick, Winn, & Morelli, 1985), believe that parental caregiving systems evolved in response to the infant's biological and physiological needs. Caretaking is thought, therefore; to be constrained by phylogeny into a prototypical form.

A recent version of this position conceptualizes the infant somewhat differently (Tronick, Als, & Brazelton, 1980). It views the infant as influencing the caretaker's behavior through a relatively precocious communication system. This communication system elicits specific types of care from the infant's caregivers and is assumed to be a biological characteristic of our species. Although this revised view allows for a good deal of modification of the caretaker's behavior by the infant, it is still a species-specific control system. In its strongest form, this position also argues that there is a prototypical system of child care independent of the differences in infant behavior that exist among cultures.

In our view, these positions are too single-minded, and it is unlikely that any one factor or process determines the relationships between infant behavior and cultural practices. We see no a priori reason to raise infant behavior, culture, or any other factor such as social ecology or phylogeny to a preeminent position. Rather, we see development as resulting from the interaction of a multiplicity of factors, including evolutionary or historical processes, physiological and bio-medical variables, ecological and social factors, organismic characteristics, child-rearing practices, and culture. These factors mutually influence one an-other, and it is the task of the investigator to specify the nature of this mutual influence (Tronick, Morrelli, & Winn, 1987).

We have found LeVine's (1977) model to be particularly useful in aiding our understanding of the relationship between infant behavior and cultural practices because it emphasizes cultural, behavioral, and biomedical variables. LeVine argues that a culture's caretaking strategy—parental investment strategy— evolves in response to the predominant environmental hazards encountered by members of the culture (LeVine, 1977). Caretaking is seen as a hazard preven-tion strategy, and is a distillate of the society's experience that allows parents to act as conforming members of society without having to generate their own strategy.

LeVine posits three universal goals for parents and parenting practices. The first goal is to insure the survival and health of the child, including the develop-ment of the child's normal reproductive capacity. The second is the development of the child's capacity for economic self-maintenance at maturity. And the third goal is the development of the child's behavioral capacities for maximizing cultural values. In order to fulfill these goals, parents select a set of caretaking practices from those made available to them by the culture; there is no best caretaking practice.

This view is compatible with Hinde's (1983) argument that evolution operated to produce specific capacities for generating strategies of caretaking that effec-tively deal with situational factors (i.e., culture, infant behavior, social ecology, physical constraints, etc.), and not a single prototypical form of human caretaking.

Of course, understanding the interaction between infant behavior and cultural practices is not simple, because different factors operate over different time scales. The time it takes for infant behavior to influence caretaking differs by several orders of magnitude from the time it takes for infant behavior to influence culture or the gene pool, if such influences occur. Over an individual's lifetime, a factor may vary in the nature and strength of its effect. Furthermore, factors vary in importance across cultures. These complications severely limit the type of inferences a researcher can draw from any given study.

Nevertheless, while recognizing these difficulties we have hypothesized that the patterns of caretaking observed among the Efe would be consonant with the goals of parenting outlined by LeVine. To examine this hypothesis, we chose to look at the relationship of infant birthweight, infant behavior, and group size, to caretaking practices. Our findings are interpreted in terms of Efe cultural values and goals. How did we decide on these factors?

Following LeVine's theory that the first goal of parenting is to insure the survival of the infant, we felt that birthweight might be an infant characteristic used to guide the caretaking of newborns during their most vulnerable period. Birthweight is a tangible characteristic, assessable by a caretaker without the use of any apparatus, and its importance on caretaking is well documented (Field, Sostek, Goldberg, & Shuman, 1979). Our observations revealed that birthweight is also an infant characteristic of concern to the Efe. The Efe use infant weight and size as a measure of the infant's vitality. This was particularly evident during infant examinations. When we announced an infant's weight, the figure was repeated by those present and echoed until everyone in camp heard it. The heavier the infant, the more positive the response.

Several factors influenced our decision to investigate the relationship between group size and infant caretaking. The Efe engage in a system of child care that draws on the help of nonfamily members (Tronick, Morelli, & Winn, 1983). It was also our impression that for all group members, and observers as well, day-to-day life in a large group was very different from that in a small group. Individuals living in a large group have more opportunity to interact socially and are exposed to a greater number of activities at any given time. Other researchers also report that patterns of child care are shaped by the cultural and situational context in which the behavior occurs (Chisholm, 1983; Munroe & Munroe, 1971). Indeed, for LeVine the social ecological setting is the setting in which economic self-maintenance and culturally appropriate behavior must be nurtured and come to fruition.

Lastly, on the basis of LeVine's notion that one of the goals of parenting is to develop the child's behavioral capacities for maximizing cultural values, we expected that there would be a relationship between these values, certain new-born and infant behaviors, and the caretaking an infant received. Before specifying the types of infant behaviors observed, we need to present more information on the Efe and their cultural practices and beliefs.

The Efe: Cultural Practices and Beliefs

The Efe[1] are one of four groups comprising the Mbuti (Pygmies) who inhabit the Ituri Forest of northeastern Zaire. Characterization of the Efe ancestral homeland and mode of subsistence is the subject of much speculation. It is not known whether the Efe once lived deep within the forest or on the forest/savannah edge, and whether they subsisted solely by hunting and gathering or were in association with horticulturalists. But however their ancestors lived, in all probability that life-style was unlike the Efe way of life today.

Although the Efe hunt and gather forest foods, they rely mainly on cultivated foods for their caloric intake (Bailey & Peacock, in press). These foods are

---

[1] Efe is pronounced "ef-*fay*." Balese is pronounced "bah-less-*say*."

acquired predominantly from an associated population of Sudanic-speaking horticulturalists, the Balese. The Balese use food as immediate payment for Efe
services or as a credit to be redeemed at some later time. In general, a long-
standing, reciprocal relationship exists between members of an Efe band and a
single Balese village, except during periods of food scarcity, when an Efe band
may draw on the resources of several villages.

The Efe move camp every 4–6 weeks to exploit the seasonally available forest
foods and for health or personal reasons. The new campsite is often located at or
near previous campsites. Efe camps rarely exceed a day's walk from the village
and are more often within a 1–3 hr walk. Camp location and hunting occurs
within a designated area, or home range, which appears to be associated with a
given Efe band from generation to generation.

Camp membership ranges from 6–50 people and is often made up of one or
several extended families. Because the Efe are virilocal, each family consists of
brothers and their wives, children, unmarried sisters, and parents. Women leave
their group around the age of 18. This emigration is attributable to the practice of
"sister exchange." Women from one band are exchanged by their male relatives
for women of another band in order to provide these relatives with wives.
Members of the extended family build their huts close to one another. But the
extended family is not the basic social unit of the Efe band. The basic social unit
is the nuclear family. When changes in camp composition occur, the nuclear
family, but not necessarily the extended family, remains intact.

Because of the way the Efe shape their physical environment and use their
living space, their life is one of continuous social interaction and exposure. The
Efe clear a small area in the forest in which to build their camp, making it free of
physical barriers. Huts tend to be small—1.5 m in diameter and 1.25 m in
height, with dim interiors that contain few material goods. Hut use is limited to
sleeping, food storage, and protection from the rain. This living arrangement
means that an individual's activities—eating, cooking, bathing, child care—and
an individual's moods are public information. In addition, most out-of-camp
activities are also shared with other individuals. It is very unusual to find an Efe
in a solitary setting or engaged in a solitary task.

Child care is a responsibility shared by group members. The Efe engage in a
system of multiple caretaking that begins at birth and continues for at least the
first 18 weeks of life (Tronick et al. 1983; Tronick et al., 1985). Efe infants
spend a large portion of the daylight hours in physical contact with individuals
other than their mothers; they are passed frequently among camp members and
are also exposed to a large number of individuals. At 3 weeks of age Efe infants
are cared for by individuals other than the mother 39% of the time, are passed an
average of 3.7 times per hours, and encounter an average of 3.6 individuals per
hour. At 18 weeks of age these figures have increased such that infants are cared
for by others 58% of the time, are passed 8.3 times per hour, and encounter 4.6
individuals per hour. As already noted, there is individual variability in each of

Photo 1.   Efe mother and infant.

these measures, so whereas an Efe caretaking pattern can be identified, it should not be overcharacterized; differences in individual parenting styles exist.

Caretaking among the Efe is significantly different from that observed in American and other Western societies. But Efe caretaking, like other systems of parental care, is shaped by various constraints (e.g., biological, cultural) acting on the individual. The differences observed in caretaking practices across cultures bring into question the assumption that certain patterns of care are critical for the normal socioemotional development of the infant.

The Efe value their infants highly. Though they often complain about the pain and danger associated with childbirth, Efe women say that "to hold a child, to look into his eyes, is good." Part of an infant's value to the Efe is undoubtedly related to her potential economic contribution to the family. Efe infants are also seen as future social companions. This is especially true for male infants, who will remain with their families. The infant's value is reflected in the infant's participation in Efe life. Infants are fully integrated into Efe society. They are included in the routines of everyday life and partake in all social functions. In fact, infants play a role in some of these functions. During a funeral, for example, infants are passed over the grave. This practice is believed to insure the well-being of all camp members.

Descriptively the Efe engage in a pattern of care that is consonant with their values and beliefs concerning infant needs and abilities. One quality valued by the Efe and used in their assessment of the infant's well-being is strength, or *ngufu*. This refers to infant weight or heaviness but incorporates other qualities as well, including size and muscle tone. A floppy, or *teke teke* infant, is often

singled out as being different, and perhaps requiring a special form of care.
When an infant's *ngufu* falls below the culturally accepted norm, adjustments are
made in the treatment of the infant. The parents may apply potions to the infant's
body and clothe the infant with charms believed to impart strength. Yet even
when the newborn's *ngufu* falls within the culturally accepted range, the child is
still viewed as vulnerable.

During the newborn period the infant experiences few physiological stresses
or social demands. The infant is fed often, is comforted quickly following a fuss
or cry, and is rarely engaged socially. These practices allow the infant to achieve
the goals set by the culture. These goals are expressed by one of our Swahili-
speaking informants, Imatofi. In her statement, Imatofi, a Lese woman, captures
the belief held by both the Efe and Balese on the young infant's needs: "Kazi ya
mtoto iko kulala . . ." (The work of the infant is to sleep. He sleeps until he gets
strong and gains weight; and then he begins to open his eyes.)

Child-care practices begin to change when the infant reaches 4–5 months of
age. These changes reflect changes in the Efe perception of the needs and
developmental status of the infant. When growth is proceeding normally, concerns about the infant's *ngufu* become less important and more attention is paid
to the infant's budding sociality. The transition in emphasis from biological to
social issues is brought about by the belief that a 4–5-month old "ikonaanza
kupata akili" (is starting to become aware). Infant smiling and babbling, as well
as certain motor advances (e.g., grasping and mouthing objects), are the developmental markers used to indicate the onset of this social awareness. It is our
experience, however, that many of these indices occur at an age earlier than that
articulated by the Efe.

Once this age of social awareness is reached, the Efe begin to view their

Photo 2.   Efe women and babies.

infants as individuals capable of learning and as social beings capable of interacting. Although more is expected of the 4-month-old than the 3-week-old, the 4-month-old still experiences few frustrations. In fact, demands are kept to a minimum during the first year of life. This period of grace, however, is short-lived. By 2–3 years of age, the Efe child is expected to cope with many frustrations. The manner in which these changes come about is currently being examined.

We used this knowledge of Efe cultural values and goals to formulate hypotheses on the relationships of newborn and older infant behavior to caretaking practices. Because the Efe believe that it is best for a newborn to remain quiet and asleep, we expected that more aroused or reactive neonates would receive a different pattern of care than their quieter cohorts. Because the Efe also respond quickly and attempt to quiet fussing infants throughout the first half-year, we expected that older infants who fussed more would receive a different pattern of care than infants who fussed less.

Procedure

The study presented in this chapter is part of a larger study on infant and early childhood development among the Efe and Balese.[2] Twenty-two Efe infants were born during our 2-year stay in Zaire. Of these 22 infants, 3 were excluded from the study. One mother died of labor complications; 1 infant was later found to have severe developmental disabilities; and 1 mother refused to participate, saying we should "come back when the baby is stronger." The remaining 19 infants were judged to be healthy, full-term newborns. Descriptive data on these 19 mother-infant pairs are presented in Table 1.

Birthweight

Infants were weighed as soon after birth as possible. In some cases we were not notified of an infant's birth for several days, while in other cases we were unable to get to an infant until 3 or 4 days after birth. Only weights obtained within 36 hr after birth are included as birthweights.

Newborn Arousal and Reactivity

Measures of newborn arousal and reactivity were based on examination of infants using the Brazelton Neonatal Behavioral Assessment Scale (hereafter,

---

[2] The study of child development among the Efe and Balese is part of a larger collaborative project which includes biological anthropologists, ecologists, public health practitioners, physiologists, and biologists. Work to date has provided complete demographic and anthropometric data on the study population, information on their health status and their sanitary practices, data on forest productivity, and descriptions of adult activity patterns and social exchanges.

Table 1.   Descriptive Characteristics of the 19 Efe Mother-Infant Pairs

	M	SD	Range	N^a
Mothers				
Age (years)	28.0	5.8	20.0–38.0	19
Gravida	3.9	2.2	1.0–8.0	19
Parity	2.7	2.1	0.0–6.0	19
Height (cm)	134.9	3.7	126.4–140.0	18
Weight (kg)	38.2	5.5	30.5–50.0	15
Head circumference (cm)	52.6	2.0	49.0–55.2	15
Prior birth interval (months)	37.6	15.2	17.0–74.0	12
Infants				
Birthweight[b] (kg)	2.4	.4	2.0–3.4	12
Birth length (cm)	43.4	2.3	39.4–47.2	16
Head circumference (cm)	34.0	1.3	31.0–36.4	17

[a]Missing data excluded. [b]Within 36 hr of birth.

BNBAS; Brazelton, 1973). The BNBAS was administered to 16 of the 19 Efe newborns within 60 hr after birth (mean age = 34 hr; range 7–53). The 3 remaining infants were examined 5–6 days after birth. The data on them are excluded from this analysis because we chose to present data on Efe newborns' earliest behaviors.

Fifteen of the 16 exams were administered in Efe huts. Huts are dim and often have a small fire burning, making them warm and smoky. Mothers were always present for the exam, and typically the hut was filled with other camp members. People watched with interest and responded positively to many test items, particularly when an infant "crawled," "walked," or turned his or her head to follow the examiner's face. Mothers were given a small piece of cloth and some soap for their infants in appreciation of their cooperation.

Several modifications in the administration and scoring of the exam were necessary. The placing reflex was omitted because Efe huts typically lack furniture. The pinprick item was also omitted. We felt that this item would be too intrusive and difficult to justify to the people watching the exam.

Other variations in administering the exam were due to the early caretaking practices of the Efe. Efe newborns are nursed several times each hour. This practice makes examining an infant 1–2 hours postprandial impossible. Furthermore, Efe newborns are almost always in physical contact with another person. They are seldom, if ever, put down or left alone. When we broke physical contact to examine the infants, 10 of them woke up fussing or crying.[3] For this reason, the habituation items were omitted from these 10 exams.

---

[3] As we have noted in previous reports (Tronick et al., 1985) the Efe infants' small size places them at greater risk for temperature instability. Breaking physical contact between infants and caretakers may have put stress on the young infants' thermoregulatory capacity.

These procedural modifications necessitated changes in scoring the exams. The pinprick item is included in the scoring of two BNBAS items: Rapidity of Buildup and Irritability. To score Rapidity of Buildup, therefore, we substituted "not until foot reflexes" for "not until pinpricks." To score Irritability, the pinprick item was left out of the list of aversive stimuli on which the score is based.

Exams were administered by the three authors. To maintain standardization of test administration in the field, two or three examiners periodically attended the exams. Interobserver reliability was determined before, during, and after field work. Reliability was maintained at or above 90%.

Two summary measures were generated to analyze the relationship of newborn arousal and reactivity to caretaking practices. The first summary measure, the Arousal cluster score, is reported in other studies (Lester, Als, & Brazelton 1978; Osofsky & O'Connell, 1977). This measure is the summation of scores from four BNBAS items: Rapidity of Buildup, Irritability, Peak of Excitement, and Lability of States.

The second summary measure ranks the newborns according to their degree of "reactivity." The measure includes: Predominant State, Irritability, Peak of Excitement, Rapidity of Buildup, Lability of States, and Consolability. Comments from the descriptive paragraph that reflect newborn irritability and the amount of handling needed to keep the newborn from crying were also considered when ranking these infants. Low-ranking, least reactive newborns were essentially asleep throughout the exam. Middle-low–ranking newborns were awake and quiet. High-middle–ranking newborns were alert and irritable, and high-ranking newborns were upset throughout the exam.

Newborns were ranked independently by two experienced examiners. Disagreements in ranking were discussed and a final ranking was achieved. Behavioral data from the BNBAS exams are presented in Table 2.

Infant Fussiness at Older Ages

Measures of infant fussiness were based on naturalistic observations of the infants. Ten infants, 6 females and 4 males, were included in the observational study of infant behavior. Infants were observed for 2 hr at 3 weeks of age (mean age = 23 days; range 13–31); 2 hr at 7 weeks (mean age = 51 days; range 43–57); and 4 hr at 18 weeks (mean age = 137 days; range 120–152). For data analysis, observations at 3 and 7 weeks were combined. Infants from 7 different camps were observed for a total of approximately 70 hr. Observations took place in the Efe camps and were evenly divided between the early morning and the late afternoon when most people were in camp. Each observation session lasted 1 hr.

Observations were recorded with an event sequence format, with the infant as focal subject. The scoring system coded infant behavior, affect, position, caretaking received, caretaker identity, and other social or physical interactions

Table 2.   Means and Standard Deviations of the 26
BNBAS Scores

Item	M	SD	N
1. Response decrement to light	6.0	1.6	4
2. Response decrement to rattle	5.8	1.3	5
3. Response decrement to bell	7.2	1.3	5
4. Response decrement to pinprick[a]			
5. Orientation inanimate visual	4.5	1.5	10
6. Orientation inanimate auditory	5.6	1.1	11
7. Orientation animate visual	5.9	1.6	12
8. Orientation animate auditory	5.6	1.4	12
9. Orientation animate visual and auditory	7.0	.6	12
10. Alertness	5.2	1.6	13
11. General tonus	5.6	1.0	15
12. Motor maturity	4.3	1.3	14
13. Pull-to-sit	5.7	1.8	15
14. Cuddliness	5.3	1.4	14
15. Defensive movements	5.8	2.6	13
16. Consolability	4.6	1.7	9
17. Peak of excitement	5.7	1.8	13
18. Rapidity of buildup	5.5	2.6	8
19. Irritability	4.2	2.2	15
20. Activity	4.7	1.2	15
21. Tremulousness	5.4	2.1	16
22. Startles	3.8	1.4	15
23. Lability of skin color	3.4	1.9	14
24. Lability of states	1.5	1.0	15
25. Self-quieting activity	5.2	2.1	14
26. Hand-mouth facility	5.9	2.2	12
27. Smiles	.4	.2	16

[a]Item omitted.

involving the infant. Interobserver reliability was 90% or above for all of the
observations included in these analyses.

Infant fussiness at 3 & 7 and 18 weeks was assessed by counting the number
of 1-minute intervals during which the infant fussed or cried at least once. This
measure is derived from the total number of intervals that the infant was awake.

Group Size

Group size was determined by including all individuals living in the camp during
the period of time in which observations were made. The size of the 7 groups in
which our infants were observed ranged from 8 to 45 individuals (mean = 28;
$SD = 14$). In future work we will extend this analysis to include the relationship
between group composition and infant care.

Caretaking

The measures of Efe caretaking used as dependent variables in this study were also derived from infant observations at 3 & 7 and 18 weeks of age. Measures included time with mother, transfer rate, transfers to mother, number of different caretakers, and latency of response to fussing (see Table 3 for a description of these behaviors).

Results

Despite the fact that all infants born during our 2-year stay in the field were included in the study, the small number of births, coupled with some unavoidably missing data (due to, e.g., time delays in being informed about a birth), results in relatively small sample sizes for many of the following analyses. Because of this we include some findings that do not reach significance but are in agreement with the pattern of significant results obtained.

Birthweight and Caretaking

There is a strong relationship between birthweight and time spent with mother and percent of passes to her (see Table 4). When compared to higher-birthweight infants, lower-birthweight infants spend more time with their mothers ($r = -.70$; $p = .039$), and are passed back to them a greater percentage of times ($r = -.63$; $p = .066$) at 3 & 7 weeks of age.

These data indicate that birthweight and caretaking are related at 3 & 7 weeks of age. Mothers of lower-birthweight infants play a greater role in caregiving than do mothers of higher-birthweight infants. Lower-birthweight infants spend

Table 3. Behavioral Definitions of Caretaking Measures

Time with mother	The percent of time the infant is in actual physical contact with mother. This includes being carried or lying with mother. Infant state is not considered.
Transfer rate	The number of times per hour an infant in passed from one person to another whether or not that person has already held the infant.
Pass to mother	The percentage of total infant transfers to mother.
Total caretakers	The number of different individuals with whom the infant is in physical contact (held, carried, etc.) during the observation. This figure does not include people who interact with, but do not hold or take care of, the infant.
Response time to Infant fuss or cry	The elapsed time between the infant's fuss or cry, and the first response by the caretaker to the fuss. Scored as: (1) within 10 seconds; (2) within 30 seconds; (3) within 1 minute; or (4) greater than 1 minute.

Table 4. Pearson Correlations of Infant Characteristics and Group Size with Caretaking Measures

	Birthweight	Arousal cluster score	Reactivity ranking	Fussing during behavioral observations	Group size
Time with mother					
3 & 7 weeks	−.70**	—	—	.58**	—
	(7)			(9)	
18 weeks	—	—	—	.79***	−.70**
				(9)	(9)
Transfer rate					
3 & 7 weeks	—	—	—	—	.50**
					(9)
18 weeks	—	—	—	—	.51*
					(9)
Transfers to mother					
3 & 7 weeks	−.63*	—	—	.51*	—
	(7)			(9)	
18 weeks	—	—	—		—
Total caretakers					
3 & 7 weeks	—	—	—	—	.48*
					(9)
18 weeks	—	—	—	−.49*	.66**
				(9)	(9)

$*p < .10.$ $**p < .05.$ $***p < .01.$

more time with their mothers and are more likely to be passed back to them. Heavier infants, on the other hand, spend less time in the care of their mothers and are less likely to be passed back to them. The relationship of birthweight to caretaking diminishes by the time the infants reach 18 weeks of age.

Newborn Arousal and Reactivity and Caretaking

The Arousal and Reactivity Ranking scores derived from the BNBAS are not strongly correlated to caretaking at 3 & 7 weeks (see Table 4). A moderate correlation exists between Arousal cluster score and transfer rate ($r = -.49$; $p = .11$). Infants with higher Arousal cluster scores are transferred less often. There is no relationship between Arousal cluster score, or Reactivity Ranking, and time with mother, total number of different caretakers, or passes to mother. At 18 weeks there is no relationship between the newborn measures and caretaking.

Caretaking and these two newborn behavioral measures appear unrelated. The failure to find a relationship among these measures may be the result of one or more factors. The measures of caretaking were not contemporaneous with the assessment of newborn behavior. When contemporaneous measures of infant fussiness at 3 & 7 weeks and 18 weeks and caretaking are analyzed, a relationship is found (see below). Moreover, newborn behavior and caretaking may be strongly related in ways not examined in this study. These issues are discussed below.

Intercorrelations of infant measures show a strong relationship between Arousal cluster score and the Reactivity Ranking ($r = .85$; $\rho = .002$), and between the ranking and observed infant fussing at 3 & 7 weeks ($r = .55$; $\rho = .078$). But there is no relationship between Arousal cluster score and observed infant fussing at this age.

Infant Fussing at Older Ages and Caretaking

Infant fussing during behavioral observations is strongly related to several dimensions of caretaking at 3 & 7 weeks (see Table 4). Infants who fuss more at 3 & 7 weeks spend more time with their mothers ($r = .58$; $\rho = .040$), and are passed to them a greater percentage of the time ($r = .51$; $\rho = .082$). There is no relationship between fussing and total number of different caretakers, or transfer rate.

The relationship between infant fussing and caretaking pattern gets stronger by 18 weeks. At this age, fussier infants spend more time with their mothers ($r = .79$; $\rho = .005$), are cared for by fewer individuals ($r = -.49$; $\rho = .089$), and tend to be passed to their mothers more often ($r = .45$; $\rho = .113$). There is still no relationship between fussing and transfer rate. These findings are in contrast to those for the relationship between birthweight and caretaking practices, which decreases in strength over time.

The low correlations between fussing and transfer rate are qualified by other features of Efe caretaking. The Efe do not typically pass an infant in response to a fuss. They do, however, respond to a fussing infant, and quickly. Data on latency of response show that a comforting response is made within 10 seconds of a fuss for over 85% of observed fussing at 3 & 7 weeks, and over 75% at 18 weeks. This indicates a great sensitivity on the part of the caretakers, and reflects the belief that infants should be kept quiet—"their work is to sleep."

A second feature of Efe caretaking that clarifies the low correlation between fussing and transfer rate is the pattern of infant transfer. Fussier infants may not be transferred more often, but their fussiness does influence to whom they are passed. Figure 1 shows the relationship between infant state (fussing vs. not fussing), and the person to whom the infant is passed (mother vs. other caretaker). Infants are passed to their mothers more often if they are fussing than if they are not fussing. When infants are passed because of fussing at 3 & 7 weeks, they are passed to their mothers 49% of the time. But when the infants are passed for reasons other than fussing, they are passed to their mothers only 33% of the time. At 18 weeks infants are passed to their mothers 43% of the time when fussing, and only 26% of the time when not fussing.

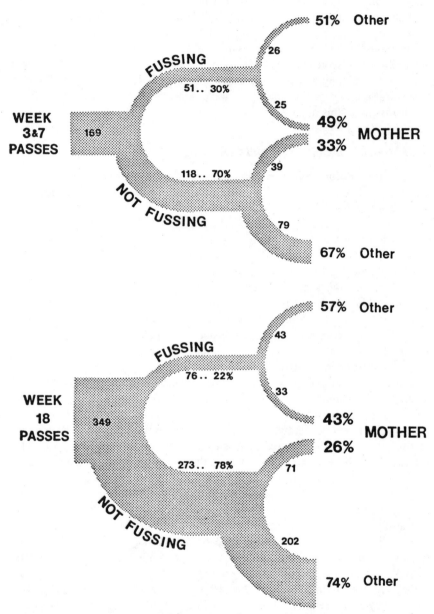

Figure 1.   Infant state and patterns of passing

We also found that when a mother receives her infant, the infant is more likely to have been fussing than when other caretakers receive the infant. At 3 & 7 weeks, 40% of all transfers to mother are preceded by infant fussiness. This figure falls to 32% at 18 weeks. Other caretakers receive fussing infants only 24% of the time. This figure also falls to 18% at 18 weeks. This pattern of care holds for 6 of the 9 mother-infant-group triads.

Note that although fussing infants are more likely to be passed to their mothers than are nonfussing infants, fussing infants are in fact passed to their mothers less than half the time. These findings are in keeping with the cultural pattern of multiple caretaking.

These data suggest that fussier infants, like lower-birthweight infants, receive a pattern of care in which the role of the mother increases.

Group Demography and Caretaking

The data show that group size tends to be related to 3 of the 4 caretaking measures at 3 & 7 wks. Infants in larger groups tend to spend more time away from their mothers ($r = -.44$; $\rho = .119$), are transferred more frequently ($r = .50$; $\rho = .086$), and are cared for by a greater number of different people ($r = .48$; $\rho = .093$). Although not reaching significance, there was a high correlation between birthweight and group size ($r = .49$; $\rho = .131$). The heavier infants in our sample were born into the larger groups. This finding led us to question whether the correlation between birthweight and caretaking was due to their relationship to group size. Partial correlations, however, showed that both birthweight and group size are independently related to caretaking. For example, when controlling for group size, time with mother and birthweight remain correlated ($r = -.62$; $\rho = .093$), and when controlling for birthweight, group size and time with mother remain significantly correlated ($r = -.72$; $\rho = .055$).

At 18 weeks the relationship of group size to caretaking practices gains strength. Infants in larger groups spend less time with their mothers ($r = -.70$; $\rho = .019$), are transferred more often ($r = .51$; $\rho = .081$), and have a greater number of different caretakers ($r = .66$; $\rho = .026$). Passes to the mother are not significantly related to group size at either age.

Discussion

These results illustrate the complexity of the transactions among behavior, social ecology, physiological factors, and cultural values and goals. The Efe use birthweight to guide their caretaking during the early weeks of life. It is easy to understand how this factor became a useful part of a hazard-prevention strategy. Birthweight is tangible and has a strong relationship to mortality and morbidity during the neonatal period (Lubchenco, 1976). The Efe appear to know this as they refer to the heavier infant as being more *ngufu*. Moreover, they enact this knowledge behaviorally. Lighter infants are passed to their mothers more often and spend more time with them. Thus, these more vulnerable infants still experience the Efe multiple caretaking system, but in a modified form. This modified form of care may offer certain benefits to these infants. For example, since infants are often nursed when they are returned to the mother, we would expect that this pattern of care serves to meet the nutritional needs of more vulnerable infants. If this is accurate, then we would expect lighter infants to nurse more and show a greater growth velocity than heavier infants. We are currently examining the data for these effects.

Our analyses indicate that there is no significant relationship between infant irritability and arousal, as measured by the BNBAS during the newborn period, and caretaking. This may be because we lacked a contemporaneous measure of newborn caretaking, or because our hypothesis that neonatal irritability influences Efe caretaking was incorrect. Certainly other aspects of Efe infant behavior need to be examined. But a more speculative interpretation of these findings is as follows. Efe infants were often fussy during the Brazelton exam, perhaps because it involved a pattern of handling extremely different from the one the infants normally receive. Specifically, the infant was often not in close physical contact with the examiner, the position which typifies Efe caretaking. Thus, to the extent that the Brazelton test was accurate in characterizing the infants as fussy, the lack of a relationship between fussing during the exam and later caretaking may have been due to the Efe having already modified their caretaking practices to reduce infant fussiness. This would be consistent with the value the Efe place on nonfussy infants, and this interpretation is supported by the finding that the Efe respond rapidly and alter their pattern of passing to soothe a fussing infant.

Fussiness in older infants is certainly an infant characteristic to which the Efe are sensitive. When measures of infant fussiness at older ages and caretaking were examined, strong relationships between these measures were found. Fussier infants spend more time with their mothers, encounter fewer caretakers, and are more likely to be passed to their mothers. This pattern of care is similar to the one observed for lower-birthweight infants at 3 & 7 weeks. But we believe that the factors which determine the care that lower-birthweight infants receive are different from those which determine the care that fussier infants receive. The Efe do not perceive the fussier infant to be more or less *ngufu* than the quiet infant. Fussiness is not seen by the Efe as a hazard to survival in LeVine's (1977) sense. Rather, we think it is seen as an aspect of the infant's personality that is worthy of change. In that sense it is a cultural hazard because fussier infants are more difficult to care for, are disruptive of camp life, and may be on their way to becoming difficult adults. And note that it is not our goal to portray the Efe infant as overly fussy.

The finding that certain infant behaviors elicit forms of caretaking which in turn modify the original behaviors is demonstrated in other cultures as well. In the United States, for example, Als and Lewis (1975) found that hyperreactive and lethargic infants are handled in different ways to encourage awake, alert, and generally well organized behavior. In Mexico, the Zinacantecos pay no attention to, and place little value on, their neonates' sensory capacities (Brazelton, 1972). Brazelton felt that this was due to the Zinacantecos' goal of minimizing any form of independence or autonomy. These findings emphasize the need for additional research on how and why cultural practices foster or discourage certain infant behaviors.

The strength of the relationship of birthweight to caretaking fades over time. This change is not because birthweight is unimportant, but because birthweight becomes a less useful measure of vulnerability for surviving infants. This pattern also occurs in Western cultures, where birthweight is a measure of prime importance during the newborn period, but loses force with development (Field et al., 1979). We would predict that the more mother-centered pattern of care given to a lower-birthweight Efe infant at 3 & 7 weeks would be maintained if that infant did not gain weight appropriately. Papousek and Papousek (1983) argue that as a species we have an intuitive knowledge of the type of caretaking required by our young. These findings on caretaking modifications based on birthweight suggest that birthweight might be innately recognized as an indicator of vulnerability. It is important to determine whether other cultures also use birthweight as a guide for caretaking.

The role that infant fussiness plays in modifying Efe caretaking practices increases over the period from 3 & 7 to 18 weeks. This occurs at about the same time the Efe see a major change occurring in the infant. At 4–5 months of age infants are viewed as becoming aware. At this time infants begin to gain more control over when and to whom they are passed. Similar types of changes in parental perception and infant control occur in other cultures. Brazelton (1969) describes how in the United States 3-month-old infants are viewed as beginning to have a will of their own; and suggests that at this time parents had best modify their caretaking practices if they are to win this battle of wills. These changes in adult perception of the infant occur around the time that major developmental shifts take place. This coincidence raises the question as to whether there is a universally recognized change, and if so, what behavior or behaviors are used to identify this change.

The decreasing importance of birthweight, coincident with the increasing importance of infant fussiness, can be viewed in terms of LeVine's (1977) goals of parenting. These changes reflect a shift from caretaking practices that emphasize survival to caretaking practices that are more concerned with the transmission and maintenance of cultural values and goals. This clearly supports LeVine's view that there is a "natural" hierarchy to these goals.

Group size is another factor found to influence the care an infant receives. It is a complicated social-ecological factor which establishes the context for the multiple caretaking pattern observed in the Efe. Efe infants born into larger groups are likely to spend less time with their mothers and encounter a greater number of different caretakers. Similar observations on the relationship between group size and caretaking have been made by Chisholm and the Munroes.

Chisholm (1983) found that Navajo infants living in nuclear families spent more time with their mothers and were in the "presence of fewer other individuals" than infants in extended families. Munroe and Munroe (1971) found that among the Logoli of East Africa, household density influenced infant caretaking. In larger households the mother was less likely to be the caretaker of her infant. Thus group size is a factor related to caretaking in a number of societies. Nevertheless, it should not be overemphasized. In other societies such as the !Kung the mother remains the almost exclusive caretaker of her young infant (Konner, 1976), even though a number of caretakers are available. For the !Kung, the pattern of care can be explained by taking other factors such as cultural values, maintenance systems, and ecology into account.

What do these results tell us about the Brazelton exam? The exam is described as a way of interacting with an infant that typifies, in condensed form, the caretaking that an infant experiences in a typical day. The behaviors observed during the Brazelton exam are expected to evidence some continuity and be related to the caretaking the infant receives. But when the behaviors elicited by the exam do not parallel the behavior elicited by the culture's caretaking routines, the behavior is less likely to be related to caretaking. Brazelton found this to be true for alertness in his study of the Zinacantecos, and we found this to be true for irritability in our study of the Efe. Efe caretaking does not stress the infant in the same manner that the Brazelton exam does. The irritability observed during the examination, therefore, was not related to the Efe caretaking situation.

These findings highlight the fact that caretaking values and standards of behavior in the United States may be implicitly embedded in the Brazelton examination. Although this is understandable, we suggest that for certain purposes and questions it may be necessary to modify the Brazelton exam according to a particular culture's practices. The expectation would be that the "Brazelton-in-culture" form would better predict continuities in behavior and the effect of infant behavior on the caretaker. The Brazelton exam works well in the United States because it mimics American caretaking practices well. If Brazelton had only considered BNBAS scores in his study of the Zinacanteco, he might have failed to explain the lack of a relationship between alertness and caretaking. Only his understanding of the culture allowed him also to understand its relationship to infant behavior.

Culture and Behavior: An Overview

A culture's predominant parental investment strategy is designed for, and influenced by, a multiplicity of factors. These factors limit the range of developmental experiences. But within this range, individual variability in caretaking exists, and this variability allows for differences in the developmental histories of individuals. Efe infants, for example, vary along several dimensions, including birthweight, behavior, and the size of the group into which they are born. Because of these differences they will be cared for differently. To the extent that these differences influence the development of an individual's behavioral style, as well as representation of self and environment, individuals will differ.

Central to an understanding of the development of behavioral differences among people of the same culture and between people of different cultures, then, is a specification of the process regulating the exchanges that take place between the individual and the environment, and how that process is represented within the individual. The representation may take different forms depending on the individual's developmental status. For example, in the young infant this representation may be in the form of particular sensorimotor or sensori-affective schemes, while in the older child it may be in the form of conscious and unconscious symbolic representations. But whatever its form, the representation is specific to the individual. This is because each individual combines unique organismic qualities with a social ecology that reflects unique historical and accidental factors.

Furthermore, following Spitz (1965), an individual's representation will be most strongly influenced by reiterated forms of interchange between that individual and the environment. Culture is one factor leading to reiterated experiences which result in individuals sharing a representation that is culturally based. But factors such as fussiness or group size may vary within a culture, modifying each individual's representation. Paradoxically, then, culture both constrains and varies individuals' representations.

In conclusion, we propose that the mutual influence among culture, behavior, and other factors finds its interface in the actual exchanges between individuals and their environment. These exchanges modify and are modified by the individuals' representation of these exchanges. They occur over periods ranging from moments to generations, and they permit the mutual influence of such disparate factors as culture and behavior.

References

Als, H., & Lewis, M. (1975, April). *The contribution of the infant to the interaction with his mother*. Paper presented at the meeting on the Society for Research in Child Development, Denver, CO.

Bailey, R. C., & Peacock, N. R. (in press). Efe Pygmies of northeast Zaire: Subsistence strategies in the Ituri Forest. In I. de Garine & G. A. Harrison (Eds.), *Coping with uncertainty in food supply*. Oxford: Oxford University Press.

Benedict, R. (1949). Child rearing in certain European countries. *American Journal of Orthopsychiatry, 19*, 342–350.

Bowlby, J. (1969). *Attachment and loss: Vol. 1. Attachment.* New York: Basic Books.

Brazelton, T. B. (1969). *Infants and mothers.* New York: Delta.

Brazelton, T. B. (1972). Implications of infant development among the Mayan Indians of Mexico. *Human Development, 15,* 90–111.

Brazelton, T. B. (1973). *Neonatal Behavioral Assessment Scale.* London: Spastics International Medical Publications/Heinemann Medical Books.

Campbell, S., & Taylor, P. (1980). Bonding and attachment: Theoretical issues. *Seminars in Perinatology, 3,* 3–14.

Caudill, W., & Weinstein, H. (1969). Maternal care and infant behavior in Japan and America. *Psychiatry, 32,* 12–43.

Chisholm, J. S. (1983). *Navajo infancy.* New York: Aldine.

Field, T. M., Sostek, A. M., Goldberg, S., & Shuman, H. H. (Eds.). (1979). *Infants born at risk.* New York: Spectrum.

Freedman, D. G. (1974). *Human infancy: An evolutionary perspective.* Hillsdale, NJ: Erlbaum.

Freedman, D. G., & Freedman, N. (1969). Behavioral differences between Chinese-American and European-American newborns. *Nature, 224,* 122.

Goldberg, S. A. (1977). Social competence in infancy: A model of parent–infant interaction. *Merrill-Palmer Quarterly, 23*(3), 163–177.

Hinde, R. A. (1983). *Biological bases of the mother-child relationship.* Unpublished manuscript.

Konner, M. J. (1976). Maternal care, infant's behavior and development. In E. B. Lee & I. DeVore (Eds.), *Kalahari hunter-gatherers* (pp. 218–245). Cambridge, MA: Harvard University Press.

Lester, R., Als, H., & Brazelton, T. B. (1978). *Scoring criteria for seven clusters of the Brazelton Scale.* Unpublished manuscript, Children's Hospital Medical Center, Child Development Unit, Boston.

LeVine, R. A. (1977). Child rearing as cultural adaptation. In P. H. Leiderman, S. R. Tulkin, & A. Rosenfeld (Eds.), *Culture and infancy: Variations in the human experience.* New York: Academic Press.

Lubchenco, L. O. (1976). *The high-risk infant.* Philadelphia: Saunders.

Mead, M. (1953). *The study of culture at a distance.* Chicago University of Chicago Press.

Munroe, R. H., & Munroe, R. L. (1971). Household density and infant care in an East African society. *The Journal of Social Psychology, 83,* 3–13.

Osofsky, J. D., & Danzger, B. (1974). Relationships between neonatal characteristics and mother-infant interaction. *Developmental Psychology, 10,* 124.

Osofsky, J. D., & O'Connell, E. J. (1977). Patterning of newborn behavior in an urban population. *Child Development, 48,* 532–536.

Papousek, H., & Papousek, M. (1983). Biological basis of social interactions: Implications of research for an understanding of behavioral deviance. *Journal of Child Psychology and Psychiatry, 24*(1), 117–129.

Rubin, J. Z., Provenzano, F. J., & Luria, Z. (1974). The eye of the beholder: Parents' view on sex of newborns. *American Journal of Orthopsychiatry, 44,* 512–519.

Schwartz, G. G., & Rosenblum, L. A. (1983). Allometric influences on primate mothers and infants. In L. Rosenblum & H. Moltz (Eds.), *Symbiosis in parent-young interactions.* New York: Plenum.

Spitz, R. A. (1965). *The first year of life: A psychoanalytic study of normal and deviant development of object relations.* New York: International Universities Press.

Tronick, E., Als, H., & Brazelton, T. B. (1980). The infant's communicative competencies and the achievement of intersubjectivity. In M. R. Key (Ed.), *The relationship of verbal and nonverbal communication* (pp. 261–274). The Hague: Mouton.

Tronick, E. Z., Morelli, G. A., & Winn, S. (1983, November). *Multiple caretaking and personality formation in an environment of human adaptiveness.* Paper presented at meeting of the Boston Institute for the development of Infants and Parents, Boston.

Tronick, E. Z., Morelli, G. A., & Winn, S. (1987). Multiple caretaking of Efe (Pygmy) infants. *American Anthropologist, 89,* 96–106.

Tronick, E. Z., Winn, S., & Morelli, G. A. (1985). Multiple caretaking in the context of human evolution: Why don't the Efe know the Western prescription for child care. In M. Reite & T. Field (Eds.), *Psychobiology of attachment,* (pp 293–322). New York: Academic Press.

Whiting, B. B., & Whiting J. M. (1975). *Children of six cultures.* Cambridge, MA: Harvard University Press.

CHAPTER 5

The Consequences of Teenage Childbearing in Traditional Puerto Rican Culture

Cynthia T. Garcia Coll

Brown University Program in Medicine
and
Women and Infants Hospital of Rhode Island

"The really interesting sight is that of grandmothers walking arm-in-arm with their teenage granddaughters, who are obviously pregnant. It is easy to tell that she is proud; she will be a great-grandmother soon. At the same time, it is clear that she is confused. . . . Yes, she was pregnant when she was a teenager, but she was married first." (Wilma Montanez, as quoted in Martinez, 1981, p. 336)

Adolescent pregnancy and childbearing are considered negative life events for both mother and child. The consequences of teenage childbearing have been documented not only on the subsequent economic, social, and emotional status of the mother, but also on the developmental outcome of the child (Baldwin & Cain, 1980; Furstenberg, 1976). Three different sets of factors have been identified as contributors to the high-risk status of the adolescent mother and her child: biological, social, and caretaking. This high-risk status is not evolutionarily borne out, however, since the history of human reproduction indicates that teenage pregnancy and childbearing are the norm, rather than the exception.

In this chapter I will review the high-risk factors associated with teenage childbearing and argue, on the basis of a series of studies carried out in San Juan, Puerto Rico, that the social and cultural contexts of teenage pregnancy and childbearing are the major determinants of the consequences (positive, negative, or mixed) for mother and child.

Biological Risk Associated with Teenage Pregnancy

The incidence of adolescent pregnancy has been termed "epidemic" by many, including the Select Committee on Population of the 95th Congress of the United States of America (Lincoln, 1979). The report suggests that "very young women . . . are biologically too immature for effective childbearing" (Lowe, 1979). The initial medical evidence supported this view, since a series of obstetric risk factors were found to be more pronounced at a younger maternal age than at an older one. Among these were pregnancy-induced hypertension, especially toxemia (Harris, 1922). A recent review of the literature reveals an incidence of toxemia usually in the range of 7–23% among adolescents, compared to 5% for the general population (Carey, McCann-Sanford, & Davidson, 1983).

Anemia is another pregnancy complication that appears to be more prevalent in adolescent than in older women. Osofsky (1970) reported that in a group of pregnant low-income teenagers, the rate of anemia was 52% and that 90% of the sample showed evidence of nutritional inadequacy. Other complications, such as cephalopelvic disproportion and prolonged labor, have been associated repeatedly with teenage pregnancies (Elster & McAnarney, 1980).

In addition, infants of adolescent mothers tend to be lighter, of shorter gestational age, and smaller for gestational age (Hardy & Mellits, 1977; Hoffman, Lundin, Bakketeig, & Harley, 1977). It seems that the extra nutritional requirements associated with pregnancy, coexisting with adolescent growth and economic disadvantage, may be possible additional growth-retarding factors for infants of teenage mothers (Heald & Jacobson, 1980).

Biological risk can be reduced through appropriate preventive and intervention practices, however. Recent data point out that the so-called "biologic risk" associated with teenage pregnancy is not simply a reflection of inherent health problems in younger women but, rather, is indicative of a life-style that may negatively affect pregnancy outcome (Carey et al., 1983). It is now recognized, for example, that early antenatal care improves the outcome of teenage pregnancy (Baldwin & Cain, 1980; Briggs, 1962). In two studies of infants of black teenagers of low socioeconomic status (SES) who were receiving adequate prenatal care, the rate of toxemia was similar to that of the average population in Chicago (Zanckler, Andelman, & Bauer, 1969), and in New Haven, Connecticut, low rates of complications were reported, with a 5% rate of toxemia and a 10% rate of prematurity (Sarrel & Klerman, 1969). Some investigators even have concluded that the ideal time to give birth, from a medical point of view, would appear to be between the ages of 16 and 19, provided the mother is given adequate prenatal care (Lawrence & Merritt, 1983; Merritt, Lawrence, & Naege, 1980). Therefore, factors such as SES, early prenatal care, and other health habits might have a more profound impact than does the mother's age on the obstetric experience and perinatal outcome of teenage pregnancy.

Social Risk Associated with Teenage Childbearing

A major concern about teenage pregnancy lies in the consequences for population growth (Bogue, 1977). For example, it has been found that later marriages lengthen the period between generations and slow population growth (Ravenholt & Lyons, 1979). If later marriage is accompanied by smaller family size preferences, the potential for reduced population growth is significantly increased. During most of human experience, it has been desirable from a demographic and a survival-of-the-species point of view that young women commence reproduction soon after puberty (Ravenholt, 1977). As mortality levels decrease among societies, however, there develops a need to curb fertility and population growth toward levels commensurate with the current distribution of resources. Therefore, teenage pregnancy and childbearing become a "problem," especially if we consider that having a first child at a very young age increases the likelihood of additional children within a short period of time (Lowe, 1977).

The adverse social consequences for the teenage mother herself have also been documented. In comparison to women who delay their first child, adolescent mothers have reduced educational and occupational attainment, lower income, and increased dependency (Card and Wise, 1978; Moore & Waite, 1977). They also tend to have higher rates of marital separation, divorce, and remarriage later on (Rolfe & Roosa, 1979). There is evidence to suggest that some of these social consequences can be alleviated through appropriate interventions. Field, Widmayer, Greenberg, and Stoller (1982) found that teenage mothers who were trained as teachers' aides had lower repeat pregnancy rates and higher return-to-work/school rates than adolescent mothers who did not receive training. Although it is not clear which of the additional benefits of this intervention made the difference (the paycheck, the job training, etc.), it is clear that the course these mothers followed was very different from that followed by most other adolescent mothers within this culture.

Caretaking Risk Associated with Teenage Pregnancy

The third source of risk associated with teenage childbearing concerns the mothering skills displayed by teenage mothers with their children. It has been argued that because of their young maternal age and the characteristic of their own stage of development (see Sahler, 1983), adolescent mothers cannot provide an adequate caretaking environment for their children. A number of studies describe adolescent mothers as impatient, insensitive, and prone to punish their children (DeLissovoy, 1973; Furstenberg, 1976; Montagau, 1981). In comparison to older mothers, they show less optimal evaluation of their infant's temperament and less realistic developmental milestones and child-rearing attitudes (Field, Widmayer, Stringer, & Ignatoff, 1980).

There is evidence to suggest that these attitudes and lack of knowledge about child rearing are related to specific differences in maternal behaviors between adolescent and nonadolescent mothers (Field, 1979). McAnarney, Lawrence, and Aten (1979) found that the younger the adolescent mother, the less she utilized typical maternal behaviors of touching, high-pitched voice, synchronous movements, and closeness to the infant. Other studies of mother-infant interaction have suggested that adolescent mothers differ from older mothers in the amount of time they spend with the infant and the amount of verbal interaction with the infant (McLaughlin, Sandler, Herrod, Vietze, & O'Connor, 1979; Osofsky & Osofsky, 1971). Thus, the effect of teenage childbearing on infant development may be an interaction between the mother's responsiveness and the infant's greater impact on a younger caregiver, as a result of the latter's lesser familiarity with children and less realistic developmental and child-rearing attitudes.

The question that remains is whether the mother's chronologic age is the critical determinant of her mothering skills. Several studies have found that other factors are stronger predictors of maternal behaviors than is the mother's age per se. SES and education have been implicated repeatedly in determining the characteristics of the caregiving environment or developmental outcome of infants of adolescent mothers (Garcia Coll, Hoffmann, & Oh, 1987; Roosa, Fitzgerald, & Carlson, 1982). The mother's own stage of development, in terms of ego strength, has also been implicated as permeating the individual differences observed among teenage mothers (Levine, Garcia Coll, & Oh, 1985; Wise & Grossman, 1980). In addition, several studies have shown that the negative effects of having an adolescent for a mother may be muted by the presence of a father and/or an extended family (Field et al., 1980; Furstenberg, 1976; Mednick, 1979).

Although we do not know if the presence of an extended family support affects the actual maternal practices of the adolescent, or merely provides a substitute, more responsive caregiver, or does both, it is clear that the caretaking risk associated with teenage parenting can be lessened through this mechanism.

Teenage Childbearing in Traditional Puerto Rican Culture

Let us shift to an examination of adolescent motherhood in traditional Puerto Rican culture. In order to place these events in an appropriate social, historical, and cultural context, we have to examine briefly Puerto Rico, its recent history, and its cultural evolution.

Puerto Rico is the smallest of the major Antilles, surrounded in the south by the Caribbean Sea and in the north by the Atlantic Ocean. Its relatively small size

(5 × 6 km) underscores its strategic military placement, which has made it a desirable possession for colonial powers since its discovery by the Spaniards in 1493. At that point it was populated by Taino Indians, who were exterminated quickly through forced labor, epidemics, and intermarriage. Their legacy remains in the language and in the physical features of the Puerto Rican people today.

Colonial Spanish culture was dominant in Puerto Rico from the 15th through the 19th centuries. Blacks were brought onto the island as slaves in order to perform the agricultural work originally done by the Indian population. The present Puerto Rican culture reflects a mix of Indian, Spanish, and black cultures, which results in a unique Creole or Caribbean blend.

In 1898 possession of Puerto Rico was transferred from Spain to the United States as a result of the former's losing the Spanish-American War. Since then the island has undergone a series of drastic political and economic changes. As a colony of the United States it has been transformed rapidly from an agrarian, rural, isolated society into a fairly industrialized one. U.S. companies are now the primary source of employment for both men and women. This process, which happened primarily between 1940 and 1970, also created a rapid migratory pattern from the rural into the urban areas. The majority of these migrants moved to San Juan and eventually to the U.S., concentrating (although not exclusively) in New York City.

This rapid economic growth has not been paralleled with a smooth cultural evolution. The traditional Puerto Rican culture, which is based on strong family ties, permeates the superficially Americanized, modern Puerto Rican society. This may be because the Americanization process has been too fast or because the cultural identity of Puerto Ricans has been too strong and resistant to change. Despite all these changes, the traditional values of family life and strict sex and age roles remain prevalent in determining behavior and ideology, and in causing conflict with the newer ways of being.

The traditional Puerto Rican culture placed an important value on family life. The family, the primary economic unit in the agricultural society, was composed of several generations and was the most important vehicle for the transmission of values and beliefs. During periods of crisis, the extended family network was mobilized quickly. Female family members helped each other during pregnancy, after childbirth, and with the children's day care (Leavitt, 1974). Emergency housing or financial assistance, care of the elderly, handicapped, or mentally afflicted were among other needs fulfilled by the family members.

Very strict behavioral roles were defined for each family member according to the sex and age of the person. The traditional family was patriarchal, with the male head of house fulfilling a very strong authoritarian role and the female a passive-submissive role (Ortiz, 1973; Stycos, 1955; Wolf, 1952). The roles and responsibilities of each member were clearly delineated. The male head of household was responsible for financial maintenance of the family, determining discipline and making all major decisions. Females, in turn, were responsible for child rearing, maintaining the home, and making the minor decisions that might have an impact on the family. Grandparents were consulted on major decisions and might be responsible for various duties (e.g., child care, cooking, etc.).

Traditional Sex Roles and Teenage Pregnancy

The clearly defined sex roles within traditional Puerto Rican families have tremendous implications for the acceptability of teenage pregnancy and childbearing within this community. The Puerto Rican woman lived in a world where the role of mother had an extremely high social value (Martinez, 1981). At the same time, however, it was demanded of the young woman that she have an attitude of so-called purity and remain a virgin up to the moment of marriage (Viel, 1977). Thus, teenage pregnancy and childbearing were very common, as long as they took place within the context of marriage. Early marriage, in a way, served the dual purpose of starting early the woman's "reproductive career" and controlled premarital sexual relations. This pattern also prevented the young female from losing her honor and dignity and destroying the family's reputation and respect in the community, traits very highly valued within Puerto Rican families (Delgado, n.d.). As a consequence, there were two classes of women: the "pure" ones (for marriage) and the others, the "impure" (with whom men acquired their premarital or extramarital experience) (Viel, 1977). Within this framework it was clear that early pregnancy and childbearing would promote the fulfillment of the woman's role within that traditional society. No other "acceptable" alternatives were provided to the woman for her to accomplish the goal of development as an adult.

Although Puerto Rican women and Puerto Rican society in general have undergone tremendous changes in terms of educational and occupational achievements within this century, the traditional ideals of the woman's role and development are still prevalent. This is more the case within the lower socioeconomic groups where, in contrast to an existence of high unemployment and inadequate educational opportunities, the so-called "alternative" of early motherhood may become a highly desirable one, even if the child is conceived out of wedlock.

What is the reaction of the Puerto Rican family to an unexpected teenage pregnancy? As long as the *dignidad* and *respeto* of the group is maintained, through marriage, the crisis is overcome. By the time the child is born, the family rejoices and celebrates the newcomer. The adolescent assumes her mothering role, thereafter surrounded by her family members. The exchange of goods and services continues among all family members as if nothing had happened. Only the mother's life has changed drastically, since her educational and other occupational attainments are usually discarded for life.

Although teenage pregnancy and childbearing might seem the norm in the "old days" (i.e., two generations ago) and not today, the statistics reveal quite a different picture. For example, among Puerto Ricans living in the U.S., 23.2% of the total births are to mothers under 20 years of age, as compared to 12.3% for white American women (Ventura & Heuser, 1981). Even within a society in which contraception is more widely advocated among teenagers, Puerto Rican women still procreate at early ages. This trend is backed up not only by the social value placed on motherhood, and by the lack of alternatives provided to young Puerto Rican women, but also by the general attitudes of Puerto Rican society toward women's sexual behavior and contraception. Abortion is not an alternative for most Puerto Rican adolescents; nor is adoption. The use of contraceptives would be an admission that one is sexually active and that one is planning one's sexual acts, which is considered improper, wrong, and unromantic. Avoidance of contraception might be due to the sense of guilt felt for expressing sexual needs. The strong Judeo-Christian and Victorian moral tradition, along with a religious resistance, contributes to this behavioral pattern (Ruarca-Marino, 1977). In a way, the longing for independence from parents, along with sexual maturity and the cultural pressure against extramarital sexual relations, make adolescent childbearing the most natural choice for Puerto Rican women.

Empirical Studies

For the past 7 years we have been conducting a series of investigations on the consequences of teenage pregnancy within an urban, low-socioeconomic Puerto Rican population in San Juan, Puerto Rico. It is important to keep in mind these characteristics, since it is our argument that the consequences of teenage childbearing will be a function of the particular sociocultural environment, rather than of the mother's age per se.

Extrapolating from the existing literature, and unaware of the sociocultural context of this population, we originally proposed to test the following hypotheses:[1]

1. Teenage pregnancy, both in Puerto Rico and within a lower-socioeconomic black population in Florida, would be associated with higher obstetric and perinatal risk than in comparison groups of older mothers from the same population.
2. Teenage childbearing in both populations would have negative effects on the neonate's behavior as measured by the Brazelton Neonatal Behavioral Assessment Scale (Brazelton, 1973).

---

[1] The reader is referred to previous publications for further details of these studies (Garcia Coll, Sepkoski, & Lester, 1982; Lester, Garcia Coll, & Sepkoski, 1982, 1983).

3. Teenage childbearing would have negative long-term effects on the infant's development, as measured by standardized tests and assessments of temperament at 1 year of age.

Much to our surprise, the negative effects of teenage pregnancy and childbearing on these areas were negligible. We can summarize our findings as follows:

A greater number of nonoptimal obstetric conditions were associated with teenage pregnancy, but only in our mainland sample. Black teenage mothers from a lower socioeconomic background had more maternal and fetal nonoptimal conditions than did the mothers in the comparison group. No difference was found in the obstetric and perinatal outcome of teenage and older mothers in Puerto Rico. Since prenatal care has been implicated as a major determinant of pregnancy outcome for adolescent mothers, we inferred from these data that the Puerto Rican mothers had better prenatal care. Our knowledge of both health care systems, however, pointed out that the services available to both populations were comparable and that the differences between the two populations might be on the utilization of the services available to them.

Concerning our second hypothesis—the impact of teenage childbearing on neonatal behavior—we found that it was a function of both the number of other nonoptimal conditions present and the cultural group. Comparisons by maternal age and the number of obstetrical complications showed that for the Puerto Rican group, infants with fewer obstetrical complications were better able to regulate their crying and active states. Infants of teenage mothers with fewer complications had a higher level of arousal than did infants of older mothers with fewer complications. Infant behavior in the mainland sample did not vary by maternal age or complications. Multiple regression analyses indicated that the combination of biomedical variables significantly predicted neonatal behavior in both cultures. The mother's age was not correlated separately with neonatal behavior but was repeatedly combined with other variables in predicting significant neonatal behavior. These findings suggest that infants of teenage mothers in Puerto Rico may differ from infants of older mothers, particularly in the organization of state behavior, and that the effects of maternal age on neonatal behavior are increased in the presence of biological risk factors. The effects of maternal age were subtle, however, and mostly within the normal range of newborn behavior.

The next question we addressed was that of the consequences of teenage parenting on the infant's behavior at 1 year of age. One-year follow-up assessments of mental and motor development and temperamental ratings by both examiners and mothers showed no significant differences between infants born to teenage mothers and those born to older mothers. The pattern of correlations, however, between neonatal variables and 1-year outcome indicated more consistent relationships for the infants born to teenage mothers, particularly along state-related dimensions. Thus it seems that infants of teenage mothers may differ along temperamental dimensions during the first year of life. None of the differences observed between teenage mothers and their infants and older mothers and their infants substantiate the expected detrimental effects of teenage pregnancy and childbearing, however. In Puerto Rico, within this socioeconomic group, early marriage and childbearing seem to be accepted as part of normal adolescent growth and development. This might affect compliance to prenatal care, nutrition, and the balance between life stress and social support, and would in turn affect the associations of maternal age with an additive adverse effect on the newborn's behavior and subsequent development.

Sociocultural Context of Teenage Childbearing in Puerto Rico

In our last study, in January–February 1983, we decided to assess more directly the sociocultural context of teenage childbearing within this population. As part of a larger study of adolescent mothers and the nutritional status of their infants, we tried to assess several aspects of the social environment that might permeate the consequences of teenage childbearing for both mother and child. Among those suggested by the literature we chose to address the following areas: childcare support and life stress (Crockenberg, in press; Field et al., 1980); maternal attitudes (DeLissovoy, 1973; Field et al., 1980); and beliefs about the implications and consequences of adolescent motherhood.

The sample consisted of primiparous women having their children at two hospital sites: Children's Hospital, San Juan, Puerto Rico, and Women and Infants Hospital, Providence, Rhode Island (the comparison group). The 30 women delivering in San Juan were all Puerto Ricans of lower to middle socioeconomic status. Fifteen were adolescents (13–17 years of age) and 15 were nonadolescents (20–29 years of age). Most of the mothers in both groups were married and were not in school or working at the time. The 30 women delivering in Providence were all American Caucasian mothers from lower to middle SES. Thirteen were adolescents (14–17 years of age) and 17 were nonadolescents (21–29 years of age). Most adolescents were single and had not completed high school. Most nonadolescent mothers were married and had completed high school. Both samples were selected as part of ongoing studies of the impact of adolescent motherhood on the infant's development.

Similar procedures were used in both sites. An experimenter reviewed the charts daily in order to identify prospective subjects. Inclusion criteria included the mother's age, cultural background, parity, and condition of the infant at birth (i.e., that the infant did not require any special care). In addition, for nonadolescent mothers, education and SES factors were also considered. In both sites, however, we found that primiparous, nonadolescent mothers remained in school and therefore had a higher education level.

Recruitment was done at the time of the infant's delivery. Informed consent was obtained from the mothers after explanation of the study design. During the recruitment period, in Puerto Rico 95% of the adolescent mothers and 100% of the nonadolescent mothers agreed to be in the study. In Providence 52% of the adolescent and 57% of the nonadolescent mothers agreed to participate in the study. Reasons for refusals included moving, returning to school or work, or problems with the time commitment required for the study.

Thus, in both sites, compliance rates were similar between adolescent and nonadolescent mothers. The difference in percentages between the sites could be due to the fact that the study in Providence required a two-year commitment, whereas in Puerto Rico, where there is no rooming-in, participation in the study was very attractive because it allowed the mother longer contact with the baby during her hospital stay.

Data on social support, life stress, and maternal attitudes were gathered by the author, in conjunction with a female research assistant who was fluent in English and Spanish, as necessary.

The interview on child-care support was an adaptation of Crockenberg's format (Crockenberg, 1981, 1987). For the child-care network, the mother was asked who and how old the persons were who would be involved in some aspect of child care (changing diapers, baby-sitting, etc.), and in how many different child-care activities and how frequently these persons would be helping out. For each category (except for number of persons), an average score was determined. To document the characteristics of the life stress within the last year, a list of 39 life events was read to the mother. This was a modified version of a 37-item stress checklist derived from Cochrane and Robertson (1973), previously utilized by Crockenberg (in press) in a study with adolescent mothers. If these stressful events had happened since the infant was born, the mother was asked to rate them on a 6-point scale to determine how stressful they were. The number of events and the average perceived stress were derived as summary scores. Reliability between two coders was determined on 10 questionnaires; it ranged from 87 to 100, with an average of 96.

To assess maternal attitudes toward rearing a young child, we used a shortened version of the Maternal Attitude Scale (Cohler, Weiss, & Grunebaum, n.d.). The shortened version consisted of the items with the highest loading on the six main rotated factors, based on a principal component analysis of the entire item pool of the Maternal Attitude Scale (Cohler et al., n.d.). These factors were maternal satisfaction, nonacceptance of the child's impulses, maternal moderation of the child's aggressive challenges, maternal flexibility, concerns regarding the performance of the maternal role, and encouragement of positive interactions with the child. The scale consisted of 65 items and was translated into Spanish for use in Puerto Rico. A score for each factor was determined by multiplying each item's score by its loading on that factor and adding those new weighted scores for all the items comprising a factor.

In addition, a section of the Maternal Developmental Expectations and Childbearing Attitudes Survey (MDECAS) (Field, n.d.) was administered. This is an assessment of the mother's knowledge of the average age in which developmental milestones (e.g., smiling, crawling, walking, and talking) are achieved. This instrument consisted of eight questions, which also were translated into Spanish for the Puerto Rican sample.

Finally, we designed a questionnaire to assess beliefs about teenage pregnancy and its consequences for mother and child. The five questions addressed the following: the best age for a woman to have her first child; the best option for a pregnant teenager to exercise; the quality of support given to a teenage daughter who is pregnant; and the long-term consequences for mother and child. These also were translated for use in Puerto Rico (see the English version of the questionnaire in Figure 1).

In order to test for cultural (American, low-SES, urban, Caucasian population vs. Puerto Rican, low-SES, urban population) and maternal age (adolescent vs. nonadolescent mothers) effects, a series of 2 × 2 analysis of variance (ANOVA) was performed on the following variables: child-care support network, life events and perceived stress, Cohler's Maternal Attitude Scale, Maternal Developmental Expectations and Childbearing Attitudes Survey (MDECAS), and beliefs about teenage childbearing. Significant main effects or interactions were followed by t tests.

These results will be discussed in terms of the original hypotheses regarding cultural differences in the perceptions of adolescent motherhood and its consequences. Specifically, we were expecting adolescent mothers in Puerto Rico to expect more child-care support and to experience less life stress than adolescent

1. What is the best age for a woman to have her first child?
   _____ 13–17 years   _____ 23–27 years
   _____ 18–22 years   _____ 28–32 years
2. If a teenager gets pregnant, she should do the following:
   _____ remain single and have her child
   _____ get married and have her child
   _____ give it up for adoption
   _____ have an abortion
3. If your teenage daughter becomes pregnant, you would:
   _____ withdraw your support to her
   _____ leave her alone and try to understand
   _____ help her as much as you can
4. If a teenager has a child, she will:
   _____ regret it later
   _____ manage with the help of her family and/or husband (boyfriend)
   _____ naturally become a good, responsible mother on her own
5. The child of a teenage mother will:
   _____ not have any problems in school
   _____ not have any problems if they live with her family and/or
          husband (boyfriend)
   _____ always have problems

Figure 1.   Beliefs About Teenage Pregnancy

mothers in Providence; for adolescent mothers in Providence to have less optimal attitudes about childbearing than nonadolescent mothers in Providence; for such an age effect not to be present in Puerto Rico; and for Puerto Rican mothers to reflect more positive beliefs about teenage childbearing than mothers in Providence.

Results

Child-Care Support Network

Table 1 shows the means for adolescents and nonadolescents in Providence and Puerto Rico for the child-care support network.

It is interesting to note that adolescents in both cultures report relying more on peers than on adults for their child-care support. A total of 85% of adolescents in Puerto Rico and 55% of adolescents in Providence include the baby's adolescent father as an important source of support. This might have tremendous implications for the quality of the caregiving requirement provided by adolescent mothers in both cultures. Since other adolescents (e.g., the baby's father, friends, relatives, etc.) will be the major source of help, will the caregiving environment be quite different from that provided by adults? Future research might address this question.

Nonadolescent mothers from Puerto Rico reported the lowest frequency of help. In contrast, adolescent mothers from Puerto Rico reported the highest frequency of help from their network. In their descriptions they reported expecting help with their baby, as an average, on a daily basis. Thus, their perception was of a supportive environment for the care of their infants. If they actually *do* receive more frequent help from their network than the other three groups, it is not a question addressed by this study. What is important is that their perception was of a frequently supportive involvement from the members of the network.

Life Events and Perceived Stress

Table 2 shows the means for adolescents and nonadolescents in Providence and Puerto Rico for the life events and perceived stress.

Nonadolescent mothers from Providence reported the lowest frequency of life events, whereas adolescent mothers from Providence reported the highest frequency of life events within the last year. This finding supports the conceptualization of pregnancy during adolescence as a more stressful event within this culture than in Puerto Rican culture. The specific life events that happened most frequently for the Providence group were dropping out of school, moving, and problems with families and boyfriends. Thus, adolescent mothers in Providence not only expected to receive less frequent help from their network, but also have

Table 1.   Child-Care Support Network

Variable	Providence Adolescents	Providence Nonadolescents[a]	Puerto Rico Adolescents	Puerto Rico Nonadolescents[a]	F	$p <$
Number of adults	2.85	4.94	2.67	4.27	1.76[b]	.001
Number of adolescents	2.77	0.00	1.13	.60	34.2[b]	.001
Kind of help	5.74	5.22	6.04	5.66	—	—
Frequency of help	4.73	3.75	5.04	4.87	14.9[c]	.01
					8.8[b]	.01
					4.4[d]	.05

[a]Means. [b]Age effect. [c]Cultural effect. [d]Culture × Age interaction.

experienced more life events within the last year, including problems with their own family involving their pregnancy.

The cultural difference in perceived stress was unexpected. Puerto Rican mothers, irrespective of their age, reported experiencing more life stress. A possible explanation for this difference is that of the specific life events these mothers reported; the Puerto Rican population reflected a lower SES than the Providence population, because of the higher unemployment rate within the working class in Puerto Rico at the time of the study (unofficial reports put it at 33%). The higher perceived stress might be coming from a more drastic change in their lives, in terms of their husband's recent change of work status and subsequent financial problems.

Maternal Attitudes

Table 3 shows the group's means for the six summary scores of Cohler's Maternal Attitude Scale.

Very few maternal age effects were found in maternal attitudes as measured by the abbreviated Cohler's Scale. Two out of the six subscales reflect lower scores for adolescents: in Providence for maternal moderation of the child's impulses, and in both cultures for encouragement of positive interaction with child. Thus we do not find major differences in maternal attitudes between adolescent and older mothers. This is in contrast with other previous reports

Table 2.   Life Events and Perceived Stress

Variable	Providence Adolescents	Providence Nonadolescents[a]	Puerto Rico Adolescents	Puerto Rico Nonadolescents[a]	F	$p <$
Number of life events	9.15	5.65	7.80	8.00	4.3[b]	.05
Perceived stress	2.78	2.20	2.89	3.11	5.4[c]	.02

[a]Means. [b]Culture × Age interaction. [c]Cultural effect.

Table 3. Cohler's Maternal Attitude Scale

Variable	Providence		Puerto Rico			
	Adolescents	Nonadolescents[a]	Adolescents	Nonadolescents[a]	F	$p <$
Maternal satisfaction	15.44	18.15	12.64	12.78	24.03[b]	.001
Nonacceptance of child's impulses	16.10	15.68	18.31	15.57	—	—
Maternal moderation of child's aggressive challenge	12.54	15.01	11.32	10.07	4.20[c]	.05
Maternal flexibility	15.80	16.89	12.19	11.13	38.80[b]	.001
Concerns about maternal role	14.05	14.83	12.04	11.90	17.73[b]	.001
Encouragement of positive interaction with child	6.58	9.50	6.02	7.16	4.90[b]	.01
					6.80[d]	

[a]Means. [b]Cultural effect. [c]Culture × Age interaction. [d]Age effect.

(DeLissovoy, 1973; Field et al., 1980) of major differences between adolescent and nonadolescent mothers' maternal attitudes. This discrepancy might be due to differences in population (blacks vs. Caucasians and Puerto Ricans) or the instruments used. There was a trend for teenage mothers in Providence to differ more from their older counterparts than the was the case of the comparison groups in Puerto Rico, as expected.

In five out of the six subscales, however, significant cultural effects were found. Puerto Rican mothers reported lower maternal satisfaction, maternal moderation of the child's aggressive challenges, maternal flexibility, concerns about maternal role, and encouragement of positive interaction with the child. These cultural differences should be interpreted cautiously since the differences in SES might be permeating them. They also might point out the cross-cultural differences in maternal attitudes that might not be necessarily maladaptive, suggesting caution in the use of this instrument as a clinical tool in another culture.

The group's means on the MDECAS are shown in Table 4.

Minimal effects of maternal age also were found in the MDECAS. Adolescent mothers in both cultures reported infants smiling at a later age than did infants of nonadolescent mothers. This was the only difference observed. Again, this is in contrast to the results obtained by Field et al. (1980), which used the same instrument with a black population.

Only one cultural effect was found: Puerto Rican mothers reported later ages for when a child should begin to obey when told "No." The ages reported are almost twice the number of months derived from the reports from the mothers from Providence. This difference is consistent with findings in the literature of "infantilizing" in Puerto Rican mothers (e.g., Badillo-Ghali, 1982).

Beliefs about Teenage Childbearing

Our last comparison concerned the beliefs about teenage childbearing. Table 5 shows the frequency distribution of responses on the five questions dealing with beliefs about teenage childbearing.

As expected, Puerto Rican mothers reported more positive beliefs around teenage childbearing. They reported more often that the best age for a woman to have her child is earlier in her life, that the teenage mother naturally will become a good, responsible mother on her own, and that a child of a teenage mother will not have any problems if mother and child live with her family and/or husband. These responses might be an indication of the supportive cultural context of teenage childbearing within this population. It is interesting to note that both adolescent and older mothers share this view, even if the nonadolescent mothers are having their first child at over 20 years of age. A few of the mothers had actually told us that they were having their child at this "late" age because of previous miscarriages or for reasons of infertility, rather than by choice.

In addition, adolescent mothers in both cultures shared some aspect of their

Table 4. Maternal Developmental Expectations and Childbearing Attitudes Survey (MDECAS)

Variable	Providence		Puerto Rico		F	$p <$
	Adolescents	Nonadolescents[a]	Adolescents	Nonadolescents[a]		
Crawling	5.78	5.43	6.71	5.73	—	—
Smiling	2.08	1.87	2.0	1.67	4.09[b]	.04
Standing	9.63	7.96	9.0	8.87	—	—
Walking	11.83	10.99	11.53	10.73	—	—
Toilet training	20.70	22.37	28.60	23.60	—	—
Sitting	6.98	7.19	9.23	7.47	—	—
First words	12.42	11.49	12.79	14.8	—	—
Obey	15.40	11.29	34.71	22.00	9.63[c]	.003

[a]Means. [b]Age effect. [c]Cultural effect.

Table 5. Frequency Distribution of Responses of Beliefs about Teenage Childbearing

Variable	Responses	Providence		Puerto Rico		X^2	$p <$
		Adolescents	Nonadolescents[a]	Adolescents	Nonadolescents[a]		
Best age to have first child (in years)	13–17	2	0	3	1		
	18–22	8	2	10	9	6.97[a]	.05
	23–27	4	15	2	5	7.45[b]	.05
	28–32	0	0	0	0		
Options for pregnant adolescent	remain single	4	9	0	8		
	get married	9	5	15	7		
	adoption	0	2	0	0		
	abortion	0	1	0	0	9.23[b]	.05
Teenager's daughter's pregnancy	withdraw support	0	0	0	0		
	leave her alone	0	0	0	2		
	help her	13	17	15	13	n.s.	—
	will regret it	0	2	0	1		
Teenager having a child	manage with family help	10	15	5	7		
	become a good mom on her own	3	0	10	7	10.11[a]	.01
Child of teenager	no problems in school	2	3	1	4		
	no problems if family involved	3	7	14	10		
	always a problem	8	7	0	1	11.14[a]	.01

[a]Culture effect. [b]Age effect.

belief system: Younger ages are better for a woman to have her first child, and the best option for a pregnant adolescent is to get married. This positive attitude toward early marriage by both groups is interesting, since most adolescent mothers in Providence were single. It might be that the birth of a child out of wedlock might generate more conflict than the actual mother's age per se. This view is not shared by the nonadolescent mothers in either culture, however. Marriage might seem, for adolescents, a way of insuring support of their new role, something that only they can appreciate.

Conclusions

These findings support the notion that the cultural context of adolescent childbearing within a low-SES, urban Puerto Rican population is supportive and positive. These findings do not imply that early childbearing is the best option for these women. It is clear that early childbearing has tremendous implications for population growth and for the educational and economic attainments of women. Until cultural evolution encourages other options for women, and the economic and educational systems provide such alternatives, adolescent childbearing will constitute the norm rather than the exception.

Various implications are derived from these findings:

1. Adolescent motherhood does not necessarily have to constitute a negative life event for mother and child. A supportive environment might lessen the negative consequences for both infant and mother.
2. The high incidence of teenage pregnancy among Hispanics in the U.S. might reflect the "mixed" messages received by adolescents from their traditional Hispanic culture. Migration might exacerbate adherence to traditional values when adolescents are in contact with a more liberal society, especially regarding sex roles and women's alternative.
3. In providing services to the Hispanic female adolescent, her own personal adherence (and her family's adherence) to traditional values of woman's role and development should be an important determinant of intervention practices. Sex education, use of contraception, abortion, marriage, return to school, and the importance of an education as a priority will vary accordingly.
4. Finally, if we want to prevent teenage pregnancy, the major task is to provide adolescents with viable alternatives, ones that are congruent with the culture's expectations for adolescence and women's development. A fine balance will have to be achieved between maintaining cultural traditions and discarding some that are not necessarily adaptive and valuable any longer. Perhaps our children will grow up in a world where the cultural expectations are more

sincerely conducive to providing a variety of choices for women and men as they fulfill their developmental tasks. Time will tell.

References

Badillo-Ghali, S. (1982). Understanding Puerto Rican traditions. *Social Work, 27*,(1), 98–102.

Baldwin, W., & Cain, V. (1980). The children of teenage parents. *Family Planning Perspectives, 12*(1), 34–43.

Bogue, D. J. (Ed.). (1977). *Adolescent fertility*. Chicago: University of Chicago Press.

Brazelton, T. B. (1973). *Neonatal Behavioral Assessment Scale*. London: Spastics International Medical Publications/Heinemann Medical Books.

Briggs, R. M. (1962). Pregnancy in the young adolescent. *American Journal of Obstetrics and Gynecology, 84*, 436–441.

Card, J., & Wise, L. (1978). Teenage mothers and teenage fathers: The impact of early childbearing on the parents: Personal and professional lives. *Family Planning Perspectives, 10*(4), 199–205.

Carey, N. B., McCann-Sanford, J., & Davidson, E. C. (1983). Adolescent age and obstetric risk. In E. R. McAnarney (Ed.), *Premature adolescent pregnancy and parenthood*. New York: Grune & Stratton.

Cochrane, R., & Robertson, A. (1973). The life events inventory: A measure of the relative severity of psycho-social stressors. *Journal of Psychosomatic Research, 17*, 135–139.

Cohler, B. J., Weiss, J. L., & Grunebaum, H. U. (n.d.). *The Maternal Attitude Scale* (preliminary manual). Unpublished manuscript.

Crockenberg, S. (1981). Infant irritability, mother responsiveness, and social support influences on the security of infant-mother attachment. *Child Development, 52* 857–865.

Crockenberg, S. (1987). Support for adolescent mothers during the post-natal period: Theory and research. In Z. Boukydis (Ed.), *Research on support for parents and infants in the postnatal period*. Norwood, NJ: Ablex.

Delgado, M. (n.d.). Child care staff and Hispanic children: Implications for service delivery. Unpublished manuscript.

DeLissovoy, V. (1973). Child care by adolescent parents. *Children Today, 35*, 22–25.

Elster, A. B., & McAnarney, E. R. (1980). Medical and psychosocial risks of pregnancy and childbearing during adolescence. In E. R. McAnarney (Ed.), The pregnant adolescent. *Pediatric Annals, 9*(3), 11–20.

Field, T. M. (1979). Interactions of preterm and term infants born to lower and middle class teenage and adult mothers. In T. M. Field et al. (Eds.), *High-risk infants and children: Adult and peer interactions*. New York: Academic Press.

Field, T. M. (n.d.). *The Maternal Developmental Expectations and Childrearing Attitudes Survey* [MDECAS]. Unpublished manuscript.

Field, T. M., Widmayer, S., Greenberg, R., & Stoller, S.: (1982). Effects of parent training on teenage mothers and their infants. *Pediatrics, 69*(2), 703.

Field, T. M., Widmayer, S. M., Stringer, S., & Ignatoff, E. (1980). Preterm infants: An intervention and developmental follow-up. *Child Development, 51,* 426–436.

Furstenberg, F. (1976). The social consequences of teenage parenthood. *Family Planning Perspectives, 8*(4), 148–164.

Garcia Coll, C., Hoffman, J., & Oh, W. (1987). The social ecology and early parenting of Caucasian adolescent mothers. *Child Development, 58,* 955–963.

Garcia Coll, C., Sepkoski, C., & Lester, B. M.: (1982). Effects of teenage childbearing on neonatal and infant behavior in Puerto Rico. *Infant Behavior and Development, 5,* 227–236.

Hardy, J. B., & Mellits, E. D. (1977). Relationships of low birth weight to maternal characteristics of age, parity, education, and body size. In D. M. Reed & F. H. Stanley (Eds.), *The epidemiology of prematurity.* Baltimore: Urban & Schwarzenberg.

Harris, J. W. (1922). Pregnancy and labor in the young primipara. *Bulletin of John Hopkins Hospital, 33,* 12–16.

Heald, F. P. & Jacobson, M. S. (1980). Nutrition. In E. R. McAnarney (Ed.), The pregnant adolescent. *Pediatric Annals, 9*(3), 21–30.

Hoffman, H. J., Lundin, F. E., Bakketeig, L. S., & Harley, E. E. (1977). Classification of births by weight and gestational age for future studies of prematurity. In D. M. Reed & F. H. Stanley (Eds.), *The epidemiology of prematurity.* Baltimore: Urban & Schwarzenberg.

Lawrence, R. A., & Merritt, T. A. (1983). Infants of adolescent mothers: Perinatal, neonatal, and infancy outcome. In E. R. McAnarney (Ed.), *Premature adolescent pregnancy and parenthood.* New York: Grune & Stratton.

Leavitt, R. R. (1974). *The Puerto Ricans: Culture change and language deviance.* Tucson, AZ: Viking Fund Publications in Anthropology.

Lester, B. M., Garcia Coll, C. T., & Sepkoski, C. (1982). Teenage pregnancy and neonatal behavior: Effects in Puerto Rico and Florida. *Journal of Youth and Adolescence, 11,* 385–402.

Lester, B. M., Garcia Coll, C. T., & Sepkoski, C. (1983). A cross-cultural study of teenage pregnancy and neonatal behavior. In T. M. Field & A. Sostek (Eds.), *Infants born at risk: Physiological, perceptual, and cognitive processes.* New York: Grune & Stratton.

Levine, L., Garcia Coll, C., & Oh, W. (1985). Determinants of mother-infant interaction in adolescent mothers. *Pediatrics. 75,* 1, 23.

Lincoln, R. (1979). Is pregnancy good for teenagers? Testimony before the Select Committee on Population, 95th Congress, 318.

Lowe, C.. U. (1977). Health implications of adolescent pregnancy. In D. J. Bogue (Ed.), *Adolescent fertility.* Chicago: University of Chicago Press.

Lowe, C. J. (1979). Fertility and contraception in America. Adolescent and pre-adolescent pregnancy hearings before the Select Committee on Population, 95th Congress, Second Session, 570.

Martinez, A. L. (1981). The impact of adolescent pregnancy on Hispanic adolescents and their families. In T. Ooms (Ed.), *Teenage pregnancy in a family context.* Philadelphia: Temple University Press.

McAnarney, E. R., Lawrence, R. A., & Aten, J. J. (1979). Premature parenthood: A preliminary report of adolescent mother-infant interaction. *Pediatric Research, 13,* 328.

McLaughlin, F. J., Sandler, H. M., Herrod, K., Vietze, P. M., & O'Connor, S. (1979). Social-psychological characteristics of adolescent mothers and behavioral characteristics of their firstborn infants. *Journal of Population, 2*(1), 69–73.

Mednick, B. R. (1979, January–July). Consequences of family structure and maternal state for child and mother's development (Progress report to National Institute for Child Health Development [NICHD]).

Merritt, T. A., Lawrence, R. A., & Naege, R. L. (1980). The infants of adolescent mothers. *Pediatric Annals, 9,* 32–52.

Montagau, A. (1981). The adolescent's unreadiness for pregnancy and motherhood. *Pediatric Annals, 10,* 507–511.

Moore, K., & Waite, L. (1977). Early childbearing and educational attainment. *Family Planning Perspectives, 9,* 220–225.

Ortiz, C. B. (1973). *Esperanza: An ethnographic study of a peasant community in Puerto Rico.* Tuscon: University of Arizona Press.

Osofsky, H. (1970). Nutritional status of low-income pregnant teenagers. *Journal of Reproductive Medicine, 5,* 18–24.

Osofsky, H. J., & Osofsky, J. D. (1971). Adolescents as mothers: Results of a program for low-income pregnant teenagers with some emphasis upon infant development. In S. Chess & A. Thomas (Eds.), *Annual progress in child psychiatry and child development.* New York: Brunner/Mazel.

Ravenholt, R. T. (1977). Demographic implications of adolescent pregnancy. In D. J. Bogue (Ed.), *Adolescent fertility.* Chicago: University of Chicago Press.

Ravenholt, R. T., & Lyons, T. C. (1979). Demography and population control. In *McGraw-Hill yearbook of science.* New York: McGraw-Hill.

Rolfe, D., & Roosa, M. (1979). Court-ordered evaluation of young teenage applicants for marriage licenses: Follow-up of a pilot study. *Council. Courts Rev., 17*(2), 25–29.

Roosa, M. W., Fitzgerald, H. E., & Carlson, N. A. (1982, May). A comparison of teenage and older mothers: A systems analysis. *Journal of Marriage and the Family,* 367–377.

Ruarca-Marino, R. (1977). Psychological issues of adolescent pregnancy: The Latin American reality. In D. J. Bogue (Ed.), *Adolescent fertility.* Chicago: University of Chicago Press.

Sahler, O. J. Z. (1983). Adolescent mothers: How nurturant is their parenting? In E. R. McAnarney (Ed.), *Premature adolescent pregnancy and parenthood.* New York: Grune & Stratton.

Sarrel, P., & Klerman, C. (1969). The young unwed mother. *American Journal of Obstetrics and Gynecology, 105,* 575–578.

Stycos, J. M. (1955). *Family and fertility in Puerto Rico.* New York: Columbia University Press.

Ventura, S. J., & Heuser, R. L. (1981). Births of Hispanic parentage, 1978. *Monthly Vital Statistics Report, 29*(12), 1–11.

Viel, B. (1977). View from Latin America. In D. J. Bogue (Ed.), *Adolescent Fertility.* Chicago: University of Chicago Press.

Wise, S., & Grossman, F. (1980). Adolescent mothers and their infants: Psychological factors in early attachment and interaction. *American Journal of Orthopsychiatry, 59*(3), 454–468.

Wolf, K. L. (1952). Growing up and its price in three Puerto Rican sub-cultures. *Psychiatry, 15,* 401–433.

Zanckler, J., Andelman, S., & Bauer, F. (1969). The young adolescent as an obstetric risk. *American Journal of Obstetrics and Gynecology, 103,* 305–312.

Chapter 6

Black American Infants: The Howard University Normative Study*

Pearl L. Rosser**

*Professor of Pediatrics,
Howard University College of Medicine*

Suzanne M. Randolph***

*Assistant Professor of Pediatrics,
Howard University College of Medicine*

This chapter reports, from a larger longitudinal study, newborn and 1-month data for 80 black, healthy, full-term infants. The specific aims of the study are to understand the influence of infant biomedical characteristics on neonatal behavior, to describe the behavioral repertoire of a normative sample of black neonates, and to examine the relationship between specific maternal characteris-

---

*This study was supported in part by Maternal and Child Health (Social Security Act, Title V) Grant MCJ-110461 awarded by the Division of Maternal and Child Health, Bureau of Health Care Delivery and Assistance, Health Resources and Services Administration, Public Health Service, Department of Health and Human Services, and by the Department of Pediatrics and Child Health, College of Medicine, Howard University.

The authors express thanks and appreciation to the staff (Doris Baytop and DeLois Ward) and research consultants of the Howard University Normative Study, the nursing and medical staffs of the Howard University Hospital (HUH) Newborn Nursery Service, and the HUH second-year pediatric house officers. A special thank you is offered to Mrs. Mary Lofton, Mrs. Wanda Mitchener-Colston, and Ms. Alison Baytop for secretarial support. Special gratitude is also extended to Mr. Samuel Gorden, Ms. Adah Kennon, Ms. Jennifer Jackson, Mr. Michael Currie, and the many other students who assisted in managing the data for this project. We are especially grateful to the families who allowed us to become a part of their lives.

**Current Address: 2222 Westview Dr., Silver Spring, MD.

***Currently Asst. Prof. of Family & Community Development, Univ. of Maryland, College Park, MD.

tics, infant characteristics, and environmental/cultural characteristics to later cognitive motivational behaviors. To achieve these aims the Howard University Normative Study (HUNS) is following 100 black mother-infant pairs from the infants' birth to age 3 years.

Data gathered at ages 2 days and 1 month, which describe the abilities of black newborns on the Brazelton Neonatal Assessment Scale (BNBAS; Brazelton, 1973), are the focus of the current presentation. In addition, mothers' expectations for development, their perceptions of their infants' abilities, and their confidence in their caregiving roles also are examined. The study uses an approach in which researchers, who are themselves black, consider the influences of black mothers' child-rearing practices and attitudes on their children's behavior.

HUNS was designed to be a longitudinal and descriptive study. It was not designed as a cross-cultural study nor as a black/white comparison paradigm. It is our belief that before any such studies are undertaken again, there is a need for normative data on normal black infants. Such data must be collected not only for black infants of a lower socioeconomic status (SES), but for middle-SES black infants as well. The major concern of HUNS is to fill this existing information gap by exploring questions such as whether the environment is different for black infants, not only quantitatively but also qualitatively. The choice of variables was dictated by unanswered questions in the research literature, by questions related to what is normal development in black infants, and by the need to determine those factors that seem to account for any variations from this norm.

At least five bodies of literature bear directly on HUNS. There is information concerning the Brazelton Neonatal Behavioral Assessment Scale (hereafter, BNBAS), particularly its administration, capacities, and interpretations (Als, Tronick, Lester, & Brazelton, 1979). The second body concerns the transactional model of interaction in child development (Sameroff & Chandler, 1975). In this model, both the child and the environment are seen as actively engaged with each other, changing and being changed by their interactions. The third source of literature concerns culture and infancy (Leiderman, Tulkin, & Rosenfeld, 1977; Lester & Brazelton, 1981; Myers, Rana, & Harris, 1979; Super, 1981a, 1981b; Yarrow, 1973) and the need for ethnomethodological studies (Peters, 1981).

A fourth body of literature relates to maternal expectations, child-rearing practices, and later cognitive development (Bartz & Levine, 1978; Brown et al., 1975; Carew, 1980; Clarke-Stewart, 1973; Field, Widmayer, Stringer, & Ignatoff, 1980; Geber, 1958; Golden & Birns, 1968, 1976; Kamii & Radin, 1967; Kaufman & DiCuio, 1975; Slaughter, 1983). Finally, there is literature that relates to cross-cultural comparisons in which Black infants were studied (Brazelton, Koslowski, & Tronick, 1976; Garcia Coll, Sepkoski, & Lester, 1981; Geber & Dean, 1957). These studies will be discussed as they relate to the findings of the HUNS.

Background

Despite progress in our understanding of infancy, theoretical formulations regarding the importance of early experience, and numerous facts about normative development, there have been virtually no studies of the normative behavior of black American infants. For decades the primary research focus of students of infancy was to compare the development of black infants to that of white infants (Hess & Shipman, 1965; Zegiob & Forehand, 1975) or to examine mother-infant interaction patterns, typically with black inner-city samples (Brown et al., 1975) and teenage mothers (Field et al., 1980). It is important to note that traditionally these investigations have largely been atheoretical and without consideration of the variability of black culture, socialization practices, or value systems.

The use of race-comparative paradigms, and the almost exclusive focus on low-SES-status blacks, has limited rather than expanded the knowledge base of infant behavioral development (Howard & Scott, 1981; Ogbu, 1981). Thus, data reported from many of these investigations have not yielded information appropriately generalizable to black populations with differing socioeconomic backgrounds and early experiences. Social class is a complex variable which significantly shapes the nature of early experience and thereby becomes a powerful determinant of child outcome (Sameroff & Chandler, 1975). Typically the variable of social class indexes the "at risk" status of black infants in traditional research with this population.

This investigation of black middle-class infants is the first of its kind to assess a normative "optimized" black sample defined by socioeconomic status and medical variables. It also is significant that the sample is drawn from Washington, D.C., which has one of the highest rates of newborn mortality and morbidity in the United States.

For some time now, research on black American infants, particularly during the newborn period, has been assumed to be culture-free, outside the direct influence of specific environmental and cultural shaping. Also, precocious motor development has been most often cited (Geber & Dean, 1957) as the prominent behavioral difference between black American and Euro-American samples. The present study represents an interdisciplinary focus on a greater understanding of the variability inherent in the development of black infants. The Brazelton (1973) Neonatal Behavioral Assessment Scale affords an initial look at infant performance following birth, and the cluster scoring allows an individual difference approach to assessment. A wealth of medical data on the newborn contributes to structuring the biological factors that influence behavioral development. A second set of assessments at 1 month of age allows a comparative examination of the effects of the caregiving environment on performance. All these data are considered against the background of the cultural experiences and behavior of this particular sample.

Sameroff's (1983) transactional model provides the theoretical backdrop for evaluating and describing the constitutional and environmental variables that influence each other over time. Parental conceptualization of the infant and expectations for progressive development are complex variables that importantly influence infant outcome (Sameroff, 1983). Recent studies of parenting behavior have focused on parental knowledge of child development and how attitudes and behavior relate to specific characteristics of children (Bee et al., 1982; Gottfried & Gottfried, 1983). Such studies exemplify the recognition of the child's unique contribution to the outcome of interactions with parents. Thus, an investigative interest in parenting styles and their elicitation of positive or negative responses from particular children has gained popularity. The manner in which parents think about and behave toward their infants ultimately plays a significant role in child development. When parental perceptions of the child, environmental influences, medical variables, and specific infant behavioral characteristics are examined in the context of a particular culture (i.e., Afro-American culture), prediction and understanding of the developmental outcome is enhanced.

Since the 1960s, research on the development of black children has been popular in the sociological and anthropological literature. In general, our current understanding of the dynamic processes of infancy has come from the collection and interpretation of a large body of facts about normative development and its relationship to social and biological influences (Super, 1981a). It is quite legitimate to argue that the process of scientific knowledge requires inquiry that refers to a "normative" standard. Traditional research designs, however, have consistently defined the behavior of black children in terms of white normative behavior, which perpetuates the idealization of the white norm while yielding little information about the black child's normative behavior (Hall, 1974).

Myers et al. (1979) point out that despite the rigorous statistical methodologies, white norms are representations of particular societal values and ideologies. As such they are convenient, pragmatic points of reference and are not objective, immutable facts. Myers and colleagues further argue that the pragmatic usefulness of white norms as reference points perpetuates the denial of variability in behavioral and developmental patterns among black children within the phenomenal realities of black people. It is logical to believe that better knowledge of black children ultimately will depend upon measures taken from black populations.

A related methodological problem has been the consistent practice of comparing the behavior of low-income black children to that of middle-income white children (McLoyd & Randolph, 1983). Such a design confuses social class with race and perpetuates the incorrect implicit assumption that characteristic behaviors of black lower-SES are normative and representative of the behavior of all black children (Myers et al., 1979). Even today there is significant reluctance to relinquish this model. Currently, some research is guided by the idea that if one controls for social class, especially during infancy, one should not expect to find ethnic or cultural differences in the behavioral development of black and white children (Myers et al., 1979). Some information exists to the contrary, however. Bartz and Levine (1978) interviewed three cohorts of Anglo-American, black, and Chicano parents ($N = 114$) in order to investigate cultural child-rearing patterns. When social class was controlled, significant ethnic differences in child-rearing patterns could still be discerned.

Tulkin (1977) has questioned the adequacy of comparative research in which cultural factors which distinguish one group from another are not taken into account (i.e., parental understanding of child development processes, values, etc.). Also, because the race-comparative paradigm emphasizes the race of the subjects or personal characteristics associated with race, it promotes personal-blame interpretations of behavior, rather than thoughtful treatments of the roles of situational and systematic factors (Boykin, 1977; Caplan & Nelson, 1973; McLoyd & Randolph, 1983; Nobles, 1981; Oyemade & Rosser, 1980). Super (1981b) further noted that a major problem with a great majority of cross-cultural comparative research of newborns has been inadequate control of variables known to influence newborn behavior (i.e., state, physical and social setting, characteristics of examiners, examiner interpretations, maternal feeding methods, gestational age, poverty, complications of pregnancy, and delivery factors). Despite various inadequacies in methodological procedures, however, in most such studies reasonable evidence exists to point to differing patterns of behavior within the first days of life in various subgroups of infants (Super, 1981a). At present, the major difficulty lies in the interpretation of differences in patterns of behavior and the theoretical conclusions and behavioral models drawn from these differences. This problem would be alleviated if there were greater interest in descriptive studies from which hypotheses could be formulated to provide a rich data base for understanding the development of children from different cultures.

Methods

Sample

The sample for the current report consisted of 80 black, healthy, full-term infants recruited from the Newborn Nursery Service at Howard University Hospital (HUH). Prospective mother-infant pairs were identified through hospital records using the criteria described later. If eligible, mothers were approached on the second day after delivery by one of the project staff who provided a brief introduction to the overall study. If mothers agreed to participate, formal written consent was obtained and mother-infant pairs were assigned an identifying study number. Of the infants born at HUH, approximately 10% met the eligibility criteria. Of the mothers thus eligible, about half agreed to participate in the study.

Of the 80 infants who were enrolled in the study, 18 were lost at 1 month. These included 10 whose mothers' home addresses had changed and who could not be contacted by telephone or mail; 6 mothers who were avoiding contact by not returning messages or responding to requests for appointments; and 2 mothers who asked to be withdrawn from the study for personal reasons.

Table 1 shows descriptive statistics for selected sample characteristics. The 80 black neonates (41 females, 39 males) were between 41 and 74 hr old when first observed ($M = 53.85$; $SD = 9.62$). All infants were born at Howard University Hospital in Washington, D.C. Infants were from low to lower-middle ($n = 49$) and middle ($n = 31$) SES families. Stringent criteria were used to select a normative "optimized" sample. Infants were selected to meet the following criteria: (a) full-term (38–41 weeks gestation; $M = 40.25$; $SD = 1.09$); (b) birthweight between 2,500 and 4,000 g ($M = 3,246.30$; $SD = 370.48$); (c) size appropriate for gestational age (AGA); (d) Apgar scores of 8 or above at 1 min and 9 or 10 at 5 min; (e) delivery by spontaneous vaginal delivery ($n = 62$) or by elective cesarean section ($n = 18$); (f) healthy as defined by a normal newborn physical exam; (g) single birth; (h) born to mother between the ages of 18 and 38 years ($M = 25.70$; $SD = 5.02$). The mean ponderal index was within average ranges ($M = 2.58$; $SD = 0.34$). The sample included 31 infants of primiparous (first child) mothers and 49 infants of multiparous mothers. All mothers had received prenatal care during at least the second half of their pregnancies. Most mothers (85%) had a total of not more than 4 (of 41) risk conditions on the Obstetrical Complications Scale (OCS).

Family structure included: nuclear (53%); single parent and child or children (9%); and extended (38%), including single parents living at home with parents or other relatives. Many extended families were headed by females. There were no mother-infant pairs in augmented family arrangements. Mothers were from various educational and occupational backgrounds, ranging from welfare recipient to medical professional.

The Hollingshead (1975) 4-factor index of social status was used to estimate the SES of the sample. Although this is the scale most often used in research, it has been argued that it is not satisfactory for black adults because it places greater emphasis on occupation than it does on education (Baldwin, 1973; McAdoo, 1977). Therefore, in addition to coding each family in the standard way, some reseachers have recommended another coding procedure, one that reverses the weights for education and occupation. Greater emphasis is placed on education, to take into account the inequity in job and income status. This modified procedure has only been used with the earlier version of the scale (Hollingshead, 1958), which has ratings of 1–7 for each of occupation and education. The reversed weighting could not be used with the 1975 version because of a difference in rating systems.

By standard Hollingshead estimates, 49 mothers were of low to lower-middle SES, and 31 were of middle SES. These estimates were checked against back-

Table 1. Descriptive Statistics for Selected Sample Characteristics

Characteristics N = 80	n	M	SD
1. Sex of infant			
Males	39		
Females	41		
2. Birth statistics			
Weight (g)		3,246.30	370.48
Length (cm)		50.15	2.42
Head circumference (cm)		34.23	1.23
Apgar at 1 min		8.73	0.45
Apgar at 5 min		9.03	0.16
Ponderal index		2.58	0.34
Gestational age (weeks)		40.25	1.09
3. Mother's history			
Age (years)		25.70	5.02
Delivery:			
Vaginal	62		
C-section	18		
Birth order:			
(1)	37		
(2)	21		
(3)	17		
(4)	4		
(5)	1		
Parity:			
Primiparous	31		
Multiparous	49		
SES:			
Low/Lower-middle	49		
Middle	31		
Feeding:			
Breast	30		
Bottle	50		
4. Infant's age at BNBAS			
1st test (hrs)	80	53.85	9.62
2nd test (days)	61	32.31	4.47

ground information used by the staff to estimate SES (from education, occupation, working vs. nonworking status, welfare status, family income, residency, etc.). The distributions were unchanged.

Older mothers (26 years and over) tended to be of middle SES and have fewer children, although the proportion of multiparae in both lower- and middle-SES groups was similar (65% and 61%, respectively). About 30% of the lower-SES mothers breast-fed their babies, in comparison to 48% of the middle-SES mothers (difference not statistically significant). About 43% of primiparae were breast-feeding, compared to 35% of the multiparae (difference not statistically significant). Most mothers were from Washington, D.C., proper (73%), while the remainder were from the surrounding Maryland suburbs.

The sample population was culled from Howard University Hospital (HUH), which is a 500-bed hospital located at the Howard University College of Medicine in Washington, D.C. HUH is the main clinical, training, and research center for the University's College of Medicine. Both the professional staff and the patient population are predominantly black and are from Washington, D.C., whose residential population is 85% black.

The number of births at HUH range from 1,350 to 1,500 annually, with a 13% incidence of low-birthweight infants. Approximately 40% of the deliveries at HUH are private patients, while 60% are considered "staff" deliveries. Compared to many other hospitals, the philosophical approach of the HUH obstetrical service to medication, anesthesia, and instrumentation is a conservative one, and it may account somewhat for some of the findings of this study. Very little medication is used during labor and delivery and the use of anesthesia is rare. The use of forceps at HUH is almost nonexistent (below 1.5%), and vacuum extractions are not used at all. C-sections are performed in 24% of deliveries. Natural childbirth classes at the hospital are on the rise.

Project staff. The project staff consisted of two principal investigators, a full-time research coordinator, a part-time research associate, and two full-time research assistants, all of whom were black females. This team was multidisciplinary with backgrounds covering pediatric medicine; developmental, clinical, educational, and pediatric research psychology; and maternal and child health nursing. The team was supplemented by three consultants who provided various technical assistance with the study design, instrument selection, data collection procedures, and data management and analyses. Consultants from Children's Hospital Medical Center in Boston made on-site visits for these purposes, and for the purpose of training the staff to reliability on administration and scoring of the BNBAS.

Although all six team members were trained to reliability on the BNBAS by the consultant, a core staff consisting of the research coordinator and research assistants had primary responsibility for administration and scoring of the BNBAS for study infants. This core staff was also responsible for collecting data through maternal interviews and feeding observations.

Data-collection activities were coordinated through weekly staff meetings of the research coordinator and research assistants. During these meetings, progress was monitored for sample selection and recruitment, reasons for attrition and ways to slow it were discussed, data collection procedures were reviewed, and problems were examined. Overall project activities were coordinated through monthly staff meetings of the principal investigators and the research design, recruitment process, and data collection procedures were modified as necessary.

Input from the statistical consultants was also incorporated into project design and operations. The research coordinator provided the communication link between the core staff and the principal investigators.

Measurements

Infant measurements. Infants routinely received Dubowitz assessments and a ponderal index calculation. The Dubowitz Assessment of Gestational Age (GA) is a cumulative scoring system that assesses newborn GA, with a 95% confidence limit for ± 2 weeks (Dubowitz, Dubowitz, & Goldberg, 1970). The assessment consists of 10 neurologic items based on muscle tone and neurologic maturation, and 11 external characteristics that measure the maturity of the dermatologic component of the fetus/newborn. The ponderal index is a measurement to define the end results of fetal growth and nutrition (Miller & Hassanien, 1971). It is a ratio of birthweight to body length (birthweight in grams × 100 divided by the cube of crown-to-heel length in centimeters). Malnutrition is defined as a ponderal index of 2.00 as opposed to 2.20 at 37 wk.

The BNBAS was administered at 2 days of age in the hospital nursery and again at 1 month of age in the home. The BNBAS is widely used to tap the behavioral repertoire of normal, healthy, full-term infants and consists of 27 behavioral items and 20 elicited responses (Brazelton, 1973).

Maternal measurements. An Obstetrical Complications Scale (OCS) was used for all mothers who participated in the study. Historical data were obtained from the medical record and supplemented by personal interview as needed. In an effort to maintain comparability with earlier Brazelton studies (Als et al., 1979), Littman and Parmelee's *Manual for Obstetrical Complications* (1974) was used. This was developed for assessing the occurrence of any complicating factors in the maternal medical history. A total of 41 separate items based on the Prechtl system of optimal scoring are used. Each item is scored after consulting the manual, and at the conclusion of scoring the optimal responses are totaled. Since information is not always available for each item, the number of optimal responses is divided by the number of items scored. Raw scores have been converted to a standard mean score of 100 and a standard deviation of 20. Higher scores are the more optimal scores.

The Seashore Self-Confidence Scale (Seashore, Leifer, Barnett, & Leiderman, 1973) and the Newborn Behavior Inventory (Anderson & Standley, n.d.), which measures mothers' perceptions of their infants were administered at 2 days in the hospital and at 1 month in the home. A Developmental Milestones Expectations scale developed for this study was administered at the same time.

Mother-infant dyad measurement. Mother-infant interactions were measured using a feeding observation scale developed by Gerson, Glantz, and Gaiter (1983).

Procedure

Infants were first examined with the BNBAS within day 2 or 3 of life. Males were observed before circumcision, if this procedure was to be done. The BNBAS was administered by an examiner in a dimly lit room adjacent to the newborn nursery. Examiners were black females who had been trained to reliability in administration and scoring of the exam by a member of the training team of Children's Hospital Medical Center in Boston. A second exam was also administered to 62 of the infants who were available at 1 month of age. This administration took place in the infant's home with the mother observing. An examiner administered the BNBAS while a scorer kept notes on the infant's performance and explained the behavior to the mother. Lighting and noise level conditions in the home were kept as similar to nursery conditions as possible (i.e., dimly lit and quiet). To the extent possible, infants were seen during mid-feeding for both exams.

Reliability on the BNBAS was checked periodically by having examiners score the same infant and comparing interscoring agreement within 1 point for the behavioral items and qualifiers, and as perfect for the reflexes. The two principal investigators served as judges in determining the interscorer agreement and arriving at consensus where there was more than 1 point of difference. Intercoder agreement ranged from .85 to 1.00 ($M = .91$).

The scoring system developed by Lester, Als, and Brazelton (1978) was used to combine 26 of the behavioral items into six clusters and 16 of the reflexes into a seventh cluster. The BNBAS curvilinear scale items are rescored as linear, and the mean of the rescored items is used to define the behavioral clusters. The six behavioral clusters are: Habituation, response decrement to the repeated presentation of a light, rattle, bell, and pinprick (environmental "noise"); Orientation, responses to animate and inanimate stimuli and overall alertness (availability for social interaction); Motor Performance, integrated motor acts and overall muscle tonus; Range of State, the rapidity, peak, and lability of state changes; Regulation of State, efforts to modulate or control the infant's own state (without assistance from the examiner/caregiver); Autonomic Stability, signs of physiological stress seen, such as tremors, startles, and changes in skin color (in response to maneuvers during the exam).

Higher scores indicate better performance on all behavioral clusters. The Reflexes Cluster is defined as the total number of deviant reflex scores. For this seventh cluster, higher scores indicate more deviant responses. BNBAS items were summarized into these seven clusters to facilitate comparisons with other studies in which cluster scores are reported (see Garcia Coll et al., 1981).

Mothers were interviewed when their infants were 2 days old in the hospital, and at home when the infants were 1 month old, about their perceptions of their infants' abilities, expectations for mastery of developmental milestones, their child-rearing practices and attitudes, and their self-confidence in caregiver roles.

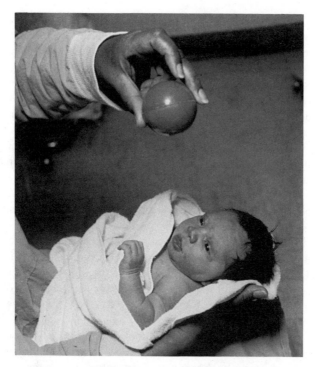

Photo 1.   Infant following vertically moving ball.

Mother-infant interaction was captured through observations of feeding situations.

The Neonatal Behavior Inventory (NBI) was used to obtain mothers' perceptions of their infants' behavior in 2 of the 27 behavioral areas measured by the BNBAS. For example, the NBI item for BNBAS item Response Decrement to Light reads: "When my baby is sleeping and a light is turned on, this disturbs his/her sleep." The responses to the NBI are: "This is (1) not at all like my baby; (2) somewhat like my baby; and (3) very much like my baby." BNBAS items were rescored as linear, using the cluster scoring criteria so that higher scores reflected better performance and could be used to interpret the direction of correlation coefficients to be calculated. The home administration of the NBI took place before the BNBAS was administered.

At the same sessions the Seashore Self-Confidence instrument and Developmental Milestones Expectations instrument were administered to the mothers by the interviewer. For each instrument only the responses in which the mother had to choose between herself and another were considered (e.g., "yourself-pediatrician," "yourself-father," etc.). On the Developmental Milestones Expectations instrument, mothers indicated the age at which an "average" infant should be expected to master various motor, cognitive, social, and self-help milestones. Responses were scored as realistic or unrealistic (earlier/later than expected) by comparing mothers' expectations with the Bayley Scales of Infant Development, the Kent Infant Development Scale, and others.

At infant ages 2 days in the hospital and 1 month (at home), mothers and infants were observed during feeding; a continuous recording procedure was used that allowed observers to record maternal and infant behaviors as simultaneous or successive within 10-second intervals throughout the feeding sessions. Observers wore earphones connected to a portable cassette tape player which beeped at 10-second intervals; at each beep, observers drew a line on the coding sheet immediately under the last behavior recorded.

Reliability on the feeding observations was established by first having core staff code behaviors while concurrently viewing segments of videotaped feeding sessions. An outside consultant, responsible for development of the code scheme, trained observers and clarified any confusions in definition of the codes. The core staff then observed mother-infant pairs who were not in the sample during feeding. Reliability was assessed by determining the agreement between observers for the number of instances recorded for each category of behavior. Reliability on these pre-study observations ranged from .82 to .94 with a mean .87. Reliability was checked periodically by having core staff code a different segment of videotape from any used in the prestudy training or previous reliability checks. Periodic reliability ranged from .88 to .95 with a mean of .91.

For the purpose of this analysis we were interested only in the proportions of behaviors recorded for each mother-infant pair. Incidences of behavior represented discrete instances of behavior recorded (e.g., 2 instances of mother giving food, 24 instances of maternal looking, 3 instances of baby looking, and so on). Proportions were calculated separately for maternal behaviors and infant behaviors by dividing the instances of behavior for a particular category by the total number of behaviors recorded for either mother or infant as appropriate (e.g. if 100 total mother behaviors were recorded, the 2 "gives food" would be .02 in proportion units, the 25 "looks at baby" would be .25, and so on). These proportions were used as the units of analysis. Means and standard deviations for proportions for each category of behavior were then calculated.

Results

The independent variables in this full-term newborn/1-month report are age of mother, parity, birthweight, medical status, gestational age, appropriateness of size for gestational age, Apgar score, and socioeconomic status. The dependent variables are Brazelton behavioral cluster scores, parental perceptions of infants, developmental expectations, mother-infant interactions and maternal self-confidence.

Table 2.   Means and Standard Deviations on Brazelton Scale Cluster Scores for HUNS Sample at 2 Days and 1 Month and Garcia Coll et al. (1981) Sample at 2 Days

Cluster	n[b]	HUNS Sample[a]				Garcia Coll et al. 2 Days (n = 24)	
		1 Month		2 Days			
		M	SD	M	SD	M	SD
Habituation	27	4.74	2.14	5.19	1.78	5.89	1.51
Orientation	62	7.76	1.43	6.93	1.69*	5.89	1.48
Motor Performance	62	6.18	0.82	5.87	0.63*	4.92	0.78
Range of State	62	3.62	0.90	3.79	0.54	3.22	0.70
Regulation of State	62	4.80	1.28	5.85	1.32**	5.34	1.36
Autonomic Stability	62	6.92	1.11	6.61	0.98	4.69	1.48
Reflexes	53	0.74	1.15	0.53	0.97	1.95	1.32

[a]Pairwise t tests were used to examine differences between 2 days and 1 month for the HUNS sample.

[b]Some ns differ, as not all infants could be tested on every item because of state behaviors (i.e., changed to an alert state or higher) or as items were not administered.

*$p \leq .01$.   **$p \leq .001$.

Infant Assessment

Although 80 infants were tested at 2 days, data at 1 month are available for only 62 infants, because of attrition. The mean age of infants at initial testing was 53.85 hr ($SD = 9.62$) and at second testing 32.31 days ($SD = 4.47$). Table 2 shows means, standard deviations, and t tests on BNBAS cluster scores for the HUNS sample at 2 days and 1 month, along with Garcia Coll et al. (1981) 2-day findings. Table 3 shows individual item scores for the 2-day BNBAS. As shown in Table 2, infants show significant recovery in Orientation ($t(62) = 3.08$, $\rho \leq .003$) and Motor Performance ($t(62) = 2.73$, $\rho \leq .008$). However, there is a decrease in the Regulation of State cluster ($t(62) = 4.55$, $\rho \leq .0001$), suggesting that something is interfering with infants' ability to control themselves at 1 month.

Inspection of individual items (Table 3 and Figure 1) indicates that at 1 month infants improved in (a) Orientation Animate Visual, Inanimate Visual, and Animate Visual and Auditory, as well as Alertness—items that partially comprise the Orientation cluster; and (b) General Tonus, Motor Maturity, Pull-to-Sit, and Activity—items which comprise the Motor Performance cluster. Also, it appears that Hand-Mouth Facility and Self-Quieting Activity show a decrease; these two items, along with Consolability and Cuddliness, comprise the Regulation of State cluster. There were no significant changes in any of the other clusters at 1 month. In these other clusters it appears that the infants in the HUH sample start out "good," and remain so, through the neonatal period.

Some group differences (SES, sex of infant, age of mother, delivery) were

Table 3. Mean Scales, Standard Deviations, and Ranges on BNBAS Items at 2 Days for HUNS Sample

Items (A–G, by Cluster)	n^a	M^b	SD	Range
A. Habituation				
1. Response decrement to light	56	7.34	1.32	4–9
2. Response decrement to rattle	49	7.53	1.47	2–9
3. Response decrement to bell	32	7.88	1.04	5–9
4. Response decrement to pinprick	35	5.83	1.29	2–8
B. Orientation				
5. Inanimate visual	75	6.97	1.76	1–9
6. Inanimate auditory	78	7.51	1.33	4–9
7. Animate visual	78	7.06	1.60	1–9
8. Animate auditory	79	7.94	1.26	3–9
9. Animate visual and auditory	78	7.23	1.43	1–9
10. Alertness	80	6.64	1.48	2–9
C. Motor Performance				
11. General tonus	80	5.85	0.60	3–6
12. Motor maturity	79	6.18	1.32	3–9
13. Pull-to-sit	80	5.74	1.57	2–9
15. Defensive movements	80	7.13	1.72	1–9
20. Activity	80	4.70	0.77	1–5
D. Range of State				
17. Peak of excitement	78	3.55	0.75	1–5
18. Rapidity of buildup	77	3.21	0.83	1–5
19. Irritability	79	5.04	1.28	1–6
24. Lability of states	80	3.54	1.01	1–5
E. Regulation of State				
14. Cuddliness	80	5.99	1.37	4–9
16. Consolability	67	6.91	1.45	2–9
25. Self-quieting activity	79	5.58	2.30	1–9
26. Hand-mouth facility	77	6.31	2.20	1–9
F. Autonomic Stability				
21. Tremulousness	80	6.44	2.27	2–9
22. Startles	79	7.27	1.27	1–8
23. Lability of skin color	80	6.38	0.92	2–7
G. Reflexes (number of deviations)				
Other				
27. Smiles	80	0.51	1.48	0–9
Age (in hours)		53.85	9.62	32–73

[a]Frequencies vary, as not all infants could be tested on every item, because of state behaviors or no response.

[b]Individual scale items were rescored as linear and then averaged (per Lester, Als, & Brazelton, 1978).

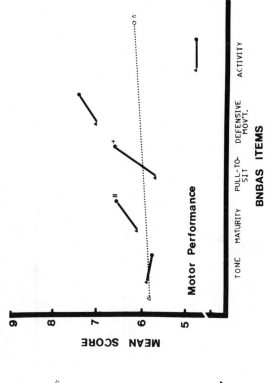

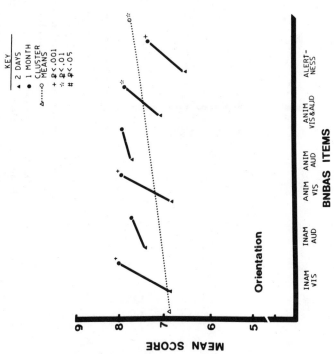

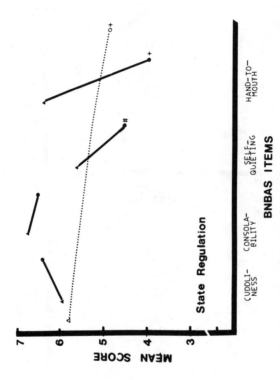

Figure 1. Mean scores on individual BNBAS items at 2 days and 1 month for the three clusters that showed significant change over time. Significant time effects for individual items are indicated. INAM VIS = Inanimate Visual; INAM AUD = Inanimate Auditory; ANIM VIS = Animate Visual; ANIM AUD = Animate Auditory; ANIM VIS & AUD = Animate Visual and Auditory.

obtained for the clusters. Autonomic Stability was better at 2 days for middle-SES infants ($\rho \leq .04$) and was better for female infants at both 2 days ($\rho \leq .01$) and 1 month ($\rho \leq .001$). Infants of younger mothers had better Range of State at 1 month ($\rho \leq .02$) and infants delivered vaginally fewer abnormal reflexes at 1 month than did infants delivered by C-sections ($\rho \leq .003$).

In general, the major descriptive and related findings of this study indicate that 2-day-old HUH infants showed good ability to shut out noises while they slept (Habituation); were controlled in their motor ability (Motor Performance); were alert and oriented toward their social environment (Orientation); and were able to keep themselves quiet and organized (Regulation of State). These infants used highly sophisticated strategies in organizing their behavior, including hand-mouth activity and locking onto visual and auditory stimuli. Their physiological systems did not seem to be particularly stressed.

These findings are different from those of other studies which indicate that black infants do not show these high levels of performance at 2 days (e.g., Garcia Coll et al., 1981). Table 2 depicts cluster means and standard deviations for the HUH sample at ages 2 days and 1 month, along with the same data for 2-day-old black infants in the Garcia Coll et al. (1981) sample (which included all lower to lower-middle SES mothers). The higher levels of performance of the HUH infants are attributed to several optimal conditions for mothers during pregnancy and delivery. Previous studies have focused on black mothers with problems or less optimal prenatal and perinatal courses.

At 1 month, HUH infants continued to show good social ($\rho \leq .003$) and motor ($\rho \leq .008$) abilities. However, something happened to their ability to keep themselves quiet and organized ($\rho \leq .001$). A possible explanation is that mothers interfered with normal hand-to-mouth behavior (confusing it with thumb-sucking), which is a key ability used by infants to control themselves. The interviews on developmental expectations support this explanation, in that 25% of the mothers reported that children should be discouraged from birth from sucking their fingers, and more than 50% said they should be discouraged before 6 months. In addition to helping infants regulate their state, hand-to-mouth behavior is also viewed as a precursor to eye-hand coordination and an indicator of neuromotor integration (Parker & Brazelton, 1981). Interference with this inborn ability at very early ages (from birth) may also affect other developmental outcomes, although this has not been systematically investigated.

Mother's perceptions, expectations, and child-rearing practices. Pearson product moment correlations were calculated for the 24 NBI items and their corresponding BNBAS items at infants ages 2 days and 1 month. In general, there were few significant correlations at 2 days and only one at 1 month, suggesting that there is very little relationship between mothers' reports of what they perceive their infants to be capable of, and standardized assessments of infants' capabilities. However, chi-square analyses of frequency data reveal that significant shifts in perception do occur over time, with most mothers changing

Table 4.   Newborn Behavior Inventory: Percentages and Significant Chi-Squares for Mothers' Responses to Items of 2 Days and 1 Month

| NBI Item | Time | Percentage of mothers responding | | | $X^2(4)$ | p |
		Not at all	Somewhat	Very much		
1. In dressing, muscles	2 days	54.8	19.4	25.8	13.8	.008
became stiff and limbs	1 month	17.7	24.2	58.1		
hard to flex						
2. Is likely to cry when	2 days	29.0	43.5	27.4	13.5	.009
uncovered, undressed,	1 month	14.5	35.5	50.0		
or diapered						
3. Have noticed limbs	2 days	43.5	32.3	24.2	12.51	.014
trembling or chin	1 month	22.6	40.3	37.1		
quivering						
4. Shows a startle reflex	2 days	27.4	16.1	56.5	11.10	.03
when moved suddenly	1 month	9.7	19.4	71.0		
5. Shows abrupt shifts or	2 days	56.5	27.4	16.1	10.23	.04
changes in mood	1 month	45.2	32.3	22.6		
6. When fussing comforts	2 days	11.5	32.8	55.7	10.87	.03
self by sucking on	1 month	4.90	34.4	60.7		
tongue or hand						
7. Often brings hand to	2 days	6.5	19.4	74.2	17.33	.002
face and puts fingers in	1 month	6.5	29.0	64.5		
mouth						

Note. N = 62.

their two-day responses from "not at all like my baby" to "somewhat" or "very much like my baby" at 1 month (see Table 4).

From these data it appears that mothers gain a greater awareness of their infants' behaviors and capabilities. However, correlational analyses may not reveal these changes. Although some methodological problems limit the usefulness of this approach, it proves to be a valuable line of inquiry, if for no other reason than to provide insight into the degree to which mothers perceive (or misperceive) their infants' capabilities. Information gained in this way can be used to help identify mothers with serious misperceptions, and then to help them understand better their baby's individual style and behavioral repertoire. Information of this sort can also provide hints about the adequacy of the mother-child interaction.

Self-confidence. For each of the four instruments five "yourself" responses (self-choices) were possible, and for all instruments a total of 20 "yourself" responses was possible. Mothers were asked at infant ages 2 days and 1 month about whether they felt confident (as compared to others) in two social and two instrumental caregiving roles. In addition, two other scores were generated. The

Table 5.   Seashore Self-Confidence: Means, Standard Deviations, and t Tests on Self-Choice Scores for Time of Administration, SES, and Mother's Age

Item[a]	n	2 days M	2 days SD	1 month M	1 month SD	t	p
		A. Time of administration					
1. Understand/Respond	57	4.39	1.03	4.72	0.56	2.88	.006
2. Bathe	62	4.08	1.41	4.53	0.86	2.66	.01
3. Calm	61	4.57	0.90	4.69	0.70	0.93	n.s.
4. Feed	61	4.64	0.91	4.78	0.59	1.43	n.s.
5. Overall	55	17.62	3.48	18.67	2.34	2.79	.007
6. Total social	57	8.42	2.13	9.21	1.31	3.24	.002
7. Total instrument	60	9.22	1.59	9.48	1.20	1.46	n.s.

	n	Lower		n	Middle			
			B. Socioeconomic status (SES)					
1. Understand/Respond (2 days)	44	4.30	1.17	28	4.75	0.52	2.25	0.28
2. Calm (2 days)	45	4.49	0.99	29	4.86	0.44	2.21	.031
3. Overall	44	17.43	3.75	27	19.00	1.71	2.40	.091
4. Total social	44	8.32	2.37	28	9.21	1.20	2.12	.038

	n	≥ 26 years		n	≤ 25 years			
			C. Age of mother					
1. Total social (2 days)	38	9.15	1.48	32	8.13	1.20	2.07	.044

[a]Total possible score equals 5 for understand, bathe, calm, and feed; 20 for overall; and 10 for total social and total instrumental. Total social combines bathe and feed.

"understand/respond" and "calm" items were combined to get a score for social items, and the "feed" and "bathe" items comprised an instrumental score. Table 5 shows the mean number of self-choices given for each instrument across the entire sample at 2 days and 1 month. At 2 days, lower-SES mothers expressed less confidence in themselves than did middle-SES mothers for the two social functions, understanding and responding to what their babies want ($t(70) = 2.21$, $p < .031$).

The "yourself" responses were further analyzed to see if mothers' confidence differed by parity, sex of infant, socioeconomic status, and mother's age. There were no significant differences found for parity or sex of infant. However, SES and mother's age revealed a few differences in the mothers' degree of confidence (see Table 5). Lower-SES and younger mothers were more likely (than middle-SES and older mothers, respectively) to report others (e.g., pediatrician, nurse, baby's grandmother) as better able to perform these social functions. No differences were found in the way groups viewed themselves as handling instrumental functions (i.e., bathing and feeding their babies). These findings may be some-what confounded in that lower-SES mothers tended to be of younger ages. In effect, it is as yet undetermined whether SES or age of mother is the more influential factor affecting mothers' confidence in themselves as caregivers (al-though these low-SES young mothers also tended to be multiparous).

Mothers were more confident with social tasks at infant age 1 month than at 2 days ($t(56)$ = 3.24, $\rho \leq$ .002). Mothers felt very confident with instrumental tasks at both 2 days and 1 month. However, when compared to social functions, the difference was significantly higher for instrumental tasks only at 2 days ($t(70)$ = 3.47, $\rho \leq$ .001). By 1 month, mothers were feeling just as confident with both social and instrumental tasks. It seems that for the instrumental score, mothers' confidence with the feeding tasks (more than with the bathing tasks) accounts for the high level of "yourself" responses at 2 days (because mothers felt more able to calm ($\rho \leq$ .05) and to understand ($\rho \leq$ .05) than to bathe at 2 days). At 1 month, there were no differences by SES or age on either the social or the instrumental tasks. All mothers reported high levels of self-confidence. The lack of differences at 1 month for age and SES emphasizes the adaptability of these black mothers and suggests that the pervasive interventions introduced from birth suggested by some other researchers (e.g., Field, 1981) may not be needed to realize improvements in maternal caregiving competency.

Expectations. Table 6 reports the mean age at which mothers reported they expected infants to master various motor, cognitive, social, and self-help ac-tivities, for each of which is also included percentage of mothers who were realistic in their reports. Most mothers were realistic about ages at which they expected their child to smile (94%), learn numbers (75.6%), sit up alone (75.3%), and at which to send their child to nursery or preschool (72.7%). Few mothers were realistic about ages they expected babbling (7%), finger sucking (12.7%), imitating acts (20%), and weaning from the breast or bottle (23.7%) to stop. Mothers were more realistic about the ages they expected motor items—crawling, sitting up alone, taking steps alone—than they were about ages for cognitive milestones—babbling, speaking two-word sentences, learning ABCs and colors ($t(df)$ = 4.64 (78), $\rho \leq$ .0001).

Lower-SES mothers weaned earlier than expected (χ^2 (2) = 5.85, $\rho \leq$ .05). Sex-of-infant differences appeared in mothers of males who expected holding-a-spoon-to-feed to happen later (61%), while mothers of girls were largely realis-tic (52%), or expected this to happen early (30%) (χ^2 (2) = 6.06, $\rho \leq$ .05). These findings suggest that mothers may expect the emergence of self-help skills to develop earlier among girls than boys.

Mother-Infant Interaction

The feeding situation was used to observe mother-child interaction (Gerson et al., 1983). Instances of maternal behaviors (e.g., looking, talking, social hand-

Table 6.   Developmental Milestones Survey: Mean Age Expected and Percentage of Mothers Having Realistic Expectations

Milestone: At what age would you expect child to	Age expected (in months)		Percentage of mothers having realistic responses
	M	SD	
1. Smile	.42	1.15	97.4
2. Be discouraged from finger sucking	13.21	17.10	12.7
3. Be weaned	8.00	8.83	23.7
Motor			
4. Crawl	6.47	6.42	61.0
5. Sit up alone	6.51	1.99	75.3
6. Pull up using furniture	8.13	1.73	57.1
7. Step alone	10.28	1.82	43.4
8. Hold own bottle	5.49	2.60	51.1
9. Pull a toy behind	12.13	5.64	57.8
10. Hold a spoon to feed	18.64	10.10	40.0
11. Stack two blocks	13.71	6.87	35.6
12. Roll from stomach to back	3.77	6.26	38.6
13. Switch objects from hand to hand	8.60	4.22	46.7
Cognitive			
14. Speak two-word sentences	13.09	4.53	31.2
15. Try to learn ABCs	18.00	9.34	39.0
16. Try to learn numbers	20.62	10.07	75.6
17. Babble	5.26	2.92	7.0
18. Imitate acts seen	18.33	12.52	20.0
19. Look for a toy dropped out of sight	12.36	9.31	28.9
20. Go to nursery or preschool	34.00	12.40	72.7
21. Try to learn color names	22.93	10.75	53.3
22. Point to common names	15.76	6.26	62.2
23. Point to parts of face named	20.44	8.59	53.3

ling, playing) and infant behaviors (e.g., looking, vocalizing, holding on) were coded. Table 7 shows the means and standard deviations for proportions of mothers' and infants' behaviors at infant age 2 days and 1 month. With the exception of giving and taking or stopping food, behaviors for mothers at 2 days were limited to looking (24%) and vocalizing (35%), and for infants to looking (14%) and holding on (16%). At 1 month, mothers continued to vocalize (29%) and look (26%), and infants continued to look (24%) and hold on (19%). However, t tests indicated that mothers vocalized less ($p \leq .04$) and played more ($p \leq .0004$), while infants showed more looking ($p \leq .006$) and more vocalizing ($p \leq .003$).

There were no differences by parity. Age of mother, SES, and type-of-feeding showed related differences. Breast-feeding mothers played with their infants more at 2 days and 1 month than did bottle-feeders ($t(35) = 2.83$), $p \leq$ .01, and $t(50) = 2.43$, $p \leq .02$, respectively). Also, breast-feeders showed more social behaviors (rocking, rubbing) at 1 month than did bottle-feeders ($t(34) = 2.07$, $p \leq .05$). Cross-tabulations of the data indicated that breast-feeders comprised 43% of the primiparae and 35% of the multiparae; 30% of the lower SES and 48% of the middle SES; 44% of the younger age group (25 years or less) and 31% of the older age group. There were no statistical differences for any of these distributions. The only sex-of-infant difference that obtained was for crying: boys cried less than girls at 1 month ($p \leq .01$).

With respect to SES, several interesting findings were obtained: at 2 days, mothers vocalized less in the lower-SES group ($p \leq .04$); at 2 days infants of lower-SES mothers cried less ($p \leq .003$) and held on to parts of their mothers' bodies less ($p \leq .04$); and at 1 month, lower-SES mothers used less social behaviors (rubbing, patting, rocking) ($p \leq .02$). It may be that lower-SES mothers view the feeding situation as mainly an instrumental one and do not use the opportunity for social interaction (or at least to a lesser extent than middle-SES mothers do), or that since babies of middle-SES mothers cried more, they may have elicited more social responses. Correlations between feeding behaviors and BNBAS scores on individual items and the cluster scores revealed only that at 2 days infants' looking is related to the Orientation cluster score ($r(68) = .20$,

Table 7.   Feeding Behaviors: Mean Proportions and Standard Deviations for Mothers and Infants at 2 Days and 1 Month

		2 Days		1 Month		
Behavior	*n*	*M*	*SD*	*M*	*SD*	$t(60)$[a]
Maternal						
1. Gives food	61	.13	.07	.13	.07	.08
2. Stops food	61	.11	.07	.11	.07	.23
3. Burps baby	61	.07	.05	.08	.04	.67
4. Social (pat, rock)	61	.05	.05	.06	.07	.79
5. Looks at baby	61	.24	.15	.26	.16	1.10
6. Vocalizes to baby	61	.35	.18	.29	.18	2.14*
7. Kisses baby	61	.02	.04	.02	.05	.18
8. Plays with baby	61	.03	.05	.05	.06	3.01*
Infant						
1. Cries	61	.02	.05	.02	.06	.47
2. Holds on	61	.16	.14	.19	.14	1.11
3. Vocalizes	61	.00	.00	.03	.07	3.13**
4. Looks	61	.14	.18	.24	.19	2.84**
5. Burps	61	.17	.13	.15	.09	.73
6. Stops food	61	.04	.08	.03	.07	.62
7. Takes food	61	.47	.22	.33	.17	4.35***

[a]Two-tailed tests of significance.
*p $\leq$ .05.   **p $\leq$ .01.   ***p $\leq$ .001.

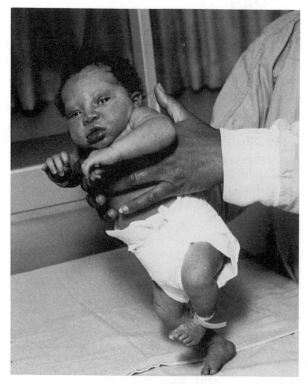

Photo 2.   Infant responding to Elicited Response 6, Walking.

$p \leq .05$), but at 1 month the Orientation cluster score is related to mothers' looking ($r(59) = .24. p \leq .034$). These relationships did not vary as a function of SES.

Discussion

This study expands previous research on black infants in several ways. First, infants and mothers were selected according to a set of stringent criteria to ensure a normative and more representative sample than previously used in studies of black infants. Second, additional data were gathered from mothers about their perceptions of their infants, their expectations for normal development, and their confidence in caregiving roles. These additional data were used in examining the results of behavioral assessments of the infants on two occasions to determine ways in which maternal child-rearing practices significantly influence patterns of development. Third, this composite of infant assessments and maternal perceptions was supplemented by observations of mother-child interactions in an effort to understand not only the ways the caregiving environment shapes infant behavior, but also the ways in which the infant may be a dynamic interacter with the environment—a person who influences, and is in turn influenced by, the caregiving environment.

It is significant that the Howard University Normative Study was conducted in Washington, D.C., a city with one of the highest infant mortality rates in the United States. In 1982, the infant mortality rate in the District of Columbia was 23.1 per 1,000 live births, or over twice the national average (11.2 per 1,000 live births). This figure represents a reduction from the 1980 rate of 24.6 per 1,000 (Morse, 1981). Most of these deaths were neonatal deaths, occurring within the first 28 days of life. Although the latter commonly reflect biologic conditions (Kessner et al., 1973) and problems associated with perinatal events, the influence of socioeconomic, socioenvironmental, and sociocultural factors cannot be overlooked.

Despite the high infant mortality rate, it was not impossible or difficult to collect at one site a sample that met the stringent criteria for normal newborns for this study. However, regardless of socioeconomic status, the approaches to parenting and child-rearing in black families have grown out of the exigencies of the unique economic, cultural, and racial circumstances in which they have lived. In order for studies to capture this sociocultural milieu and to attempt to understand the Afro-American family system, such factors as the influence of kin, the flexibility of family roles, and the flexibility and elasticity of family boundaries must at least be explored. In this study, looking at culture became a way of broadening the perspective on underlying processes of development and provided a matrix for understanding the adaptive capabilities and strategies of infants. The results of the current study are discussed in this section by relating findings to previously reported research on black infants (American and African) and comparing these data to that collected on nonblack groups.

Previous Research on Black Infants

The problems with previous research on black infants have been detailed earlier. The present study represents an attempt to fill the void in information that exists for black infants by using an approach in which: (a) a sample of black infants was studied which was normative and more representative than samples used in previous research; (b) a large percentage of middle-SES mothers was also included; (c) the cultural integrity of Afro-American family dynamics was considered in the design; and (d) the design was longitudinal and descriptive, in contrast to previous research which took only one sample of behavior or compared black infants to white or other nonblack infants.

Some of the findings of this study fit well with previous research on black infants, both American and African. Other findings suggest what is possible if normative and optimized samples of black infants are selected for study. The neonatal precocity of black infants has often been described in terms of motor maturity and responsiveness (Geber & Dean, 1957; Lester & Brazelton, 1981; Super, 1981a). Brazelton and his colleagues (Brazelton et al., 1976; Garcia Coll et al., 1981; Lester & Brazelton, 1981) have demonstrated repeatedly that black infants show superior motor performance over infants from other cultural groups. This higher performance of the black infants has been attributed by these authors to improvement in the infants' physical conditions (rehydration and nutrition) and mothers' expectations for early motor and interactive development. In addition, in a study of Kenyan infants, Brazelton and his colleague go so far as to state that African babies' motor precocity was facilitated by cultural child-rearing practices that were built on the infant's responsiveness to being handled in the neonatal period (Lester & Brazelton, 1981).

This motor precocity of black infants, which is well documented in previous research through the first year of life (Scott, Ferguson, Jenkins, & Cutter, 1955), was also evident in our study. HUH infants showed good pull-to-sit, had good tone, demonstrated few jerky movements, and were observed to swipe toward midline during defensive movements. Consistent with Lester and Brazelton's (1981) observation that child-rearing practices may facilitate early motor development, the maternal interview data in this study revealed that mothers hold realistic expectations for their infants' motor development and even expect mastery for some items much earlier than do published norms. To this extent, it seems that mothers might promote or encourage developmental advance earlier in some areas than others. Also, the motor excitement of black infants should greatly influence such maternal behavior.

Earlier comparative studies of black infants with nonblack groups showed that African infants did not show higher levels of motor performance until day 5 or 10 (Lester & Brazelton, 1981). It should be noted that in these earlier studies Black infants were at risk medically, as indicated by maternal obstetrical factors, and their patterns of recovery may have reflected intrauterine stress. In the present sample and an earlier study by Garcia Coll et al. (1981), black infants were selected to meet optimal criteria for the normal *healthy* newborn, and high levels of motor maturity were observed from as early as 2 days after birth.

Although the Garcia Coll et al. (1981) sample did not show higher levels of performance on any other clusters, the HUNS sample showed high levels of performance on Orientation, Autonomic Stability, and Reflexes. One difference in sample selection may account for this. In the Garcia Coll et al. sample, all mothers had received analgesia and pudendal block and/or infiltration or local anesthesia for episiotomy. In the HUNS sample, 41% of the mothers received no medication during labor and delivery. The effect of medication on infant behavior in general and on BNBAS performance in particular has been reported in previous research (Bakeman & Brown, 1977; Bowes, Brackbill, Conway, & Steinschneider, 1970; Horowitz et al., 1977; Lester, Als, & Brazelton, 1982;

Stechler, 1964). Some authors have reported noticeable effects at 1 month (Bowes et al., 1970; Horowitz et al., Gallas, 1973). Consistent with the findings of the Garcia Coll et al. study (1981), however, none of the correlations combining biomedical variables into a multiple regression on cluster scores reached statistical significance.

One major overall finding of the HUNS runs counter to previously established notions about black infants and their relationships with their mothers. This major finding concerns the few differences in socioeconomic status found for infant behaviors, maternal expectations and perceptions, and mother-infant interactive measures. Previous research had suggested that infants of low-income mothers would respond less optimally on the BNBAS than infants of middle-income mothers (Brazelton et al., 1976); that low-income mothers would be considerably less interactive than middle-income mothers during feeding (Lewis & Wilson, 1972); and that low-income mothers would hold less realistic expectations for development (Frank & Barrett, 1981) and more inaccurate perceptions of their infants (Field, 1981) than would middle-income mothers.

We found only that infants of middle-SES mothers scored better than infants of lower-SES mothers on the Autonomic Stability Cluster. As noted earlier, the lack of other cluster differences are attributed to the optimal conditions of the sample. These findings also suggest that research that observes behavior of low-socioeconomic status black samples with high obstetrical risk, as compared to middle-socioeconomic-status white samples with low obstetrical risk, confounds notions of environmental effects. For example, prenatal conditions such as fetal malnutrition may already have influenced infant outcome before extrauterine environmental or cultural influences can take effect. Yet some researchers using the comparative approach have accounted for behavioral differences in terms of genotypic and inherent traits that typify infant behavior, and thus conclude that differences are racial rather than cultural or environmental.

In the present study, when race and obstetrical risk factors were controlled, similar patterns of development and behavior were noted for infants in both the lower and middle socioeconomic groups. Also, the inclusion of biomedical and other independent variables in this study allowed us to look at variations (individual differences) in behavior even within the same cultural group. Moreover, maternal interview data allowed us to attribute specific neonatal behavior to environmental influences and cultural expectations rather than to genotypic influences. Unlike comparative research approaches, the value in this approach lies in the fact that typical infant behavior can be described within a particular cultural context, while individual differences in behavior can also be observed within that same cultural group. From this vantage point, we can move forward in comparing other infants from this same cultural group against these baseline data, and examining their environments for clues about how the infant is shaping or being shaped by it.

This study revealed that although lower-SES and younger mothers were less confident in caregiving roles (social tasks) at infant age 2 days, by 1 month they report the same high levels of confidence as middle-SES and older mothers. It may be that since, although they are younger, lower-SES mothers were likely to have other children, they have some experience with what to expect during the first month of life and therefore expect caregiving during this very early period to be somewhat challenging. Middle-SES mothers, who tended to be primiparous and older, may have been overly confident at 2 days in stating their caregiving abilities. As there was no real way to check perceived competence (self-confidence) against actual competence, the meaning of this finding remains unclear.

The findings for maternal-infant interactive behaviors were also not consistent with previous research. Although some socioeconomic-status differences did obtain, these were limited to lower-SES mothers showing fewer vocalizations at 2 days and less social handling at 1 month than middle-SES mothers, and to infants of lower-SES mothers crying less and holding on to mothers' bodies less than infants of middle-SES mothers at 2 days. Mothers did not show more vocal or tactile responsiveness to male infants than to female infants, even among lower-SES mothers, as has been indicated in previous research (Bakeman & Brown, 1977; Brown et al., 1975). Also, correlations between mother-infant interactive behaviors and BNBAS cluster scores did not vary as a function of socioeconomic status or sex of infant. Moreover, the lack of socioeconomic-status differences and age differences throughout the study suggests that the previous interventions recommended for use with low-income mothers from as soon as just after delivery may not be totally warranted.

Previous Research on Nonblack Infants

To understand the meaning of these findings in the general context of infant development, Sameroff's transactional model of development is considered in this discussion. Some data from the present study lend support to the notion of the infant as a dynamic interacter—a person who influences and is also influenced by the caregiving environment. In particular, it was found that at 2 days infants' looking during the feeding session is related to the Orientation cluster, but at 1 month infant Orientation behavior is related to mothers' looking. Could it be that socially interested and alert infants at 2 days are shaping their mother's behavior by eliciting reciprocal responses? If so, are these responses used by the infants to fuel themselves, and to participate actively in the social interaction? Mothers indicated on the Neonatal Behavior Inventory (maternal perception of infant) that at both 2 days and 1 month items corresponding to BNBAS Orientation Animate and Inanimate items very much describe their infants. In addition, examiner scoring of the BNBAS Qualifiers, an additional summary scale, indicated that at 2 days HUNS infants were generally robust, showed good qualities of alertness, and were socially attractive without much examiner facilitation during the exam. Examiners had to use few facilitating strategies, yet performance on the Orientation cluster was quite high. As would be expected, correlational data indicated that infants who were not as alert or who were not observed looking as much during the feeding session showed poorer performance on the Orientation cluster.

Additional support for the transactional notion of development is found in the data for Motor Performance and mother's expectations for motor development. As suggested by Lester and Brazelton (1981), the motor excitement of infants may elicit intense social handling from their caregivers which in turn promotes accelerated developmental advance in motoric skills. Mothers' early expectations for mastery of motoric milestones (as found in the HUNS) could be influenced by their experience with infants and cultural expectations for this observed motor excitement. In these ways, infants are both influencing and being influenced by the caregiving environment.

Summary and Conclusions

Data are reported from behavioral assessments of 80 black infants at two times— 2 days and 1 month of age. This study attempts to describe how patterns of performance over time may provide insight into the interaction between behavioral organization of the infant and the mother's cultural practices and expectations. It is presumed that newborns are biologically predisposed to certain behaviors, but over time infants will make adaptations as part of a cultural matrix that modifies expressed behavior (Garcia Coll et al., 1981). This includes adaptive responses to the environment as well as to the caregiver. In this study, the cultural matrix included mothers' perceptions of infants, expectations for development, self-confidence, feeding practices, child-rearing practices and attitudes, family structure, SES, age, and parity.

The results of this study show that under optimal conditions, 2-day-old black infants perform well on standard behavioral assessment scales. This finding is different from those of previous studies of black infants which show that, except for motor ability, high levels of performance do not obtain until later (e.g., at 10 days). The optimal prenatal and perinatal conditions for mothers were cited as possible explanations for this higher level of performance in the HUH sample. Previous studies tended to use low-income samples with varying degrees of prenatal care, medication at time of delivery, and less than optimal biomedical conditions.

The results of this study suggest that the BNBAS is an appropriate assessment tool for use with black infants in that it is first used at a time when cultural bias has not had a chance to influence performance, that it is sensitive to changes in behavior over time, and that it may give some clues as to environmental influences that impinge on behavior. It has shown, for example, that while a 1-month-old infant showed improved social and motor abilities, something mothers do interferes with their own natural ability to keep themselves quiet and organized (and thus available for social interaction). By 1 month, mothers' child-rearing practices or expectations for development may be influencing infants' abilities. In this sense, the infant is being shaped by the environment. An infant's high level of motor ability, however, may be shaping his or her caregiver or environment. The motor precocity of black infants, which is well documented in previous research (e.g., Scott et al., 1955), was also evident in this study. It seems that black mothers hold more realistic expectations for motor development than they do for cognitive development, and this should greatly influence the extent to which they promote certain developmental activities.

Changes in infant behavior that may be due to environmental influences do not appear to be related to SES differences in mothers as has been suggested by previous research. In fact, few SES differences were found for infant behaviors or mothers' perceptions and expectations. Whether SES differences in child-rearing practices emerge at later ages (as seen in other research) and act to influence behavior remains to be seen. This study will follow mother-infant pairs through age 3 years, and will investigate these relationships at a later point.

This information is significant. It will change outdated theoretical concepts about a critical age period as it relates to black newborns. It also points out what is possible if normative and more representative samples of black mothers and infants are selected for study. It is expected that the results of the Howard University Normative Study will provide new normative expectations for black newborns and insight into the infant as a dynamic interacter—that is, a person who influences and is influenced by both environment and caretaker. The study should also be useful in revising teaching methods for infants, toddlers, and preschoolers where needed; enable concerned individuals to mobilize preventive efforts and to institute effective interventions for infants when needed; and foster the strengthening of those rich and positive influences of black cultural heritage on child-rearing practices and parenting.

References

Als, H., Tronick, E., Lester, B., & Brazelton, T. B. (1979). Specific neonatal measures: The Brazelton Neonatal Behavioral Assessment Scale. In J. D. Osofsky (Ed.), *The handbook of infant development*. New York: Wiley.

Anderson, R., & Standley, K. (n.d.). *Newborn behavior inventory*. Washington, DC: United States Department of Health, Education, and Welfare, National Institute of Mental Health.

Bakeman, R., & Brown, J. V. (1977). Behavioral dialogues: An approach to the assessment of mother-infant interaction. *Child Development, 48*, 195–203.

Baldwin, C. (1973). *Comparison of mother-child interaction at different ages and in families of different education levels and ethnic backgrounds*. Paper presented at the annual meeting of the Society for Research in Child Development, Philadelphia.

Bartz. K. W., and Levine, E. S. (1978). Childrearing by black parents: A description and comparison to Anglo and Chicano parents. *Journal of Marriage and the Family*, 709–719.

Bee, H. L., Barnard, K. E., Eyres, S. J., Gray, C. A., Hammond, M. A., Spietz, A. L., Snyder, C., & Clark, B. (1982). Prediction of IQ and language skills from perinatal status, child performance, family characteristics, and mother-infant interaction. *Child Development, 53*, 1134–1156.

Bowes, W. C., Brackbill, Y., Conway, E., & Steinschneider, A. (1970). The effects of obsterical medication on fetus and infant. *Monographs of the Society for Research in Child Development, 35*(4, Serial no. 137).

Boykin, A. W. (1977). Black psychology and the research process: Keeping the baby but throwing out the bath water. *Journal of Black Psychology, 4*, 43–64.

Brazelton, T. B. (1973). *Neonatal Behavioral Assessment Scale*. Philadelphia: Lippincott.

Brazelton, T. B., Koslowski, B., & Tronick, E. (1976). Study of the neonatal behavior in Zambian and American neonates. *Journal of the American Academy of Child Psychiatry, 15*, 97–107.

Brown, J. V., Bakeman, R., Snyder, P. A., Fredrickson, W. T., Morgan, S. E., & Hepler, R. (1975). Interactions of black inner-city mothers with their newborn infants. *Child Development, 46*, 677–686.

Caplan, N., & Nelson, S. D. (1973). On being useful: The nature and consequences of psychological research on social problems. *American Psychologist, 28*, 199–211.

Carew, J. (1980). Experience and the development of intelligence in young children at home and in day care. *Monographs of the Society for Research in Child Development, 45*(6–7, Serial No. 187).

Clarke-Stewart, K. A. (1973). Interactions between mothers and their young children: Characteristics and consequences. *Monographs of the Society for Research in Child Development, 38*(6–7, Serial No. 153).

Dubowitz, L. M. S., Dubowitz, V., & Goldberg, C. (1970). Clinical assessment of gestational age in the newborn infant. *Journal of Pediatrics, 77*, 1–10.

Field, T. M. (1981). Intervention for high-risk infants and their parents. *Educational Evaluation and Policy Analysis, 3*, 69–78.

Field, T. M., Widmayer, S. M., Stringer, S., & Ignatoff, E. (1980). Preterm infants: An intervention and developmental follow-up. *Child Development, 51*, 426–436.

Frank, D. A., & Barrett, D. E. (1981). Mothers' expectations of developmental milestones. *Pediatric Research, 15*, 448.

Garcia Coll, C. T., Sepkoski, C., & Lester, B. (1981). Cultural and biomedical correlates of neonatal behavior. *Developmental Psychobiology, 14*, 147–154.

Geber, M. (1958). The psycho-motor development of African children in the first year and the influence of maternal behavior. *Journal of Social Psychology, 47*, 185–195.

Geber, M., & Dean, R. F. (1957). The state of development of newborn African children. *Lancet, 1*, 1216–1219.

Gerson, L., Glantz, M., & Gaiter, J. (1983). Predicting maternal responsiveness through contextual and infant personality characteristics. Paper presented at the biennial meeting of the Society for Research in Child Development, Detroit, MI, April.

Golden, M., & Birns, B. (1968). Social class and cognitive development in infancy. *Merrill-Palmer Quarterly, 14*, 139–149.

Golden, M., & Birns, B. (1976). Social class and infant intelligence. In M. Lewis (Ed.), *Origins of intelligence*. New York: Plenum.

Gottfried, A. W. & Gottfried, A. E. (1983). Home environment and mental development in young children of middle-class families. In A. W. Gottfried (Ed.), *Home environment and early mental development: Longitudinal research*. New York: Academic Press.

Hall, W. S. (1974). Research in the Black community: Child development. In J. Chunn (Ed.), *The survival of Black children and youth*. Washington, DC: Nuclassics & Science Publishing.

Hess, R., & Shipman, V. (1965). Early experience and the socialization of cognitive modes in children. *Child Development, 36*, 869–886.

Hollingshead, A. (1975). *Four-factor index of social status*. Unpublished manuscript. Yale University, New Haven, CT.

Hollingshead, A. (1958). Index of social position. Appendix [developed 1957]. A. Hollingshead, A. & F. C. Redlich, *Social class and mental illness: A community study*. New York: Wiley.

Horowitz, F. D., Aleksandrowicz, M., Ashton, L. J., Tims, S., McCluskey, K., Culp, R., & Gallas, H. (1973, April). *American and Uruguayan infants: reliabilities, maternal drug histories, and population differences using the Brazelton Scale*. Paper presented at the biennial meeting of the Society for Research in Child Development, Philadelphia, PA.

Horowitz, F. D., Ashton, L. J., Culp, R., Gaddis, E., Levin, S., & Reichmann, B. (1977). The effects of obstetric medication on the behavior of Israeli newborn infants and some comparisons with Uruguayan and American infants. *Child Development, 48*, 1607–1623.

Howard, A., & Scott, R. S. (1981). The study of minority groups in complex societies. In R. H. Munroe, R. L. Monroe, & B. Whiting (Eds.), *Handbook of cross-cultural human development*. New York: Garland.

Kamii, C., & Radin, N. (1967). Class differences in the socialization practices of Negro mothers. *Journal of Marriage and the Family, 29*, 302–310.

Kaufman, A., & DiCuio, R. (1975). Separate factor analyses for the McCarthy Scales for groups of black and white children. *Journal of School Psychology, 13*, 10–18.

Kessner, D. M., et al. (Eds.) (1973). *Infant death: An analysis by maternal risk and health care (Vol 1)*. Washington, DC: Institute of Medicine, National Academy of Science.

Leiderman, P. H., Tulkin, S. R., & Rosenfeld, A. (Eds.) (1977). *Culture and infancy: Variations in the human experience*. New York: Academic Press.

Lester, B. M., Als, H., & Brazelton, T. B. (1978). *Scoring criteria for seven clusters of the Brazelton scale*. Unpublished manuscript, Children's Hospital Medical Center, Child Development Unit, Boston.

Lester, B. M., Als, H., & Brazelton, T. B. (1982). Regional obstetrical anesthesia and newborn behavior: A reanalysis toward synergistic effects. *Child Development, 53*, 687–692.

Lester, B. M., & Brazelton, T. B. (1981). Cross-cultural assessment of neonatal behavior. In H. Stevenson & D. Wagner (Eds.), *Cultural perspectives on child development*. San Francisco: Freeman.

Lewis, M., & Wilson, C. D. (1972). Infant development and lower-class American families. *Human Development, 15,* 112–127.

Littman, B., & Parmelee, A. H. (1974). *Manual for obstetrical complications*. Los Angles: UCLA School of Medicine.

McAdoo, H. P. (1977, December). The impact of extended family variables upon the upward mobility of Black families (Final report to the USDHEW). Columbia, MD: Columbia Research Systems.

McAdoo, H. P. (Ed.) (1981). *Black families*. Beverly Hills, CA: Sage.

McLoyd, V. C., & Randolph, S. M. (1983, April). Secular trends in the study of Afro-American children: A review of Child Development 1936–1980. Paper presented at the biennial meeting of the Society for Research in Child Development, Detroit, MI.

Miller, H. C., & Hassanien, K. (1971). Diagnosis of impaired fetal growth in newborn infants. *Pediatrics, 48,* 511.

Morse, W. W. (1981). *Infant mortality and morbidity in the District of Columbia: Statistical report*. Washington, DC: Department of Human Services.

Myers, F., Rana, P. Y., & Harris, M. (1979). *Black child development in America 1927– 1977: An annotated bibliography*. Westport, CT: Greenwood.

Nobles, W. W. (1981). African-American family life: An instrument of culture. In H. P. McAdoo (Ed.), *Black families*. Beverly Hills, CA: Sage.

Ogbu, J. U. (1981). Origins of human competence: A cultural-ecological perspective. *Child Development, 52,* 413–429.

Oyemade, U. J., & Rosser, P. L. (1980). Development in Black children. *Advances in Behavioral Pediatrics, 1,* 153–179.

Parker, S., & Brazelton, T. B. (1981). Newborn behavioral assessment: Research, prediction, and clinical uses. *Children Today, 10,* 2–5.

Peters, M. F. (1981). Parenting in Black families with young children: A historical perspective. In H. P. McAdoo (Ed.), *Black families*. Beverly Hills, CA: Sage.

Sameroff, A. J. (1983). Systems of development: Contexts and evolution. In W. Kessen (Ed.), *History, theories and methods*. In P. H. Mussen (Ed.), *Handbook of child psychology (Vol. 4)*. New York: Wiley.

Sameroff, A. J., & Chandler, M. D. (1975). Reproductive risk and the continuum of caretaking casuality. In F. D. Horowitz (Ed.), *Review of child development research*. Chicago: University of Chicago Press.

Scott, R. B., Ferguson, A. D., Jenkins, M. E., & Cutter, F. F. (1955). Growth and development in Negro infants: V. Neuromuscular patterns of behavior during the first year of life. *Pediatrics, 16,* 24–29.

Seashore, M. J., Leifer, A. D., Barnett, C. R., & Leiderman, P. H. (1973). The effects of denial or early mother-infant interaction on maternal self-confidence. *Journal of Personality and Social Psychology, 26,* 369-378.

Slaughter, D. T. (1983). Early intervention and its effects on maternal and child development. *Monographs of the Society for Research in Child Development, 48*(4, Serial No. 202).

Stechler, G. (1964). Newborn attention as affected by medication during labor. *Science, 144,* 315–317.

Super, C. M. (1981a). Behavioral development in infancy. In R. Munroe, R. L. Munroe, & B. Whiting (Eds.), *Handbook of cross-cultural human development*. New York: Garland.

Super, C. M. (1981b). Cross-cultural research on infancy. In H. C. Triandis & A. Heron (Eds.), *Handbook of cross-cultural psychology, Vol. 4: Developmental psychology*. Boston: Allyn & Bacon.

Tulkin, S. R. (1977). Dimensions of multicultural research in infancy and early childhood. In P. A. Leiderman, S. R. Tulkin, & A. Rosenfeld (Eds.), *Culture and infancy: Variations in the human experience*. New York: Academic Press.

Yarrow, L. J. (1973). *Cultural and social influences in infancy and early childhood: Mother-infant interaction and development in infancy*. New York: Wenner-Gren Foundation for Anthropological Research.

Zegiob, L., & Forehand, R. (1975). Maternal interactive behavior as a function of race, socioeconomic status, and sex of the child. *Child Development, 46*, 564–568.

PART II

MOTHER-INFANT INTERACTION IN THE FIRST YEAR OF LIFE

CHAPTER 7

A Psychobiological Study of Infant Development in South India*

Cassie Landers

*Department of Comparative Human Development,
Harvard University,
Cambridge, Massachusetts*

The growing emphasis on culture, as one of the many variables to be investigated in developmental research, has broadened our perspective and appreciation for the underlying processes of development. The opportunity is a challenging one. It forces us to explain our definition of normality as we witness culturally varying modes of organization. The systematic study of infant development across cultures demands the formulation of multidimensional models to account for the interrelationships among complex sets of variables. These paradigms must be able to describe and document the interactions between environmental conditions of the culture, the effects of these conditions on the mother and fetus, and the nature of the individual infant.

In response to this challenge, the psychobiological model was designed by Lester and Brazelton (1982). Upholding the assumption of a transactional or holistic model (Sameroff & Chandler, 1975) of development, they suggest that behavior is only interpretable by viewing the functioning of the organism in the caregiving environment. The infant is viewed as both a biological and psychological system which proceeds developmentally from less complex to increasingly differentiated levels of organization. A second assumption implicit in the model is that behavior is adaptive. The neonate comes equipped with a programmed response repertoire which is designed to maximize the survival of the

*The author is indebted to Dr. A. Venkatesh and Dr. R. S. Iyer of the Kasturba Medical College, Department of Pediatrics, Manipal, South India. This research was supported by the Professional Studies Program, University of California, Berkeley, and the Ford Foundation. The author is currently a consultant in Early Child Care and Development, UNICEF, N.Y.

individual and the species. The form of adaptation reflects both the evolutionary history of the species and the particular or ontogenetic history of the individual.

Development is influenced by several classes of variables. These include the obstetrical and reproductive history of the mother, the genetic endowment, and the prenatal environment. In addition, the infant characteristics of gestational age, size, weight, and sex must also be considered. These forces act synergistically to produce a behavioral phenotype; the expression of a genetic endowment within a particular environment. The infant elicits from the environment the responses necessary for his or her survival and, at the same time, is affected by environmental forces, which include methods of care and handling, family structure, and physical setting, as well as the larger goals and expectations of the culture (Lester & Brazelton, 1982).

In an effort to contribute to the growing body of comparative infancy research, the psychobiological model was applied to a group of 30 full-term infants born in a rural village in South India. The investigation was carried out with two goals in mind: (a) to describe and document the behavioral profile of a group of full-term Indian infants throughout the first 3 months of life; and (b) to illustrate the complex relationships between biomedical and social variables and neonatal behavior, and discover how these relationships may vary in different cultures. To address the first goal, the Brazelton Neonatal Behavioral Assessment Scale (BNBAS; Brazelton, 1973) was administered to each of the 30 infants on days 1, 2, 3, 4, 5, 7, 10 and 30 of life in an effort to document both the change and the stability in neonatal performance within the first month of life. To monitor the path of early infant growth, the Bayley Scales of mental and motor development were administered at 3 months of age (Bayley, 1969).

Investigation of the relationship between the physical and behavioral characteristics of these infants and the circumstances surrounding their birth was the second goal of the study. The hypothesis to be tested here was that the potential influence of biomedical and social factors may vary in different populations so that some populations may be more resistant to the effects of biological and social risks than others. It was hoped that this set of analyses would generate a culture-specific profile of relative infant risk as it relates to and interacts with the caregiving adaptations exhibited by this community.

Demographic and Social Characteristics of The Research Site

The study described here took place within the villages surrounding Udupi in the South Kanara district of Karnataka state. This area may be broadly defined as the region in southern India inhabited predominantly by Kannada-speaking people.

The coastland of Karnataka, known as Kanara, is approximately 320 km long. Its northern width varies from 13 to 32 km; its southern, from 48 to 64 km. This lowland region of the western coast is crossed by several traverse ridges and spurs of the western Ghats. Malpe, a village 1.5 km from Udupi, was the major site of the study. Covering an area of 9.12 square km, it has 2,110 occupied households and a population of 17,000 (Census of India, 1971). Although Malpe is predominantly a fishing village, agriculture accounts for a large portion of its economic activity. The maximum temperature reaches 34.9°C and falls to a minimum of 18.6°C during December and January. The months of March, April, and May are the hottest, followed by the heavy monsoon rains which fall in January, July, and August, and which yield an annual rainfall of 4,187 mm. The area has approximately 20 km of roads and an open surface drainage system.

The government-run educational facilities include six primary schools, two middle schools, and a secondary school. Reflecting the high literacy rate of South Kanara, Malpe has an overall rate of 52%. Of the literate population, 57% are males, while 43% are females. A total of 75% of the population are Hindu; 14% practice some form of Christianity; and 11% are classified as Muslim (Census of India, 1971). The predominant language is Tulu, followed by Kannada, the official state language. Tulu is a highly developed Dravidian language with a rich vocabulary capable of expressing the most subtle shades of meaning . It does not have a script, however, and Kannada is used when writing (Diwakar, 1968).

Rice is the main crop in the alluvial patches of the coastland and in the irrigated areas of the eastern plateau; coconut is the chief crop on the sandy coastal soils. Jowar, a type of wheat, and ragi, a cereal, are grown in the poorer soils, which require moderate rain. Fishing, fish curing, fruit canning, salt making, wood cutting, ship building, and ivory carving are the chief industries of the coastland region of Kanara (Hukkerikar, 1955). The three most important imported commodities include rice, salt, and clay, while the three most important exports are fish, fish meal, and coir (a fiber) products. The goods manufactured within the village include: canned fish and fish meal, tiles and bricks, coir products, and wicker baskets. Of the total population, 33% are employed, with women constituting approximately 34.7% of the labor supply (Census of India, 1971).

While there is a wide range of economic levels within the fishing community, most of India's small-scale traditional fisherman are poor. Two major factors inherent in the economic structure of fishing in India have been cited as the major cause of their relative poverty: inequality in assets holding, and exploitation and malfunction of the market system (Kurien, 1980). There is a tremendous skewing in the distribution of equipment, and the distribution of proceeds favors the owner of capital rather than the laborer. Depending on the type of equipment, the owner receives about a fifth to a half of the total catch in addition to his shares as worker (Norr, 1975).

The second major factor lies in the failings inherent in the market system. The marketing of fish, whether it involves small-scale disposal over short distances, bulk disposal over long distances, or export disposal, is a breeding ground for middlemen. For every middleman on a marketing chain there is a proportionate decrease in the returns to the fisherman and an increase in the supply to the consumer. Although these problems still plague Malpe's fisherman, several achievements in the past two decades have enabled economic growth to occur in the village. These include the introduction of mechanized fishing, imported infrastructure, and the availability of foreign markets for export.

Until recently, traditional fishing methods, involving dug-out canoes and plank boats, accounted for approximately 75% of Malpe's total fish yield. At present, the village has several hundred power boats which are distributed to small groups of fishermen on a loan subsidy basis. The traditional methods, with an operational range of only 3 km from the coast, restricted the available catch to the shoals located near the shore giving rise to tremendous seasonal and annual variation. With the advent of advanced fishing techniques, the markets have stabilized at dramatically higher levels of productivity. Moreover, the introduction of modern technology to fish handling and preservation has led to the development of foreign markets. Currently, frozen prawns and lobsters from Malpe reach Japanese and American markets.

The rapid transformation of the traditionally oriented coastal fishing industry results in part from the modernization of the infrastructure that is required to support other realms of fish production. Facilities such as ice and freezing plants, and canning and fish-meal plants, were installed through the use of 100 km of approach roads, transport vehicles, and marketing facilities. In spite of the prevailing economic difficulties, these facilities provide the villagers with a realistic vision of future economic prosperity.

Members of Malpe's fishing community are from the same low caste, know in the village as "Mogaveras." Their housing consists of small one-room huts with thatched roofs, mud or bamboo walls, and dirt floors. The more prosperous fishermen have homes with tiled roofs and brick walls or mud walls. Few of the homes have electricity, and most are no larger than two rooms. Cooking and food preparation take place either outside or in a small area of the home reserved for these purposes. With a few exceptions, members of this community grow up in some form of extended family organization. The most common form in this village is the joint family, with two or more married brothers living together with their wives and children but without their parents, and the generational family, which consists of parents and only one of their married children and his spouse and children (Kakar, 1978).

The extended family is a cooperative unit with members engaged in the many activities necessary to enable its survival and to protect its members from the uncertainty and threats of the outside world. In determining an acceptable division of labor, and articulating the relationships between its members, the family essentially relies upon the hierarchical principal inherent in all of Indian society. For the Indian family this process is traditional and well defined. The organization of relationships within the family and the values it generates are constantly reaffirmed through the celebration of transitional points within an individual's life cycle. Much of an Indian's social activity centers around this ritualistic punctuation of both minor and major occasions. These traditional ceremonies celebrate the individual's place and importance within his particular family, providing him with keen awareness that he belongs. Such events also continually reaffirm the belief that the family is the most reliable, durable, and moral of all social relations (Kakar, 1978).

Thus the economic realities of village India, coupled with the intense social consideration of prestige, status, and reputation inherent in the caste system, powerfully reinforce and strengthen the family bond. An individual's worth and, indeed, recognition of his identity are intimately interwoven with the reputation of his family. The expressed patterns of behavior and action are not the product of individual effort, motivation, or even conflict, but emerge out of and reflect the individual's family circumstances and reputation in the wider society. Within this environment, conformity to both caste and family norms is the admired behavior; to embark upon an individually chosen path is to invite not only ostracism but pity (Kakar, 1978).

To the Western observer, it is rather striking that in spite of the economic uncertainties confronting the inhabitants of Malpe, there is a pervasive sense of joy in small rewards and accomplishments of the day, and hope that the fruits of their labor will be reaped later in life. Perhaps this world view not only reflects the teaching of the culture but is influenced and conditioned by their dependence on the power, uncertain rewards, but unyielding constancy of the sea.

Indian Early Childhood

According to the reality of childhood and identity development of the Indian child, the psychosocial definition of infancy extends to years 4 and 5 of life, when the capacity for reasoning, cognition, and judgment are firmly established. Infancy is characterized by an extended and deep attachment to the maternal figure. Although this attachment is not an exclusive one, given the nature of the extended family and the presence of other potential caregivers, the infant's attachment to his biological mother is by far the most poignant. This intimacy is reflected in the physical proximity of the mother and child within the early years of a child's life. During the day infants are carried on the mother's hip and are actively engaged with her as she performs most of her daily chores. Continuously held, cuddled, and talked to, the infant's exposure to the world is characterized by a maternal relationship of duration and intensity not usually found in the Western world (Kakar, 1979).

The mother's indulgence to her infant's demands appears to be extended past the time when the infant is biologically capable of independent functioning. For example, breast-feeding is on demand at all times of the day and night, continues often until the child is 2 or 3 years of age, and only gradually comes to an end. Accordingly, detachment from the mother-infant bond takes place gradually, and the development of a strong independent ego is not a feature of the Indian model of child rearing. Motor, cognitive, and linguistic development proceed at their own pace according to a course directed by the child. Developmental accomplishments, independent of the rate or dexterity with which they occur, are responded to with delight or affectionate tolerance. It appears, moreover, that minimal demands are placed on the Indian infant to explore and master the world independent of his mother.

What is emphasized in the early years of childhood is the avoidance of infant frustration and enjoyment between the infant and others within his environment. The young child is relatively free from external pressures to conform to a rigid structure of behavior. The parental agenda of early child development in India contrasts sharply with that valued in the West, where a child's development is channeled, molded, and shaped to fulfill a set of predetermined goals. The Indian mother emphasizes the positive aspects of her child's behavior and accedes to the child's demands rather than attempting to control and structure them.

Methodology

Over a 2-month period, 30 infants were selected for study from the population of normal deliveries at the Kasturba Medical College Hospital and a rural maternity health center. The center is one of six that operate under the direction of the Kasturba Hospital. Infants were eligible for study if they were healthy, full-term, born of uncomplicated deliveries, and mothers with an uncomplcated medical history. The selection criteria for the study of healthy newborns was adapted from the standards defined by Als, Tronick, Lester, and Brazelton (1979). Each mother-infant dyad selected for study was assessed according to the measures outlined in Table 1. As is evident from Table 1, the areas under study included behavior, medical, sociocultural, psychometric, and sociocultural factors.

The Brazelton Neonatal Behavioral Assessment Scale

The BNBAS formed the major part of the study during the first 30 days of life (Brazelton, 1973). In order to measure the pattern of adaptation and coping strategies of the neonate, each infant was examined on days 1, 3, 5, 7, 10, and 30 of life. The first two or three examinations were performed at the delivery site, while subsequent ones were administered at home.

Table 1.   Selected Measures for Cross-cultural Infancy Research

Behavior organization	Brazelton Neonatal Behavioral Assessment Scale: Days 1, 3, 5, 7, 10, 30	
Medical factors	Infant	Mother
	Anthropometric measures (length, weight, head circumference)	Prenatal history
		Reproductive history
		Obstetrical history
	Ponderal index	Anthropometric measures (height, weight, arm circumference)
Sociocultural factors	Socioeconomic status/Family Wealth Index	
	Family structure and social-support system	
Psychometric factors	Bayley Scale of Infant Development	

The BNBAS is based on the concept of the healthy newborn as a complex, competent, well-organized being adapted to the environment, able to interact with it and elicit from it the stimulation necessary for species-specific motor, emotional, and cognitive development (Als et al., 1979). Through the administration of 16 reflexive and 26 behavioral items, the infant's capacity for social interaction, motoric organization, physiologic response to stress, and state control are described and recorded. The reflex items are scored as follows: 0 = absent, 1 = low, 2 = medium, 3 = high, with a 2 considered normal for most of the reflexes. The 26 behavioral items are rated on a 9-point scale. The BNBAS uncovers infants' major capacities to organize themselves when confronted with the intense physiological demands for recovery from labor, delivery, and exposure to the environment outside the uterus. Infants are manipulated in such a fashion that within the half-hour examination they demonstrate their ability for physical, cognitive, social, and temperamental function, as well as psychophysiological intactness.

To analyze the data, the individual items were grouped according to the behavioral clusters developed by Lester, Als, and Brazelton (1982). This system, which seeks to perserve the dynamic conceptualization of the infant, combines the 26 behavioral item into six behavioral clusters and uses the 16 reflexes to generate a seventh cluster (see Table 2). To derive the six behavioral clusters, the curvilinear scale items are rescored as linear. The cluster score is the mean of the rescored items used to define the cluster, with higher scores indicating "better" performance. The six behavioral clusters are: Habituation, including response decrement to repeated auditory, visual, and tactile stimulation; Orientation, including response to animate and inanimate stimuli and overall alertness; Motor Performance, comprising integrated motor acts and overall muscle tone; Range of State, which assesses the rapidity, peak, and lability of state changes; Regula-

Table 2. Brazelton Neonatal Behavioral Assessment Scale—Seven Cluster Scoring Criteria

Item[a]	Cluster
	Habituation
1. Light .... Raw score	
2. Rattle .... Raw score	
3. Bell .... Raw score	
4. Pinprick .... Raw score	
	Orientation
5. Inanimate visual .... Raw score	
6. Inanimate auditory .... Raw score	
7. Animate visual .... Raw score	
8. Animate auditory .... Raw score	
9. Animate visual and auditory ..... Raw score	
10. Alertness .... Raw score	
	Motor Performance
11. General tonus .... Recode: 9/1 = 1; 8/2 = 2; 7/3 = 3; 4 = 4; 5 = 5; 6 = 6	
12. Motor maturity .... Raw score	
13. Pull-to-sit .... Raw score	
15. Defensive movements .... Raw score	
20. Activity .... Recode: 9/1 = 1; 8/2 = 2; 7/3 = 3; 4/6 = 4; 5 = 5	
	Range of State
17. Peak of excitement .... Recode: 9/1 = 1; 8/2 = 2; 4/3 = 3; 7/5 = 4; 6 = 5	
18. Rapidity of buildup .... Recode: 9/1 = 1; 8/2 = 2; 7/3 = 3; 4 = 4; 5 = 5; 6 = 6	
19. Irritability .... Recode: 9/1 = 1; 8 = 2; 7 = 3; 6 = 4; 5 = 5; 2, 3, 4 = 6	
24. Lability of states .... Recode: 1, 7, 8, 9 = 1; 5, 6 = 2; 4 = 3; 3 = 4; 2 = 5	
	Regulation of State
14. Cuddliness .... Raw score	
16. Consolability .... Raw score	
25. Self-quieting activity .... Raw score	
26. Hand-facility mouth .... Raw score	
	Autonomic Stability
21. Tremulousness .... Recode: invert: 9 = 1 (1 = 9); 8 = 2 (2 = 8); etc.	
22. Startles .... Recode: if 1 drop; otherwise invert 2 − 9 on 8-point scale	
23. Lability of skin color .... Recode: 9, 1 = 1; 8 = 2; 7 = 3, 6 = 4; 5 = 5; 3, 4 = 6; 2 = 7	
	Reflexes
	An abnormal score is defined as 0,1, or 3 for all reflexes except clonus, mystagmus, or TNR where 0,1, and 2 are normal and 3 is abnormal. Reflex score = total number of abnormal reflex scores

Note. Table taken from "Regional Obstetric Anesthesia and Newborn Behavior: A Reanalysis Towards Synergistic Effects," by B. M. Lester, H. Als, and T. B. Brazelton, 1982, *Child Development, 53,* pp. 687–692.

[a]Numerals represent Brazelton Scale item numbering.

tion of State, or efforts to modulate the infant's own state control; and Autonomic Regulation, including signs of physiological stress seen as tremors, startles, and changes in skin color. The seventh, or Reflex cluster is the total number of deviant reflex scores such that higher scores indicate a greater number of deviant reflexes.

Performance on the BNBAS for each of the 30 Indian infants will be presented and discussed under two major headings; (a) group analysis of cluster scores and their pattern of change during the first month of life; and (b) correlational analysis between selected maternal and infant biomedical factors and BNBAS performance.

Medical Assessments

Maternal medical information consisted of obstetrical and reproductive histories and the anthropometric indicators of height, weight, and arm circumference. For the infant the anthropometric indicators, length, weight, and head circumference were measured at birth, at 1 month, and at 3 months, with additional measurements of chest and arm circumference at 3 months. The ponderal index, a ratio of weight and length at birth, useful in defining the end results of fetal growth and nutrition, was also calculated.

Sociocultural Data

Through a series of both formal and informal interviews, an attempt was made to describe the particular sociocultural setting surrounding each mother and infant. Information regarding the family support system and kinship structure and the educational level of the parents was obtained. Based on the work of Levinson (1974), an overall index of family wealth was calculated, which included the following: housing, occupation, sanitation, and the number of various household possessions.

Psychometric Functioning

The Bayley Scales of Infant Development were administered to each infant at 3 months (Bayley, 1969). The primary value of this tool for the infant lies in its ability to determine a child's current level of functioning and the degree of deviation from normality. The scales are divided into two complementary areas of developmental functioning, namely mental ability and psychomotor ability. The mental scale is designed to assess sensory-perceptual activities, discrimination and the ability to respond to these; the early acquisition of object constancy and memory, learning, and problem solving, vocalizations, and the beginning of verbal communication; and early evidence of the ability to form generalizations and classifications, which is the basis of abstract thought. The motor scale assesses both gross and fine motor control, the degree of balance, tone, and flexibility.

Norms for the Bayley Scales are based on a sample of 1,262 children ranging in age from 2 to 30 months. In standardizing the scale, the mental and motor items were arranged in approximate order by age placement (the age at which 50% of the children passed a given item). The Mental Development Index (MDI) and the Psychomotor Development Index (PDI) were derived by administration of the respective scales. The distribution of raw scores at each level was converted to a set of normalized standard scores with a mean value of 100 and a standard deviation of 16. The standard score range of 50 through 150 covers more than three standard deviations on either side of the average MDI or PDI for each of the 14 chosen age groups tested in the standardization design.

Sample Characteristics

Delivery Characteristics and Early Infant Environment

Of the 30 infants, 12 were delivered by a physician at the Kasturba Medical College Hospital, while the remaining births took place at a rural health center with a midwife attending the delivery. Infants were delivered without medication and were placed alongside the mothers immediately after birth, though mothers at the rural health center had the option of placing their infant in a cradle located at the foot of the bed. The average length of the hospital stay was 5–7 days, while mothers who delivered at the rural center returned home between days 3 and 5. The new mother was constantly surrounded by female members of her extended family throughout the duration of her stay. Breast-feeding was initiated usually within 24–48 hr of birth. Initial feeds were supplemented on days 1–3 with a jaggery (a brown sugar from palm sap) water administered by spoon. The tradition of not giving colostrum, recommended by ancient Indian physicians and still practiced by 85–90% of rural mothers (Agarwal & Agarwal, 1981), was not widely practiced by the study population. Breast-feeding was frequent and on demand at all times of the day and night.

Day 10 of the infant's life is memorable. It is at this time that the infant is named and a cradle made out of wood or straw is hung from the center of the hut. A silver belt, or piece of string in poorer families, is placed around the infant's waist and used to measure and monitor the child's growth. Children are named after their grandparents, the patron deity of the family, or some object known for strength and purity. The name is usually selected jointly by the elder members of the family. Until day 10 or 11 after delivery, mothers are considered impure. This state of impurity is remedied by a bath, as running water is considered the great purification agent. Traditionally assigned to the washerwoman, this task is currently performed by the maternal grandmother. Following the purification bath, the new mother is reintegrated into the family. Within the first week of life, the infant is given an elaborate bath and oil massage, followed by tight wrapping in an old piece of sari.

Throughout the first month of life, infant and mother rest in a corner of the hut. As women often return to their native home for delivery, remaining there from 3 to 6 months, the maternal grandmother plays a major role in the early life of the infant. In cases where the maternal grandmother was absent, she was replaced by a female relative or, in two cases, an elderly woman in the community. It is a time when all of the new mother's energies are directed toward the care of her infant and she is comforted and strenghtened by the security of her familial environment. From the moment of birth, the Indian infant is greeted and surrounded by constant physical ministrations and the Indian mother is highly responsive to her infant's demands (Kakar, 1978). Reflecting the stoicism, endurance and dedication of her culture, the Indian woman gives to infancy its mystical aura and marked impact on development.

The characteristics of the Indian mothers are shown in Table 3. The mean height was 155.6 cm (59.0 in), with a weight of 47.2 kg (103.8 lb) and an arm circumference of 23.0 cm (8.8 in). Both mean height and mean weight were below the 5th percentile of American standards for women aged 25–34 years (National Center for Health Statistics, 1979b). However, when weight was assessed in terms of height (weight for height), the mean fell between the 10th and 25th percentile. The range of weight for height was from the 3rd to 75th percentile (National Center for Health Statistics, 1979a). Since height is influenced strongly by malnutrition, infection, and other types of stress centered in infancy and childhood and extending into adulthood, the low values for height and weight may be indicative of suboptimal maternal health and nutrition. They also are likely to influence weight gain during pregnancy (Mata & Wyatt, 1971). The

Table 3.   Mean, Standard Deviation, and Range of Selected Maternal Characteristics

Variable	M	SD	Range
Height (cm)	155.6	6.6	141.0–168.0
Weight (kg)	47.2	6.3	37.5–59.2
Arm circumference (cm)	23.0	2.0	20.0–27.0
Age	28.2	5.5	19.0–45.0
Gravida	3.7	2.4	1.0–9.0
Parity	2.4	2.3	0–8.0
Family Wealth Index	149.0	57.7	51.8–294.8
Maternal literacy[a]	2.3	.8	1.0–3.0

[a]Literacy: 1 = illiterate; 2 = semiliterate; 3 = literate.

diets of these women were typical of a South Indian community, consisting of rice, ragi, wheat, pulses, vegetables, buttermilk, and coconut milk. Rice and fish characterized the diets of the nonvegetarian mothers from the fishing community.

Ages ranged from 19 to 45, with a mean of 28.2 years. Approximately 46% of the mothers were between the ages of 20–29 years. Gravida and parity were found to be 3.7 and 2.4, respectively, with 17% of the mothers delivering their first child. In terms of educational status, 18.5% were illiterate, 29.7% were semiliterate, and 51.8% were literate.

Measurement of selected environmental variables permitted computation of the Family Wealth Index, useful in separating families into categories of differing socioeconomic status. The observed limits of dispersion ranged between 51.8 and 294.8, with a mean of 149 and a standard deviation of 57.7. As indicated by the wide range of scores, the families included in the study represented the poor, lower-middle, and middle socioeconomic classifications.

Several of the maternal characteristics were significantly interrelated as indicated in Table 4. Weight and height were positively related, as were weight and arm circumference. Age, parity, and gravida are highly interrelated and suggest that older mothers have a greater number of children. The maternal anthropometric characteristics also were examined with respect to Family Wealth Index and maternal literacy rate. Maternal literacy was positively related to the Family Wealth Index, and negatively related to the maternal factors of gravida and parity.

Newborn Characteristics

Infants weighing less than 2,500 g were included in the study and not considered low birthweight as according to criteria laid down by the World Health Organza-

Table 4.   Correlations Within Maternal Characteristics Matrix

	Gravida	Parity	Height	Weight	Arm circumference	Family Wealth Index	Literacy
Age	.435*	.582**	−.34	−.41	−.33	.16	−.21
Gravida		.970***	−.43*	−.40	−.32	−.21	−.587**
Parity			−.41	−.39	−.34	−.19	−.582**
Height				.600**	.33	−.07	.01
Weight					.844***	.07	−.02
Arm circumference						−.01	−.00
Family Wealth Index							.341*

*.05 ≤ p ≤ .10
**p ≤ .01
***p ≤ .001

Table 5.   Mean, Standard Deviation, and Range of Selected
Newborn Characteristics

Variable	M	SD	Range
Weight (g)	2,777	353.0	2,000–3,500
Length (cm)	49.1	2.7	44.0–53.0
Head circumference (cm)	33.7	1.6	31.0–36.0
Ponderal index[a]	2.36	.32	1.88–3.28

[a]Weight in grams $\times$ 100/(length in centimeters)^3.

tion. The average birthweight of full-term infants in India is about 500 g less than that in Western countries; therefore, the international low birthweight (LBW) criterion cannot be accepted for the Indian infant. Various Indian investigators have suggested 1,800–2,500 g as the criterion for LBW infants, with the majority approving 2,000 g as the cutoff point (Bhargava & Ghosh, 1974; Datta Banik, 1978; Ghosh, 1970).

The newborn characteristics are presented in Table 5. All infants were between 37 and 40 weeks gestation. The birthweights ranged from 2,000 to 3,550 g with a mean of 2,777. Male infants were slightly heavier than female infants– 2,834 and 2,773, respectively. These findings are in agreement with the mean birthweights reported by various investigators throughout India (Bhargava, Kumari, Choudhury, & Lall, 1980). According to U.S. birthweight standards for males, 60% of the Indian infants were at or below the 10th percentile, while 40% were at or below the 50th percentile. The corresponding figures for females were 41% at or below the 10th percentile, and 59% at or below the 50th percentile (Gairdner & Pearson, 1971).

In the present study the average crown-to-heel length in cm of 49.1 cm is in agreement with that reported by other Indian investigators (Ghai & Sandhu, 1968; Uklonskaya, Puri, Choudhari, Luthra, & Kumar, 1961). This figure corresponds to the 50th percentile of U.S. standards (Gairdner & Pearson, 1971). The mean head circumference was 33.7 cm, a figure slightly less than that reported by Ghai and Sandu (1968), and is below the 10th percentile for U.S. newborns (Gairdner & Pearson, 1971).

The ponderal index (PI), a ratio of birthweight to body length, can be used to define the end results of fetal growth and nutrition. It is a unique and useful measure for, unlike birthweight, the ponderal index is not confounded by race, sex, fetal age, or parity in defining malnutrition. By taking length into consideration, babies who are long, with a relatively small amount of soft tissue mass, can be seen as having experienced a late gestation nutritional insult (Brazelton, Parker, & Zuckerman, 1976). On the basis of research in the United States, a PI less than 2.3 has been used to define fetal malnutrition in full-term infants. The mean PI for the Indian infant in the present study was 2.36, with a range from 1.88 to 3.28. Using 2.3 as as the cutoff point, 45% of the infants would be

defined as malnourished or small for gestational age (SGA). An important research question is to determine whether the behavioral characteristics typical of
an SGA infant are manifested by these Indian infants who, by means of a low of
a low PI, would be defined as such.

Several of the medical factors for the newborn were interrelated. The significant correlations between them are shown in Table 6. As may be expected, the
heavier infants are also longer and have a larger head circumference. Infant
length at birth also was negatively related to PI, which suggests that low PI
infants have a longer birth length. The PI, however, was not significantly correlated with weight at 1 month. The anthropometric measures of weight, length,
and head circumference at birth were positively correlated with weight at 1
month. Thus, infants who are larger at birth are also larger at 1 month, which
supports the notion that growth in the early months is a biological function of
infant status at birth.

Results of BNBAS Cluster Scores

The means and standard deviations for the seven BNBAS cluster scores are
presented in Table 7. In order to test the overall equality of means across time, a
one-way repeated-measure analysis of variance test with days as the factor was
applied (Bruning & Kintz, 1977). The results of the analysis, presented in Table
8, indicate that for five of seven clusters, the overall F ratio is highly significant.
Mean scores for the Habituation, Motor Performance, Regulation of State, Autonomic Regulation, and Reflexes clusters show significant variation throughout
the first month of life, whereas the variation for both the Orientation and Range
of State clusters was not significant. The relationship between the mean scores as
they change over time was described by trend analysis. Orthogonal polynomial
coefficients designed for unequal intervals were tested to determine the presence
of linear, quadratic, cubic, quartic, and quintic components (Dickson, 1981;
Kirk, 1968).

Table 6.   Correlations Within Infant Characteristics Matrix

	Length	Head circumference	Ponderal index	Weight (1 month)
Birthweight	.636***	.489**	.20	.562**
Length		.497**	−.619***	.434*
Head circumference			−.06	.510**
Ponderal index				.03

*$p \leq .05$.   **$p \leq .01$.   ***$p \leq .001$.

Table 7.   Means and Standard Deviations on Seven BNBAS Clusters on Days 1, 3, 5, 7, 10, 30: Indian Sample

	Day 1		Day 3		Day 5		Day 7		Day 10		Day 30	
Cluster	M	SD	M	SD	M	SD	M	SD	M	SD	M	SD
Habituation	6.6	1.7	7.2	1.2	7.5	1.3	7.5	1.2	8.0	.7	8.0	1.7
Orientation	4.7	1.4	4.5	1.5	4.7	1.4	4.8	1.8	5.5	1.8	5.1	1.7
Motor Performance	4.3	.7	5.0	.9	5.3	.8	5.1	.9	5.4	1.0	6.0	.8
Range of State	3.6	1.0	3.7	.9	3.5	.8	3.2	1.0	3.2	1.0	3.6	.9
Regulation of State	6.5	1.2	5.8	1.4	6.3	1.1	6.1	1.5	6.2	1.3	4.9	1.6
Autonomic Regulation	7.0	.7	7.2	.7	7.4	.5	7.6	.5	7.5	.6	7.5	.6
Reflexes	2.2	1.6	1.5	1.5	1.5	1.3	1.9	2.0	1.4	1.5	.5	1.2

Habituation

The newborn is equipped at birth with a capacity to shut out repetitious and disturbing visual, auditory, and tactile stimulation that might otherwise make excessive demands on his or her immature physiologic system. The BNBAS assesses this capacity by measuring the decrement that occurs in response to a flashlight, bell, rattle, and pinprick. The pinprick, however, was not administered to the Indian infants. As evident from the mean scores for the Habituation cluster presented in Table 7, this sample of Indian infants is performing in the optimal range. Their behavior could be characterized by shutdown of body movements, diminution in blinks and respiratory changes after four to six presentations of stimuli. Moreover, their performance changes significantly throughout the first month, as identified in the results of the analysis of variance (ANOVA) on this cluster, presented in Table 8. The pattern of mean scores indicates that the scores increase over time. In addition to the linear increase, the quadratic function indicates that the scores remain the same on days 5 and 7, increase on day 10, and remain the same on day 30. The linear component accounts for 48.9% of the change, while the quadratic component accounts for 45.8% of the variation in scores.

Indian infants' capacity to shut out disturbing visual and auditory stimulation serves them well when confronting the demands of their environment. From the moment of birth these infants are exposed to the continuous stream of intense animate and inanimate stimulation that characterizes the small, crowded, and open huts. Their optimal performance on this cluster reflects the adequacy of their habituation center to adapt to the demands of a stimulation-rich environment. This optimal habituation response may be due to the use of swaddling, a technique practiced by this community. It is generally believed that swaddleing has a calming, restraining influence on infants inducing and extending sleep by reducing the number of startles which may lead to waking (Chisholm, 1978).

Table 8.   Summary of Repeated-Measure Analysis of
Variance BNBAS Cluster Scores on Days 1, 3, 5, 7, 10, 30

Cluster	SS Error	df	F	p
Habituation	141.57	175	13.17	.0001
Orientation	371.19	175	2.03	.07
Motor Performance	85.25	175	21.69	.0001
Range of State	150.18	175	1.81	.1132
Regulation of State	267.93	175	7.58	.0001
Autonomic Regulation	43.00	175	8.03	.0001
Reflexes	384.45	175	4.31	.001

Perhaps the most significant medical research on the effects of swaddling with or without the use of the cradleboard has been conducted by Lipton, Steinschneider, and Richmond (1965). On the basis of experimental evidence, they noted that swaddled infants slept more, had reduced levels of motor activity in response to stimulation, fewer startles, and lower heart rate variability than did nonswaddled infants. According to these authors, the motor restraint imposed by swaddling reduces the overall arousal level by decreasing afferent proprioceptive stimuli to the central reticular formation of the brain stem. The findings from this investigation seem to support the hypothesis that both the effects of swaddling and the constant stimulation provided by the environment are related to these infants' exceptional ability to shut out disturbing and physiologically threatening environmental stimulation.

Orientation

At birth infants are equipped with a capacity for processing complex visual information and for demonstrating visual motor movements that enable them to follow and fixiate on an appealing stimulus. The BNBAS items used to measure this capacity are the visual and auditory orientation to inanimate objects (bell, ball) and responsiveness to the examiner's face and/or voice. Although large within-group variation was found, overall scores fell at the low-to-mid-range level of the scale. Behavior can be characterized by stilled and quiet alerting to the stimulus with smooth or jerky visual tracking for at least a 30° arc. Only a few of the infants were able to follow the stimulus with eyes and head 60° horizontally and 30° vertically, which is characteristic of a more optimal orientation response. As identified in Table 7, the items comprising this cluster show no significant change over the first 30 days of life ($p < .07$). There is, however, a slight increase over time, with the means fluctuating between a low of 4.7 on day 1 and a high score of 5.5 on day 10.

In interpreting the low-to-mid-range orientation performance which does not improve significantly over time, two hypotheses may be offered. One difficulty in applying the BNBAS in cross-cultural research is the experimenter's lack of control over environmental circumstances (de Vries & Super, 1978). For example, the administration manual states explicitly that the examination should be performed in between feeding and in a quiet and dimly lit environment (Brazelton, 1973). As the Indian infant is fed on demand and as the examinations were often performed in small, dark huts, amid the confusion of daily activities and the enthusiastic support of as many as 20 observers, the atmosphere was less than ideal. Thus it may be suggested that the demands of the environment made it more difficult for the examiner to bring the infant to the quiet alert state needed to elicit the infant's optimal orientation response. Greater control over the conditions under which the examination is performed would perhaps enable the overall mean scores to show some improvment.

A second hypothesis is that the mother's expectations for the social responsivity of her infant may be low. In the first month of life there was little evidence of en-face behaviors between a mother and her infant, and little expectation of infant response during feeding. The typical feeding position, moreover, with the infant seated sideways against the mother's outstretched legs, exacerbated the lack of en-face regard. Maternal energy seemed directed toward ministering to the infant's physiological needs, in contrast to the verbal and visual interaction characterizing mother-infant behavior in Western societies.

Motor Performance

During the neonatal exam, motor behavior was assessed according to the maturity, tone, and vigor of motoric movements as well as the capacity for head and neck control. The repeated-measure ANOVA for the Motor cluster found a significant increase throughout the first month ($p \le .0001$). The linear,quadratic, and cubic components were significant and accounted for 72.16%, 16%, and 4.9% of the variation, respectively. There was an overall increase from a mean of 4.3 on day 1 to 6.0 on day 30. The variation in scores between days 3 and 10 accounted for the quadratic and cubic variation.

The type and kind of motor activity exibited by this group could be qualitatively described as mature, somewhat hypertonic, and resistant with an air of deliberate intensity. Movements were not the jerky restricted arcs of the immature infant, nor were they the smooth, well-controlled movements typifying the healthy, full-term infant. Rather, they were vigorous, intensely driving responses indicative of the strong motoric potential of these infants. Largely controlled by state behavior, most motor activity was seen when the infant was roused to an active state 5 to 6. When infants were resting or were in a quiet alert state, random, nonpurposeful activity was rarely seen, and a position of flexion for both arms and legs was the preferred position. These intensely motorically active infants could be easily consoled through appropriately supportive tactile maneuvers. Once in a high arousal state, they were brought back easily to the resting position of flexion in both upper and lower extremities through the restraining tactile responses of the examiner. Thus, through these motor responses the infants would communicate their preference for the type and kind of handling they needed to stabilize their physiologic state.

Mothers typically administered to the infant's needs with quick, abrupt, and vigorous movements. Grandmothers, who provided most of the care during the first month of life, were especially rough in their handling of these small but motorically active infants. This type of motor stimulation was most noticeable during bathing (Hopkins, 1976; Leboyer, 1976). The Indian bath is an elaborate, formal routine of daily massage which starts in the first few days of life and continues throughout the first year (see Figure 1). It begins with the infant lying prone on the mother's outstretched legs. Each part of the infant's body is stretched and prodded. Then, with tepid water and soap, the feet and legs are massaged, followed by the arms, back, abdomen, neck, and face. Exhausted from the intensity of this stimulation, the infant is swaddled and then enters into a prolonged sleep.

The abrupt handling of the infant was observed only during caregiving activities; at other times no efforts were made to stimulate the infant motorically. Infants were not played with, nor engaged in en-face play behaviors. Moreover, their motor activity was usually interpreted as a signal of distress to which the

Photo 1.   Daily infant bath and massage performed by maternal grandmother.

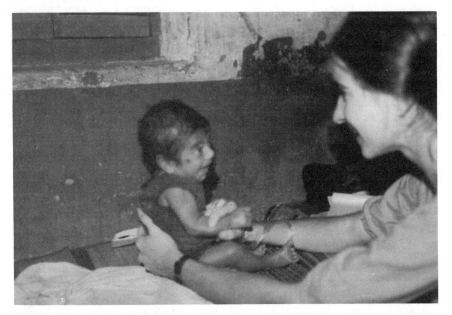

Photo 2.   One month old infant showing marked head control during pull-to-sit.

mothers responded with feeding and/or rocking. To console by rocking, the infant was placed upright on the mother's outstreched legs. Continuous rocking movements were instigated by tapping the infant's back, and the infant was required to maintian adequate head and neck control.

The effect of this early and constant motor stimulation on the pattern of the Indian infants' development is apparent from the comparative data from a group of Caucasion American middle-class infants (Landers, 1983). On the individual item Pull-to-Sit, which measures girdle strength as well as the degree of balance between flexor and extensor muscles, the American infant performed significantly better than the Indian infant on day 1. By day 10, however, this pattern was reversed, with the mean for Indian infants reaching a high of 7.1, in comparison to a U.S. mean of 6.0 ($p \leq .005$). It was suggested that the superior performance of the Indian infants by day 10 is evidence for the interplay between their given biological potential for early motor development and the type and quality of environmental stimulation they received (see Figure 2).

Range of State

The items comprising this cluster assess the difficulty in rousing certain infants from a sleep state to an alert state with disturbing stimuli, the rapidity with which they go from sleep to crying, and the lability that certain infants demonstrate as they move rapidly from one state to another.

For this sample, the ANOVA did not show any significant change in the Range of State cluster. The overall mean score of 3.5 suggests that these infants are performing on the lower end of the rapidity, peak, and lability of state changes scale. Generally speaking, the infants were somewhat irritable, and also hypersensitive to stimulation as they moved rapidly into an intense crying state in which they did not respond or interact with the external environment. The lack of improvement in the mean scores of this cluster over time is particularly disturbing. However, there is a large standard deviation for this cluster, which may point to potentially strong within-group differences.

Regulation of State

This cluster assesses the neonate's use of state behavior, and the infants are assessed for their capacity to shut out disturbing stimulation. The ANOVA for this cluster was significant and shows a generally decreasing linear trend over time from a mean score of 6.5 on day 1 to a score of 4.9 on day 30. The decrease in mean score on day 30 may indicate the scale's upper limit for this cluster, which these infants reached on day 10. Perhaps at 1 month the infant requires increasingly complex and demanding stimulation from the environment in order to maintain an alert and active state. Throughout the first few days of the infants' lives, they performed in the mid-to-upper range of the scale. They reacted almost instantly to being cuddled by the examiner by leaning on the examiner's shoulder and nestling their heads in the crook of the examiner's neck. Less optimal behaviors would have been characterized by active resistance or passive involvement. This responsiveness to the examiner is an important source of rewarding feedback and indicates the infant's positive contribution to the infant-caregiver relationship. An additional indicator of state regulation is the infant's capacity to exhibit self-quieting behaviors. Even during the first or second exam infants would spontaneously bring his or her state under control by hand-to-mouth movements.

Autonomic Regulation

This cluster assesses infants response to the physiological demands of their immaturity and the stresses of labor and delivery. In this exam, autonomic stability is measured by tremulousness, amount of startle during exam, and lability of skin color. As seen in Table 8, the ANOVA for this cluster was significant and the difference in mean scores accounted for by both the linear and quadratic trends. Scores were in the optimal range on day 1 and increased throughout the first seven days. By day 7, the scores had stabilized and reached a mean of 7.6. In general, these infants showed few startles and tremors and had healthy skin color that changed only minimally throughout the exam.

As suggested by the results of the Habituation cluster, the optimal autonomic regulation exhibited by these infants may be related to the practice of swaddling. These data support the results of previous investigators (Brackbill, 1973; Giacoman, 1971; Lipton et al., 1965) and suggest that the technique of swaddling is related to a decrease in the number of startles seen in the newborn period. It is suggested that this occurs because of the decreased afferent proprioceptive stimuli to the central reticular formation of the brain stem, which reduces the overall arousal level. It is further argued that the constant tactile proprioceptive stimulation of the swaddling material may be an important motor restraint.

Reflexes

The Reflex cluster, which is the total number of abnormal reflex scores such that a higher score indicates a greater number of deviant reflexes, shows a significant linear trend ($p \leq .001$). The decrease in mean scores from a high of 2.2 to a low of .5 shows the pattern of recovery in reflex activity during the first month of life. Of the 16 elicited reflexes, an increased sucking and rooting response, as well as decreased walking, stepping, and incurvation response, accounted for most of the deviation in the early days of life. The exaggerated sucking and rooting response can be related to hunger and rate of milk flow (Brazelton et al., 1976), and in the early exams these infants did show signs of hunger. The hypotonic walking and stepping responses seen early on may also be the result of the depleted nutritional stores as a result of poor intrauterine growth. Incurvation of the trunk often did not appear until day 5 or day 7. Asymmetry also was apparent, with the response first emerging on one side only. According to Prechtl and Beintema (1964), this response is often weak or absent in the first few days and thus this decreased response was not indicative of any abnormality. In general, the reflex activity of these infants was evidence in favor of an intact central nervous system.

In summary, the repeated-measures analysis of variance provided a description of the BNBAS performance of a group of 30 healthy South Indian newborns in the first month of life. The most salient finding is the increase in performance over time on the Habituation, Motor Performance, Autonomic Regulation, and Reflex clusters. For each of these clusters, optimal performance was seen on day 30, following a general systematic up and down pattern on days 5, 7, and 10. On two of the seven clusters, Habituation and Autonomic Regulation, the infants performed in the optimal range. Mid-range performance was seen initially on both the Orientation and Range of State clusters and showed no significant improvement throughout the first month. This behavior and the neurological development profile was interpreted as an interaction of environmental forces and cultural practices.

In particular, the analysis focused on the following three aspects of the environment: the effects of swaddling on infant development; the type and quality of motor stimulation; and the mother-infant interaction and its effect on the infant's social responsivity. It was suggested that the optimal performance on the Habituation and Autonomic Regulation clusters was related to the restraining and calming influences of the swaddling techniques employed by this community. Maternal behaviors seemed to contribute to the development of infant motor activity, specifically the combination of vigorous motor stimulation coupled with constraining and consoling behaviors. Finally, it was suggested that the poor orientation responses exhibited by these infants was related to the lack of maternal expectations for social responsivity and the less than ideal circumstances under which the exam was performed.

Maternal Factors and Brazelton Scale Performance

It has been suggested that BNBAS performance is affected by several infant and maternal biomedical factors and that these factors may vary within different cultural groups (Lester & Brazelton, 1982). In an effort to determine how these forces operate within this sample of infants, BNBAS performance was correlated with a number of maternal and infant variables. Maternal factors included in the analysis were age, parity, height, weight, arm circumference, family wealth, and literacy. Infant behavior was measured by performance on BNBAS cluster scores at three time periods throughout the first month. Exams performed on days 1 and 3 characterized an early exam; the middle period consisted of exams on days 5, 7, and 10, with the final or late exam performed on day 30. Several of these correlations were significant and the results are presented in Table 9.

Maternal Age and Parity

An increased number of deviant reflex scores were significantly associated with both increasing maternal age and parity. These correlations reached significance at the $\rho \leq .005$. The Range of State cluster was negatively associated with parity, which suggests that the infants of multiparous mothers were more irritable, hypersensitive to environmental stimulus and rapidly came to an alert state during the administration of an exam. The Habituation cluster, however, was correlated with parity in the opposite direction, but reached statistical significance only during the early examination period (days 1 and 3). This association suggested that infants of older multiparous mothers demonstrated greater competence in shutting out disturbing stimuli when in the sleep state. Thus, in spite of a behavioral profile characterized by irritability, hyperexcitability, and rapid shifts of state, these infants demonstrated an ability for sleep-state regulation. This relationship between parity and BNBAS performance was described by Dixon, Tronick, Keefer, and Brazelton (1982) as being characteristic of the infants born to older multiparous Gusii mothers of Kenya. With the exception of the Range of

Table 9. Correlations: Maternal Medical/Social Factors and Infant Behavior (BNBAS)

Brazelton Scale Cluster	Age			Parity			Height			Weight			Arm circumference			Family Wealth Index			Literacy		
	E	M	L	E	M	L	E	M	L	E	M	L	E	M	L	E	M	L	E	M	L
Habituation	.40*																.45**				
Orientation																					
Motor Performance																.52*			.40*		
Range of State					-.36*	-.43*				-.58*			-.66***								
Regulation of State															-.55*						
Autonomic Regulation								-.60**		-.50*	-.53*		-.64**				.40*			.48**	
Reflexes	.66***	.67***			.62***			-.50*			-.53*										

Note. Early exam performed on days 1, 3; middle exam performed on days 5, 7, 10; late exam performed on day 30.
*p ≤ .05.   **p ≤ .01.   ***p ≤ .005.

191

State cluster, these relationships between parity and maternal age and BNBAS performance were not significant in the final examination.

Maternal Size

Maternal size as measured by height, weight, and arm circumference was significantly correlated with several of the BNBAS clusters. The number of deviant reflexes was found to increase as maternal height and weight decreased. There was no significant relationship between maternal arm circumference and the number of deviant reflexes. The two clusters describing the infant's range of state and regulation of state were negatively associated with maternal weight and arm circumference. This suggests that lighter mothers were more likely to produce quiet, passive infants who were easily consoled when brought to higher levels of state activity. Autonomic regulation, which includes the lability of skin color and the number of startles and tremors during an exam, was negatively associated with both maternal height and weight. Thus the lighter mothers delivered infants who showed little or no signs of physiologic stress during an exam. As is evident from the data in Table 9, none of the correlations between maternal size and infant behavior reached statistical significance on the final exam.

Socioeconomic Status and Education

Socioeconomic status, as measured by the Family Wealth Index and maternal literacy rate, was positively related to infant behavior during the early and middle examination periods. Increasing education, as well as higher socioeconomic status, was positively associated with both the autonomic regulation and motor clusters. Thus the more literate mothers from wealthier families were more likely to produce motorically mature and active infants who showed few signs of physiologic stress during an exam. The Family Wealth Index was also positively correlated with the infant's ability to shut out disturbing stimuli as measured by the Habituation cluster during the middle examination periods.

In summary, this normal infant sample demonstrated several interesting relationships between behavior outcome and maternal status. It appears that an increase in the number of deviant reflexes was significantly related to both increasing age and parity and decreasing maternal size. As Prechtl and Beintema (1964) have suggested, deviant reflexes do not immediately imply neurological dysfunction but only identify those infants who may be suspect for future abnormalities. It is interesting, therefore, that by the late examination period none of the correlations with the Reflex cluster reached statistical significance, suggesting that whatever abnormalities had been observed initially had been overcome by the organism. The correlation between the Range-of-State cluster and maternal perinatal factors was not in the originally anticipated direction. It was found that high-risk maternal factors such as increasing age and parity and small maternal stature were associated with increased performance in the infants' capacity for state control. This behavior is in contrast to the more intense and demanding behaviors characterizing the infant whose mother did not exhibit seemingly high-risk maternal factors. These infants of were effective in eliciting maternal responsivity through the use of rapid-state swings. By crying, they demanded to be held, cuddled, or fed, while the infants of lower-weight mothers were less likely to use their state behaviors to elicit maternal responsivity. It was interesting to note the positive effects of increasing maternal education on infant performance in terms of motor, habituation, and autonomic regulatory capacity. The only cluster not affected by the investigated perinatal factors was Orientation. This fact is of particular interest and suggests that the given biological capacity for responsive behaviors is not significantly affected by the perinatal factors, at least within the range exhibited by this sample of mothers.

As is evident from the data in Table 9, the relationship between maternal factors and BNBAS performance is strongest in the middle exam period (days 5, 7, 10) which suggests that the environmental factors are beginning to exert their influence over the biological influences present at birth. The infant's behavior immediately after birth is erratic, and the effects of environmental influence are less likely to be manifested. A more consistent picture of the infant behavioral profile as shaped by genetic and intrauterine experiences emerges after an initial reorganization period following birth (Dixon et al., 1982). Moreover, by the middle exam period, the infants are adapting to their home environments, and the impact of maternal and environmental variability is more likely to be seen.

Infant Physical Characteristics and Brazelton Scale Performance

As is evident from the data in Table 10, only a few of the infants' physical characteristics were significantly correlated with the BNBAS cluster scores, most of which occurred during the middle examination period.

Birthweight had the most effect on BNBAS outcome, and an interesting behavioral profile typifying the smaller infants began to emerge. Negative associations were found for the Habituation and Range of State clusters. This suggests more optimal performance by the lower-weight infant in the ability to shut out disturbing stimuli and the capacity to move slowly from one state to another. Thus the lower-weight infants could maintain deep-sleep states and were somewhat less vulnerable to the manipulations and ministrations of the examiner. Because of their optimal state regulation they were less easily excited, and came to and maintained an alert state 4 for longer periods. An increase in the number of deviant reflexes was related to low birthweight, an association which is significant on both middle and late exams.

The association between motor performance and birthweight was positive, which suggests that the heavier infants had more optimal motor behavior, as assessed by tone, maturity, pull-to-sit behavior, defensive movements, and ac-

Table 10.   Correlations: Infant Physical Characteristics[a] and BNBAS Performance

Brazelton Scale Cluster	Birthweight			Length			Ponderal Index			Weight (1 month)		
	E[b]	M	L	E	M	L	E	M	L	E	M	L
Habituation	−.41*											
Orientation												.46*
Motor		.41*			.49**							
Range of State		−.42*										
State of Regulation								−.43*				
Autonomic Regulation												
Reflex		−.49**	−.41*				−.38*				−.38*	

[a]Head circumference was not significant.
[b]Early exam performed on days 1, 3,; middle exam performed on days 5, 7, 10; late exam performed on day 30.
*$p \leq .05$.   **$p \leq .01$.

tivity. An enhanced motor performance also was positively related to birth length during the middle examination periods. There were no significant associations between head circumference and infant behavior. Weight at 1 month was positively correlated to the Orientation cluster on the final exam and negatively correlated to the Reflexes cluster during the middle period. Thus, those infants who weighed the most at 1 month exhibited better alerting, orienting, and following responses to both inanimate and animate stimulation.

The relationship to the Reflex cluster implies that the number of deviant reflexes seen in the middle examination period was greater for those infants who weighed less at 1 month. The ponderal index (PI) was computed for each infant and correlated with BNBAS cluster scores (Brazelton et al., 1976). The PI is used in the assessment of fetal malnutrition, and a low PI score indicates thinness, and a high score, obesity. The PI was associated in the early examination period with the Reflex cluster, and with the State of Regulation cluster in the middle exam period. These correlations suggested that a low PI, indicative of thinness, was associated with an increased number of deviant reflex scores and a decreased capacity for state regulation. These infants were somewhat more irritable, hypersensitive to stimulation, and less able to console themselves when upset.

These data suggest that the low-PI and lighter-weight infants in the sample are somewhat, although not dramatically, distinct—and curiously so, as their associations to BNBAS cluster scores were not always in the direction anticipated. It appears that the low-PI infants had less capacity for state regulation and an increased number of deviant reflexes and poorer motor performance than the heavier infants in this sample.

In order to obtain a more complete understanding of the effects of birthweight and PI on infant behavior, a one-way repeated-measure ANOVA was performed to see if either birthweight or PI had any effect on BNBAS performance. Infants were divided into three groups according to the 75th, 50th, and 25th percentile distribution for birthweight and ponderal index as defined by this sample.

In this analysis, BNBAS outcome was measured by the rate of change in performance as estimated by the slope of the best-fitting regression line for each of the clusters (Landers, 1983). The slope of the best-fitting regression line, computed for each of the seven BNBAS clusters, was used to indicate the rate of change on that cluster over the first month of life for each of the three birthweight groups, as well as each of the three PI groups. As a result of these two analyses, it was found that neither birthweight nor PI had any significant effects on the rate of change in BNBAS cluster scores. The trend observed from the correlational analysis between BNBAS performance and infant factors were not apparent upon further inspection of the data. In light of this information, the variability in BNBAS performance as measured by the rate of change in cluster scores exhibited by this sample of infants cannot be accounted for by the singular effects of either birthweight or ponderal index.

The simple correlation analysis of maternal, infant, and environmental factors on infants in the first 3 months indicated several important relationships that may be operating within this sample. This analysis, however, was based on the assumption that there are clear sequences of linear causality between variables of infant-risk status and later developmental outcome. Given the results of reviews of single-factor studies and their inability to explain relations between risk factors this approach has inherent limitations (Clarke & Clarke, 1976; McCall, Hogarty, & Hurlburt, 1972; Sameroff & Chandler, 1975). In contrast, risk scores that are based on multiple factors produce clearer results (Hobel, Hyvarinen, & Okada, 1973; Prechtl, 1968). It is suggested that the combination of risk variables will account for a greater amount of the variability exhibited by this sample. For a more complete understanding of the interaction between the biologic, cultural and social factors, the reader is referred to the multiple-factor analysis performed on this data set (Landers, 1983).

Infant Development at 3 Months

Anthropometric indicators

In an effort to monitor the path of early infant growth, anthropometric data and Bayley scores were obtained at 3 months. All assessment procedures were performed within the home environment. The means, standard deviations, and

Table 11. Mean, Standard Deviation, and Range of Outcome Measures at 3 Months

Measure	M	SD	Range
Weight (kg)	5.92	1.0	4.0–8.0
Length (cm)	61.3	2.5	55.0–66.0
Head circumference (cm)	40.3	2.2	37–47
Bayley Mental Developmental Index (MDI)	108.6	13.9	72–131
Bayley Psychomotor Developmental Index (PDI)	129.2	20.5	50–150

ranges for these items are presented at Table 11. The weight at 3 months ranged from 4.0 kg to 8.0 kg, with a mean of 5.92 kg. Males are slightly heavier than females with a mean of 6.0 kg and 5.84 kg, respectively. When weights were compared to U.S. standards, the following picture emerged. For male weight distribution, 22% were above the 90th percentile, 33% fell between the 50th and 90th percentiles, 22% fell between the 10th and 50th percentiles, and 22% fell below the 10th percentile. For female weight distribution, 33% fell above the

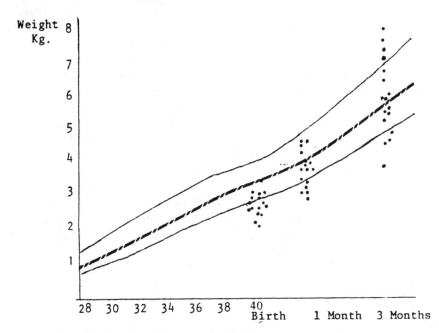

Figure 3. Boys Weight at Birth, One and Three Months: 90, 50, 10 centiles[1]

[1] Chart based on Western standards. Prepared by Drs. D. Gairdner and J. Pearson. Published and distributed by Castleread Publications, Castleread, Hertford, England, 1971.

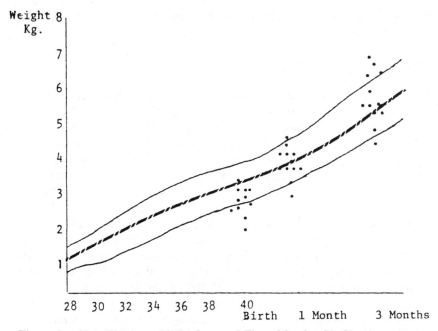

Figure 4.   Girls Weight at Birth, One, and Three Months: 90, 50, 10 centiles[1]

[1] Chart based on Western standards. Prepared by Drs. D. Gairdner and J. Pearson. Published and distributed by Castleread Publications, Castleread, Hertford, England, 1971.

90th percentile, 33% fell between the 50th and the 90th percentiles, and 1 child fell below the 10th percentile. Figures 3 and 4 graphically display this distribution.

As the graphs portray, the speed of growth from birth to 3 months is quite remarkable. The average gain in weight was 3.16 kg, compared to an average gain of 2.5 kg for American infants (Lowrey, 1973). In the Indian sample, 65% of the infants had doubled their birthweights by 3 months. The two additional measures of infant growth, length and head circumference, showed similar increases throughout the first 3 months. The mean crown-to-heel length was 61.3 cm, which corresponds to the 90th percentile of U.S. standards. Similarly, the mean head circumference for this group (40.3 cm) corresponded to the 50th percentile. By comparison, it is interesting to note that at birth the mean head circumference for this sample fell below the U.S. 10th percentile.

The mean weight for this sample is slightly higher than the weights reported by various investigators throughout India (Currimbhoy, 1963; Ghai & Sandu, 1968; Swaminathan, Jyothi, Singh, Madhavad, & Gopalan, 1964; Udani, 1963). The all-Indian mean weight for 3-month-old infants was 4.0 kg, while the higher mean reported for this sample stems in part from the selection of only healthy full-term infants and in part from the sample's longitudinal design. Moreover, the majority of Indian investigations have been cross-sectional and have included infants of all birthweights.

Bayley Performance

The Bayley Scales were administered to each infant, and the Mental Development Index (MDI) and Psychomotor Development Index (PDI) were calculated (Bayley, 1969). These indices are a normalized standard score with a mean of 100 and a range from 50 to 150, which covers more than three standard deviations on either side of the mean. For this sample, the mean MDI was 108.6, with a range of 72–131. The psychomotor index yielded a slightly higher mean score of 129.2 and a range that spanned the entire scale. It was further noted that 23% of the Indian infants had a motor index of 140 or above, a score achieved by less than 10% of the U.S. infants. While Indian infants performed similarly to American infants on tasks of cognitive development, specific items on the motor scale were in advance of the norms. These included the gross motor abilities such as head balance, unassisted upright sitting, and the ability to roll over from back to stomach. At 3 months of age more than 50% of the Indian infants had these abilities, in comparison to the mean age of 4.2, 5.3, and 6.4 months, respectively, for each of the abilities in the standardized U.S. sample. In fine motor performance, partial thumb opposition while holding a cube was more advanced for the Indian infants. These data support the notion of an enhanced motor development, which was suggested by the analysis of Brazelton data in the first month of life.

Table 12 presents the correlations between the 3-month outcome measures. As indicated in the table, the MDI and PDI were highly correlated at .64, which supports the premise that early motor and cognitive development are highly correlated. It is argued that motor development, through its emphasis on and concern with the development of sensory and motor processes associated with active movement and physical exploration of the extended environment, provides the basic foundation for the development of higher-ordered informa-

Table 12.   Correlation Matrix of 3-Month Outcome Measures

	Length	Head circumference	MDI	PDI
Weight	.53****	.66****	.30	.53****
Length		.11	.26	.39**
Head circumference			.16	.32*
MDI				.64****

*.05 ≤ p ≤ .10.   **p ≤ .05.   ***p ≤ .01.   ****p ≤ .005.

tion-processing system upon which more sophisticated perceptual and cognitive processes are ultimately built. The evidence suggests that the feedback provided to the young infants as a result of their active exploration of and interaction with the environment is a stimulation for continued perceptual and cognitive growth (Williams, 1983). While there were no significant correlations between the MDI and anthropometric variables, the PDI was correlated with both the infant's weight and length at 3 months, suggesting that the larger infants were more motorically advanced than the smaller infants. Furthermore, the PDI was significantly correlated to weight at 1 month and positively although not significantly related to weight at birth.

In summary, the data described the growth of a group of healthy infants, characterized by a dramatic rate of physical growth, advanced motor performance, and patterns of cognitive development, similar to that of a group of American infants. This pattern of development mirrors the course of adaptation evidenced by this sample in the first month of life.

Discussion

On the basis of conceptions of high-risk perinatal factors developed in the United States (Hobel et al., 1973; Prechtl, 1968), many of the mothers in this sample would have been placed in a high-risk category. These factors would be low weight, small stature, high parity, poor weight gain during pregnancy, nonantiseptic techniques, and unmonitored deliveries, added to the environmental conditions of crowded, dark huts. In spite of these circumstances, the infants produced were small but motorically organized and physically intact. Those infants with a low PI, indicative of intrauterine malnutrition, did not exhibit to the same degree the hypersensitive, irritable behaviors characterizing full-term but undernourished American infants. The pattern of recovery exhibited by this group of infants throughout the first month of life was even more dramatic by 3 months of age. Their developmental profile was characterized by increased speed of physical growth, advanced motor development, and patterns of cognitive performance that were similar to standards set by American infants at 3 months of age.

Although exploratory in nature, findings from the data presented here challenge a number of widely accepted assumptions concerning the relationship between prenatal and perinatal circumstances and infant growth. These data lend themselves to the consideration of three perspectives: the efficacy and adaptability of the biological organism to overcome the demands of a stressful environment; the effectiveness of culturally different infant-rearing patterns; and the unique psychological makeup and identity development of the Indian woman.

Biological Adaptability

The behavior of this group of infants exemplifies the adaptability of the human infant, when confronted with continued and persistent stress, in returning to a predetermined developmental pathway. Nutritional, obstetrical, and social stress factors of the maternal prenatal and perinatal environment should not be under-emphasized. But this behavior underscores the awesome capacity of the species to adjust in accordance with the degree of stress imposed. The developmental pattern described by this group of infants emphasizes the preadapted variablity in the human infant, especially as it functions to overcome the obstacles to growth under less than ideal circumstances. The infants demonstrated the ability of the human species to overcome deflection and to return to a predetermined develop-mental pathway which, as Waddington (1962) has suggested, is in itself a biolog-ical goal. This process was particularly salient in the dramatic catch-up weight gain exhibited by this sample during the first 3 months of life. By 3 months of age, 58% of the infants were above the 50th percentile of weight based on U.S. standards, while at birth only 1 infant was above the 50th percentile and 48% fell below the 10th percentile.

The pattern of infant feeding displayed by this community was characterized by constant maternal proximity and availability, which enabled breast-feeding on demand. It has been argued that the biologic capacity for catch-up growth is inherent in our species, and the maternal feeding practices described here al-lowed this preprogrammed adaptability to unfold. For example, the antibodies, lysozomes, lymphocytes, macrophages, and other components of colostrum and transitional breast milk serve to defend against infection, which may have been major "predator" during evolution (Goldman & Smith, 1973; Gyorgy, 1967; Jelliffe & Jelliffe, 1971; Lozoff, Brittenham, Trause, Kennell, & Klaus, 1977; Stohiar, Pelley, Kaniecki-Green, Klaus, & Carpenter, 1976). Because of these properties, a significantly enhanced resistance to enteric infection has been ob-served among breast-fed babies not only when the environment is favorable but also when the environmental sanitation was at less than acceptable levels (Mata, 1978; Mata & Wyatt, 1971).

In addition the composition of the breast milk is particularly well suited to the pattern of feeding exhibited by the mothers of this community. In species that nest or cache their infants, breast milk is high in protein and fat, mother-infant contact is intermittent and feedings are spaced from 2 to 15 hours apart (Dumo-nd, 1975). By receiving their total nutritional requirements in short periods, these infants are adapted for long separations.

In contrast, species in which infants are carried by, hibernate with, or follow their mothers have low-fat, low-protein breast milk, constant maternal-infant contact, and essentially continuous feeding (Ben-Shaul, 1962). Human milk is low in fat and extremely low in proteins. Since human infants are immobile at birth, the insights of comparative physiology have identified the pattern of human care as that of carrying and continuous feeding (Blurton Jones, 1972). Thus the culturally determined patterns of continuous feeding, made possible through constant maternal availability, support, reinforce, and enhance the biologic pre-adaptability of our species. When viewed in this light, the ability of these infants to exhibit catch-up growth is simply part of the developmental script of the human species.

Another enlightening point raised by these data relates to our understanding of developmental deviations and suggests that early deviations from expected patterns of growth occur as a result of the environmental forces that constrain and defeat the organism's self-righting tendencies and inherent ability to return to the path of normality (Sameroff, 1975).

Child-Rearing Patterns

A second conceptual issue raised by the data relates to the role of the child-rearing environment and its ability to influence the developmental pathway. In this highly supportive environment, it seems that even the most vulnerable infants were integrated into the family in a manner which fostered their capacity for recovery. In commenting on this issue, LeVine (1977, p.16) states that "cultural evolution within human populations also produces standardized strategies reflecting environmental pressures from a more recent past, encoded in customs rather than genes and transmitted socially rather than biologically." The patterns of infant rearing exhibited by this community and their effects on development address specifically the quality and quantity of tactile-kinesthetic stimulation and the degree and kind of maternal social responsivity. The possible effects of these behaviors on early infant development is suggested by these data.

As described earlier, the motoric stimulation received by these infants, reflected in the elaborate daily bath and massage, seemed particularly well suited to these motorically precocious infants and paved the way for increasingly complex motor organization. At 3 months of age the infants are above U.S. standards for motor development as measured on the Bayley Scales, with certain items involving head control 2–3 months ahead of U.S. norms. Active motoric stimulation was complemented by swaddling techniques which seemed to be related to an increased capacity to habituate to disturbing stimulation and maintain autonomic regulation as measured by the Brazelton Scale throughout the first month. It was suggested that these tactile-kinesthetic ministrations are directly related to the advanced motor performance characterizing this group of infants in the early months of life. Rapid motor development in infancy has been reported by other cross-cultural investigators (Super, 1981a; 1981b). Fundamental to all these cultures is the increased amount of kinesthetic stimulation, maternal proximity, and rapid response to distress signals.

Experimental studies of the human infant given supplemental kinesthetic stimulation confirm these findings. Kinesthetic stimulation was found to exert a reinforcing effect on the smiling response of 4-to-5-month-old infants (Brossard & DeCarie, 1968) and to be more effective than tactile stimulation in soothing the neonate (Korner & Thoman, 1972). In another study, premature infants given supplementary kinesthetic stimulation by rocking for 30 minutes each day had significant weight gains when compared to matched controls (Freedman, cited in Ambrose, 1969). Scarr-Salapatek and Williams (1973), investigating the effects of early stimulation on low-birthweight infants, found that infants who received increased visual tactile and kinesthetic stimulation in the first year had better grasp reflexes, greater alertness, and increased weight gain at age 4 weeks, and higher Cattel scores at 1 year. In a study of 6-month-old infants, Yarrow, Rubenstein, and Pederson (1975) found that among all the sensory modes investigated, kinesthetic vestibular stimulation was of singular importance.

A second idea in which the culture of Indian infancy exhibits an adaptive pattern of response focuses on the type and quality of maternal social responsivity. Mothers, following rather than leading while interacting with their infants, responded instantly to the slightest indication of infant distress. In the early months of life, distress signals are interpreted as a hunger call and the infants are pacified by feeding. Particularly apparent was the paucity of maternal vocalizations directed toward the infant. Although their environment exposes them to a constant stream of human speech, infants are rarely the direct recipients of vocal exchange. The adaptive element of maternal behaviors concealed in patterns of child rearing is suggested by these observations. The Indian mother's immediate response to her infant's distress may be an adaptive reaction to the pressures of a harsh physical environment and threats of high rates of infant mortality. At the same time, her behavior conforms to the culture's emphasis on and value for dependency at the expense of behaviors which would shape the infant toward autonomous, creative, and individualized functioning.

A number of investigators have been concerned with the specific effects of contingent responsiveness to distress on infant development. Lewin and Goldberg (1969) suggested that the infant's awareness of a contingent relationship with the caregiver promotes cognitive development. They reported a significant relationship between maternal contingent behavior and the infant's habituation to a redundant stimulus, a measure believed to be a primary indicator of cognitive development. In a study of the maternal resposiveness to an infant's cry, it was found that a decreased latency of response resulted in a decreased amount of crying in the first year. Speculating that the infant's use of the cry as social communication is enhanced by the maternal contingent response, the authors rejected the notion that a rapid response to crying may interfere with the child's level of competence (Yarrow et al., 1975). A study of 6-month-old infants reported by Yarrow et al. (1975) found that a high level of maternal contingent response to distress was associated with higher scores on the Bayley Scales. In addition, three measures of cognitive motivation were positively associated and included goal directedness, reaching and grasping, and secondary circular relations. In interpreting these results, Lewin and Goldberg (1969) speculated that immediate response to an infant's distress may facilitate the infant's motivation to interact with the environment. Goal directedness (a measure indexing persistent attempts to secure objects not immediately available) and secondary circular reactions (behaviors involving the repetition of actions to produce feedback) may be early expressions of the infant's attempt to master the environment. The observations of this study support the results of past investigators and suggest that rapid maternal response to an infant's cry reinforces active coping with the infant's environment and enhances the infant's persistence in eliciting feedback.

In describing the beliefs and practices typifying early infant care in this South Indian community, the analytical framework of childrearing as cultural adaptation defined by LeVine (1977) is particularly applicable. The data presented here support his conclusion that culture no less than biology contributes to the way in which parents perceive the tasks of child rearing. Moreover, these ways are rational and contain information about environmental contingencies previously experienced by the population and assimilated into its cultural tradition. Parents who rigidly conform to customary prescriptions may not be aware of their past or present efficacy but may view them as religiously or ethically ordained. Finally, as LeVine states, if we are to understand the constraints within which cultural values operate and to assess the prospects of change, the adaptive component concealed in child-rearing customs must be clarified (LeVine, 1977, p. 17).

Maternal Commitment

The observed ability of these infants to meet the demands of their environment warrants the investigation of the powerful psychosocial commitment of the Indian mother to the survival of her infant and the confidence with which she ministers to the infant's needs. It is argued that the psychosocial development of the Indian mother evolved from the interplay between universal processes of human development and the set historical trends, religious ideals and social institutions unique to the Indian culture. It is further suggested that the mother's response to the demands of her infant reflect both her deeply rooted emotional stance toward her infant and the culture's perception and value of the child. The Indian mother's psychosocial commitment to her child emerges out of an extended family system which instructs, rewards, and supports her in these efforts. According to Kakar's (1978) analysis, this deference and indulgence in Indian motherhood has psychological origins in the identity development of the Indian woman. As a daughter, an Indian girl is merely a sojourner in her own family, and in marriage her status is changed to daughter-in-law rather than wife. It is only with motherhood that she comes into her own and can establish her position within the family, community, and life cycle. Her role from thence forward is a powerful one. As reflected in the popular devotional Krishna mythology, the child is traditionally perceived as a completely innocent being, a gift of the gods, towards whom one is expected to shower deepest protection, affection and indulgence (Kakar, 1979). Also, according to traditional Hindu thought, it is the child, with spontaneity and intense capacity for sorrow and joy, who comes closest to the divine state. It is the adult who must learn what it is the child has to teach (Kinsley, 1977).

In conclusion, these data emphasize that the application of universal risk factors in development must be viewed with caution since the mechanisms through which they exert their effect varies both between and within cultures. For a given factor, the degree of risk imposed is directly related to the culturally defined structures and institutions that have evolved to buffer its impact. Thus, we must continue in our efforts to construct paradigms that allow for the systematic analysis of the contexts that directly and indirectly influence the developmental pathway.

References

Agarwal, K. N., & Agarwal, D. K. (1981). Infant feeding in India. *Indian Journal of Pediatrics, 49*, 285.

Als, H., Tronick, E., Lester, B., & Brazelton, T. B. (1979). Specific neonatal measures: The Brazelton Neonatal Assessment Scale. In J. D. Osofsky (Ed.), *The handbook of infant development*. New York: Wiley.

Ambrose, A. (Ed.) (1969). *Stimulation in early infancy development*. New York: Academic Press.

Bayley, N. (1969). *Manual for the Bayley Scales of Infant Development*.New York: Psychological Corporation.

Ben-Shaul, D. (1962). The composition of the milk of wild animals. *International Zoo Yearbook, 4*, 33.

Bhargava, S. K., & Ghosh, S. (1974). Nomenclature of the newborn. *Indian Pediatrics, 11*, 443.

Bhargava, S. K., Kumari, S., Choudhury, P., & Lall, U. B. (1980). A longitudinal study of physical growth from birth to six years in children with birth weights of 2501g. or more. *Indian Pediatrics, 17*, 495.

Blurton Jones, N. (1972). Comparative aspects of mother-child contact. In Blurton Jones (Ed.), *Ethological studies of child behavior*. London: Cambridge University Press.

Brackbill, Y. (1973). Continuous stimulation reduces arousal level: Stability of the effects over time. *Child Development, 44*, 43.

Brazelton, T. B. (1973). *Neonatal Behavioral Assessment Scale*. London: Spastics International Medical Publications/Heinemann Medical Books.

Brazelton, T. B., Parker, W., & Zuckerman, B. (1976). Importance of behavioral assessment in the neonate. In L. Gluck (Ed.), *Current Problems in Pediatrics, 7*, 2.

Brossard, L. M., & DeCarie, T. G. (1968). Comparative reinforcing effect of eight stimulations on the smiling response of infants. *Journal of Child Psychology and Psychiatry*, *9*, 51.

Bruning, J., & Kintz, B. L. (1977). *Computational handbook of statistics*. Chicago: Scott, Foresman.

Census of India (1971). Series-14 Mysore Part VI-A, Town Directory. Mysore: Padmanabha, I.A.S.

Chisholm, J. S. (1978). Swaddling, cradleboards and development of children. *Early Human Development*, *2*(3), 255.

Clarke, A. M., & Clarke, A. D. (1976). *Early experience: Myth and evidence*. London: Open Books.

Currimbhoy, A. (1963). Growth and development of Bombay children. *Indian Journal of Child Health*, *12*, 627.

Datta Banik, N. D. (1978). A study of the incidence of different birth weight babies and related factors. *Indian Pediatrics*, *15*, 327.

de Vries, M., & Super, C. (1978). Contextual influences on the Neonatal Behavioral Assessment Scale and implications for its cross-cultural use. In A. J. Sameroff (Ed.), Organization and stability of newborn behavior: A commentary on the Brazelton Neonatal Behavioral Assessment Scale. *Monographs of the Society for Research in Child Development*, *43* (5–6, Serial No. 177), 92–101.

Dickson, W. J. (Ed.). (1981). *B.M.D.P. Statistical Software*. Berkeley: University of California Press.

Diwakar, R. R. (1968). *Karnataka through the ages*. Bangalore, India: Government of Mysore.

Dixon, S., Tronick, E., Keefer, C., & Brazelton, T. B. (1982). Perinatal circumstances and newborn among the Gusii of Kenya. *Infant Behavior and Development*, *5*, 11.

Dumond, D. E. (1975). The limitation of human population: A natural history. *Science*, *187*, 713.

Gairdner, D., & Pearson, J. (1971). *Growth charts*. Hertford, England: Castlemead Publications, 1971.

Ghai, O. P., & Sandu, R. K. (1968). Study of physical growth of Indian children in Delhi. *Indian Journal of Pediatrics*, *35*, 92.

Ghosh, S. (1970). Low birth weight [Editorial]. *Indian Pediatrics*, *7*, 65.

Giacoman, S. L. (1971). The effects of hunger and motor restraint on arousal and visual attention in the infant. *Child Development*, *42*, 605.

Goldman, A. S., & Smith, C. W. (1973). Host resistance factors in human milk. *Journal of Pediatrics*, *83*, 1082.

Gyorgy, P. (1967). Human milk and resistance to infection. In *Nutrition and Infection* (Ciba Foundation Study Group No. 31). Boston: Little, Brown.

Hobel, C. J., Hyvarinen, M. A., & Okada, D. (1973). Prenatal and intrapartum high risk screening. *American Journal of Obstetrics and Gynecology*, *1*, 1171.

Hopkins, B. 1976). Culturally determined patterns of handling the human infant. *Journal of Human Movement Studies*, *2*, 1.

Hukkerikar, R. S. (1955). *Karnataka Darshana*. Bombay: Perfecta Printing Works.

Jelliffe, D. B., & Jelliffe, E. F. P. (1971). The uniqueness of human milk. *American Journal of Clinical Nutrition*, *24*, 968.

Kakar, S. (1978). *The Inner World*. New York: Oxford University Press.

Kakar, S. (1979). *Indian Childhood: Cultural Ideals and Social Reality*. London: Oxford University Press.

Kinsley, D. (1977). *The sword and the flute*. Berkeley: University of California Press.

Kirk, R. (1968). *Experimental Design: Procedures for the Behavioral Sciences*. California: Wadsworth.

Korner, A. F., & Thoman, E. B. (1972). The relative efficacy of contact and vestibular-proprioceptive stimulation in soothing neonates. *Child Development, 43*, 443.

Kurien, J. (1980). Social factors and economic organization of the traditional small-scale fisherman of India. *Social Action, 30*, 111.

Landers, C. (1983). *Biological, social, and cultural determinants of infant behavior in a South Indian fishing village*. Unpublished thesis, Harvard Graduate School of Education.

Leboyer, F. (1976). *Loving Hands*. New York: Knopf.

Lester, B. M., Als, H., & Brazelton, T. B. (1982). Regional obstetrics anesthesia and newborn behavior: A reanalysis towards synergistic effects. *Child Development, 53*, 687.

Lester, B. M., & Brazelton, T. B. (1982). Cross-cultural assessment of neonatal behavior. In D. A. Wagner & H. W. Stevenson (Eds.), *Cultural perspectives on child development*. San Francisco: Freeman.

LeVine, R. A. (1977). Child rearing as cultural adaptation. In H. Leiderman, S. Tulkin, & A. Rosenfeld (Eds.), *Culture and infancy*. New York: Academic Press.

Levinson, F. J. (1974). *Morinda: An economic analysis of malnutrition among young children in rural India*. Cambridge, MA: MIT Press.

Lewin, M., & Goldberg, S. (1969). Perceptual-cognitive development in infancy: A generalized expectancy model as a function of the mother-infant relationship. *Merrill-Palmer Quarterly,15*, 81.

Lipton, E. L., Steinschneider, A., & Richmand, J. B. (1965). Swaddling, a child care practice: Historical, cultural and experimental observations. *Pediatrics, 35* (Supplement), 521.

Lowrey, G. H. (1973). *Growth and development of children*. Chicago: Yearbook Medical Publishers.

Lozoff, B., Brittenham, G., Trause, M., Kennell, J., & Klaus, M. (1977). The mother-newborn relationship: Limits of adaptability. *Journal of Pediatrics, 91*.

Mata, L. J. (1978). *The Children of Santa Maria Cauque: A prospective field study of health and growth*. Cambridge, MA: MIT Press.

Mata, L. J., & Wyatt, R. G. (1971). Host resistance to infection. *American Journal of Clinical Nutrition, 24*, 976.

McCall, R. B., Hogarty, P. S., & Hurlburt, N. (1972). Transitions in infant sensorimotor development and the prediction of childhood IQ. *American Psychologist, 27*.

National Center for Health Statistics. (1979a). *Weight by age and height for adults 18–74 Years: United States, 1971–1974* (U.S. Vital Health Statistics Series, *201*).

National Center for Health Statistics. (1979b). *Weight by age and height for adults 18–74 years: United States, 1971–1974* (U.S. Vital Health Statistics Series, *208*).

Norr, K. (1975). The organization of coastal fishing in Tamil Nadu. *Ethnology, 14*, 357.

Prechtl, H. F. (1968). Neurological findings in newborn infants after pre- and paranatal complications. In Jonxis, Visser, & Troelstra (Eds.), *Aspects of prematurity and dysmaturity*. Leiden, Holland: Stenfert Kroese.

Prechtl, H. F., & Beintema, O. (1964). *The neurological examination of the full term newborn infant.* London: Heinemann.

Sameroff, A. J. (1975). Early influences on development: Fact or fancy? *Merrill-Palmer Quarterly, 21,* 267.

Sameroff, A. J., & Chandler, M. J. (1975). Reproductive risk and the continuum of caretaking casuality. In F. Horowitz (Ed.), *Review of Child Development Research* (Vol. 4). Chicago: University of Chicago Press.

Scarr-Salapatek, S., & Williams, M. L. (1973). The effects of early stimulation on low-birthweight infants. *Child Development, 44,* 94.

Stohiar, O. A., Pelley, R. P., Kaniecki-Green, E., Klaus, M. H., & Carpenter, C. C. (1976). Secretory IgA against enterotoxins in breast milk. *Lancet, 1,* 1258.

Super, C. M. (1981a). Behavioral development in infancy. In R. H. Munroe, R. L. Munroe, & B. B. Whiting (Eds.), *Handbook of cross-cultural human development.* New York: Garland.

Super, C. M. (1981b). Cross-cultural research in infancy. In H. C. Triandis & A. Heron (Eds.), *Handbook of cross-cultural psychology: Vol. 4. Developmental Psychology.* Boston: Allyn & Bacon.

Swaminathan, M. C., Jyothi, K. K., Singh, R., Madhavad, S., & Gopalan, C. (1964). A semi-longitudinal study of growth of Indian children and related factors. *Indian Pediatrics, 1,* 255.

Udani, P. M. (1963). Physical growth of children in different socio-economic groups in Bombay. *Indian Journal of Child Health, 12,* 593.

Uklonskaya, R., Puri, B., Choudhari, N., Luthra, D., & Kumar, R. (1961). Physical development of infants in New Delhi in the first year of life. *Indian Journal of Child Health, 10,* 211.

Waddington, E. (1962). New patterns in genetics and development. New York: Columbia University Press.

Williams, H. (1983). *Perceptual and motor development.* Englewood Cliffs, NJ: Prentice-Hall.

Yarrow, L., Rubenstein, J., & Pederson, F. (1975). *Infant and environment: Early cognitive and motivational development.* New York: Wiley.

CHAPTER 8

The Effects of Extended Contact in the Neonatal Period on the Behavior of a Sample of Portuguese Mothers and Infants*

João C. Gomes Pedro

*Child Development Unit,
Clinica Pediatrica Universitaria,
Hospital de Santa Maria,
Lisbon, Portugal*

Introduction: The Cultural Context of Portugal

The origin of Portugal as an independent country goes back to the beginning of the 12th century, specifically 1143. Limited geographically by Spain on one side and the Atlantic Ocean on the other, and lacking sufficient internal resources, Portugal turned its attention to maritime exploration. The era of the discoveries that began in the 15th century marks the most glorious period of Portuguese history. The effects of this era are still with us in the strong cultural ties maintained between Portugal and nations of every continent. The high emigration rate to European countries, North America, and Brazil during the last few decades

---

*This research was supported in part by the Milupa Company.

I wish to express my gratitude to Dr. T. Berry Brazelton, M.D., of Boston; Prof. J. Kennell of Cleveland; and Prof. M. L. Levy and Prof. Salazar de Sousa of Lisbon for the support, confidence, and encouragement they all gave me during this research.

My thanks go also to Dr. K. Nugent, who trained me in the BNBAS, and to all on the team of Unidade de Desenvolvimento Infantil, Hospital de Santa Maria, Lisbon, Portugal: J. Bento de Almeida, C. S. Costa, A. Barbosa, M.J. Lobo Fernandes, N. Lacerda, F. Torgal, and R. Gouveia, who joined me in this research.

Fig. 1.   "Peixinheiras" de Lino António (1898–1976), oil, courtesy of National Museum of Contemporary Art, Lisbon.

has been one of the factors contributing to Portugal's continuing contact with other nations.

The Portuguese language is spoken by approximately 150 million people throughout the world. The Portuguese population, estimated to number about 10 million at present, are not uniformly distributed, the highest concentration being to the north of the Tagus River and along the coast. In fact, the sea stretching out from the 832 km of Portuguese coast has always been one of the horizons of this nation and has inspired most of the literature and art of Portugal.

Fishing and associated industries thus constitute a major part of the tertiary activities and represent in terms of employment one third of the total working population in Portugal. The country's 1983 Gross National Product per capita was U.S. $2,352, and the unemployment rate was 7.6% (Banco de Portugal, economic indicators, 1983).

The political system is a semipresidential democracy based on the sovereignty of the people, on the respect for and guarantee of fundamental rights, and on freedom of speech within political and religious organizations, though Portugal is traditionally a Catholic country.

In Portugal fertility has been declining steadily over the years. While in 1930 a woman married at age 20 could expect to have 6.1 children during her life, in 1970 the compound figure was down 26%, to 4.4 children. Similarly, the gross reproduction rate fell from 1.83 in 1930 to 1.06 in 1979. In addition, the proportion of births among older women has been dropping steadily. In 1931, 23.6% of all births were to women 35 years and over, but in 1979 this figure was down to only 10.7%. The average annual birth rate fell from 31 per 1,000 in 1900-1909 to an average of 16 per 1,000 by 1980 (average number of births/year: 154,000). This decline in fertility went hand in hand with a steady decline in mortality, with the mortality rate falling from 20 per 1,000 in 1900-1909 to 10 per 1,000 in 1980 (International Statistical Institute, *World Fertility Survey*, 1980). In terms of statistical data on child health, the infant mortality rate in Portugal was 26.02 per 1,000 in 1979 while the neonatal mortality rate was 15.74 per 1,000 in the same period (Statistical Department, Direcção Geral de Saúde, 1980). Two of the major causes of neonatal mortality continue to be obstetric trauma and neonatal anoxia. The conditions of affection that influence the mother and her child in the early neonatal period are clearly conditions of risk in child development in Portugal.

Modern Portuguese society does not provide adequate support for the mother-to-be. Moreover, the existence of the extended family is quite rare: The grandparents either have already died or live far away, making it difficult for them to give help to the new family. In most cases, the future parents have never had the opportunity to take care of a newborn baby and, further, this subject is not part of any school curriculum.

Having been in close contact over several years with labor wards, I have been able to consider the levels and nature of the woman's "stress", especially during the periods involving one of the most significant moments of her life: the birth of her child. In Portugal it still is common for the expectant mother to enter the ward alone, having said good bye to her husband or some other relative or friend at the door. The doctor or nurse who has dealt with her throughout the pregnancy generally is not present. Usually, the expectant mother knows no one around her. When she needs to talk, she can only do so with the expectant mother in the next bed, who is equally alone and anxious. She is forbidden to walk and, often, to change position, even when she states that this is what she feels like doing.

In the labor ward the expectant mother continues to be alone. She is obliged to stay in a routine position. Often she feels confused and sleepy as a result of the medications administered. Under these conditions, she can only partially cooperate; episiotomies and the use of forceps for delivery are frequent. When the baby is born the mother can have only a glance at the infant, and she is told that in a few hours she will be together with her child in the ward, where she will be visited by her husband.

I feel that the strict adherence to such a routine is the antithesis of natural human expression, and in itself may represent one of the first risks to child development, insofar as the bond between mother and child is concerned. To argue this case, especially from a clinical point of view, and with prevention as a priority, it is necessary to identify and then to strengthen the factors that are most directly linked with the process of bonding, and which can influence positively the interaction between the mother and her baby. I believe that one of these factors is the physical contact between the two immediately after birth (i.e., the newborn baby on the abdomen and chest of the mother, dressed or naked under a heat source).

The relevance of cross-cultural studies in child development has shown me the potential importance of investigating, with a defined Portuguese social group, the influence of early mother-infant contact on behavior. A review of the literature suggests that there are indications of a synergistic relationship between the biological and psychological variables in the background and social culture of the mother, and the behavior of the infant as evaluated by level of complex organization in the aspects emphasized by the Brazelton Neonatal Behavioral Assessment Scale (BNBAS; Brazelton, 1984).

The dynamic demonstration of this reality is framed by Bowlby's (1958, 1972, 1978) interactive model which implies that each research project in this field has to take into account not only the evaluation of the behavior of the mother and child but also its interactive character.

Having conducted this research from a clinical, pedagogic, and cross-cultural point of view, I am convinced that the unequivocal demonstration of the effects of early mother-child contact on the behavior of both, in such important areas as the interactive processes, may modify principles and practices in our maternity wards and contribute to a different kind of birth and life experience (i.e., at least its beginning) in Portugal.

To put early mother-infant contact and its probable influences into perspective necessarily implies having a concept of the mother's behavior during both pregnancy and birth, defining the most relevant factors in the behavior of the baby that influence communication with the mother, considering the ideas that make up the notion of bonding. Judging the scientific data that support the concept of the sensitive period, making a detailed analysis of the investigations into early mother-child contact, and finally, associating the determining factors in the interactive system of the dyad are central to the task.

Maternal Behavior During Pregnancy and Childbirth

The mother's behavior during pregnancy and childbirth includes *all* the behaviors of the woman who is expecting a child, especially as regards her expecta-

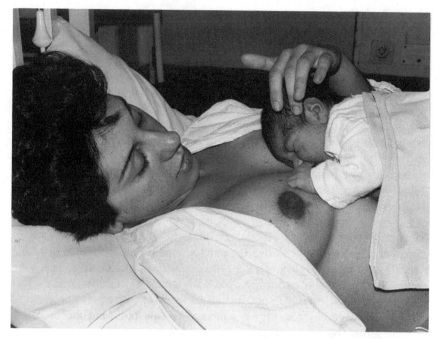

Figure 2.   Early mother–infant contact, Hospital Santa Maria, Lisbon.

tions and attitudes during her pregnancy and in the phases which, in time, make up the phenomenon of the birth.

Expecting a baby, especially the first one, is one of the most important events in a woman's life and without doubt represents a challenge to her maturity and to the structure of her personality. It also is an opportunity for new responsibilities with a new being, and from the beginning the woman feels involved in a relationship of mutual dependence and progression.

In Portuguese society there are very few sources of help to prepare the woman for all that constitutes the beginning of family organization. The pediatricians, in their role as family consultants, are among the mother-child health experts who possess the greatest opportunities to give support and advice to the future mother. If a woman has had a pediatrician since her own childhood and regards him or her as a unique friend, when she knows she is pregnant she will seek support from her pediatrician.

Being pregnant places an enormous physical as well as psychological strain on the woman. The readjustment of various organs that are responsible for the maintenance of the psychological and biological homeostasis of the pregnant woman consumes most of her available energy. The most dramatic changes in the life-style of the pregnant woman occur once she is aware that she has stopped being a girl who is basically responsible for herself, and is now to be responsible for her child. This responsibility is also progressively assumed by the couple, to the extent that both become aware of the division of their time and attention with another person, already real, although not yet present.

During the first 3 months of pregnancy the woman is mostly worried about the changes to her body. Dreams and fantasies take up a large part of her life for the rest of the pregnancy and it is during this period that she draws on all her psychological resources to guarantee her psychic energy and to fight against her own doubts about her capacity to take on the primary role in the family structure. In this phase of pregnancy, the woman often visits and attempts to get closer to her mother, questioning her about her own childhood. The opportunity to resolve old conflicts also frequently arises, as does the opportunity to return to a relationship of warm parental dependence which has changed over many years as a consequence of her own struggle for autonomy during adolescence.

Throughout the pregnancy there is evidence to suggest that the fetus is being influenced by its mother's experiences; the fetus itself also develops a wide repertoire of sensorimotor skills. The mother senses that already there is some synchronization between her and her child as she begins to identify sleep-wake cycles. She begins to discover her child's adjustment to her own rhythm. This forms one of the bases of their progressive discovery of each other. The mother's progressive awareness can help her prepare for the birth and the inevitable physical separation.

The future mother's anxiety, especially during the last month of pregnancy, can be interpreted in a different light, in view of researchers' determination (on the basis of prenatal interviews) that it is indeed a pathological state. Brazelton (1981) considers that most prenatal anxiety and distortion of maternal fantasies may be healthy mechanisms of adjustment to a new psychological homeostasis and that the fear reactions may constitute a form of alarm reaction which can contribute to the reorganization of the woman in the face of her new role. This adaptation demands rapid adjustment to a child with whom the mother is not yet completely familiar. In this way, the roles of the obstetrician and pediatrician are fundamentally those of giving support for this adjustment.

As long as all the conditions of physiological control are secured, a birth that has good psychological conditions is one of the guarantees that good mother-infant bonding will take place. Associated with the psychological control and regulation of pain during the birth is the prevention of solitude during the most crucial phase which precedes the birth. Even though in the last 10 years members of the family, especially the father, have been allowed to enter the labor wards in a great number of countries, in Portugal a significant number of women stay alone in the maternity wards.

The role of the father of the child, during the pregnancy and at the birth, seems to be one of the most relevant aspects influencing both the mother's behavior and the whole process of mother-infant bonding in the postnatal period. The time of the birth offers special conditions for performing that role. The father's function as mediator of the mother's anxiety during the pregnancy assumes characteristics which are important to develop in the new sociological contexts of family formation and motivation.

During the birth the father can also play an active participatory role, an aspect which may have important implications in Portugal in relation to less-privileged families or in cases in which the mother is very young and not sufficiently prepared.

The symbiotic parasite-host relationship between the fetus and the mother, as Mahler and Laperriere (1965) called it, becomes a new type of relationship after the birth. Here, the investment of the mother coincides with the establishment of a new kind of body unity with her baby. The birth, then, is not only the end of the pregnancy but the beginning of a strong and unique contact in the continuation of mother-child liaison. After the birth, the relationship enters into a new phase. Before birth the mother considered the baby as an organic part of herself, while being aware of his or her individual reactions, movements, and waking and sleeping cycle. After the birth the mother continues to identify with the baby but now must distinguish between the physical separation and the psychological individualization that follows it.

Even though lack of maternal differentiation in relation to the baby seems to be an essential aspect in the first maternal transactions, there also is an acceptance of the baby as autonomous and possessing individual characteristics.

The Behavior of the Newborn Infant

Specialists in human behavior who come into clinical contact with the child— pediatricians, psychologists, psychiatrists, and others—now believe that many serious problems during development, in the long run, may be prevented by accurate diagnosis of early disturbances in the behavior and interaction of the newborn child. Research into mother-child interaction, for example, shows that the baby plays an important part in communication. The baby influences and stimulates the various aspects of the mother's behavior. Schaffer (1978, 1979) has made a detailed study of the child's social relationships, and his research suggests that the essentials of the functions of attachment are illustrated by the tendency of the infant to seek out the proximity of other members of its species. There is no finer proof of this need than an analysis of individual behavior when there is evidence of removal of this proximity.

The social dimension of man differs from the social relationships of other, nonhuman primates in its ability to adapt to culture. This is essential to survival. We therefore can understand why the evolutionary significance of early patterns of social behavior is becoming increasingly important. Als (1979) understands the behavior of the newborn child as a pattern that represents a continuity in the evolution of the organization of development, and in which there are stages whose order corresponds to the systems of interaction between mother and baby.

Brazelton's (1984) technique for evaluating the behavior of the newborn child works on the principle that the newborn child shapes its environment to a great extent. This principle has had a tremendous impact on the quality of child care and on the way in which doctors have come to view early interaction between mother and baby. Through the use of the BNBAS, more and more people have come to realize, as a result of their own experiences, that the newborn baby is capable of seeing, hearing, and paying attention to objects—both animate and inanimate—for prolonged periods. It now is generally accepted that the baby can isolate itself from harsh noises and other unpleasant stimuli. It also has become clear that the baby can coordinate certain movements, begin an activity while adapting to new stimulations, and become aware of its needs while trying to communicate with them. Experts in mother-child medical care have no doubt whatsoever that the baby indeed influences its environment, particularly in the way in which it communicates with its mother.

The dimensions defined by Lester, Als, and Brazelton (1978)—Regulation of State, Range of State, Motor Performance, Habituation, Autonomic Regulation, and Orientation—bring together the results of the evaluation of the various items and reflexes of the BNBAS. In the course of an analysis of 60 newborn babies who were continually assessed during the first month of life, we concluded that it may be possible to predict certain aspects of infant behavior through the classified study to these dimensions (Gomes Pedro, 1982). We discovered that there was a relative stability throughout the first month of life with regard to the baby's Regulation of State and Range of State. We also observed, however, an overall and increasing improvement in the motor processes, interactive and sensorial orientation, and the organization of the baby's ability to cope with stress.

These considerations, together with known factors about maternal behavior, may serve as part of the basis for studies on the establishment of mother-child bonding.

Bonding

When the newborn baby is first handed to the mother, there is a tendency for her to easily and quickly "fall in love" with the baby. The maintenance of this feeling, however, implies a long process of learning, both in relation to the mother herself and to the newborn child, who requires stimulation and protection.

Much of the literature written during the last decade on the theory of attachment (i.e., research into the interaction between the mother and the infant) is based on the theory originally formulated in 1958 by Bowlby in his article, "The Nature of the Child's Tie to His Mother." This theory developed out of the confluences of various important currents in the biological and social sciences. Bowlby used the term *attachment* to describe the affective tie of a person or animal to another specific individual, and to define the child's relationshp with his or her mother. This term, although not a synonym, has the same connotations as the designations *object relations* (dynamic psychology) and *dependence* (social science).

Bowlby observed that just like the young of other species, the human baby shapes for itself, during the first weeks and months of life, a series of instinctive, complex, and well-balanced responses, the purpose of which is to insure that the parental attention necessary for the baby's survival will be provided. The mother thus becomes a central figure toward whom all the baby's responses are directed, implying that there is a process of specific integration, which Bowlby (1958, 1972, 1978) calls "affective behavior."

In recent years, clinical data have been collected (though much of the data have not yet been integrated into consistent psychological theories) concerning the importance of physical contact in the first moments of life. Although it is clearly impossible to equate the twin concepts of dependence and attachment, they do have certain common characteristics, principally during the first weeks of life. I believe that this is what led Ainsworth (1969) to understand *love* as a synonym for *attachment*, almost 10 years after Harlow and Suomi (1974) had entitled their first study on bonding, "Nature of Love—Simplified." With this in mind, we can perhaps understand the affectionate behavior between mother and newborn child in the wider context of *love contact*, a term more readily acceptable and comprehensible to doctors and other experts more closely involved in this association.

Babies, from the first seconds of life, have a genetic propensity to interact with other people. Their sensory equipment reacts to stimuli, which in turn activate many of their behavior systems. The newborn infant experiences its first social contact with the mother, precisely when both are particularly ready and eager for this contact. This is the *raison d'etre* of a sensitive period, which conditions many of the effects of the first mother-child contact and thus facilitates the bonding link in particular.

The Sensitive Period

It now seems certain that in animals, from insects to primates, certain events related to environmental conditions which take place in early periods of life have irreversible effects on future behavior. The period of maximum vulnerability in infancy does not correspond entirely to the period in which the animal is dependent on its mother for survival, and can only be limited to the place in which the influence of the environment has been understood to be wholly subordinated to the process of maturation.

Lorenz (1970a, 1970b) maintains that the fundamental concept to keep in mind is the critical period, the time during which the nature of the object to which the young animal is briefly exposed has far-reaching and lasting effects on its social behavior. The biological need for such a period is comprehensible in the context of the problem of animal survival. The duration of the period varies considerably in species, ranging from a few hours in birds to several weeks in dogs. The onset of the critical period is related to the ability of the young creature to follow its mother, and this depends not only on the maturation of motor capacities but also on faculties of perception—whether the young animal can see and hear the object of its attachment.

Research carried out on various aspects of animals has led Klaus and Kennell (1976a, 1976b) to conclude that there seems to be a postnatal sensitive period that differs from species to species and during which the females may adopt the young of another mother; this adoption usually does not occur once the sensitive period has passed, and the environmental factors affect the process of adoption.

Klaus and Kennell (1976a, 1976b) also suggest that there is a pattern of transition between hormonal and nonhormonal mechanisms in the control of maternal behavior, and they are of the opinion that the most fixed and rigid biological mechanisms are replaced at an early stage by more flexible behavior mechanisms. This idea of transition provides an explanation, in evolutionary terms, for the survival of the species in environmental conditions potentially hostile to the establishment of balanced patterns of mother-child attachment and to their resulting interaction.

Klaus and others (Klaus & Kennell, 1970, 1976a, 1976b, 1979; Klaus, Kennell, Plumb, & Zueheke, 1970; Klaus, Jerauld, Kreger, McAlpine, Steffa, & Kennell, 1972) have been responsible for the term *bonding* and a theoretical model based on etiological analogies connected with the notion of the critical or sensitive period. This concept has been defended in a variety of ways, and although apparently it is more widely manifested in other mammals, it also is accepted as existing in humans. It refers, generally speaking, to an early period of ontogenesis in which the young organism rapidly assimilates organized experiences, including the specific characteristics of the species of its progenitors, during which an important social attachment is established between the parents and the offspring. This process would be the equivalent, in part, to the phenomenon of imprinting, which has been described in animals and birds (Lorenz, 1970a, 1970b).

The effects of the influence of early contact may mean the reconstruction of a human maternal form of behavior characteristics of the species, through the awakening of an innate system imprinted in women over the centuries. With this in mind, Klaus and Kennell (1979) maintain that keeping the mother and child together immediately following birth has the effect of triggering a series of hormonal, immunological, and behavioral mechanisms essential to attachment.

Studies carried out in recent years on the influence of early contact in the human species and on the period in which it takes place, whether or not with the connotation of a critical or sensitive priod, confirm the etiologial principles which were a fundamental source of research and a determining factor in mother-infant interaction.

Mother-Infant Contact

Mother and baby need a strong attachment in order to establish the patterns of confidence which are indispensable to the physical and emotional development of the child. Some mothers have strong feelings of attachment early and manage to maintain these ties with their children, even after an enforced period of separation. This ability is related, possibly, to the quality of the maternal care the mothers themselves received during childhood. Other mothers experience difficulties in establishing these ties and thus need reinforcing factors that may release potential maternal feelings that may not have reached complete maturity by the time of the birth (Valman, 1980).

Among these factors the most suitable and the easiest to achieve is mother-infant body contact immediately after birth. This specific kind of contact provides various ways in which the mother-child attachment is likely to be strengthened. Three types of research have been conducted on the influence of mother-child contact after birth: the effects of early mother-child separation, especially with premature babies, or newborn babies in intensive care units; the effects of "rooming-in" on the behavior of mother to child; and the effects of early contact in the neonatal period on the mother and the newborn baby.

Until 1970 research work on the subject of mother-infant contact was exclusively concerned with rooming-in. This term was first used by Gesell and Ilg in 1943, even though the practice has an earlier history. Rooming-in, which implies a hospital atmosphere, is a system in which the newborn baby is placed in a crib at the side of the mother, who will be motivated to take care of the baby as soon as she feels able to do so. Generally, rooming-in presupposes that the mother and child stay together only some time (a few hours) after birth. The conventional routine, still applied in many Portuguese maternity wards, involved the separation of the mother from her child who, immediately after birth, was taken to a nursery until leaving the hospital, being taken to the mother for periods of time (usually for feeding) at fixed intervals which differed from hospital to hospital. The studies made by Montgomery, Steward, and Shenk (1949), Greenberg and Rosenberg (1973), and O'Connor, Sherrod, Sandler, and Vietle (1978) demonstrate the positive effects of rooming-in, thereby leading the way for this system to be put into practice all over the world.

As can be seen in Table 1, however, until 1983 there were only three references to research efforts to determine the effects of rooming-in on the mother's or child's behavior. In another three studies, the object of the investigations was the effect of early mother-infant contact, but the authors gave the experimental groups additional opportunities for rooming-in—a minimum of 6 hr. The remaining seven pieces of research, in which rooming-in was not taken into consideration, are represented in more detail in Table 2. For my purposes, I have established, after analysis of several studies and as a criterion, that rooming-in should only be considered as the child staying with the mother for more than 6 hr daily.

Table 1. Early Contact and Rooming-In in the Experimental Groups of the Different Studies

Author	Early Contact (first 3 hr)	Rooming-in[a]			
		Day 1	Day 2	Day 3	Other days
Klaus & Kennell, 1970	1 hr				
Greenberg & Rosenberg, 1973					
Hales et al. (2 studies), 1975, 1977	45 min				
de Chateau & Wiberg, 1977a, 1977b	10–15 min				
Carlsson et al., 1978	1 hr				
O'Connor et al., 1978					
Kontos, 1978	45 min				
Curry, 1979	1 hr				
Svedja et al., 1980	1 hr				
Siegel, 1982	45 min				
Ali & Lowry, 1981	45 min				
Anisfeld & Lipper, 1983	45–60 min				

[a]Rooming-in was considered to be more than 6 hr daily only.

Table 2 shows that until the end of 1983 only one study on the effects of early contact was conducted in which methods geared to the observation of individual mother-child contact were used.

During the last 10 years, the positive effects of rooming-in have been considered as certain, and the majority of current researchers have turned their attention to the unknown area of the effects of mother-infant contact immediately after birth. The objective of these studies has been to define what makes that period a special or sensitive phase, sufficiently influential for the experimental

Table 2. Studies of the Effects of Mother-Infant Early Contact During the First Month of Life

Number of groups	Authors	Date & place	Number of cases	Objectives	Methods
2	Salk	1970 U.S.A.	401	Study on the side on which the mother holds the baby	Direct observation, interview
2	Klaus & Kennell	1970 U.S.A.	28	Study on maternal behavior	Direct observation, interview, video
2	Trause et al.	1972 (1978) U.S.A.	14	Study on maternal behavior	Photography
2	Sousa	1973 Brazil	200	Study on influence on the type of feeding	Interview
2	Hales et al.	1975 Guatemala	19	Study on maternal behavior	Direct observation
2	Whiten	1975 Great Britain	21	Study on maternal behavior	Direct observation, diary
3	Hales et al.	1977 Guatemala	60	Study on maternal behavior	Direct observation
3	De Chateau & Wiberg	1977 (a,b) Sweden	62	Simultaneous study on maternal and infant behavior	Direct observation
3	Carlsson et al.	1977 Sweden	62	Study on maternal behavior	Video
4	Kontos	1978 Canada	48	Study on maternal behavior	Direct observation, interview
2	Curry	1979 U.S.A.	20	Study on maternal behavior (wrapped and naked babies)	Direct observation, interview
2	Svedja et al.	1980 U.S.A.	14	Study on maternal behavior	Video
2	Jones et al.	1980 U.S.A.	40	Study on maternal behavior (influence of maternal age)	Video
4	Siegel	1980 (1982) U.S.A.	321	Study on maternal behavior	Direct observation, interview

(*continued*)

Table 2.   (*Continued*)

Number of groups	Authors	Date & place	Number of cases	Objectives	Methods
2	Ali & Lowry	1981 Jamaica	100	Study on maternal and infant behavior individually	Direct observation, interview
2	Anisfeld & Lipper	1983 U.S.A.	59	Study on maternal behavior	Direct observation, interview

groups in these studies to have revealed positive differences from the control groups associated with the traditional routine. Table 2 shows that there are differences in the methods used in each study, especially with respect to the beginning of early contact and rooming-in, and also to their respective duration.

An interpretation of the results of the known works on early contact associated with the data on the influences of rooming-in is complex, given the differences in methodology, objectives, and statistical treatment in the various investigations; yet it seems reasonable to verify that greater mother-infant contact in the first 3 days of life is correlated with more optimal maternal behavior. There also is a suggestion that when this contact is established in the first hours of life, there are differences in the mother-child behavior of those who had contact, compared to those who did not have this contact. Early contact seems to be, therefore, a determining factor in the structural conditioning of mother-infant interaction.

Mother-Infant Interaction

The way a baby relates to the world and in particular to its mother develops in the context of the culture and social organization to which the baby's family belongs. Anthropologists recognized the importance of the perinatal period and the role of the culture as a supplier of specific systems of social support to both the mother and the baby. The developing human interacts not only with a natural atmosphere, but also with a specific culture associated with a social order transmitted to him or her by significant people responsible for his or her survival. The characteristics of the baby contribute toward the dynamic relationship between the baby's individual differences and the cultural continuity of humanity.

Interaction has been one of the most elusive and neglected concepts in research on child development. The consensus that a mutual flow of influences exists in the mother-child relationship has been progressively established, along with the necessity to study the direction of influences in this interaction (Bromwich, 1976). Brazelton, Koslowski, and Main (1974) have demonstrated that the interaction is made up of positive and negative cycles, as far as attention and affectionate behavior are concerned, seemingly like a homeostatic system. Tronick and others (Tronick, Als, & Brazelton, 1977, 1980) suggest that interaction is a structured system of units of mutual behavior regulated reciprocally. In this way, the interaction is divided into behavior units that supply information about who is acting, what he or she is doing, and when he or she is doing it. These units are denominated in monadic phases considered as the structural units of interaction, which are analyzed with this presupposition.

From the first days of life, individual interaction patterns, dependent on various factors connected both with the other and the child, are established. According to Ainsworth and Bell (1969), these early interactive patterns last throughout subsequent periods of life, and the independence of the newborn child from these stems from a still undefined overall necessity for stimulation.

Brazelton and Als (1979) refer to a homeostatic domination reached by the baby during the first stage of interaction development over various systems of control of stimuli. The infant is able to set off and interrupt simple stimuli, so as to regulate his physiological states and equilibrium. With this model of development, we can understand the reciprocal ties between mother and infant as a bilateral circuit of flexibility, of rupture and modulation, in successive and organized cycles. Condon and Sander (1974) state that the newborn infant moves in a synchronized way with the structure of human language which they consider to be like a dance with rhythm and pauses. This expression of interaction takes place independently of the language used.

Another way in which the interaction may be expressed is eye contact, when the baby is in an alert state with no ocular irritation. The eyes seem to be the most stimulating infant characteristic for the mother. Eye contact helps the mother feel less strange with her baby and gives her the sensation that her baby is a real person who can establish a social relationship, awakening in her the positive feelings that are indispensable to interaction.

Bonding processes, especially through early mother-infant contact during the sensitive period after the birth, are based on numerous facets of interaction of the child. The way to understand them progressively better is by assessing them.

Basis for the Investigation

In Portugal, mothers seldom have the opportunity to get to know their infants immediately after birth. The infant often is separated from the mother until the first feed, which usually takes place 6 hr after delivery. Erikson (1950) and Valman (1980) have shown the influence of different factors on interaction and development of the mother's full potential of affection. Among these factors, mother-infant body contact immediately after birth, with all the subsequent opportunities, has been considered to be more likely to strengthen attachment. In fact, short-term differences between infant-mother pairs have been attributed to variation in the experience during and shortly after birth (Ali & Lowry, 1981; Anisfeld & Lipper, 1983; Carlsson et al., 1978; de Chateau & Wiberg, 1977a, 1977b; Klaus et al., 1972; Kontos, 1978). Studies on this subject, however, have not yet clarified the true influence of postdelivery contact on behavior in the dyad, especially that of the newborn infant. In addition, specific assessment methods of individual behavior of the newborn infant were not used in any of the studies.

According to Klaus et al. (1972), differences between experimental and control groups consisted of 1 hr of extra contact during the first 3 hours of life and of 5 hr extra every day of rooming-in for the experimental group, whereas for de Chateau and Wiberg (1977a, 1977b), groups differed only with relation to early contact. In both studies' groups, newborn infants were with mothers from half an hour to 2 hr after birth. After the research of Klaus et al. in 1972, it was still doubtful whether the better results found in the experimental group were due to extra contact only, or whether rooming-in contributed to these results. According to de Chateau and Wiberg (1977a, 1977b), early mother-infant contact for 15-min periods seemed to explain the results obtained in the experimental group. It should be pointed out that differences between groups referred only to items of mother's position observed 36 hr after delivery.

The study by Hales, Lozoff, Sosa, and Kennell (1977) seems to confirm the importance of early mother-infant contact, although the differences found between pairs in relation to the interval between birth and beginning of rooming-in (due to a fixed daytime schedule) may have influenced results in the control group. Svedja, Campos, and Emde (1980) did not find differences between experimental and control groups in the 28 items they chose, but their method calls for some comment. In addition to presenting only a small number of cases, their control group mothers were allowed to hold their infants for 5 min after birth, as were those in the control group in the study by Carlsson et al. (1978). Mothers in the experimental group, however, started extra contact with their infants half an hour after birth, and they also had 10 hr extra of rooming-in during the first 36 hr of life. The fact that Svedja et al. found no differences may be due to the fact that their observations took place at 36 hr after birth, now considered to be too early.

Curry (1979) studied only the effects of early contact with either wrapped or naked infants and there were no control groups of late contact mothers. In addition, results were studied only on day 3 of life. Kontos (1978) found a cumulative effect of extra contact and rooming-in on mother's behavior assessed 1 and 3 months after birth. Distribution of mothers in 2 of the 4 rooming-in groups, however, was not aleatory, and part of the observation was carried out by the author, who knew to which group the mothers belonged. Ali and Lowry (1981) observed dyads only 6 and 12 weeks after birth, which makes it difficult to interpret their results with relation to the newborn infant.

Recently, a study by Anisfeld and Lipper (1983) indicated that mothers who were given their infants to hold for an extended period of time immediately after delivery exhibited more affectionate contact behavior to their infants at 2 days of age than did mothers who were not given any opportunity. According to Lamb (1982a, 1982b), although early contact may have modest but beneficial short-term effects in some circumstances, some findings have been equivocal and obtained in methodologically suspect studies.

In our studies we have tried to give attention to methodological conditions, namely selection criteria of sample, enhancement of the early contact variable by rigorous control of conditions distinguishing the experimental and the control groups. It was our purpose to study the newborn infant's behavior specifically, using an appropriate scale (the BNBAS). Since rooming-in already was a standard policy in our country, we intended to find out whether early contact had an additional effect, especially on mothers' affectionate behavior and on infants' performance on the BNBAS. Therefore, we studied the influence of early extended contact on newborn infants as well as on mothers' behavior in the same rooming-in conditions, on three different occasions (days 1, 3, and 28) during the first month of life.

Methods and Materials

Selection Criteria for the Sample

The study involved 60 primiparous mothers and their newborn infants from the maternity ward of the Hospital de Santa Maria in Lisbon, Portugal. Of the mothers, 91.6% were under 30 years of age; average gestational age was 40.14 weeks (SD = 1.05); 80% of the mothers were given analgesic drugs 3–6 hr before delivery; 90% of the newborn infants had an Apgar score of 10 at 1 min.

The criteria for the choice of mother-infant pairs included the following: intention to breast-feed; white mothers of Portuguese nationality; ages between 18 and 35; living with baby's father for at least 1 year; social class IV (low medium) on Graffard's International Social Classification[1]; uncomplicated pregnancy excluding hemorrhage, blood pressure above 140/90, hemoglobin values below 10 gr, drug ingestion, hyperglycemia, and pelvic disproportion; pregnancy of 38–42 weeks; labor not lasting more than 24 hr; identical analgesic medication—50 mg Pethidin and 100 mg Prometazin given at mid-dilation; vaginal delivery; healthy newborn infants with minimum Apgar score of 8 at 1 min (Apgar score of 10 at 5 min); infant weight percentile between 10 and 90.

No significant differences were found between the experimental group and the control group as far as the selection criteria age of mothers, gestational age,

---

[1]This scale includes five items: level of education, professional status, income, type of dwelling, and place of residence.

analgesia before delivery, duration of labor, Apgar score, weight percentile. Sex distribution was equal in spite of not having been controlled.

Definition of Groups

Mother-infant dyads were randomly assigned before delivery to one of two groups:

Experimental group (N = 30). After section of the umbilical cord the newborn was aspirated, clothed and immediately placed on the mother's chest and abdomen for 30 minutes. Both were protected with a small sheet to prevent cooling, but allowing the mother to explore her baby. After 30 minutes the infant was taken to another room and given the normal routine care, then placed in the neonatal nursery until six hours old.

Control group (N = 30). Routine: After birth the infant was shown briefly to the mother, and immediately taken to another room in order to receive routine admission care. From there, the infant was taken directly to the nursery, where he or she remained until 6 hr of life.

At 6 hr of age, newborn infants of both groups were taken to their mothers' rooms, where they remained until discharge (all rooms had two beds and were identical). The staff on the ward did not know to which group the infants belonged and followed their usual routine. Choice of mothers for each group was made randomly, by pick-up envelopes, before delivery. After the delivery, a blind observer asked the mother to participate in the study and it was explained that the intention was to observe the behavior of healthy babies during the first month of life. No refusals were encountered in either group.

Assessment Methods

BNBAS. Several studies have revealed the hitherto unknown capacities of the newborn (Brazelton 1961a, 1961b, 1963; Goren, Starty, & Wu Pyk, 1975). In order to assess newborn infants, the BNBAS was chosen and used on days 1 (between 2 and 6 hr of life), 3, and 28 (Brazelton et al., 1974).

We considered classification of each time, as well as grouping of items in four dimensions (interacting processes; motor processes; organizing processes related to state control; and organizing processes related to physiological response to stress) in order to obtain a global and evolutionary view (Als et al., 1979). A 3-degree classification was used: excellent; adequate; deficient. The first two assessments were carried out in the hospital and the third in the mother's home, by pediatricians trained to reliability on the scale and blind to the babies' group status. Mothers were not present at the first two assessments, which were performed when the newborn infants were in the nursery. Both assessments were performed in the same room (next to the nursery) and only the pediatrician and the baby were present. The conditions of light and temperature were identical in all the observations. After the second assessment, pediatricians gave the mothers of each group identical brief information, such as "All is well with your baby." After the third assessment, which was carried out in the mother's presence, the pediatrician explained the procedure and was available to clarify any doubts about the infant. Pediatricians were blind to which group the infants belonged to.

Direct observation. Direct observation in a feeding situation was carried out on days 3 and 28. Observations were carried out on day 3 of life in the maternity ward, and on day 28 in the home. This observation lasted 15 min and started as soon as the mothers picked up the baby for feeding. The observer was placed so that he or she could see the profiles of mother and infant. Periods of observation and of recording were given with signals transmitted by an earpiece connected to a small tape recorder (16×8 cm) placed in the observer's pocket. Observation periods of 15s each were followed by a 30-s period during which behavior was registered. Mothers' behavior items were grouped in four dimensions: affectionate behavior, proximity, care of newborn infant, and attention (see Table 3).

Choice of items was based on studies from Hales et al. (1977) and from Richards and Bernal (1976), and items were recorded by hand on appropriate forms (Hales et al., 1977; Richards & Bernal, 1976). During recording periods, the presence or absence of each behavioral item was recorded once for each 15-s period, even if it occurred more often. After each observation, the number of occurrences of each behavior was totaled. The newborn infant's behavior items observed during feeding situation are listed in Table 3. Scores of each group of items were obtained by the addition of individual classifications of separate behaviors and were compared for each group.

To minimize mothers' feelings of being observed, it was explained to them beforehand that our aim was to study the behavior of healthy newborn infants during feeding. For training, 30 observations were carried out at the hospital by two observers who were psychologists. They obtained an 87% interobserver reliability on eight observations. During reliability training, both observers were present at each feeding situation, and they recorded behaviors independently. For the study, one observer at each feeding situation did not know to which group infants belonged. Recording of items in each observation was globally submitted to the following concordance criteria (Richards & Bernal, 1976): the number of concordances divided by the number of concordances, plus the number of discordances and the number of omissions:

$$\frac{C}{C + D + O}$$

Mother's behavior during application of the BNBAS. During application of the scale by the pediatrician in the home, on day 28, mother's behavior was recorded by the psychologist who observed the feeding situation. Three items,

Table 3.   Direct Observation of Mothers' and Infants' Behavior

Mother

Dimension 1: Affectionate behavior

Kisses:	any type of contact of mother's mouth with newborn infant (including licking and biting)
Smiles:	smiles while looking at newborn infant (baby may have eyes closed)
Vocalizes:	any type of sound, including speech, directed at newborn infant
Looks:	looks at any part of newborn's body
En-face:	positions her face so that her eyes meet baby's eyes on the same vertical plane
Facial expression:	change of facial expression, with the purpose of stimulating or imitating baby's behavior (except smiling)
Touches:	contact of mother's hand or fingers with newborn infant's skin or clothing, without any movement of hand or fingers
Caresses:	contact of mother's hand or fingers with newborn infant's skin or clothing, with hand or finger movement
Rocks:	rhythmic movements (repeatedly to and fro)

Dimension 2: Proximity (way of holding baby)

Encompassing:	front part of newborn infant's body in contact with front part of mother's body, and baby is encompassed by both her arms (mother may be lying down, sitting, or standing)
Holds:	mother sitting or standing: newborn infant in mother's arms, more or less at waist level
	mother lying down: mother with one or both arms around baby, with no contact between front parts of newborn infant's and mother's bodies
Newborn infant in lap:	mother sitting with newborn lying in her lap
Newborn infant on mother's arm or on mother's bed:	baby in crib or on mother's bed, when mother is not lying down

Dimension 3: Care of newborn infant

Stimulates suckling:	soft tapping, patting or any other form of stimulating newborn infant, as well as accommodation of teat or nipple to baby's mouth
Burping:	mother puts newborn infant in burping position
Cleanliness of face:	mother cleans newborn infant's eyes, nose, or mouth, using a cloth or her own hand
Diapers:	diaper changing
Clothes:	dressing, undressing, or changing newborn infant's clothes; covering baby or arranging clothes which cover the newborn infant

Dimension 4: Mother's attention

Talks to others:	talks to anyone present, including observer
Looks away:	mother looks away from baby (looks at other object or person)
Nipple or teat out of newborn infant's mouth:	nipple or teat comes out of baby's mouth, because of mother's distraction

Table 3.   (*Continued*)

Infant
State[a]
Cries
Smiles
Looks at mother's face
Spits up
Chokes
Hiccups
Nipple/teat out

[a]Classification of the state was based on the BNBAS.

scored from 0 to 2, were studied: Mother's attention—(a) mother not interested at all; (b) intermediate situation; (c) mother close to pediatrician; Mother's behavior regarding infant's crying—(a) mother never tries to soothe baby; (b) intermediate situation; (c) mother tries to soothe baby consistently; and Mother's curiosity (a) mother never asks questions; (b) intermediate situation; (c) mother asks questions about the scale. Observers were blind regarding group status.

Statistical Analysis

Variables relating to selection criteria in both groups (experimental and control) were studied by means of contingency tables and a chi-square test, which also was used to assess answers to questions and mothers' behavior during application of the BNBAS. The nonparametric Mann-Whitney test was used to compare both groups. The difference between the average values of items and dimensions of mother-infant observations was determined, and its significance was studied by means of the Student t test for independent samples (two-tailed tests were used). A probability value of .05 was chosen as the lower threshold of significance.

Results

On day 1, on the basis of the BNBAS, similar results were found in both groups of babies; only the item Hand-Mouth Facility ($z = 2.01$; $p < .05$) in the experimental group had a significantly higher score. Analysis of the BNBAS on days 3 and 38 revealed that significantly higher scores were obtained in the experimental group in the dimension Interactive Processes on both days (see Table 4). The experimental group also obtained significantly higher scores on the following single items:

Attractiveness
Need for Stimulation

Response Decrement to Light
Orientation Inanimate Visual
Orientation Animate Visual
Orientation Animate Auditory
Orientation Animate Visual and Auditory
Motor Maturity
Consolability
Rapidity of Buildup
Startles
Alertness
Cuddliness
Self-quieting Activity

Direct observation of the mothers' behavior was studied in the four dimensions as well as for each item separately (see Table 3).

On day 3, mothers in the experimental group made their infants burp significantly more often ($t(58) = 2.04$; $\rho < .05$). On day 28, mothers in the experimental group scored significantly higher than those in the control group in the Affectionate Behavior dimension ($t(58) = 2.58$; $\rho < .001$), which includes several items (e.g., Kisses, Smiles, Vocalizes, Touches, Caresses, Looks, Facial Expression, Rocks) listed in Table 3. Analysis of results, considering each item separately, revealed that mothers with postdelivery extra contact vocalized more

Table 4. Items and Dimensions that Obtained Significant Differences on Days 3 and 28 of Life

Item/Dimension	Day 3		Day 28	
	z	p<	z	p<
Attractiveness	3.23	0.001	2.55	0.025
Need for stimulation	4.08	0.001	—	—
Response decrement to light	—	—	3.12	0.0025
Orientation inanimate visual	2.87	0.005	2.66	0.01
Orientation animate visual	—	—	2.47	0.025
Orientation animate auditory	2.89	0.005	—	—
Orientation animate visual and auditory	3.55	0.001	2.43	0.025
Alertness	2.25	0.025	2.52	0.025
Motor maturity	2.47	0.025	—	—
Cuddliness	4.55	0.001	3.13	0.0025
Consolability	2.21	0.05	—	—
Rapidity of buildup	2.27	0.025	—	—
Startles	2.09	0.05	—	—
Self-quieting activity	2.31	0.025	—	—
Dimension I—Interactive processes	2.90	0.005	2.16	0.05

often (t (58) = 2.12; $p < .05$) and took greater care with the cleanliness of their newborn's face (t (58) = 2.33; $p < .025$).

No differences were found between experimental and control groups as regards the items of infant's behavior directly observed in the feeding situation.

During application of the BNBAS, mothers in the experimental group had a greater tendency to soothe their infants when they cried (item Mother's Behavior Regarding Infant's Crying; $\chi^2 = 4.27$; $df = 1$; $p < .05$).

In the first interview, which took place prior to delivery, no significant differences in answers to the 13 questions about expectancies and attitudes toward the baby's birth were found between the two groups of mothers. In the second interview, which took place in the mother's home, it was found that the mothers in the experimental group answered significantly more often "Yes, for the better" to the question, "Did your baby bring any significant change to your life?" ($\chi^2 = 6.08$; $df = -1$; $p < .025$).

Discussion

Our results seem to confirm those obtained in studies that demonstrate that additional early mother-infant contact does lead to changes in maternal behavior. As far as maternal behavior is concerned, having realized that the feeding situation could be limiting for assessing variability among mothers, we used descriptive items designed to pick up the sensitivity of the mother to the individuality of her baby. For the same reason, we assessed mothers during application of the BNBAS and interviewed each mother, in her home, on the 28th day after delivery.

In addition, we may have demonstrated for the first time the influence of mother-infant contact after birth, especially on the newborn infant's behavior. For this purpose we used the BNBAS, which seemed to be the most comprehensive instrument for the assessment of differences in the newborn infant's behavior. It seems important to stress that the dimension and items of the scale that relate to interactive processes were the ones in which significantly better results were obtained in the postpartum contact group, some of which persisted from the third to the 28th day of life (Dimension 1—Interactive Processes; Orientation Animate Visual and Auditory; Alertness; and Cuddliness). Also, on both day 3 and day 28, infants in the experimental group were considered by observers to be significantly more attractive than infants in the control group (descriptive paragraph of the scale).

Moreover, on day 3 of life, infants in the early-contact group not only had fewer startles and cried less often (items Rapidity of Buildup and Self-Quieting Activity) but also were easier to console during application of the BNBAS (item Consolability), compared to babies in the other groups.

On day 1 of life, the effort of the newborn infant to adapt to extrauterine conditions may have contributed to the fact that better results were obtained in the experimental group, on only one item of the scale (Hand-Mouth Facility).

As far as the mother's behavior, it was observed that differences between the two groups increased from day 3 to day 28 and therefore influence of contact was more evident on day 28. Although two of the behavior differences observed may appear unrelated to affectionate behavior (namely, mothers in the experimental group made their infants burp significantly more often and took greater care with cleaning the newborn's face), the other results observed on the 28th day in the experimental group on the Affectionate Behavior dimension (e.g., items Kisses, Touches, Smiles) seem to be meaningful.

We should like to point out that, as in the study by Hales et al. (1977), differences between groups were found only in relation to affectionate behavior, with higher scores for mothers in the contact group. In our study, differences still were slight on day 3, probably because it may have been too soon for the influence of early experiences to become apparent. It also is possible that infant behavior previously mentioned may have influenced the evolution of the mothers' behavior over time, although we believe additional longitudinal studies are needed to demonstrate these findings.

At the end of the first month of life, in regard to mother's behavior during application of the BNBAS, our results produced an additional finding relating to the influence of early contact on the mother. It was observed that mothers of the experimental group tended to soothe their infants more often when they cried.

Finally, we may conclude that higher scores with regards to both mothers' and newborn infants' behavior were obtained in our experimental group, which differed from the control group only in the fact that there was early mother-infant contact during 30 min after birth.

Summary

In this study I attempted to examine the effect of early mother-infant contact on the behavior of both mother and infant during the first month of life. To do this, 60 mother-infant dyads were divided into two groups: an experimental group (N = 30), which had early and extended postpartum contact, and a control group (N = 30), which followed the usual maternity routine.

The research was concerned mainly with assessment of the newborn infant's behavior, and for this purpose the BNBAS was used on days 1, 3, and 28 of life; behavior of the dyad was observed during feeding. Differences were found between the two groups of newborn infants, the higher scores being those of the infants in the experimental group, mainly in interaction processes. Greater differences were found between the mothers on the 28th day, more affectionate behavior being displayed by the mothers in the experimental group.

References

Ainsworth, M. D. S. (1969). Object relations, dependency, and attachment: A theoretical review of the infant-mother relationship. *Child Development, 40*, 969–1025.

Ainsworth, M. D. S., & Bell, S. M. (1969). Some contemporary patterns of mother-infant interaction in the feeding situation. In: J. A. Ambrose (Ed.), *Stimulation in early infancy* (pp. 133–170). London:Academic Press.

Ali, Z., & Lowry, M. (1981). Early maternal-child contact: Effects on later behavior. *Developmental Medicine and Child Neurology, 23*, 337–345.

Als, H. (1979). Social interaction: Dynamic matrix for developing behavioral organization. *New Directions in Child Development, 4*, 21–39.

Als, H., Tronick, E., Lester, B. M., & Brazelton, T. B. (1979). Specific neonatal measures: The Brazelton neonatal behavior assessment scale. In J. D. Osofsky (Ed.), *The handbook of infant development* (pp. 185–215). New York: Wiley.

Anisfeld, E., & Lipper, E. (1983). Early contact, social support and mother-infant bonding. *Pediatrics, 72*, 79–83.

Bowlby, J. (1958). The nature of the child's tie to his mother. *International Journal of Psychoanalysis, 39*, 350–373.

Bowlby, J. (1972). *Child care and the growth of love (2nd ed.).* Harmondsworth, England: Penguin.

Bowlby, J. (1978). *Attachment and loss.* Harmondsworth, England: Penguin.

Brazelton, T. B. (1961a). Psychophysiologic reactions in the neonate. I. The value of observation of the neonate. *Journal of Pediatrics, 58*, 508–512.

Brazelton, T. B. (1961b). Psychophysiologic reactions in the neonate. II. Effect of maternal medication on the neonate and his behavior. *Journal of Pediatrics, 58*, 513–518.

Brazelton, T. B. (1963). The early mother-infant adjustment. *Journal of Pediatrics, 32*, 931–937.

Brazelton, T. B. (1970). Effect of prenatal drugs on the behaviorof the neonate. *American Journal of Psych., 126*, 95–100.

Brazelton, T. B. (1981). *On becoming a family: The growth of attachment.* New York: Delacorte/Seymour Lawrence.

Brazelton, T. B. (1984). *Neonatal Behavioural Assessment Scale (2nd ed.).* London: Spastics International Medical Publications/Heinemann Medical Books.

Brazelton, T. B. & Als, H. (1979). Four early stages in the development of mother-infant interaction. *Psychoanal. Study Child, 34*, 85–117.

Brazelton, T. B., Koslowski, B., & Main, M. (1974). The origins of reciprocity: The early mother-infant interaction. In L. M. Rosenblum (Ed.), *The effect of the infant on its caregiver* (pp. 49–75). New York: Wiley.

Bromwich, R. M. (1976). Focus on maternal behavior in infant intervention. *American Journal of Orthopsychiatry, 46*, 439–446.

Carlsson, S. G., Fagerberg, H., Horneman, G., Hwand, C. F., Larsson, K., Dholm, R. M., Schallter, J., Danielsson, B., & Gundewal, C. (1978). Effects of amount of contact between mother and child on the mother's nursing behavior. *Developmental Psychobiology, 11*, 143–150.

de Chateau, P., & Wiberg, B. (1977a). Long-term effect on mother-infant behaviour of extra contact during the first hour postpartum. I. First observations at 36 hours. *Acta Paediatrica Scandinavica, 66*, 137–143.

de Chateau, P., & Wiberg, B. (1977b). Long-term effect on mother-infant behaviour of extra contact during the first hour postpartum. II. A follow-up at three months. *Acta Paediatrica Scandinavica, 66*, 145–151.

Condon, W. S., & Sander, L. W. (1974). Neonate movement is synchronized with adult speech: Interactional participation and language acquisition. *Science, 183*, 99–101.

Curry, M. A. H. (1979). Contact during the first hour with the wrapped or naked newborn: Effect on maternal attachment behaviours at 36 hours and three months. *Birth Family Journal, 6*, 227–235.

Erikson, E. H. (1950). *Childhood and society*. New York: Norton.

Gesell, A., & Ilg, F. (1943). *Infant and child in the culture of today: The guidance of development in home and nursery school*. New York: Harper & Brothers.

Gomes-Pedro, J. (1982). Unpublished doctoral thesis. Lisbon.

Goren, C. C., Starty, M., & Wu Pyk (1975). Visual following and pattern discrimination of facelike stimuli by newborn infants. *Pediatrics, 56*, 544–549.

Greenberg, M., & Rosenberg, J. L. (1973). First mothers rooming-in with their newborns: Its impact upon the mothers. *American Journal of Orthopsychiatry, 43*, 783–788.

Greenberg, N. (1965). Developmental effects of stimulation during early infancy: Some conceptual and methodological considerations. *Ann. New York Academy of Science, 118*, 831–839.

Hales, D., Kennell, J., Klaus, M., Mata, L., & Sosa, R. (1975). The effect of early skin-to-skin contact on maternal behavior at twelve hours (Abstract). *Pediatri Res., 9*, 259.

Hales, D., Lozoff, B., Sosa, R., & Kennell, J. H. (1977). Defining the limits of the neonatal sensitive period. *Developmental Medicine and Child Neurology, 19*, 454–461.

Harlow, H. F., & Soomi Suomi, S. J. (1974). Nature of love—simplified. In L. J. Stone, H.T. Smith, & L. B. Murphy (Eds.), *The competent infant* (pp. 1040–1053). London: Tavistock Publication Limited.

Jones, F. A., Green, V., & Krauss, D. R. (1980). Maternal responsiveness of primiparous mothers during the postpartum period: Age differences. *Pediatrics, 65*, 579–584.

Kennell, J. H. (1980). Are we in the midst of a revolution? *American Journal of Diseases in Childhood, 134*, 303–310.

Klaus, M. H. (1978). The biology of parent-to-infant attachment. *Birth Family Journal, 5*,: 200–203.

Klaus, M. H., Jerauld, R., Kreger, N. C., McAlpine, W., Steffa, M., & Kennell, J. H. (1972). Maternal attachment: The importance of the first postpartum days. *New England Journal of Medicine, 286*, 460–463.

Klaus, M. H., & Kennell, J. H. (1970). Mothers separated from their newborn infants. *Pediatric Clinics of North America, 17*, 1015–1037.

Klaus, M. H., & Kennell, J. H. (1976a). *Maternal-infant bonding: The impact of early separation or loss on family development*. St. Louis, MO: Mosby.

Klaus, M. H., & Kennell, J. H. (1976b). Parent-to-infant attachment. In D. Hall (Ed.), *Recent advances in pediatrics* (pp. 129–152). London: Churchill Livingstone.

Klaus, M. H., & Kennell, J. H. (1979). An early maternal sensitive period? A theoretical analysis. In D. Stern (Ed.), *Intensive care in the newborn* (pp. 381–387).

Klaus, M. H., Kennell, J. H., Plumb, N., & Zuehlke, S. (1970). Human maternal behavior of the first contact with the young. *Pediatrics, 46*, 187–192.

Kontos, D. (1978). A study of the effects of extended mother-infant contact on maternal behavior at one and three months. *Birth Family Journal*, *5*, 133–140.

Lamb, M. E. (1982a). Early contact on maternal-infant bonding: One decade later. *Pediatrics*, *70*, 763–767.

Lamb, M. E. (1982b). The bonding phenomenon: Misinterpretations and their implications. *J Pediatr*, *104*, 555–557.

Lester, B. M., Als, H., & Brazelton, T. B. (1978). *Scoring criteria for seven clusters of the Brazelton Scale*. Unpublished manuscript, Child Development Unit, Children's Hospital Medical Center, Boston.

Levy, M. L., & Gomes-Pedro, J. (in press). Avaliar para prevenir.

Lorenz, K. (1970a). Companionship in bird life. In *Instinctive behavior*. New York: International Universities Press.

Lorenz, K. (1970b). *Studies in animal and human behavior*. Cambridge, MA: Harvard University Press.

Mahler, M. S. & Laperrierre, K. (1965). Mother-child interaction during separation-individuation. *Psychoanalytic Quarterly*, *34*, 482–498.

Montgomery, T. L., Steward, R. E., & Shenk, E. P. (1949). Observations on the rooming-in program of baby with mother in ward and private service. *American Journal of Obstetrics and Gynecology*, *57*, 176–186.

O'Connor, S., Sherrod, K. B., Sandler, H. M., & Vietle, P. M. (1978). The effect of extended postpartum contact on problems with parenting: A controlled study of 301 families. *Birth Family Journal*, *5*, 231–234.

Richards, M. P. M. (1978). Possible effects of early separation on later development of children. In F. S. W. Brimblecombe, M. P. M. Richards, & N. C. R. Roberton (Eds.), *Separation and special-care baby units* (pp. 12-32). London: Heinemann Medical Books.

Richards, M. P. M., & Bernal, J. F. (1976). An observational study of mother-infant interaction. In N. Blurton Jones (Ed.), *Ethological studies of child behavior* (pp. 175–197). London: Cambridge University Press.

Salk, L. (1970). The critical nature of the postpartum period in the human for the establishment of the mother-infant bond: A controlled study. *Diseases of the Nervous System*, *31*, 110–116.

Schaffer, H. R. (1978). Early interactive development. In H. R. Schaffer (Ed.), *Studies in mother-infant interaction, 2nd ed.* (pp. 3–16). London: Academic Press.

Schaffer, H. R. (1979). *Mothering, 2nd ed.*. London:

Siegel, M. (1982). Early and extended maternal-infant contact. *American Journal of Diseases in Childhood*, *136*, 251–257.

Siegel, S. (1956). *Nonparametric statistics for the behavioural sciences*. London: McGraw-Hill.

Svedja, M. J., Campos, J. J., & Emde, R. N. (1980). Mother-infant "bonding": Failure to generalize. *Child Development*, *51*, 775–779.

Trause, M. A., Kennell, S. H., & Klaus, M. H. (1978). A fresh look at early mother-infant contact [Abstract]. *Pediatric Research*, *12*, 376.

Tronick, E., Als, H., & Brazelton, T. B. (1980). Monadic phases: A structural descriptive analysis of infant-mother face-to-face interaction. *Merrill-Palmer Quarterly*, *26*, 3–24.

Valman, H. B. (1980). Mother-infant. *British Medical Journal*, 308.

CHAPTER 9

The Effect of Different Routines in a Special Care Baby Unit on the Mother-Infant Relationship (Great Britain)*

Joanna Hawthorne Amick

Child Care and Development Group
University of Cambridge

Special care baby units (including intensive care units) in British hospitals are designed for the treatment of low-birthweight (< 2,500 g) or ill newborn babies and use specialized equipment and specially trained staff to care for these babies. In 1964, over 6% of all live newborn babies in England and Wales spent a minimum of 24 hr in a special care baby unit. This figure increased to 20% in 1979. This seems to reflect an increase in routine admissions, rather than a deterioration of overall health. In 1980 the figure was 14%, however, perhaps showing that recent opinion on high admission rates has begun to reduce them.

Advances in neonatal medicine in the last 10 years have improved the techniques and technology as well as the skill and knowledge of pediatricians and nursing staff. Emphasis usually is placed on the medical aspects of babies' treatment, and it is only recently that researchers have been concerned with the psychological effects on the mother and baby of a prolonged stay in a special care baby unit. This study investigates the separation of mothers from their low-birthweight babies and the ways in which it may affect aspects of the mother-infant relationship.

In Britain in 1975, 99% of first-born babies were born in a hospital. Technology was immediately available and resulted in childbirth becoming a medical

* This research was carried out under a three-year studentship from the Medical Research Council, London, and one year's funding from the Health Education Council. I am very grateful for the kind cooperation of the doctors and nurses at the Mill Road Maternity Hospital in Cambridge, as well as the cooperation of the parents and babies who took part in this study.

matter in Britain as well as some other industrialized countries. The mortality rate in England and Wales was 6.3 per 1,000 in 1982, with the neonatal mortality rate 11.3 per 1,000 live births. Maternal mortality is rare, and in 1976–1978 it was 11.9 per 100,000. As a reaction to the medicalization of childbirth, parents have called for the reintroduction of the human element ensuring that mothers and babies stay together and that families are a part of the birth event. A result of medical intervention was to increase the separation of mother and baby at birth, often whether or not the babies were ill. Until recently, mothers and full-term healthy babies often were separated from one another on the regular lying-in wards, especially in the United States and frequently in Britain. The babies were removed to nurseries at night and for most of the day. In some hospitals in the United States, mothers and babies were brought together only at feeding times during the day, and this is still true in many hospitals. Recently, it has become more common in Great Britain and in America for mothers and babies to stay together all day, and sometimes at night, and for babies to be fed when they demand it. Most mothers express a preference to have their newborn babies with them and there is evidence to suggest that this early contact promotes lactation and increases the mother's confidence in her caretaking abilities.

Clearly, the placing of babies in special care baby units is a more complicated matter. The baby is taken from the mother and put in an incubator or cot in a special unit. Ten years ago, when there was a greater concern about the risk of cross-infection, mothers had very little contact with their babies. Often only visual contact was allowed, and if the baby was very small and ill, separation could last for a few weeks or even months. A study at Stanford University, California in 1970 (Barnett, Leiderman, Grobstein, & Klaus, 1970) showed that an increase in parental visiting actually reduced infection rates. These researchers also found that with increased parental access to the babies mothers gained more confidence in their ability to look after the baby once they were home.

The mother's confidence was not the only reason why concern grew about the separation of mothers and special care babies. There were suggestions that distortions in the mother-child relationship could follow from these separations. Some theorists (Klaus & Kennell, 1976) hypothesized that problems would arise because of a disruption in the bonding process thought to take place at birth between mother and infant. Other theorists suggested that a mother's behavior after a separation from an infant in a special care unit could be best explained in psychological terms. A disruption in maternal feelings is brought about by the separation, which violates expectations of contact with the infant. The mother must cope with the emotional crisis of a preterm birth as well as with the inhibiting effect of hospital routines on spontaneous interactions with her baby.

The first premature baby unit in Britain was set up at the Sorrento Maternity Hospital, Birmingham, under Dr. V. Crosse in 1931. With the gradual increase in knowledge of the treatment of babies with complications at birth, pediatricians and neonatologists felt that the concentration of very small babies, or those with medical perinatal complications, into separate specialized departments under constant surveillance could reduce substantially both perinatal mortality and neonatal morbidity.

On the basis of this conclusion, in 1961 the Joint Sub-Committee on the Standing Maternity and Midwifery Advisory Committee recommended the establishment of special care units for both premature and ill newborn babies in the large maternity hospitals. An Expert Group Committee produced a report in 1971 discussing the future facilities for infants requiring special care. The committee recommended that the number of cots be increased from 4.3 cots per 1,000 live births to 6.0 cots, with at least 20 cots per unit in the 257 nurseries that existed in 1968. The group described the babies who might need treatment or observation in special care units as follows:

babies born with difficult deliveries (including cesarean section, forceps, and breech deliveries);
low-birthweight babies ($< 2,500$ gms);
perinatal deaths.

When admission rates in England and Wales rose from 6.2% of all live births in 1964 to above 18.5% in 1975, doctors and psychologists became alarmed and began the discussion of methods which might reduce admission rates (Richards & Roberton, 1978). The proportion of babies weighing under 1,500 g is only 7% nationally; thus the vast majority of infants entering special care units must be of heavier birthweight (Chamberlain, Chamberlain, Howlett, & Claireaux, 1975). Therefore, unnecessary separation of mothers and infants was taking place. Many hospitals recently have taken steps to reduce unnecessary admissions, and dramatic reductions in numbers have been seen in Cambridge and Exeter (Richards & Roberton, 1978).

There is a distinction between special care units and intensive care units, although the Cambridge unit has facilities for both forms of treatment. The following definition can be found in Brimblecombe, Richards, and Roberton (1978, p. 3):

Special care units.
Special care units were designed for three classes of infants: (1) those with illnesses which require immediate medical treatment e.g. severe congenital malformations, meningitis, fits, urinary infections, pneumonia, hypoglycaemia, vomiting, heart failure, or severe feeding problems; (2) a few infants with illnesses unique to the neonate, e.g. those with Rhesus haemolytic disease or respiratory distress syndrome, and infants of diabetic mothers; and (3) healthy infants of very low birthweight who need a special thermal environment, tube feeding, etc.
Intensive care units.
Intensive care of newborns is exactly the same as intensive care of older chil-

dren or adults, and is for those infants who require prolonged oxygen therapy with appropriate monitoring techniques, in particular, if it is by continuous positive airways pressure (CPAP) or ventilation and requires the use of arterial catheters. It also includes the management of infants with severe Rhesus incompatibility, or those who need peritoneal dialysis or intravenous feeding.

Despite the fact that in Britain and in some hospitals in the U.S. routine admissions may be decreasing, there will be some babies who will require the treatment these units can provide and so will be separated from their parents for several weeks or months at birth. Therefore, these units are places where parents and babies will first interact. But often the design, facilities, and staff attitude do not provide a satisfactory milieu in which parents can get to know their babies.

Problems Parents Face in Special Care Units

The birth of a preterm baby can be a traumatic experience, and a mother can feel guilty at producing a small, ill baby. She may react by becoming highly anxious, at one extreme, or detached, at the other extreme. She also may go through a mourning process over the loss of the expected ideal baby and the conditions she envisaged. The subsequent separation is assumed to be a stressful event for all mothers, although the degree of distress will be different for each mother. The

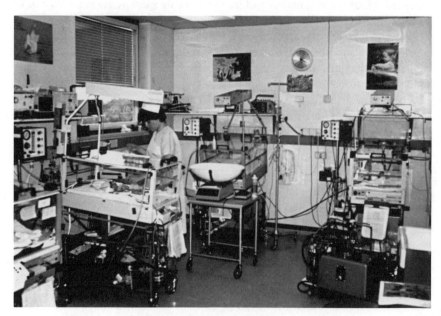

Photo 1.   Intensive care room at the Special Care Baby Unit.

nature of this distress will depend on the mother's expectations, disappointments, views of mothering, past experience, the amount of support she receives, and the other stresses in her life. There is a possibility that the separation will have some lasting effects on the mother, altering her perceptions of the child and thus showing up in her relationship with the child.

As well as these emotional considerations, parents must contend with the hospital environment and the staff attitude toward parental involvement. The baby is removed from the parents and cared for by professionals who seem so much more adept and who can unknowingly make the mother feel useless and helpless. There mothers often lack a clear role in dealing with the baby, and their maternal feelings can be thwarted by routines imposed upon them in the special care unit (e.g., not being able to handle the baby spontaneously, or to meet the baby's needs by feeding or changing, or to meet medical requirements). Staff members often are resistant to parental involvement, feeling that parents get in the way of their work. As a result the parents may feel ostracized and inhibited about visiting the baby; or they often will not know what to do when they do visit. It is only when staff members find they have a role in advising the mother that the barriers may be removed.

The effects of separation can be minimized if the routines in the special care baby unit are flexible enough to give the parents as much responsibility for their baby as possible, to give them information about their baby, to provide them with the chance to interact spontaneously with their baby, and to give them the support needed to retain their confidence and resolve their emotional distress. The parents' own perceptions of their situation will be strongly affected by the institutional context in which the separation occurs. Studies have shown that parental rates of visiting babies in special care units are low (Barnett et al., 1970; Klaus & Kennell, 1976; Hawthorne, Richards, & Callon, 1978; Rosenfield, 1980). Factors in the hospital environment that impose restrictions on the developing mother-infant relationship as well as the parents' emotional needs must be explored in order to accommodate the needs of parents more successfully. For instance, it appears from studies on parental visiting that simply allowing parents access to special care units does not always lead to an increase in parent-infant contact. It is clear that the parents' motivation to visit will be influenced by how they are treated and accepted by the special care unit staff and how they are supported in their reactions. As Richards (1978) points out, we should consider early separation from the viewpoint of the parents' psychology and the way it affects parental behavior, which in turn will have an impact on the child.

There is a great variation in the treatment of parents in special care units in Britain and the U.S., as well as in the accessibility parents have to their babies. Some units allow parents to visit 24 hr a day and to touch and to hold the baby, while other units have set visiting times and may allow only mothers to visit. Some units allow other members of the family to visit, but others are quite restrictive. Some units have facilities for parents to have a snack, whereas others have no areas for the parents to sit and rest. Some units are cheerfully decorated

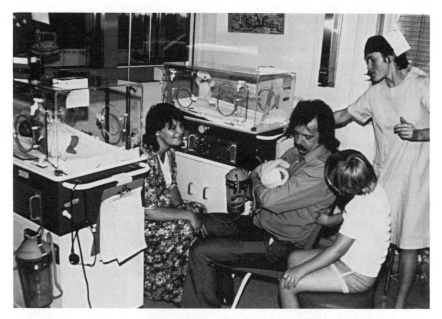

Photo 2.   Parents and sibling visiting infant at the Special Care Baby Unit.

to soften the clinical atmosphere, have colored clothes and blankets for the baby, and allow families to bring in clean toys, whereas others are quite stark and unfriendly.

While it is very pleasant to be in a cheerfully decorated unit that allows 24-hr parental visiting, the most important aspect of all is whether the members of the staff understand the parents' need to interact with their babies, and their own need to encourage and support the parents' involvement. Without this under-standing, little can be accomplished.

The aim of this study was to determine how increased contact with the baby, along with increased encouragement, information, and support at home affected the special care unit mother's relationship with her baby, her feelings of compe-tence and self-confidence, her perceptions of her baby, and her attitudes and experience with the unit. This study also aimed to describe what it is like to have a baby in a special care unit, what the caretaking issues that arise are, and in what way the experience could be made easier for the parents.

The hypothesis was that more support would help the mothers feel closer to their babies, more confident in their caretaking abilities, more relaxed with the staff, and more content with the way they coped at home, and would serve to make them report fewer difficulties with their babies. It also was hoped that areas in which hospital and community staff could help parents of babies in special care units would be pinpointed.

Methodology

Two groups of mothers and babies were recruited at the Maternity Hospital in Cambridge, England, and followed for a year. The control group ($N = 14$) was collected at first under the routines in the unit found upon my arrival (i.e., the status quo). There then was a period of 1 month during which the changes in routine were introduced to the staff, who put them into effect. The collection of the intervention group ($N = 11$) then took place under the new routines. (I had planned to collect a third group a few months later to examine whether or not the intervention program was continued after my departure, but this phase had to be abandoned because of to a viral epidemic that curtailed the collection of the sample after I had collected 11 mothers in the intervention group.)

The first group (control group) was collected under the conditions I found when I arrived in 1976. These were as follows: Parents only were allowed to visit their babies 24 hr a day. They touched their babies in incubators and held them but did not change them until they were in a cot. They did not tube-feed them at all and bathed them once or watched a demonstration bath just before taking the baby home. Breast-feeding was encouraged and a breast-milk bank had been set up in 1974. Parents received no photographs or explanatory booklets. Some parents may never have talked to a doctor. There was one Mother and Baby Room in the unit where primiparae usually stayed for one night with their babies before taking them home. The frequency of follow-up at home by community health visitors (nurses) depended upon the individual health visitor. There was a liaison system between the hospital health visitor and the mother's own local health visitor, and information was passed on twice a week during the baby's stay. This ensured that the local health visitor knew the baby's condition and discharge date.

Babies who had been ventilated for respiratory distress or who were very small at birth were seen at the hospital clinic six weeks after discharge and again if necessary. If tests on blood, weight, or bilirubin levels had to be done sooner than that, the mother took the baby to the special care unit itself to see the doctor.

On admittance to the unit, the baby was put in an incubator or cot, depending upon his or her condition. The father often visited first and would pass information on to his wife. The mother visited as soon as she was able, often a few hours later, and came in a wheelchair if necessary. Very occasionally, a baby was taken to see the mother on the postnatal ward if she was too ill to visit. When the baby's weight approached 2,100 g (before 1974 it was 2,300 g), primaparae were asked to come to the Mother and Baby Room near the unit to stay overnight with the baby before they went home together. A short leaflet was given to the parents to take home, which answered a few common questions (e.g., when to take the baby outside).

The special care unit was purpose-built, with six glass-walled rooms, of which one or two were used for intensive care. Most of the incubators were the closed type with portholes, but during my study two open incubators with over-head heating panels were bought. A plastic chair or high stool was beside most of the babies' cots or incubators. The babies' nappies, gowns, cot sheets, and cotton balls for washing the babies were kept in cupboards in each room. The unit walls were decorated at Christmastime, and each baby received a small stocking. There were no pictures or decorations at any other time of year.

The special care unit was two floors above the labor ward and one floor above one of the postnatal wards. During my study, this ward began to admit small babies who needed tube-feeding or phototherapy so they could stay with their mothers. The facilities for visitors were poor at the hospital, with no cafeteria nearby and poor car-parking facilities.

The ratio of nurses to babies was roughly 1 to 3, and in 1977 the staff consisted of:

Nursing officer (in charge of unit)   1
Nursing sisters   5
Staff nurses   7
Pediatrician in charge of day-to-day running of unit   1
Pediatric house officers   2 (stay for 6 months' duty and overlap for 3 months)
Pediatric consultants   2
Nursery nurses   6
Auxiliaries   2.5
Neonatal nursing students   4

The second group of mothers and low-birthweight babies (the intervention group) was recruited after the control group and received different treatment as follows:

increased encouragement to visit;
increased encouragement to touch, cuddle, change (nappies, clothes, sheets), tube-, bottle-, breast-feed, and bathe baby. Babies were transferred to cots at a lower weight (about 1,500 g);
a booklet "A guide for Parents of Babies in the Special Care Baby Unit";
a Polaroid photograph of the baby;
two discussions with the pediatrician, one at the baby's admission and one at discharge;
mothers stayed in the Mother and Baby Room with the baby for 2 nights before the baby went home;
health visitors visited:
    once a week before the baby came home;
    every day for the first 5 days the baby was home;
    once a week for the next month.

Sample Criteria

The Maternity Hospital in Cambridge, England, had delivered 3,324 babies in 1976, when this study began. This hospital is the regional center for East Anglia, and mothers at risk for obstetric problems are delivered there. The special care unit admits babies from about 10 other hospitals within a 50-mile radius of Cambridge, which deliver 2,061 babies per annum. There are 24 cots (including four for intensive care), and an admission rate of about 30 babies a month. It is the designated intensive care unit for the East Anglian Regional Health Authority (the counties of Norfolk, Suffolk, and Cambridgeshire). It also provides intensive care for three other counties, thus serving a population of about 2.5 million. There were 257 live premature births in 1976 (7.7% of the deliveries), and 63 babies (24.5%) were treated for respiratory distress. Of the premature live births, 32 babies weighed under 1,500 g and 21 of these babies (66%) survived.

I was interested in looking at a reasonably healthy sample of low-birthweight babies who had to stay in the special care unit for 3 weeks or more after birth, which meant that the mother would be visiting from home for at least a week. Initially, I planned to recruit second-borns where the first-born had not stayed in a special care unit, as this would have controlled for any effects of parity.

The final set of criteria for admission to the sample was as follows:

1. Low-birthweight babies (preterm, small-for-dates, or both) weighing under 1,900 g at birth and staying in the special care unit for a minimum of 3 weeks at birth.
2. Babies first- or second-born.
3. Babies with no congenital malformations and no need for artificial respiration (continuous positive airways pressure, CPAP, or intermittent positive pressure ventilation, IPPV) for more than 1 week.
4. Parents married, English-speaking, and staying in the area for a year.
5. Mothers booked at the Maternity Hospital (with special care baby unit, SCBU, upstairs).
6. Parents living within 20 miles of Cambridge.
7. Parents not receiving help from a social worker.
8. Mother who had no previous stillbirth, abortion, or a baby or child who died, but may have had a miscarriage.

I decided to concentrate on maternal reactions and interviewed the mothers only, although in some cases the father was present. The mothers were approached one or two days after the baby was admitted to the special care unit, depending on the baby's condition after birth. I explained the study and left a descriptive letter with them so they could think about it and discuss it with their husbands.

Data Collected

The main source of data was seven extensive interviews with each mother during her baby's first year. Other data consisted of the Brazelton Neonatal Behavioral Assessment Scale (BNBAS; Brazelton, 1973), performed at the baby's discharge from the hospital, when both groups had a mean gestational age of 38 weeks; the Prechtl Neurological Examination (Prechtl & Beintema, 1964) done at discharge and at conceptual age 8 weeks; the Denver Developmental Screening Test at postnatal ages 7 months and 12 months; medical information; visiting and contact rates (Hawthorne et al., 1978); observations of the mother's affectionate behavior at the baby clinic (Klaus & Kennell, 1976) at conceptual age 8 weeks, postnatal ages 7 months and 12 months; Schaffer and Emerson's (1964) brief separation index at 6 months, 9 months, and 12 months; health visitors' and nurses' reports (Hawthorne et al., 1978); and 48-hour diaries given to the mother to record the baby's behavior at five different time periods during the first year (similar to those used in Richards & Bernal, 1971).

The interviews were conducted with the mother three times before the baby went home, then at conceptual age 8 weeks, and at postnatal ages 6, 9, and 12 months. The information gained form the interviews fell into three main categories:

1. background information on mother and baby;
2. the mother's reaction to her baby and the baby's behavior during the first year;
3. the mother's attitudes toward the special care unit, the staff, and the care and support she received, and the effects this experience may have had on her or her baby.

The interview schedule and data collected are presented in Table 1.

The groups were collected one after the other, with the control group being collected from November to May and the intervention group from June to December. This avoided any contamination in treatments. The data were analyzed using nonparametric tests of significance such as the Mann-Whitney U test, chi-square test, and Fisher Exact Probability Test.

Description of the Intervention

In order to increase parents' access to their baby in the special care unit, I had to intervene to discuss the possibility of changing the routines of the nursing staff. Although there was an open visiting policy in the unit, quite often the amount of parental involvement depended on the attitude of the particular nurse on duty. I

Table 1.   Interview Schedule and Data Collected

Schedule	Data
Days 1–7 after baby's birth	Recruit mother. (Intervention group receive booklet and photograph.) Mother's and baby's medical information. Visiting and contact rates, telephone calls collected throughout baby's stay.
Mother and baby in hospital	*Interview 1*
Mother at home, baby in hospital	*Interview 2*
Just before baby's discharge	*Interview 3*
	Prechtl Neurological Examination. Brazelton Scale. Weight. Nurse's rating on baby.
Mother and baby at home 1–2 weeks	*Interview 4*
	48-hour diary. (Intervention group receive extra visits from health visitor.)
Mother and baby at home 1 month	Health visitor's report.
Baby aged 2 months (from expected date of delivery)	*Interview 5*
	48-hour diary. Clinic visit: Prechtl Neurological Examination, Mother/baby observations, Weight.
Baby aged 6 months from d.o.b.[a]	*Interview 6*
	Brief separation index. 48-hour diary.
Baby aged 7 months from d.o.b.	*Clinic Visit*
	Denver Test. Mother/baby observations. Weight.
Baby aged 9 months from d.o.b.	*Postal questionnaire*
	Brief separation index. 48-hour diary.
Baby aged 12 months from d.o.b.	*Interview 7*
	Brief separation index. 48-hour diary. Clinic visit: Denver Test, Mother/baby observations. Weight.

[a]d.o.b. = date of birth.

needed to ensure that encouraging the mothers to have early contact and handling became standard practice in the special care unit.

I was first granted access to the special care unit by the consultant pediatrician in charge. My first request was to collect data on parental visiting and telephone calls in the unit, as well as brief medical data on the mother and baby. During this phase, I was able to observe the current routines in the unit, get to know the staff, and to interview some mothers in order to find out about the experience of having a baby in a special care unit. This information then would contribute to the type of intervention I thought was necessary. There were four parts to the study:

Part 1

- Collection of data on parental visiting patterns and telephone calls and background medical data on mother and baby.
- Pilot interviews of 10 mothers.

Part 2

- Collection of the control group of mothers and babies ($N = 14$) under the status quo conditions.

Part 3

- Introduction of the intervention phase—discussions with doctors, nurses, and community health visitors.
- Collection of the intervention group of mothers and babies ($N = 11$).

Part 4 (planned but later abandoned)

- Collection of a third group of mothers and babies after a few months' gap, to see which interventions the hospital had retained.

In Part 1, I spent time getting to know the current attitudes and routines in the special care unit. Since I was an outsider to the hospital staff, I felt it was important to conform to their requirements (such as wearing a white coat) and to try to fit into the expected pattern of behavior. This required observational ability and sensitivity to the staff and their particular pressures each day. Therefore, I played the role of a participant-observer, making a special effort not to influence their routines and attitudes during this phase. I strove to establish a trust between myself and the staff (Gans, 1968).

During the collection of the control-group mothers and babies, I began discussing the intervention with the nursing officer in charge of the special care unit. We discussed how I wanted to promote even more contact between mother and baby, but it was only toward the time when the intervention was to be implemented that we determined the actual items to be introduced. From the beginning I stressed that for experimental purposes nothing should be changed until a certain date, after I had collected the control-group mothers under the conditions of the status quo.

There could be no control over things that changed apart from the intervention study or during the collection of the control group, for instance, ideas that had been considered for some time—including demand-feeding on the postnatal wards, and admission of babies weighing 2 kg to one of the postnatal wards instead of to the special care unit. These changes, along with my presence and my study of parental visiting, must have contributed in part to the changing perceptions of the staff, factors over which I had no control.

I had several discussions with the nursing officer over a period of months. The various procedures I wanted to introduce were brought up gradually, so as not to appear overwhelming. Some items were more difficult for her to accept than were others (e.g., allowing the parents to tube-feed their babies, giving an explanatory booklet about the special care unit and low-birthweight babies to the parents), and the nursing officer wanted time to think about them before she could agree to introduce a particular item. It took almost a year before the intervention items were accepted.

I described the intervention to the pediatricians, obstetricians, special care unit staff, hospital staff, community midwives and health visitors, the general practitioners, the Community Health Council, and the local branch of the National Association for the Welfare of Children in Hospital. I felt it was important to inform all health personnel who might be involved with the parents who were taking part, and the local groups that had expressed an interest in the study.

Once the intervention phase started, I played a directive role in ensuring that the appropriate variables were manipulated for each mother and baby in the study sample. The staff was keen to cooperate and often was eager to explain to me why one of the items had not yet been introduced to the parents. I was responsible for giving the photograph and the booklet to the parents, for reminding the pediatricians to talk to them, and for informing the physician in charge and the health visitor. The other intervention items soon were left for the staff to introduce, although I played a strong role in checking that the items were introduced as soon as possible.

During the intervention phase I changed my behavior in order to influence the changes in the hospital. More informal discussions took place with the staff in the unit, covering the needs of parents as well as staff comments on parental reactions. I encouraged the mothers to do as much as they could for their babies, suggesting they discuss any worries with the staff. I also gave the mothers feedback on other mothers' responses and needs.

The interest I showed in the parents' involvement in the care of their babies made a difference in the attitude of the staff. It was important to praise and encourage the staff as they began to increase the parents' involvement with the babies. Staff members were found to be very observant of parental reactions, even though they did not always perceive possible ways of alleviating parental anxiety.

I interacted with the baby in the unit during the collection of the control group and the intervention group by performing the Brazelton Neonatal Behavioral Assessment Scale (Brazelton, 1973). It may have helped the staff to see a tiny baby as a social being capable of responding to several forms of stimuli. By gaining this insight, the nurses' interest in the baby's abilities may well have passed on to the parents. The nurses also may have recognized that the baby is indeed a member of a family and therefore his or her isolation in a special care unit is all the more unusual. Staff can easily forget that the separation from the parents is enforced and can almost accept it as the status quo. Seeing the baby interacting socially may help to emphasize the baby's deprivation and increased need for a social environment. It also may encourage the staff to help the parents become more involved with their baby, in order to normalize the situation.

Results

Tables 2 and 3 show the characteristics of the sample. While the two groups were similar on the measures of background variables, there was a difference on two variables in Table 3, intubation at birth, and the levels of oxygen received in the special care unit. When a composite score for illness was compiled, there was no statistically significant difference between the two groups:

Table 2. Characteristics of Sample (Mothers)

	Control Group (N = 14)	Intervention Group (N = 11)
Mother's age		
mean	26 years	28 years[a]*
median	26 years	29 years
range	18–34 years	21–37 years
Marital status		
married	13 (93%)	11 (100%)
cohabiting	1 (7%)	0
Length of marriage (mean)	5 years	6 years
Method of delivery		
Normal delivery	4 (28%)	5 (45%)
Elective cesarean section	1 (7%)	3 (27%)
Emergency cesarean section	9 (64%)	3 (27%)
Maternal height (mean)	159 cm	265 cm[b]*
Maternal age at completion of education (mean)	16 years	16 years
Social class of husbands (Registrar General's Scale, U.K.)		
I and II	4 (28%)	6 (54%)
III WC	2 (14%)	0
III M and IV	8 (57%)	5 (45%)
Length of stay in hospital		
mean	8.2 days	8.0 days
range	2–13 days	2–12 days
Length of separation of mother and baby		
mean	27 days	25 days
range	8–57 days	10–54 days
Distance between home and hospital		
mean	20.8 km	16 km
range	1.6–43.2 km	1.6–35.2 km

Note. All results are expressed in percentages as well as in numbers solely in order to make comparison between the two unequal samples easier.
[a]$U = 47.0.$ [b]$U = 45.0.$
*$p < .10$, two-tailed.

Table 3.   Characteristics of Sample (Babies)

	Control Group (N = 14)	Intervention Group (N = 11)
Birthweight		
mean	1,555 g	1,545 g
range	1,110–1,840 g	910–1,940 g
Gestational age		
mean	33 weeks	33 weeks
range	28–38 weeks	27–37 weeks
Sex (male/female)	8/6 (57%/43%)	7/4 (64%/36%)
Under gestational age 37 weeks	12 (86%)	10 (91%)
Small-for-dates (<10th percentile in weight)	7 (50%)	5 (45%)
Firstborn	9 (64%)	6 (54%)
Length of stay in incubator		
mean	21 days	16 days
range	(5–51 days)	(6 hr–48 days)
Length of stay in SCBU		
mean	35 days	33 days
range	(21–64 days)	(19–63 days)
Days oxygen received	10.45	3.23
Severity of baby's illness		
not very ill	4 (28%)	6 (54%)
moderately ill	5 (36%)	3 (27%)
very ill	5 (36%)	2 (18%)
Diagnosed respiratory distress syndrom (RDS)	7 (50%)	4 (36%)
Baby's highest oxygen level (mean)	49%	25%†
Baby received ventilation at birth	7 (50%)	1 (9%)*
IPPV[a] in SCBU	1	0
IPPV + CPAP[b] in SCBU	2	2
IPPV/CPAP in SCBU + IPPV at birth	3	0

[a]Intermittent positive pressure ventilation.   [b]Continuous positive airways pressure.

*$p < .04$, one-tailed (Fisher Exact Probability Test).   †$p < .03$, two-tailed ($U = 38.0$).

Definition of code for severity of baby's illness

1. *Not very ill*—No oxygen, or oxygen for under 3 days only. No umbilical arterial catheter (UAC) or umbilical venous catheter (UVC).
2. *Moderately ill*—Oxygen therapy for over 3 days; UAC or UVC in use.
3. *Very ill*—Oxygen therapy at a level of 60% or more for over 3 days. Intermittent positive pressure ventilation (IPPV) or continuous positive airways pressure (CPAP), or both, in SCBU.

The condition of the infants must be taken into consideration when assessing the results of this study.

There also was a difference between the two groupps on measures of maternal height and maternal age at the $p < .10$ level (see Table 2). This could point to a difference in social class between the groups, for the intervention group mothers tended to be middle-class. We see that the variables maternal age at completion of education and social class of husbands showed no significant differences between the groups, however. These facts should be considered when assessing the results of this study.

Results of the BNBAS

The BNBAS was used to compare the two groups of babies before they left the hospital. It was performed only once, or twice if the first situation was not optimal, but one score was used. The scale was performed without the parents being present. (It is valuable, of course, to teach the parents the baby's abilities as an intervention.)

In this study the scale was used to assess the babies' characteristics in order to determine whether being in one group or the other might have been more rewarding to the mother and therefore give her a more positive feeling about her baby. It also helped me become familiar with the baby's repertoire, and to understand better the mother's reports about her baby at home.

The BNBAS scale was used since the full-term scale had been used staisfactorily for preterms who had reached gestational age of 37 weeks. Scores on each of the items were compared between the two groups and were analyzed by a two-tailed Mann-Whitney U test.

The results are shown in Table 4. There was one statistically significant difference between the two groups on the scale item Pull-to-Sit, where the control-group babies were "floppier." Of a possible scale between 1 and 9, the control group babies scored 3.7 and the intervention group babies scored 5.0. This finding, along with others pointing in the same direction, suggests that the control group babies behaved differently from the intervention group babies.

Results of the Hospital Intervention

I now shall describe the results of this study, focusing on statistically significant differences and similarities between the two groups. I also will discuss patterns that emerged with help to explain some of the group differences and similarities.

Table 4 illustrates the following results: There were no significant differences between the two groups in the total amount of parental visiting. This could be due to the fact that visiting rates in this particular special care unit were already high, with all mothers visiting at least once a day on average. While staff attitude

Table 4.   Parent-infant Visiting and Contact Rates in SCBU and Results of BNBAS

	Control Group (N = 14)	Intervention Group (N = 11)
Visiting per day (mean)		
Mother's visits	1.04	1.24
Father's visits	.72	.88
Contact per day (mean)		
Mother touches	.97	1.17
Mother holds	.70	.93*
Mother changes	.28	.58**
Mother feeds	.35	.42
Mother first saw baby in SCBU	58 hours	46 hours
Mother first touched baby in SCBU	68 hours	58 hours
Mother first held baby in SCBU	178 hours	115 hours
Mother first fed baby in SCBU	24.5 days	21.2 days
Mother first changed baby in SCBU	23.3 days	8.1 days***
BNBAS results	(n = 13)	(n = 10)
Pull-to-sit (score 1–9)	3.7	5.0†

*$p < .05$, one-tailed ($U = 45.5$).
**$p < .005$, one-tailed ($U = 29.0$).
***$p < .0003$, one-tailed ($U = 14.5$).
†$p < .05$, two-tailed ($U = 34.5$).

affects visiting rates, physical constraints such as having other children at home and transportation difficulties have more of an impact on visiting rates.

Although there was no significant difference, the control group mothers more often described themselves as being in a state of shock and disbelief over their baby, as being critical of staff members and inhibited by them, and as being frightened and scared of the baby. Babies in incubators tended to be more frightening to mothers, who had more of an incentive to visit when their babies were put in an open cot. Mothers in the intervention group spent a longer time on their visits during the second week, presumably because they had more to do for the baby in the unit.

Contact

There were significant differences in the amount of mother-infant contact between the two groups. The intervention group mothers cuddled and changed their babies significantly more often than did the control group mothers (see Table 4). The control group mothers took a longer time to touch their babies and first changed their nappies much later than did the intervention group mothers. This was a direct result of the intervention, although it was affected partially by whether or not the babies were receiving oxygen therapy. In general, the intervention group mothers tended to feel less inhibited in the special care unit and more often expressed being upset at the way their baby was being handled.

Feeding

More mothers in the intervention group tube-fed their babies, as was intended, but there was no significant difference between the two groups in the number of women who stored their milk for their babies or who went home breast-feeding their babies, although the numbers in both groups were high (see Table 5).

It was hypothesized that the intervention and increased encouragement to breast-feed would increase the number of mothers who were successful at maintaining their lactation; no increase was seen, however. Although there was a milk bank at the unit and the staff maintained a high interest in breast-feeding, it appeared from the interview comments that much more of the right kind of support and encouragement was needed, such as information on how to maintain lactation until the baby could suck.

It was evident that the severity of the baby's illness influenced the ease of breast-feeding, although anxiety about breast-feeding was not always associated with the baby's previous medical problems. Breast-feeding mothers in both groups were highly anxious about their baby's weight gain, and two mothers were very anxious and critical of the hospital staff for not giving them enough

Table 5. Other Results: Tube-Feeding, Talks with Doctor, Use of the Mother and Baby Room

	Control ($N = 14$)	Intervention ($N = 11$)
Mother tube-fed baby	2 (14%)	8 (73%)*
Mother expressed milk in SCBU	8 (57%)	9 (82%)
Mother breast-fed at home	5 (36%)	4 (36%)
	($n = 5$)	($n = 4$)
Length of time mother breast-fed (mean)	5 months	9 months
Number of primiparae	2	2
Number of multiparae	3	2
	($N = 14$)	($N = 11$)
Mother talked with pediatrician on baby's admission and discharge		
Yes	8 (57%)	9 (82%)
No	6 (43%)	2 (18%)
Use of Mother and Baby Room		
Primiparae	9 (100%)	4 (67%)
Multiparae	2 (40%)	3 (60%)
Mother stayed 1 night	10 (91%)	4 (57%)
Mother stayed 2–4 nights	1 (9%)	3 (43%)

*$p < .005$, one-tailed (Fisher Exact Probability Test).

support and encouragement to breast-feed. Mothers in both groups felt that storing their milk was the most positive thing they could do for their baby during the separation. This influenced their visiting patterns to a certain extent, as they had to bring their milk to the special care unit milk bank. The availability of breast pumps was also important, and the electric ones, which were difficult to find, seemed to be better for the mothers. The cost of hiring these pumps was considered high by some mothers, and in several cases they or their husbands had to drive up to 60–65 km to secure a pump.

The intervention helped increase the support for breast-feeding mothers and show the staff how breast-feeding made mothers feel much closer to their babies. This illustrates the importance of the need to satisfy the mother's instinct to nurture. The mothers appreciated it if one nurse spent time with them while they were breast-feeding, until they felt at ease with the situation. Special care units would benefit from having a breast-feeding counselor present to help mothers.

Other Intervention Items

Talks with a pediatrician. The doctors were asked to talk to the parents on the baby's admission and discharge from the special care unit. In the pilot study I found that parents of ill newborns spoke often to a pediatrician, but parents of healthier babies often never spoke to a doctor.

There were more mothers in the intervention group who spoke to a doctor, although the difference was not statistically significant (see Table 5). The pediatricians probably spent more time with the intervention group than the control group, as they talked to 9 of the mothers at least twice. In the cases in which the mother was ill, the father talked to the doctors and passed information on to her.

There were other non–statistically significant results to suggest that intervention alleviates tension with the staff who work along with the mother and help to make her feel more responsible for her baby. The intervention group mothers were less critical of the staff and were more likely to feel that their baby belonged to them while still in the special care unit. It is clear that staff attitudes and the ways staff members include the mother in the care of her baby may have a bearing on how the mother feels about her baby, although of course her own background and experiences also will influence her reaction.

Use of the Mother and Baby Room. The policy of the special care unit before the intervention was to encourage mothers to stay in the Mother and Baby Room for 1 night with the baby beside them, and then take the baby home the next day. Primiparae were always asked to come in, and sometimes multiparae. Mothers who were breast-feeding often came to stay for a number of days in order to establish breast-feeding.

All primiparae in the control group used the Mother and Baby Room, but it is interesting to note that 2 of the primiparae in the intervention group refused to stay there (see Table 5). They felt they knew their babies quite well, as they had been caring for them in the special care unit, and they were not eager to stay in the hospital again. Primiparae in both groups wished they had stayed longer than one or sometimes even two nights, however, when asked this question later. The Mother and Baby Room served as a halfway point between sharing the baby with the nurses and having the baby at home alone. In general, many of the primiparae in this study felt anxious and overburdened when they found themselves at home alone with their babies. A more gradual introduction to total responsibility for their baby might have helped them.

Booklet[1]. A booklet describing the special care unit and the sorts of problems a baby who needs special or intensive care might have and explaining what parents can do for their baby and how they might feel was given to the mothers in the intervention group.

The booklet was well received, with no mothers objecting to the information it contained and all reporting that they felt better informed. The information enabled the parents to understand better the procedures in the special care unit and to feel more confident about asking questions of the staff and less hesitant with them.

The initial worry about the booklet among some of the hospital staff appears to be unfounded. In this study, the working-class mothers appear to have found the booklet easy to read and the information clearly presented. No one said the booklet was too long or the information too worrying. There was also no indication that the booklet had usurped the role of the staff; instead, the booklet seems to have enhanced it. In fact, a booklet should never be used in isolation, and the staff found the booklet a valuable addition to the information they provided; parents often need information repeated, and they tend to reread the booklet several times.

Photograph. Along with the booklet, each mother in the intervention group was given a Polaroid photograph of her baby, taken soon after the baby's admission to the special care unit. All mothers were very pleased to have the photograph and said it was proof that they had a baby. The photograph was a tangible reminder of their baby, who was not beside them on the postnatal ward. When the mother was visiting from home, the photograph could reassure her of the baby's appearance so that she would not have to imagine the worst from a distance. (The photograph should be given to the mother only after she has been told what she will see, or after she has seen the baby in person, as a baby on a ventilator and monitor can be an alarming sight. The sooner the mother receives the photograph the better.)

The photograph and the booklet were useful instruments for demonstrating the desire of the staff to communicate to parents and created an overall difference in atmosphere in the special care unit. The staff may have reacted to these tools and

---

[1] For a copy of this booklet, see the appendix in Davis, Richards, & Roberton (1983).

to the changes in routine by becoming more aware of the parents' needs and realizing that the baby belongs to the parents.

Health visitor follow-up. The intervention was successful in increasing the number of visits made by the health visitors during the first 1–2 weeks that the baby was first at home, but not in the other two time periods that they were asked to visit, that is, once a week before the baby came home and once a week until the baby had been home for month (see Table 6).

The visits before the baby came home appeared to be difficult for the health visitors to make and in general were not part of their routine. The liaison health visitor at the hospital informed the mother's own health visitor of the baby's condition and several of the health visitors liked to try to meet the mother before the baby went home. Results showed that the health visitors visited both the control and intervention group mothers a similar number of times during the first month. They agreed that follow-up on mothers and babies from the special care unit was important.

While the baby is in the hospital, the mother becomes used to relying on the nurses for advice and there is a quick reduction in the advice and moral support mothers receive once their babies go home. The community health visitor can thus play a vital role in supporting mothers of special care babies. Some mothers reported that their health visitors were unfamiliar with the requirements of low-

Table 6.   Visits by Health Visitor and Hospital Admissions

	Control Group (N = 14)	Intervention Group (N = 11)
Health visitor's visits (mean)		
before baby went home	.8	1.5
1–2 weeks baby at home	2.0	5.5*
Interview 5	3.2	2.4
Interview 6	.8	1.0
9 months	1.1	.5
1 year	1.1	.4

Admissions to hospital in first year Control Group (N = 14)	Intervention Group (N = 11)
1. Inguinal hernia	1. Pyloric stenosis
2. Febrile illness (near-miss cot death?)	2. Echovirus 11
3. Bronchiolitis	
4. Vomiting and nappy rash	
5. Feeding and management	
6. Failure to thrive (+ surgery for squint)	
Total = 6 (43%)	Total = 2 (18%)

*$p < .001$, one-tailed ($U = 9.0$).

birthweight babies. It may be that a properly trained premature baby nurse should be available for mothers in the community; these exist in some areas.

The rehospitalization rate for babies from special care units in the first year, particularly low-birthweight babies weighing less than 1,500 g, was reported to be 33% by Hack, De Monterice, Merkatz, Jones, and Fanaroff (1981). In my study, 6 babies (43%) in the control group and only 2 babies (18%) in the intervention group were readmitted to the hospital in their first year. Although this was not a statistically significant difference, it is interesting to note that 3 out of the 6 control group babies were readmitted for feeding and management problems, whereas none of the intervention group babies went to the hospital for this reason (see Table 6). More health visitor follow-up may help mothers to overcome any such problems at home and this is a question for further research. It should be remembered that parents are often much more worried than doctors and nurses about their low-birthweight babies, an important fact to consider when organizing follow-up care for these families (Boyle, Giffen, & Fitzhardinge, 1977).

Results of Follow-up at Home

I followed up the mothers and babies until the babies were a year old. There were some significant differences between the two groups on follow-up. The intervention group babies weighed significantly more at 2 and 7 months of age, as shown in Table 7.

The intervention group mothers tended to breast-feed for longer (a mean of 9 months compared to 5 months in the control group, a nonsignificant difference; see Table 5). In general, the intervention group babies were thriving throughout the first year. Although this difference cannot be attributed entirely to the effects of intervention, because of the small sample size and some background differences, it is possible that intervention, providing more support for parents and thereby fostering a better parent-child relationship, could have a result such as this. Several studies show that a babies who are the appropriate weight for their age are indicative of better mother-child relationships (Kempe & Kempe, 1978).

Another finding showed a significant difference between the two groups in the amount of affectionate behavior the mothers showed to their babies during the doctor's physical examination at the baby clinic. When the baby was 2 months old (conceptual age) the intervention group mothers hugged their baby more often (see Table 7). This result is similar to that of the study by de Chateau (1976), who found that mothers who had early contact with their babies showed more affectionate behavior (en-face position and kissing) with their 3-month-old babies at home than did the control group mothers who had not had early contact. Klaus et al. (1972) also showed similar results at a doctor's physical examination where the mothers who had had early contact stood closer to the baby.

There were some differences between the two groups on measures of babies'

Table 7.   Results of Babies' Weight Gain and Behavior on Follow-up

	Control Group (N = 14)	Intervention Group (N = 11)
Birthweight		
mean	1,555	1,545 g
range	1,110–1,840 g	910–1,940 g
Babies regained birthweight (day)	13	13
Weight at discharge	2,139	2,128 g
Weight at 2 months	4,051 g	4,798 g****
Weight at 7 months	6,003 g	6,956 g***[1]
Weight at 12 months	8,560 g	8,720 g
	(n = 13)	(n = 11)
Mothers' affectionate behaviors at baby clinic at 2 months (mean frequency)	2.2	3.6**
	(N = 14)	(N = 11)
Baby has sleeping problems at 1 year	7 (50%)	1 (9%)
Baby takes Phenergan at 1 year	3 (21%)	1 (9%)
Brief Separation Index[c]		
Baby protests put in cot at night (9 months)		
yes	1 (7%)	7 (64%)*
sometimes	7 (50%)	1 (9%)
no	6 (43%)	3 (27%)
Baby protests left alone in room (9 months)		
yes	4 (29%)	8 (57%)***[2]
sometimes	7 (50%)	0
no	3 (21%)	3 (27%)
Baby fussy with food (1 year)	1 (7%)	7 (64%)

[a]Schaffer and Emerson (1964).
*$p < .04$, two-tailed ($U = 41.0$).   **$p < .03$, two-tailed ($U = 39.0$).   ***$p < .02$, two-tailed:
[1]$U = 34.5$; [2]$U = 38.5$.   ****$p < .01$, two-tailed ($U = 31.5$).

sleeping behavior. At 1 year, more control group mothers were reporting troubles with the babies' sleeping, such as trouble settling them to bed at night or their waking during the night (see Table 7). Three babies in the control group and only 1 in the intervention group were being given Phenergan, a sedative, for sleeping problems. Some factors affecting sleep patterns could have been responsible, such as the finding that perinatal factors affect night waking (Blurton Jones, Rossetti Ferreria, Farquar Brown, & MacDonald, 1978), and the control group babies' poorer condition at birth. Measures were also taken of the babies' crying and fussing behavior. At 2 months, significantly more intervention group babies were reported to be crying in the evenings. At 9 months old, significantly more babies in the intervention group always fussed when put in their cot at night and when left alone in a room. This fussiness of the intervention group babies shows up again in their fussiness over food at 1 year, suggesting that they may be more demanding than the control group babies (see Table 7).

Many of these findings suggest that the intervention group mothers tended to be more anxious and their babies fussier than the control group mothers and babies, respectively. The intervention group mothers might have been more responsive to their babies or more willing to acknowledge their babies' demands and therefore their babies were fussier. Other studies have shown that maternal anxiety is heightened by having early contact with an ill baby and the consequent parental nervousness may result in overprotectiveness (Douglas & Gear, 1976; Harper, Sia, Sokol, & Sokol, 1976). Harper et al. showed that high levels of contact with babies in a special care unit are correlated with high levels of parental anxiety at first, but 90% of the parents would have opposed any restriction of contact. Studies of conditions in which no or minimal contact has taken place produce more worrying and detrimental results about the parent-child relationship (Klaus et al., 1972). Heightened anxiety is not in itself a negative finding, as it shows that the parents are involved with the baby rather than neglecting it.

Interaction with the Staff

In general, the intervention group felt less inhibited and self-conscious with the staff, which suggests that a change in staff attitude could have taken place (see Table 8). This did not alter the fact that about half the mothers in each group thought the nurses knew their babies better than they themselves did; there was some jealousy. These findings bring up the topic of rivalry, which can arise between staff and parents when there is not enough support or opportunity for

Table 8. Mothers' Condition and Reactions to Separation

	Control Group ($N = 14$)	Intervention Group ($N = 11$)
Mother feels self-conscious/in way/shy in	6 (43%)	0**
SCBU	8 (57%)	6 (54%)
Nurses know baby better	2 (14%)	7 (64%)**
Mother had routine since baby came		
home (9 months)		
Mother took tablets in last year		
Valium	2 (14%)	0
antidepressants	1 (7%)	2 (18%)
sleeping piils	1 (7%)	0
Mother under doctor's care (1 year)	6 (43%)	5 (45%)
Mother feels baby is really hers once	11 (78%)	8 (73%)
taken home		
Mother describes baby negatively (1 year)	5 (36%)	3 (27%)
Mother overprotective, possessive (1 year)	2 (14%)	6 (54.5%)*
Mother underprotective (1 year)	0	2 (18.2%)

*$p < .04$ (Fisher Exact Probability Test).   **$p < .02$ (Fisher Exact Probability Test).

both staff and parents to air grievances. From the negative comments made about the postnatal ward staff, it would appear that all maternity hospital staff need to be better prepared for the sort of support mothers with babies in special care units need.

In this study I have not examined closely the needs of the staff in coping with their problems of working in a highly specialized field where they constantly confront human difficulties and tragedy. Their needs for airing their views, coping with their personal reactions, and learning to work alongside parents and their babies should not be underestimated (Bender & Swan-Parente, 1983). Clearly, for a special care unit to run smoothly, meeting the emotional needs of staff members is just as important as meeting those of parents.

Maternal Feelings and Family Problems

Many of the family doctors did not know about the baby's birth until the baby was at home perhaps as much as several weeks later. If they had known sooner, they might have supported the parents and provided medical attention if necessary. In the early interviews, several of the mothers in both groups reported emotional difficulties with which they usually grappled alone. They continued to struggle with feelings of guilt at having produced a small or preterm baby; anxiety over the baby's condition and over feeding (especially breast-feeding); tiredness and the rush of visiting; sadness and impatience about the separation from their baby; remoteness and detachment from the baby; and difficulties with their other child or children or relatives. The situation was stressful for several families. Often fathers had to miss days of work to stay at home with the children. One mother said her husband had been so worried and tired that he started drinking; another father asked the doctor for tranquilizers, and another started having severe asthma attacks and also was treated for depression. Some husbands reported weight loss during this period. The strain on some families in this situation should not be underestimated. It is just becoming generally recognized that parents of neonatal unit babies may need the support of psychotherapists and psychiatrists who should be members of the team caring for parents and babies in these units (Bender & Swan-Parente, 1983).

Many mothers in both groups continued to report problems later in the first year. Some remembered that while their baby was in the special care unit they felt irritable; others lost their appetite; others felt preoccupied with thoughts of the baby. Several of the mothers had family tensions such as troubles with in-laws or with their husbands. Many of the mothers were tired because their baby needed feeding often. Several mothers expressed the need for more help or support from outsiders, such as the health visitor, family doctor, or community clinic, and other mothers wished their husband would help more.

By the time the baby was 6 months old, the mothers seemed to have regained some confidence but they were still adapting to the baby's characteristics and dealing with any sickness that persisted. It is my impression that although the mothers may regain confidence in the day-to-day care of their baby, they may still need to overcome some of these remaining feelings which might prevent them from successfully adapting to subsequent stages of the baby's development.

When the baby was 9 months old, significantly more intervention group mothers felt they had established a routine since the baby came home (see Table 8). While it might be that intervention could have this effect, I must also point out that 5 babies in the control group and 2 babies in the intervention group had another stay in hospital by the age of 9 months. It would not be surprising if these admissions had caused disruption and delayed adaptation of mother and baby.

At 1 year, the mothers were asked about their feelings and their reaction to the earlier separation. The mothers reported less depression at 1 year, whereas after the baby's birth they had reported being "weepy," "down in the dumps," and said they "cried when [the baby] cried" and felt "blues and depression, and extreme anxiety." One mother in each group felt depressed for 3 months and 6 months, respectively. Some of the mothers didn't report depression, but said they were "just upset," "just exhausted and didn't feel well," "moody and cried a lot but not depressed," and one "felt awful at leaving hospital without the baby and drank a glass of sherry at 10:00 a.m. to get out of there." During the year, 2 mothers took Valium, 3 mothers took antidepressants, and 1 mother took sleeping pills (see Table 8). Tragically, one of the fathers died of a heart attack when the baby was 11 months old. Several mothers in both groups reported being fed up, lonely, or worried about their baby. One couple in the intervention group were in the process of separating and were seeing a psychotherapist once a week. Six mothers in the control group and 5 in the intervention group were under a doctor's care for certain medical problems at a year.

It is evident from these findings that mothers of special care unit babies have more than their share of personal problems and need extra support to deal with the difficulties they encounter when their baby has to stay in a special care unit.

The Mother's Relationship with Her Baby

When looking at the mother's relationship with her baby, we see that most mothers in both groups felt closer to their babies once their babies came home, but there were a few mothers who were a bit doubtful or still felt a bit detached (see Table 8). It seems that early contact alone cannot completely eradicate the emotional difficulties; this has been suggested in other studies (see Ross, 1980). Support should help to build a mother's self-confidence and treat her emotional difficulties. Some mothers in this study felt that the baby was born the day he or she came home, and this appeared to make them feel better about developing a relationship with the baby, as they felt less concerned that they had "missed out" while the baby was in the special care unit.

The Impact of the Special Care Unit Experience on the Mothers and Babies

Throughout the interviews, I asked each mother whether she thought her baby needed special treatment, whether she still thought of her baby as small or premature, and what her opinion of the effects of separation on her and her baby was. Minde (1980) has suggested that mothers who have ill or very small babies might hold a "cognitive set" of the way they first see their babies for some time. These maternal perceptions may have an effect on the relationship between mother and baby; this reaction requires further research.

It appears from this study that the very fact that the baby was in the special care unit at all may affect the mother's perception of her baby and result in her feeling "possessive" about the baby, "spoiling" the baby, or feeling that the baby needs some special treatment. The data show that a substantial number of mothers in both groups felt that the special care unit experience had affected them or their baby in some way. This provides some evidence that these mothers may have altered views of their relationship with their baby as a result of the separation. Some of the mothers thought they were more anxious, had missed out, treated the baby specially, were more protective or more remote. At 1 year, fewer control group mothers described themselves as being underprotective while more intervention group mothers felt themselves to be overprotective or possessive (see Table 8). Many of the mothers still thought of the baby as premature or small. About half the mothers in each group felt responsible for the fact their baby was premature.

This continued perception of the baby could be an important factor in the continuing relationship of the mother and baby. Although increased handling and sympathetic staff attitudes appears to alleviate some of the mother's feeling of "not belonging" when she does visit her baby, there appear to be other feelings of guilt, disappointment, and helplessness. Help in resolving the psychological reactions to the crisis of a preterm birth could mean that mothers overcome their disappointment sooner (Sherman, 1980). Mothers are able to deal better with the separation if they are given adequate factual information and emotional support.

There may be many reasons for the concern these mothers show about the effects of separation, including the fact that I was questioning them about it. Also the issue of bonding was being widely discussed by both the media and the health services during the period in which I was recruiting and following-up the sample (1976–1978), and mothers may have been influenced by this. An atmosphere of tension over the issue of early separation and an expectation of difficulties have perhaps been created which could be more damaging than the separation itself (Richards, 1979; Ross, 1980). Richards (1981) concludes that so much emphasis has been placed on the bonding issue that the real problems of the mothers may have been missed.

A sufficient reason for improving facilities for mother-infant contact is surely that mothers prefer it. The special care unit environment is not conducive to a normal relationship between mother and baby. Even though changes can be made to make the situation more normal, to reduce anxiety and increase confidence, in essence it remains an artificial environment. It is important that we do not make parents anxious about possible deleterious effects but instead help them emotionally to cope with the experience.

Discussion and Conclusion

The results of this study show that it is possible to change routines in a special care unit in order to allow parents more contact with their baby. The hospital retained many of the ideas introduced, such as the booklet, the photograph, and increased use of the Mother and Baby Room. Breast-feeding is common, and in 1979–1980, 50% of the babies were breast-feeding on discharge. Parental involvement has become standard practice, and some low-birthweight babies are also nursed on an adjoining postnatal ward beside their mothers (Whitby, de Cates, & Roberton, 1983). It is also becoming more common for nurses to recognize their role in facilitating mother-baby interaction (Boxall & Whitby, 1983). The unit welcomes grandparents, siblings, and other family members to visit the baby.

A new hospital, the Rosie Maternity Hospital, opened in Cambridge in October 1983 and provides further facilities for mothers, such as six Mother and Baby Rooms, a sitting room, and kitchen in a unit which has 18 special care and six intensive care cots. A discussion group for parents and one for staff members are being set up and a counselor will be available.

Some of the hypotheses were confirmed in this study: The intervention group mothers felt more relaxed with the staff, reported fewer difficulties at home with their babies, and felt they had a routine sooner than the control group mothers. The intervention was successful in encouraging the mothers to do more for their babies in the unit, such as tube-feed and change their babies. The booklet and the photograph helped them feel better informed and involved in their baby's care.

The majority of findings show that mothers would have welcomed even more support than was provided. Although there was a milk bank where breast milk could be frozen, and although the staff promoted breast-feeding, the majority of mothers felt there was little information on how to maintain lactation. Much more information and psychological support was needed by these mothers, who would have welcomed the advice of a nurse or midwife whose role as a breast-feeding counselor could have given them individual help and support.

It is also clear from this study that many of the mothers, or parents, would have benefited from some form of counseling or support group in order to overcome their anxiety and cope with their feelings. Although there was an open attitude to visiting, mothers lacked emotional support. It may be that with appropriate training, all the staff members in a special care baby unit could give the mother a sense of increased responsibility for her baby by helping her to feel included in the baby's care. Although this took place to a certain degree in this study, it is evident that there is the need for an appropriately trained person such as a psychotherapist or psychiatrist to be a member of the staff in special care baby units in order to help parents and staff through their difficulties. The fact that many mothers in both groups felt that the separation may have affected them or their baby in some lasting way points to the need for resolving these feelings. There is some suggestion that unresolved feelings can interfere with the development of a healthy mother-child relationship (Minde, 1980). In this society in which people worry about the effect of early child-care practices on child development and mother-infant relationships, and in which little family support is available, medical and social support is vital. Different cultures provide social support in different ways, and care must be taken not to eliminate emotional support by technological advances. American and European studies have well illustrated the consequences of emphasizing the medical in place of the social effects on babies in special care units, and care should be taken by other societies not to repeat this mistake.

Another issue arising from this study has to do with intervention itself. Clearly, changing hospital routines is not simply a matter of altering the practical aspects of parental involvement; it involves a completely new approach in staff attitude toward the inclusion of parents in the care of their baby. The sensitivity of the staff to each mother's individual needs in caring for her baby is important. Mothers may not want to become closely involved right away and it is vital to let them move at their own pace. In this study I found that some mothers preferred not to tube-feed their baby, but rather to stroke the baby or hold the baby's hand. It would be detrimental to require all parents to perform a particular activity. Parents must be given a choice in performing tasks for their baby. One mother may want to handle her ill baby, another may not. We may discover that the mother's readiness to touch her baby is more important than physical togetherness at an early stage. It is important, therefore, that the report of this study does not encourage hospitals blindly to enforce contact between parents and babies, but rather teaches hospitals to ensure that parents' individual needs are understood when encouraging contact.

This study shows that changes in staff policy cannot take place overnight; a gradual introduction to changes must occur. It took a year of my presence in the unit as well as extensive discussions with the staff before changes were accepted. The seeds of changes must have been present in the unit for me to enlist as much cooperation as I did. Other units in the country were also changing their attitudes to parental involvement because of the increased attention paid to this field by the media and the health services. Many units now use booklets and photographs and encourage parent-infant contact. Although there has been very little formal assessment of such changes as the increases in visiting and contact and communication between staff and parents, the parents' wish for close contact and information about their baby is probably a sufficient reason for this approach. It must be remembered that the baby belongs to the parents, who will be responsible for the child for many years to come.

References

Barnett, C. R., Leiderman, P. H., Grobstein, R., & Klaus, M. H. (1970). Neonatal separation: The maternal side of interactional deprivation. *Pediatrics, 45* 197–205.

Bender, H., & Swan-Parente, A. (1983). Psychological and Psychotherapeutic support of staff and parents in an intensive care baby unit. In J. A. Davis, M. P. M. Richards, & N. R. C. Roberton (Eds.), *Parent-baby attachment in premature infants* (pp. 165–176). London: Croom Helm.

Blurton Jones, N., Rossetti Ferreria, C., Farquar Brown, M., & MacDonald, L. (1978). The association between perinatal factors and later night waking. *Developmental Medicine and Child Neurology, 20*(4), 427–434.

Boxall, J., & Whitby, C. (1983). The role of the nurse in mother-baby interaction. In J. A. Davis, M. P. M. Richards, & N. R. C. Roberton (Eds.), *Parent-baby attachment in premature infants* (pp. 129–138). London: Croom Helm.

Boyle, M., Griffen, A., & Fitzhardinge, P. (1977). The very low birthweight infant: Impact on parents during the pre-school years. *Early Human Development, 1*(2), 191–201.

Brazelton, T. B. (1973). *Neonatal Behavioral Assessment Scale.* London: Spastics International Medical Publications/Heinemann Medical Books.

Brimblecombe, F. S. W., Richards, M. P. M., & Roberton, N. R. C. (Eds.). (1978). *Separation and special care baby units.* London: Spastics International Medical Publications/Heinemann Medical Books.

Chamberlain, R., Chamberlain, G., Howlett, B., & Claireaux, A. (1975). *British births 1970: Vol. 1. The first week of life.* London: Heinemann Medical Books.

de Chateau, P. (1976). *Neonatal care routines: Influences on maternal and infant behaviour and on breastfeeding.* (Umea University Medical Dissertation, New Series, No. 20). Umea, Sweden.

Davis, J. A., Richards, M. P. M., & Roberton, N. R. C. (Eds.). (1983). *Parent-baby attachment in premature infants.* London: Croom Helm.

Douglas, J. W. B., & Gear, R. (1976). Children of low birthweight in the 1946 national cohort. *Archives of Disease in Childhood, 51,* 820–827.

Gans, H. J. (1968). The participant-observer as a human being: Observations on the personal aspects of field work. In H. S. Becker, B. Geer, D. Riesman, & R. S. Weiss (Eds.), *Institutions and the person* (pp. 300–317). Chicago: Aldine.

Hack, M., De Monterice, D., Merkatz, I. R., Jones, P., & Fanaroff, A. A. (1981). Rehospitalization of the very low-birthweight infant. *American Journal of Diseases in Childhood, 135,* 263–266.

Harper, R. G., Sia, C., Sokol, S., & Sokol, M. (1976). Observations on unrestricted parental contact with infants in the neonatal intensive care unit. *Journal of Pediatrics, 89*(3), 441–445.

Hawthorne, J. T., Richards, M. P. M., & Callon, M. (1978). A study of parental visiting of babies in a special care unit. In F. S. W. Brimblecombe, M. P. M. Richards, & N. R. C. Roberton (Eds.), *Separation and special care baby units* (pp. 33–54). London: Spastics International Medical Publications/Heinemann Medical Books.

Kempe, R. S., & Kempe, C. H. (1978). *Child abuse*. London: Fontana/Open Books.

Klaus, M., Jerauld, R., Kreger, N., McAlpine, W., Steffa, M., & Kennell, J. H. (1972). Maternal attachment: The importance of the first postpartum days. *New England Journal of Medicine, 286,* 460–463.

Klaus, M. H., & Kennell, J. H. (1976). *Maternal-infant bonding*. St. Louis, MO: Mosby.

Minde, K. K. (1980). Bonding of parents to premature infants: Theory and practice. In P. M. Taylor (Ed.), *Parent-infant relationships* (pp. 291–313). New York: Grune & Stratton.

Prechtl, H., & Beintema, D. (1964). *The neurological examination of the full-term newborn infant* (Little Club Clinics in Developmental Medicine, No. 12). London: Spastics International Medical Publications/Heinemann Medical Books.

Richards, M. P. M. (1978). Possible effects of early separation on later development in children—A review. In F. S. W. Brimblecombe, M. P. M. Richards, & N. R. C. Roberton (Eds.), *Separation and special care baby units* (Clinics in Developmental Medicine, No. 68, pp. 12–32). London: Spastics International Medical Publications/Heinemann Medical Books.

Richards, M. P. M. (1979). Effects on development of medical interventions and the separation of newborns from their parents. In D. Shaffer & J. Dunn, (Eds.), *The first year of life* (pp. 37–54). London: Wiley.

Richards, M. P. M. (1981, April). *The myth of bonding*. Paper presented at a conference of the Royal Society of Medicine on "Pregnancy Care for the 1980s." London.

Richards, M. P. M., & Bernal, J. F. (1971). Social interaction in the first days of life. In H. R. Schaffer (Ed.), *The origins of human social relations* (pp. 3–13). London: Academic Press.

Richards, M. P. M., & Roberton, N. R. C. (1978). Admission and discharge policies for special care units. In F. S. W. Brimblecombe, M. P. M. Richards, & N. R. C. Roberton (Eds.), *Separation and special care baby units* (pp. 82–110). London: Spastics International Medical Publications/Heinemann Medical Books.

Rosenfield, A. G. (1980). Visiting in the intensive care nursery. *Child Development, 51*(3), 939–941.

Ross, G. S. (1980). Parental responses to infants in intensive care: The separation issue re-evaluated. *Clinics in Perinatology, 7,* 47–61.

Schaffer, H. R., & Emerson, P. E. (1964). The development of social attachments in infancy. *Monographs of the Society for Research in Child Development, 29*(94).

Sherman, M. (1980). Psychiatry in the neonatal intensive care unit. *Clinics in Perinatology, 7*(1), 33–46.

Whitby, C., de Cates, C. M., & Roberton, N. R. C. (1983). Neonatal care in the Cambridge unit. In J. A. Davis, M. P. M. Richards, & N. R. C. Roberton, (Eds.), *Parent-Baby attachment in premature infants* (pp. 232–242). London: Croom Helm.

PART III

CROSS-CULTURAL COMPARISONS IN INFANT BEHAVIOR

CHAPTER 10

Environment and Early Development: An Israeli Cross-cultural Comparison*

Judith Auerbach, Charles W. Greenbaum, Rivka Nowik,
Ruth Guttman, and Judith Margolin

*Department of Psychology,
Hebrew University,
Jerusalem, Israel*

Frances Degen Horowitz

*Department of Human Development,
University of Kansas,
Lawrence, Kansas*

The purpose of this chapter is to review the research done in Israel on neonatal behavior, and to present our study on infants from varying social groups and origins who were administered the Brazelton Neonatal Behavioral Assessment Scale (BNBAS; Brazelton, 1973). We view this effort as part of a growing tradition of cross-cultural research whose purpose is to determine which aspects

* This research was funded by grants from the Ford Foundation, the United States-Israeli Binational Science Foundation, the Irving Harris Foundation, the James Marshall Fund, and the Struman Center of Human Development.

We wish to thank the following for their generous help and assistance: Ms. Aviva Lion, Children's Service, Ministry of Labor and Social Betterment; Dr. Dov Tamir, Department of Public Health, Municipality of Jerusalem; Shoshana Alon, Mother-Child Health Care Station; Ir Ganim, Jerusalem; Rita Mansour, Mother-Child Health Care Station, Nahlaot, Jerusalem; Professor Arthur Eidelman, Department of Neonatology, Shaare Zedek Medical Center. We would also like to thank our research staff, in particular Yanit Be'er, Elisheva Mogilner, Shela Golgursky, Galia Arzi, and Ruth Pat-Horenchick, our BNBAS-K examiners. In addition, we are indebted to Tali Arbel, Schumuel Bronner, Moti Ferdman, Israel Kosowsky, and Shlomit Levy for their work on the statistical analysis of the data.

of neonatal behavior are invariant and what their possible origins are. Parallel to these questions is that of determining characteristics of behavior specific to various groups differing in ethnic or social characteristics. However, the research to be reported here is limited to cross-cultural studies within the predominantly Jewish population of Israel, though our brief review will consider studies done with Arab populations as well.

Cultural and Social Class Settings in Israel

In 1982, Israel had a population of 4,373,200, of which 3,337,200 were Jews and 690,400 were non-Jews (*Statistical Abstracts of Israel, 1983*). Most of the non-Jews are Arab (77% Moslem, 14% Christian, most of the rest Druze and Bedouin). Two large cultural groups make up the Jewish population, and membership in these groups is based on country of origin. In keeping with the most correct usage, we will consider individuals as Western if their country of origin is Europe, the Americas, or other English-speaking countries, and term as Eastern those peoples who trace their origins to North Africa, the Middle East, and India. The Eastern Jews slightly outnumber the Western Jews. At present, Eastern Jews are overrepresented in the lower socioeconomic classes and Western Jews in the middle class, although this is changing because of increasing social mobility among Eastern Jews and intermarriage between the two groups (see Curtis & Chertoff, 1973; Matras, 1965).

The majority (90%) of the Jewish population lives in urban areas of varying sizes. The rest live either in *moshavim,* which are cooperative agricultural communities, or on *kibbutzim,* which are communal agricultural settlements. The Arab population lives in locales varying from small villages to large urban areas. The Bedouin are nomadic tribes most of whom live in tents or huts, although some have now moved to towns.

Prenatal, Obstetrical, and Postnatal Care in Israel

Prenatal care for the pregnant woman is available from a variety of sources. The most easily available is provided by government-sponsored neighborhood mother-child health care stations (more popularly called *tipat halav,* literally, "a drop of milk"). Auerbach, Greenbaum, and Rosoff (1981) conducted a survey of 258 women, of whom 149 were Israeli-born, 59 Western-born, and 50 Eastern-born. Of the women who were interviewed, 48% received their prenatal care from these health care stations. The majority of Israeli or Eastern-born women attended the health care stations for prenatal care, while Western-born women preferred to receive their prenatal care from private doctors or from hospital obstetrical clinics. Years of education also played a role in the selection of

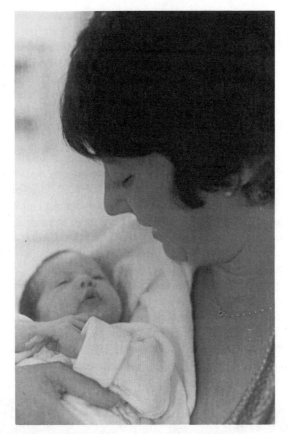

Photo 1.   Israeli mother and daughter. *(Photo by author)*

prenatal care: 54% of women with a high-school education or less go to the mother-child health care stations, as compared to 41% of women with more than a high-school education. More highly educated women were more likely to go to hospital clinics or private doctors for prenatal care than were less well-educated women (16% vs. 6%). Of the 258 women interviewed, 14 (5.4%) reported that they had received no prenatal care whatsoever and 10 of these 14 had either high-school education or less. Only 5 (3%) of Israeli-born women reported no prenatal care, as compared to 5 (10%) of Eastern-born and 4 (7%) of Western-born women.

The *Statistical Abstracts of Israel* (1983) reports that 100% of Israeli women give birth in hospitals. There are no alternative methods of childbirth available. A woman will receive a cash maternity grant from the National Insurance Institute only if she gives birth in hospital, a policy that encourages hospital delivery. Delivery typically takes place with the assistance of a midwife, although a doctor is on call in case of complications. While the use of drugs during delivery is on the increase, childbirth without drugs is still common. When asked about drugs during delivery, 37% of the 258 women reported a drug-free delivery, while 45% reported that they had received an inhalant analgesic. Fifty-five percent of Israeli-born women reported receiving an inhalant analgesia as compared to 31% of Eastern- and Western-born women. Women with more than a high school education received inhalant analgesic more often than women with less education.

The percentage of cesarean deliveries in this sample was 10.5%, but the frequency varied according to origin: 20% of Eastern-born women had cesarean deliveries, as compared to 9% of Israeli-born and 5% of Western-born women. Most cesarean deliveries in Israel are performed under general anesthetic. The average hospital stay after a cesarean delivery is 8 days, as compared to 2–3 days for an uncomplicated vaginal delivery.

Israeli working mothers receive a 3-month paid maternity leave and their jobs must be held for them for 1 year after delivery. Mothers who return to work within the first year are entitled to work 1 hour less each day for the rest of the year.

Comprehensive well-baby care through the neighborhood mother-child health care stations is provided for all infants from the time they arrive home from the hospital until they enter 1st grade. Almost all (94%) mothers use this service, especially in the infant's first year (*Statistical Abstracts of Israel,* 1983). Each

Photo 2.   Israeli mother, infant daughter, and son. (*Photo copyright: David Harris*)

health care station is staffed by public health nurses and a public health doctor. They provide the infant and the mother with routine care such as weighing, advice on infant care and feedings, inoculations, and periodic pediatric examinations. Developmental screening as well as vision and hearing tests are performed routinely. The health care stations vary widely in the additional services they provide, with most additional services being directed to the more disadvantaged neighborhoods. Psychiatrists, psychologists, and social workers are available in some of the stations. In Jerusalem, many of the stations have a play corner, usually staffed by an occupational therapist who advises parents on age-appropriate stimulation for their infants and demonstrates various infant activities. The Department of Public Health of the Municipality of Jerusalem established these play corners in order to lessen the developmental and educational delays often found in children from disadvantaged neighborhoods (Tamir, 1981).

Research on Neonatal and Infant Behavior in Israel

At least three published studies with samples of Israeli infants have included the BNBAS as one of their assessment procedures. Horowitz et al. (1977) studied the effects of medication on the behavior of Israeli newborns. In this study, 65 infants were tested five times during the first month of life, on days 1–4 and at 1 month of age. Few behavioral differences were found between infants from medicated and nonmedicated deliveries. In comparison to American babies, Israeli newborns scored higher on orientation, motor maturity, were easier to console, and demonstrated greater ability to quiet themselves when upset. Israeli infants scored higher than Uruguayan infants on some orientation items, were more easily consoled, had fewer state changes, and showed less hand-mouth facility.

In a study by Marcus, Auerbach, Wilkinson, and Burack (1981) the BNBAS was given at 3 and 14 days of age. This study investigated the first-year development of infants born to parents with serious mental disorders. As expected from a genetic model of the transmission of schizophrenia, a subgroup of infants born to schizophrenic parents were found to perform poorly on motor and sensorimotor items from the BNBAS and the Bayley Scales of Infant Development which were administered at 4, 8, and 12 months of age. According to the authors, the poor motor and sensorimotor functioning in this subgroup adds further support to the possible existence of a genetically determined neurointegrative deficit thought to be associated with schizophrenia.

The development of small-for-gestational-age (SGA) and appropriate-for-gestational-age (AGA) infants was the focus of a study by Frankel, Shapira, Arbel, Shapira, and Ayal (1982). The SGA infants weighed less than 2,500 g at term while the AGA infants weighed more than 2,500 g at term. SGA (40) and AGA (33) infants were administered the BNBAS at 2 days and between 17–21 days of age. At 4 months, their visual attention was evaluated. SGA infants who received a worrisome evaluation on the BNBAS interactive processes or who changed from an average to a worrisome evaluation on interactive processes showed an unusual pattern of visual fixation at 4 months of age.

Social and Cultural Influences

Although all the previously mentioned studies were conducted in Israel, none of them focused on the possible effects of cultural or social class membership on neonatal functioning. Horowitz (personal communication, 1983) believes that there were no differences in the study sample between infants from Western and Eastern families. However, cultural and socioeconomic class factors have been found to influence the development of Israeli infants during the first 2 years of life, with the earliest reported differences being at 3 weeks of age with the onset of the social smile (Anisfeld, 1982).

Some Israeli studies of infant development, whether it be mental, motor, or social, have compared the effects of different rearing environments on development. The samples are composed of families of Western or Eastern origin, families from the lower or middle class, or families living in a city or a rural environment. The behaviors studied have been smiling, vocalization, reaching, and mental and motor development.

Smiling, considered to be an important developmental milestone, has been extensively studied in Israel. Age of onset of the social smile has been investigated by Anisfeld (1982). In addition to finding differences between preterm and full-term infants, it was found that infants from Eastern families began to smile earlier than infants from Western families. Also, Gewirtz (1965) and Landau (1977) both report that smiling in home-reared infants is infrequent at 2 months, reaches a peak at about 4 months, and then decreases in frequency. When rate of smiling was compared for home-reared infants, Landau (1977) found that the highest rate of spontaneous smiling occurred in the lower-class and kibbutz-reared infants and the lowest rate among Bedouin infants. These differences disappeared when the mothers were asked to elicit smiling from their infants. The findings of these studies suggest that the pattern of early elicited smiling across ages in the first year is similar in different rearing environments, but that the age of onset and the rate of smiling are affected by cultural and class environments.

A similarity in pattern across rearing environments also seems to be true for vocalization. Greenbaum and Landau (1977) report that the pattern of vocalization of consonants at 2, 4, 7, and 11 months was similar for infants regardless of whether they were lower-class, middle-class, kibbutz, or Bedouin. At 11 months, there was a tendency for middle-class, kibbutz, and Bedouin infants to use more words and complex utterances than lower-class and institutional infants. For the latter infants, this was probably due to the much lower level of stimulation to which they were exposed (see Greenbaum & Landau, 1977). Differences between lower-class and other populations were smaller, both for infant and adult vocalization. Slovin-Ela and Kohen-Raz (1978) also report differences in vocalization between disadvantaged and middle-class infants, with middle-class infants showing superior vocalization at both 4 and 7 months.

Reaching and object manipulation in infants from disadvantaged and middle-class homes were studied by Slovin-Ela and Kohen-Raz (1978). The majority of 4-month-old middle-class infants were able to grasp a red ring, while none of the disadvantaged infants could do so. By 7 months, all but 1 of the middle-class infants were banging, shaking, and transferring the ring from hand to hand. The disadvantaged infants transferred the ring but only 1 of them banged it. Slovin-Ela and Kohen-Raz attribute the developmental delay of reaching and manipulation skills in the disadvantaged infants to their inadequate home environment.

In contrast to these findings, Kohen-Raz (1967, 1968) found few differences in development as measured by the Bayley Scales of Infant Development among kibbutz-reared, city-reared, and institution-reared infants until 8 months of age. Beginning at 8 months, the institution-reared infants started to fall behind on items measuring social interaction, object permanence, and verbal development. In comparing the performance of Israeli infants to American infants, Kohen-Raz reports that Israeli infants obtained high motor development scores at 1–4 months and higher mental development scores at 8–15 months than American infants.

The Brunet–Lezine Infant Test (Brunet & Lezine, 1965) has been used to assess the development of infants from Western and Eastern families. Both Ivanans (1975) and Smilansky, Shephatia, and Frankel (1976) report that until 18 months of age infants from Eastern immigrant families show more advanced development than infants from Western immigrant families. The situation is reversed at 2 years, with children from Western immigrant families performing better than children from Eastern immigrant families (Palti, Gitlin, & Zloto, 1977; Smilansky, Shephatia, & Frankel, 1976). Palti, Gitlin, and Zloto (1977) did not find cultural differences in developmental level in second-generation Israeli children. It may well be that by the time the children of immigrants have their own children, their child-rearing attitudes and practices are influenced more by the dominant trends in Israeli society than by cultural background of their families. Consequently, second-generation Israeli infants are more similar developmentally to each other than are first-generation Israeli children. Similar findings for second-generation Israeli children were reported by Lieblich, Ninio, and Kugelmass (1972) in a study of preschool children's WPPSI performance.

The impact of Israeli society on attitudes and knowledge about child rearing has been reported by Frankel and Roer-Bornstein (1982) and Ninio (1979). Frankel and Roer-Bornstein interviewed two generations (grandmother and granddaughter) of Yemenite and Kurdish women about their child-rearing ideas, showing that contemporary ideas about child rearing were influenced by both traditional and modern approaches. However, the granddaughters viewed infants as more competent and therefore capable of benefiting from earlier social and cognitive stimulation than did the grandmothers.

In her description of parents' naive theory of the infant, Ninio (1979) points out that child-rearing practices are influenced by the conception of the cognitive capacities of the infant. She found that lower-class Eastern mothers, compared to middle-class Western mothers, saw their infants as acquiring cognitive skills later and that therefore they introduced cognitively stimulating activities at later ages. She ascribes the lack of group differences in weaning from breast and bottle, as well as in toilet training, to the equalizing influence of the advice given on physical care at the mother-child health care stations. If this is so, cultural and class differences in attitudes and knowledge about development could be modified, as the health care stations continue to include information about psychological development in their sessions with mother and infant.

Both cultural and social class membership seem to exert an influence on the development of Israeli infants from an early age. However, whether these differences exist during the first month of life remains to be examined. There is some evidence from research in other cultures to show that neonatal behavior is affected by the rearing environment. De Vries and Super (1978) report that the behavior of Kenyan infants on some items of the BNBAS was related to the early child-rearing practices of their tribes. Muret-Wagstaff and Moore (this volume) studied the newborn behavior of Hmong (Laotian) and Caucasian babies in an American inner-city hospital. Hmong infants scored more favorably than the American Caucasian infants in the BNBAS clusters of Orientation, Autonomic Stability, and Range of State. These differences were attributed to the greater maternal sensitivity of the Hmong mothers.

The Israeli Study of Neonatal Behavior

The purpose of the present research is to investigate the relation between variations in rearing environment (i.e., family origin and level of parental education) and the behavior of infants 3–4 weeks old. In addition, the behavioral pattern of Israeli infants on the BNBAS-K (Brazelton Neonatal Behavioral Assessment Scale with the Kansas modifications) will be described. The BNBAS-K data for this report come from data collected by the authors for three ongoing studies.

The first study investigates the effects of a home-intervention program on parenting attitudes and behavior and on infant development. The sample is composed of young couples, with no more than 12 years of education, who are primarily of Eastern origin. All are expecting their first child. The couples will be visited biweekly until the infant's first birthday and thereafter on a monthly basis through the second year. Periodic assessments of parenting attitudes, infant development, and parent interaction provide the means of testing the programs' effectiveness.

The second study investigates the effects of adoption on parenting attitudes and behavior and child development. Adoptive and matched-control biological

Photo 3.   Israeli father and twin sons. (*Photo by author*)

parents are recruited into the study before the arrival or birth of the infant. The assessments, observations, and interviews are the same as those used in the intervention study. Most of the infants available for adoption are from Eastern lower-class families, while most of the adoptive families are middle-class and of Western origin. Since the origin of the adopted infants and the educational level of the biological mothers are not yet known to us, only the data of the control group infants are included in this report.

The third study, carried out by Nowik, is an investigation of the relationship between fetal movement and neonatal behavior. Pregnant women record the amount and kind of fetal movement during the last trimester of pregnancy. During the first postnatal month, the infant's behavior is assessed and his or her activity level observed. Most of the families participating in this study are well educated and of Western origin.

Method

Sample

The sample is composed of 83 infants. The number of infants by origin and parental educational level is given in Table 1. The infants were considered Western if their parents traced their origin to Europe, the Americas, or English-

Table 1.   Number of Infants
in Each Group

| | Education | | |
Origin	Low	High	Total
Eastern	23	7	30
Western	9	44	53
Total	32	51	83

speaking countries. Eastern infants came from families who traced their origins to North Africa, the Middle East, and India. Level of parental education is defined as high (more than 12 years) or low (12 years or less). In cases in which mothers and fathers differed as to origin or level of education, group placement was determined by the origin and the level of education of the mother. All of the infants were full-term; and all were assessed with the BNBAS-K when they were between 3 and 4 weeks old. The assessments were done in the infants' homes with at least one parent present.

The 45 infants from the adoption and intervention studies received a shortened version of the BNBAS-K. Pinprick, undress, and most of the reflex items were eliminated. The tonic neck reflex and the Moro tests were administered because of their importance as aversive stimuli. The rest of the items were eliminated because they are not used in scoring the behavioral items; they serve primarily to bring the infant to a proper state of arousal from a sleep state. Since most of our infants were awake at the beginning of the examination, this was not necessary. Shortening the procedure allowed us to include an interview of both parents, an observation session, and the BNBAS-K in one family visit. In light of these changes, the scoring for the Rapidity of Buildup, Irritability, and General Irritability items was modified slightly in order to maintain a 9-point scale. These modifications are presented in Table 2.

The 38 infants in the fetal movement study were administered the BNBAS-K and, with the exception of two items (pinprick and incurvation), the test was administered in its entirety. The original BNBAS scoring system was used.

Results

Group means, standard deviations, and results of the analyses are shown in Table 3. It can be seen that Eastern babies were more alert, had superior motor maturity, and smiled more frequently than Western babies. Infants from high-education families smiled more and were rated as more rewarding to test than infants from low-education families. For pull-to-sit, there was an origin-by-education interaction, with infants from low-education Western families performing more poorly than the infants from the other groups. Several other differences are worth

Table 2. Scoring Modifications

18. Rapidity of buildup (from 1, 2 to 6)
    1. No upset at all
    2. Not until TNR and/or Moro
    3. Not until defensive reactions
    4. Not until orientation items
    5. Not until pull-to-sit
    6. Not until uncover
    7. At the end of habituation items (auditory)
    8. During first habituation item (light)
    9. Never was quiet enough to score this
19. Irritability[a] (3,4,5)

uncover	habituation	TNR
pull-to-sit	orientation	Moro
prone	defensive reaction	

    1. No irritable crying to any of the above
    2. Irritable crying to one of the stimuli
    3. Irritable crying to two of the stimuli
    4. Irritable crying to three of the stimuli
    5. Irritable crying to four of the stimuli
    6. Irritable crying to five of the stimuli
    7. Irritable crying to six of the stimuli
    8. Irritable crying to seven of the stimuli
    9. Irritable crying to all of them
31. General irritability
    1. No irritability
    2. Only irritable to most aversive stimuli (defensive reaction, TNR, Moro); maintains control between aversive stimulation
    3. Irritable to most aversive stimuli (defensive reaction, TNR, Moro); unable to maintain control between aversive stimulation
    4. Irritability to less-aversive stimuli (prone, pull-to-sit); leads to state 6 crying, but returns to lower state spontaneously
    5. Irritability to most-aversive and less-aversive stimuli leads to state 6 crying, but with consoling returns to lower states
    6. Irritable to some of the Orientation items, may or may not have been irritable to aversive or nonaversive stimulation
    7. Irritable to most of the Orientation items, may or may not have been irritable to aversive or nonaversive stimulation
    8. Irritability begins early (somewhere around habituation, uncover, prone, pull to sit), and increases in frequency during the course of the exam. Irritability frequently results in state 6 crying
    9. Irritable to all degrees of stimulation encountered throughout the examination

[a]Irritability is fussy crying that is not of sufficient duration to be scored as state 6 (3″ but 15″). May be accompanied by increased motor activity.

noting. Eastern infants engaged in more self-quieting activity and maintained an alert state more easily than Western infants. The motor maturity and the quality of alertness of infants from high-education homes were superior to that of infants from low-education homes.

Table 3. Behavioral Performance of Israeli Infants from Differing Parental Backgrounds

| | Origin | | | | | | Education | | | | | | ANOVA Effects | | |
| | Eastern | | | Western | | | Low | | | High | | | | | |
	X̄	s.d.	n	X̄	s.d.	n	X̄	s.d.	n	X̄	s.d.	n	Origin	Education	Origin × Education
1. Response decrement to light	6.89	2.52	9	7.34	1.21	14	6.58	2.26	10	7.62	1.26	13			
2. Response decrement to rattle	7.38	2.06	13	7.44	1.41	23	7.80	1.52	14	7.18	1.71	22			
3. Response decrement to bell	4.57	3.60	7	5.85	2.81	20	5.43	3.26	7	5.55	3.02	20			
5. Orientation inanimate, visual	5.91	1.72	30	6.17	1.81	53	5.66	1.85	32	6.34	1.69	51			
6. Orientation inanimate, auditory	5.40	1.55	29	5.66	1.37	53	5.45	1.39	31	5.64	1.46	51			
7. Orientation animate, visual	5.63	1.97	29	5.72	1.26	53	5.38	2.00	31	5.87	1.15	51			
8. Orientation animate, auditory	5.68	1.52	28	5.88	1.31	53	5.71	1.44	31	5.88	1.35	49			
9. Orientation animate, visual and auditory	6.34	1.57	28	6.11	1.28	53	6.15	1.58	31	6.21	1.26	50			
10. Alertness	6.22	1.77	28	5.51	1.34	52	5.80	1.67	31	5.73	1.46	50	.02		
11. General tonus	5.66	6.7	29	5.58	.87	52	5.63	.75	32	5.59	.84	49			
12. Motor maturity	5.30	1.33	28	4.98	1.22	53	4.97	1.33	30	5.17	1.23	50	.05	.08	
13. Pull-to-sit	5.30	2.19	29	5.10	2.14	52	4.91	2.34	31	5.33	2.02	50			.05
14. Cuddliness	5.60	1.43	30	5.32	1.31	53	5.69	1.45	32	5.25	1.28	51			
15. Defensive movement	6.00	2.04	28	6.11	1.88	53	5.81	1.85	31	6.24	1.96	50			
16. Consolability	5.75	1.89	21	5.20	1.80	41	5.40	1.66	25	5.37	1.96	37			
17. Peak of excitement	5.91	1.48	28	5.65	1.33	5	5.94	1.53	32	5.60	1.27	47			
18. Rapidity of buildup	3.50	1.58	28	3.75	1.98	51	3.65	1.52	31	3.67	2.04	48			
19. Irritability	2.85	1.38	26	2.88	1.45	52	2.92	1.31	29	2.84	1.49	49			
20. Activity	4.53	.84	28	4.64	.84	53	4.44	.81	31	4.70	.84	50			

	M	SD	N	M	SD	N	M	SD	N	M	SD	N	p
21. Tremulousness	3.07	2.12	28	2.70	2.20	53	3.00	2.32	31	2.72	2.08	50	
22. Startle	1.96	.33	28	2.71	.72	53	1.94	.44	31	2.24	.69	50	
23. Lability of skin color	3.43	1.29	28	3.72	1.36	53	3.44	1.34	32	3.73	1.34	49	
24. Lability of states	3.50	1.39	26	3.42	1.53	50	3.62	1.42	29	3.34	.51	47	
25. Self-quieting activity	4.14	2.68	25	2.63	1.95	42	3.84	2.53	28	2.73	2.12	39	.08
26. Hand–mouth facility	2.97	2.61	29	2.40	1.95	53	2.53	2.36	32	2.64	2.14	50	
27. Smiles	.95	1.62	30	.46	1.03	53	.51	1.15	32	.71	1.38	51	.01
28. Orientation inanimate, visual and auditory	6.96	1.52	29	6.94	1.47	53	6.86	4.52	31	7.00	1.47	51	.03
29. Quality of infant's alert responsivity	6.00	2.08	29	5.90	1.69	53	5.62	1.94	32	6.14	1.74	50	.08
30. Examiner persistence	5.41	2.45	29	4.65	2.20	53	4.93	2.30	32	4.92	2.33	50	.08
31. General irritability	4.07	2.70	29	3.98	2.82	51	4.28	2.80	32	3.83	2.75	48	
32. Reinforcement value of infant's behavior	6.79	2.77	29	6.98	1.42	53	6.41	2.20	32	7.24	1.33	50	.02
33. Modal-orientation, inanimate visual	5.34	2.00	29	5.42	2.05	52	5.00	2.11	31	5.64	.95	50	
34. Modal-orientation, inanimate auditory	4.98	1.52	29	5.15	1.45	53	4.97	1.31	31	5.16	1.56	51	
35. Modal-orientation, inanimate visual and auditory	6.41	1.79	29	6.55	1.70	53	6.43	1.75	31	6.55	1.72	51	
36. Modal-orientation, animate visual	5.55	1.81	28	5.32	1.33	53	5.27	1.85	30	5.48	1.27	51	
37. Modal-orientation, animate auditory	5.14	1.74	28	5.33	1.45	52	5.34	1.48	31	5.22	1.61	49	
38. Modal-orientation, animate visual and auditory	5.81	1.81	28	5.64	1.56	53	5.58	1.89	31	5.77	1.44	50	
39. Modal-defensive movement	5.04	1.95	28	4.66	1.62	53	5.08	1.97	31	4.64	1.35	50	
40. Modal-consolability	5.00	1.86	19	4.63	1.55	40	4.75	1.57	24	4.74	1.72	35	

BNBAS cluster scores (Lester, Als, & Brazelton, 1982) were calculated for each of the groups. The means and standard deviations are presented in Table 4. The Habituation cluster shows that Western babies habituate faster than Eastern babies. Infants from high-education homes received higher scores than infants from low-education homes on the Motor Performance cluster. There also was a tendency for Eastern infants to score higher than Western infants in this cluster.

Two considerations should be kept in mind with respect to the group differences. First, in the analysis of the Habituation cluster and in the interaction effects for the Pull-to-Sit item the subject number is small (the low-education Western group consists of 9 infants). Second, mean differences of 1 point or less are questionable because of the way examiner reliability is calculated.

The structure of neonatal behavior. The structure of neonatal behavior was analyzed using Guttman's Facet Theory and Smallest Space Analysis (SSA; Guttman, 1968; Lingoes, 1973). According to Guttman (Gratch, 1973, p 35.), a theory is a "hypothesis of a correspondence between a definitional system for a universe of observation, and an aspect of the empirical structure of those observations, together with a rationale for such a hypothesis". The researcher must think about two things in partnership: (a) the design of the observations, and (b) the empirical structure of those observations.

An essential part of facet design is the *mapping sentence*, which makes explicit the hypothesized relationship among observations, in our case the infant's performance on the BNBAS-K. The mapping sentence includes three varieties of facets: the population (X), the content, and the range. X designates the population of subjects and, together with the facets that classify the content of the variables (A, B, C, . . . N), makes up the *domain* of the mapping sentence. The third type of facet, the *range*, is the set of response categories specified for the universe of items studied. Each respondent (x) has one response in the range for each item classified by the elements of the content facets A, B, C, . . . N. In essence, the mapping sentence serves to define a priori exactly what is being studied (the population and the content of variables), and the range of possible responses. Facets hypothesized in the mapping sentence are then tested via SSA to see if they do indeed correspond to regional partitions in space. Figure 1 contains a mapping sentence for the BNBAS-K.

The facets for this mapping sentence are the following: Facet A—time period of examination; Facet B—type of behavior; Facet C—functioning modality; Facet D—procedural condition. The range has been stated in terms of degree of involvement in the test which allowed us to retain the original scoring direction from low to high frequency of behavior.

Facet design provides the definitional system of the observations specified by the mapping sentence, together with the rationale for hypotheses. The set of intercorrelations can be subjected to SSA in which a set of intercorrelations among variables are geometrically portrayed in a space of two more more dimensions (Lingoes, 1973).

Table 4. Group Means and Standard Deviations for Lester Clusters

| | Origin | | | | | | Education | | | | | | ANOVA Effects | | |
| | Eastern | | | Western | | | Low | | | High | | | | | Origin–|
Clusters	X̄	s.d.	n	X̄	s.d.	n	X̄	s.d.	n	X̄	s.d.	n	Origin	Education	Education
Habituation	5.00	1.63	4	7.00	.77	11	6.00	1.76	4	6.64	1.23	11	.01		
Orientation	5.92	1.17	27	5.84	1.05	52	5.76	1.25	30	5.97	1.97	49			
Motor	5.31	.75	28	5.18	.79	50	5.10	.87	30	5.31	.70	48	.08	.04	
Range of State	3.80	.76	23	3.77	1.01	49	3.94	.77	26	3.69	1.01	46			
Regulation of State	4.34	1.14	20	3.93	1.04	40	4.19	.94	24	3.98	1.17	36			
Autonomic Stability	7.23	.68	25	7.20	.89	49	7.19	.83	27	7.23	.82	47			

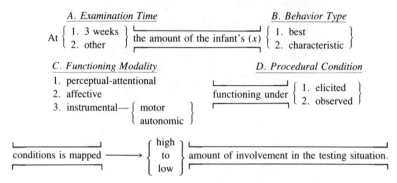

Figure 1.   Mapping Sentence for Items of the BNBAS-K

The division into *regions* comes from boundary curves determined by *structuples* of the variables. A structuple is a profile of scores on each variable, composed by selecting an element from each facet. Each facet element (for example, a_1 is an element of the facet A) is called a *struct*, and structuples are made up of one struct from each facet (Shye, 1978). For instance, the item Orientation Animate Visual on the BNBAS-K for a test done at 3 weeks examining best behavior would have the following structuple: a_1, b_1, c_1, d_1.

SSA treats each variable as a point in a Euclidean space, such that the higher the correlation between two variables, the closer the points are in space. SSA uses the smallest possible number of dimensions that will preserve the rank order of the relationships. The extent to which the space diagram reflects the original correlational relaitonships is indicated by a coefficient of alienation that ranges from 0 to 1 (Raveh, 1978). The small ther coefficient of alienation, the better the fit.

Each facet of the domain of variables corresponds to a partitioning of the SSA space into as many regions as there are elements to the facet. A region, as distinct from a cluster, is an a priori defined spatial partition in which items of the same elements of a facet fall, before empirical data are collected, as hypothesized according to the facets' roles stipulated in the mapping sentence. The a priori pattern of the items' representation defines a region. A cluster is defined simply by closeness of items according to their empirical intercorrelations. For a more detailed explanation of facet design, see Levy (1981) and Shye (1978).

Figure 2 presents a projection of the SSA space of the BNBAS-K items for the entire sample of 83 infants. The response decrement items and the Kansas modal items were not included in this analysis. The numbers in the figure correspond to BNBAS-K item numbers given in Table 3. This two-dimensional solution (coefficient of alienation = 0.26) partitions the space into three polar regions. Polar regions divide the space into wedgelike partitions, all emanating from a common point. Each region corresponds to an element of facet C, functioning modality, whose elements are perceptual-attentional, affective, and instrumental. Each of the regions appears to contain two subregions.

In our mapping sentence, two submodalities, motor and autonomic, were hypothesized for the instrumental modality. Figure 2 shows that the instrumental region is indeed composed of a motor subregion and an autonomic stability subregion. Figure 2 shows the perceptual-attentional region to be composed of a subregion of orientation items and a subregion of alertness items. The affective regions break down into what Lester calls Range of State items and Regulation of State items.

Three items appear to be misplaced. Item 28 (Orientation Inanimate, Visual and Auditory) falls in the instrumental region rather than in the perceptual-attentional region while item 17 (Rapidity of Buildup), hypothesized to appear in the affective region, also falls in the instrumental region. Item 26 (Hand-Mouth Facility), if regarded as an affective item, is misplaced by region although, if regarded as an instrumental item, it is in the appropriate region but not in the correct subregion. Reinforcement value of the infant is not easily defined in terms of modality. On the basis of its SSA placement, it appears to belong in the perceptual-attentional region.

The analysis also suggests a possible modular, that is, circular, partition for the procedural facet with the elicited behavior items appearing at the periphery and the observed behavior items appearing closer to the center of the diagram.

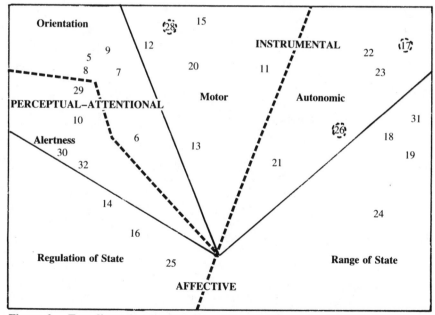

Figure 2.   Two-dimensional projection of the SSA space for the BNBAS-K items

Given a polar role for the modality facet and a modular role for the procedural facet, a two-dimensional representation (radex) of neonatal behavior is suggested. Figure 3 depicts this hypothesized structure. When we computed SSAs for the BNBAS-K with the sample divided by origin and education, we found the solution for Western infants and infants from high-education homes to be similar to that for the overall sample, at least for the modality facet. For Eastern infants and infants from lower-education homes, the affective region, particularly the Range of State subregion, and the Perceptual-Attentional region appeared, but the Instrumental region did not. This may mean that for these groups of infants, instrumental behavior is not distinct from perceptual-attentional behavior. Whether this indicates real differences in the structure of neonatal behavior for infants from differing backgrounds or is an unstable finding due to small numbers is an open question that we hope to answer eventually, when further data are available.

The facet for type of functioning was not tested in these analyses because the modal items were excluded from the correlation matrix.

Discussion

We found that 3-week-old Israeli infants from homes that vary in cultural origin and educational level are behaviorally more similar to than different from each other. The influence that the home environment may eventually have on the

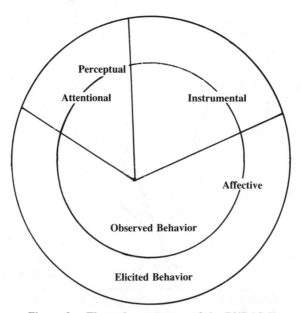

Figure 3.   The radex structure of the BNBAS-K

development of these infants is not readily apparent in the neonatal period. The behavioral similarity of infants whose parents are identifiable by origin and educational level may point to a similarity in the quality of parental care or to a commonality in child-rearing approaches in the early weeks of life. Typically, the major activity in this period is the physical care of the infant, and commonality in physical care, including breast- and bottle-feeding, is enhanced by the relationship that each family has with the neighborhood mother-child health care station.

Advice on basic child care is given to parents with young infants, and the nature of the advice is standard throughout the mother-child health care stations, even allowing for the idiosyncratic ways it may be transmitted. The majority of parents in our study are second-generation Israeli, so their approach to child rearing and early interaction with their infants may be more closely tied to shared Israeli cultural beliefs and attitudes than to the tradition of their original cultures.

These findings are consistent with the findings indicated earlier and with others reviewed by Super (1981) which show few cross-cultural differences in neonatal behavior, unless highly distinct infant-rearing practices encourage a specific early response. The data thus support a hypothesis of invariance in neonatal behavior generally. In this case, child-rearing practices common to the different cultural groups may also have played a role.

The use of clusters or factors also has implications for evaluating level of performance. There is some risk involved in taking seriously the appearance of a small number of differences between cultural groups in individual scale items, unless these items represent part of a consistent cluster or unless one has a reasonable environmental explanation. Thus, the lower level of defensive movement among Kipsigis babies, which deVries and Super (1978) found, can be understood on the basis of the Kipsigis mothers covering the child's face as a routine measure to which the infants may have become habituated. Other isolated differences such as those reported by Freedman and Freedman (1969), Horowitz et al. (1977), as well as those found in the present study, must be treated with caution unless they are replicated and their determining factors identified.

It is a commonly held belief among some Israeli parents that babies neither see nor hear, or at least not well, in the early weeks of life (Ninio, 1979). Consequently, cultural and education-related differences in the nature of interaction and type of stimulation may not become apparent until infants reach an age at which they are regarded by their parents as social beings capable of sensory perception. This change in the conception of the baby may then account for the differences that appear in the neonatal period and that have been reported by a number of investigators (Ivanans, 1975; Kohen-Raz, 1967, 1968; Slovin-Ela & Kohen-Raz, 1978; Smilansky, Shephatia, & Frankel, 1976).

The few behavioral differences that we did find favored Eastern infants and infants from high-education homes. Whether their superiority in later development (Ivanans, 1975; Slovin-Ela & Kohen-Raz, 1978; Smilansky, Shephatia, & Frankel, 1976) can be traced to these nascent differences remains a question to which our longitudinal project may eventually provide an answer. One implication of this finding is that the low-education Western group may have some special developmental or socialization problems.

Classifying origin globally as either Eastern or Western may mask early behavioral differences among babies who can trace their own origins to areas and countries as diverse as, for example, Kurdistan, Yemen, the United States, and France. As Frankel and Roer-Bornstein (1982) have shown, the child-rearing practices and parental perceptions of the capabilities of the infant are quite different for Kurdistan and Yemenite Jews, both of whom are considered to be Eastern Jews. It may be necessary to analyze separately the neonatal behavior of infatns by country of origin rather than grouping them together as Eastern or Western. As yet, our data base is not large enough to allow us to focus more precisely on country of origin, but we plan to do so in the future.

The SSA of the BNBAS-K suggests a radex structure for neonatal behavior that consists of a functioning modality and a procedural condition. Although cast in somewhat different terms, the elements in the facet of modality are similar to the behavioral clusters proposed by other investigators (Als, Tronick, Lester, & Brazelton, 1979; Lester, Als, & Brazelton, 1982). We wrote our mapping sentence specifically for the neonatal behavior as measured by the BNBAS-K. Our modality facet is a simplified version of that proposed by Marcus and Hans (1982) for their comprehensive mapping sentence of child development.

Comparing our results with the facets and clusters of these investigators, we find a regionalization of the modality facet that resembles the major regions presented to use the term *perceptual-attentional* rather than *cognitive* to describe the first modality. Looking more closely, however, the existence of two subregions within every region presents a picture of neonatal behavior that resembles Lester's conceptualization of the BNBAS and thus provides support for his conceptualization. In light of this, we have modified the modality facet to include two submodalities within each major modality as follows.

Functioning Modality:
1. perceptual-attentional (Orientation)
                         (alertness)
2. affective (range of state)
            (regulation of state)
3. instrumental (motor performance)
               (autonomic stability)

This refinement of the modality facet will now be tested in future analyses of the BNBAS-K.

The results allow us to confirm tentatively the presence of another facet of neonatal behaviors: those that are elicited by the examiner and those that are primarily observed. It is this facet, together with the modality facet in a two-dimensional representation, that suggests the structure of neonatal behavior to be radex in form. As more facets of neonatal behavior are defined and tested, the conceptualization of the structure may have to be modified accordingly. In this report, we decided to limit ourselves to the analysis of two of the hypothesized facets since high-spatial dimensionality is often needed for a multifaceted design.

At this time, it is not possible to address the issue of whether or not the structure of neonatal behavior is the same for infants from varying backgrounds. We still have too few infants in each group to provide a stable structural solution. Even so, our preliminary analyses lead us to speculate that if differences occur, they will be in the region Instrumental modality and the subregion affective Regulation of State. An SSA of neonatal behavior by country of origin would be of even more interest, but this will not be possible for some time to come. Similar analyses by other researchers and pooling of efforts would help to reach this goal.

The composition of the Perceptual-Attentional modality and the affective submodality Range of State seems to be stable cross-culturally in that it has appeared not only in our SSA of the BNBAS-K but also in factor-analytic studies of BNBAS data collected in the United States (Kaye, 1978; Osofsky & O'Connell, 1977; Sameroff, Krafchuk, & Bakow, 1978; Strauss & Rourke, 1978). In contrast, the item composition of the Instrumental modality and the affective submodality Regulation of State may play different roles in various populations of infants, and thus be population-specific. If so, the hypothesized relationships among certain of the items will need to be defined specifically for each infant population that varies as to origin, birth status, parental factors, and so on. By defining these relationships as they relate to each population, it will be possible to test for variations in the structure of neonatal behavior.

The psychometric issues raised by the results are similar to those involved in intelligence testing. More is known about the levels of performance for individual items than about the relationship of items to one another. The relations among the items, or patterns of performance, could represent the degree of behavioral organization in a sample of a particular culture. The degree of behavioral organization may differ from culture to culture. Differences among cultures may thus be investigated both in level of performance and in patterns of performance. The importance of understanding patterns of performance representing abilities among different cultures has been pointed out by Goodnow (1975), Greenbaum and Kugelmass (1980), and Guttman and Guttman (1963). Guttman and Guttman, for example, have suggested that similarities in correlation matrices across cultures may indicate a possible biological basis for the structure of abilities. Environment could serve to enhance or depress these abilities.

In conclusion, this study, like previous ones, did not find many large differences among cultural groups in level of BNBAS performance, indicating that both level and pattern of performance have characteristics common to different cultures and may be biologically based. Whether the differences found at later ages, including infancy, are due to environmental or genetic factors or some combination is an open question. It appears that neonatal performance does not reflect differences in regard to levels, and only further research may determine whether the differences between cultures exist in behavioral organization and in the predictive validity of neonatal behavior. The present study suggests that we should look more closely at cross-cultural differences in level of behavior and also at the structure of the relationship among the infants' responses.

References

Als, H., Tronick, E., Lester, B. M., & Brazelton, T. B. (1979). Specific neonatal measures: The Brazelton Neonatal Behavioral Assessment Scale. In J. Osofsky (Ed.), *The Handbook of Infant Development*. New York: Wiley.

Anisfeld, E. (1982). The onset of social smiling in preterm and full-term infants from two ethnic backgrounds. *Infant Behavior and Development, 5,* 387–395.

Auerbach, J., Greenbaum, C. W., & Rosoff, R. (1981). *Survey of prenatal care and delivery experiences in Jerusalem.* Unpublished manuscript.

Brazelton, T. B. (1973). *Neonatal Behavioral Assessment Scale.* Philadelphia: Lippincott.

Brunet, O., & Lezine, I. (1965). *Le development psychologique de la première enfance* (2nd ed.). Paris: Presses Universitaires de France.

Curtis, M., & Chertoff, M. S. (1973). *Israel: Social structure and change.* New Brunswick, NJ: Transaction Books.

deVries, M., & Super, C. M. (1978). Contextual influences on the neonatal behavioral assessment scale in several samples. In A. J. Sameroff (Ed.), Organization and stability of newborn behavior: A commentary on the ton Neonatal Behavior Scale. *Monographs of the Society for Research in Child Development, 43* (Serial No. 177), pp. 92–101.

Frankel, D., & Roer-Bornstein, D. (1982). Traditional and modern contributions to changing infant-rearing ideologies of two ethnic communities. *Monographs of the Society for Research in Child Development, 47* (Serial No. 196).

Frankel, D. G., Shapira, R., Arbel, T., Shapira, Y., & Ayal, F. (1982). The visual attention at 4 months of full-term small-for-gestational-age and full-term appropriate-weight-for-gestational-age infants. In L. P. Lipsitt & T. M. Field (Eds.), *Infant behavior and development: Perinatal risk and newborn behavior.* Norwood, NJ: Ablex.

Freedman, D. G., & Freedman, N. C. (1969). Behavioral differences between Chinese-American and European-American newborns. *Nature, 224,* 1227.

Gewirtz, J. L. (1965). The course of infant smiling in four child-rearing environments in Israel. In B. M. Foss (Ed.), *Determinants of infant behavior* (Vol. 3). London: Methuen.

Goodnow, J. J. (1975). The nature of intelligent behavior: Questions raised by cross-cultural studies. In L. Resnick (Ed.), *New approaches to intelligence.* New York: Erlbaum.

Gratch, H. (Ed.). (1973). *Twenty-five years of social research in Israel.* Jersualem: Jerusalem Academic Press.

Greenbaum, C. W., & Kugelmass, S. (1980). Human development and socialization in cross-cultural perspectives: Issues arising from research in Israel. In N. Warren (Ed.), *Studies in cross-cultural psychology,* (Vol.2). New York: Academic Press.

Greenbaum, C. W., & Landau, R. (1977). Mothers' speech and early development of vocal behavior: Findings from a cross-cultural observation study in Israel. In P. H. Leiderman, S. R. Tulkin, & A. Rosenfeld (Eds.), *Culture and infancy: Variations in the human experience.* New York: Academic Press.

Guttman, L. (1968). A general nonmetric technique for finding the smallest coordinate space for a configuration of points. *Psychometrika, 33,* 469–506.

Guttman, L., & Guttman, R. (1963). Cross-cultural stability of an intercorrelation pattern of abilities: A possible test of a biological bias. *Human Biology, 35,* 53–60.

Horowitz, F. D., Ashton, J., Culp, R., Gaddis, E., Levin, S., & Reichmann, B. (1977). The effects of obstetrical medication on the behavior of Israeli newborn infants and some comparisons with Uruguayan and American infants. *Child Development, 48,* 1607–1623.

Ivanans, T. (1975). Effect of maternal education and ethnic backgrond on infant development. *Archives of Disease in Childhood, 50,* 454–457.

Kaye, K. (1978). Discriminating among normal infants by multivariate analysis of Brazelton scores: Lumping and smoothing. In A. J. Sameroff (Ed.), Organization and stability of newborn behavior: A commentary on the Brazelton Neonatal Behavioral Assessment Scale. *Monographs of the Society for Research in Child Development, 43* (5–6, Serial No. 177), 160–80.

Kohen-Raz, R. (1967). Scalogram analysis of some developmental sequences of infant behavior as measured by the Bayley Scales of Mental Development. *Genetic Psychology Monographs, 76,* 3–21.

Kohen-Raz, R. (1968). Mental and motor development of kibbutz, institutionalized, and home-reared infants in Israel. *Child Development, 39,* 489–509.

Landau, R. (1977). Spontaneous and elicited smiles and vocalizations of infants in four Israeli environments. *Developmental Psychology, 13,* 389–400.

Lester, B. M., Als, H., & Brazelton, T. B. (1982). Regional obstetric anesthesia and newborn behavior: A reanalysis toward synergistic effects. *Child Development, 53,* 687–692.

Levy, S. (1981). Lawful roles of facets in social theories. In I. Borg (Ed.), *Multidimensional data representation: When and why.* Ann Arbor, MI: Mathesis.

Lieblich, A., Ninio, A., & Kugelmass, S. (1972). Effects of ethnic origin and parental SES on WPPSI performance of pre-school children in Israel. *Journal of Cross-Cultural Psychology, 3,* 159–168.

Lingoes, J. C. (1973). *The Gutman–Lingoes nonmetric program series.* Ann Arbor, MI: Mathesis.

Marcus, J., & Aubrey, A. (1982). Multidimensional statistical analysis: A pattern for clinical insight. *Zero to Three, 3,* 1–7.

Marcus, J., Auerbach, J., Wilkinson, L., & Burack, C. M. (1981) Infants at risk for schizophrenia: The Jerusalem Infant Development Study. *Archives of General Psychiatry, 38,* 703–713.

Marcus, J., & Hans, S. L. (1982). A methodological model to study the effects of toxins on child development. *Neurobehavioral Toxicology and Teratology, 4,* 483–487.

Matras, J. (1965). *Social change in Israel.* Chicago: Aldine.

Muret-Wagstaff, S., & Moore, S. G. (1983). *Hmong vs. American Caucasian newborn behavior and rearing practices.* Paper presented at the biennial meeting of the Society for Research in Child Development, Detroit, MI.

Ninio, A. (1979). The naive theory of the infant and other maternal attitudes in two subgroups in Israel. *Child Development, 50,* 976–980.

Osofsky, J., & O'Connell, E. J. (1977). Patterning of newborn behavior in an urban population. *Child Development, 48,* 532–536.

Palti, H., Gitlin, M., & Zloto, R. (1977). Psychomotor development of two-year-old chidren in Jerusalem. *Journal of Cross-Cultural Psychology, 8,* 453–464.

Raveh, A. (1978). Finding periodic patterns in time series with monotone trend: A new technique. In S. Shye (Ed.), *Theory construction and data analysis in the behavioral science.* San Francisco, CA: Jossey-Bass.

Sameroff, A. J., Krafchuk, E. E., & Bakow, H. A. (1978). Issues in grouping items from the Neonatal Behavioral Assessment Scale. In A. J. Sameroff (Ed.), *Organization and stability of newborn behavior: A commentary on the Brazelton Neonatal Behavioral Assessment Scale. Monographs of the Society for Research in Child Development, 43* (5–6, Serial No. 177), 46–59.

Shye, S. (Ed.). (1978). *Theory construction and data analysis in the behavioral sciences.* San Francisco, CA: Jossey-Bass.

Slovin-Ela, S., & Kohen-Raz, R. (1978). Developmental differences in primary reaching responses of young infants from varying social backgrounds. *Child Development, 49,* 132–140.

Smilansky, E., Shephatia, L., & Frankel, E. (1976). *Mental development of infants from two ethnic groups* (Research Rep. No. 195). Jerusalem: Henrietta Szold Institute.

Statistical abstracts of Israel. (1983). Jerusalem: Government Printing Office.

Strauss, M. E., & Rourke, D. L. (1978). A multivariate analysis of the Neonatal Behavioral Assessment Scale in several samples. In A. J. Sameroff (Ed.), *Organization and stability of newborn behavior: A commentary on the Brazelton Neonatal Behavioral Assessment Scale. Monographs of the Society for Research in Child Development, 43* (5–6, Serial No. 177), 81–91.

Super, C. (1981). Behavioral development in infancy. R. H. Monroe, R. L. Monroe, & B. B. Whiting (Eds.), *Handbook of cross-cultural human development.* New York: Garland.

Tamir, D. (1981). Project Kiddum: Early intervention in a health care setting. *Journal of Education, 163,* 219–227.

CHAPTER 11

The Behavior of Chinese, Malay, and Tamil Newborns from Malaysia*

R. H. Woodson

University of Texas

E. da Costa

University of London

Research Background

This chapter concerns the behavior of Chinese, Malay, and Tamil neonates. In many ways, this study was conceived and executed much as any other study of newborn behavior that might be performed in America or Europe. A widely used examination procedure—the Brazelton Neonatal Behavioral Assessment Scale (BNBAS; Brazelton, 1973)—was administered to each neonate. The same procedural strictures, such as examining the neonate midway between feeds in a quiet, dimly lit room, were observed. As far as possible, the information gathered in this study on background demographic, obstetric, and neonatal measures was that which would be gathered in any other study of the neonate's behavior.

What, then, makes this study unique and at the same time links it to the growing body of work on neonatal behavior? Obviously the answer lies in the composition of the sample and the setting in which the research was conducted. At the time this research began (1975–1976), our knowledge of newborn behavior rested largely on the rather narrow foundation provided by studies of newborns in Western cultures. To be sure, there did exist a small set of studies

* We wish to thank the Maternal and Child Health Section of the Malaysian Ministry of Health and the staff of the Hospital Bersalin, Kuala Lumpur, for their help and encouragement in this research. The Malaysian research was funded by the Harry Frank Guggenheim Foundation and the English research was funded by the Social Science Research Council of the United Kingdom.

295

concerning newborns from non-Western cultures and the yield of these studies was certainly intriguing. Geber and Dean (1957) had described what appeared to be a remarkable motor precocity in Ugandan newborns. Freedman and his colleagues had drawn our attention to the impressive state control of Chinese newborns (Freedman & Freedman, 1969) and the weak lower-limb responses of the Navajo neonate (Freedman, 1971). Brazelton, Robey, and Collier (1969) had told us of the striking alertness and controlled motor activity of the Zinacanteco newborn.

The general impression left by these and other cross-cultural studies (Brazelton, Koslowski, & Tronick, 1976; deVries & Super, 1978; Horowitz et al., 1977) was that our rapidly emerging notions concerning newborn behavior, based as they were on studies within our own culture and country, would benefit from the test afforded by a broader sampling of newborns from different environments. Without a doubt, the specific findings of the early cross-cultural investigations provided important points for replication and extension. Above all, there was a need for more programmatic studies involving sufficiently large numbers of newborns from a range of cultures. Whether the findings emerging from these studies would confirm or call into question those of the earlier studies would be of little consequence. The broadening of our knowledge base concerning newborn behavior would wholly justify the cost and complexity of performing research in different cultures.

Research Setting

The research reported here was conducted in western Malaysia, the peninsula bordered on the north by Thailand, the south by Singapore, the east by the South China Sea, and the west by the Indian Ocean. The country is situated some 4° off the equator, so its climate is tropical. A mountainous region forms the peninsula's north-south spine, the western portion being more developed than the eastern. Although the country is undergoing rapid industrial development, Malaysia's economic base is provided mainly by the production of rubber, palm oil, and rice and the mining of tin.

Malaysia's attraction for the cross-cultural researcher lies in its multicultural population. The country's three main cultural groups are the Malays, ethnically and linguistically related to the Indonesians; the Chinese, primarily second- and third-generation descendants of immigrants from southeastern China; and the Tamils, descendants of immigrants from the south Indian state of Tamil Nadu. For a variety of historic, religious, economic, and political reasons the three cultures have intermingled very little, each retaining its identity. As a consequence, Malaysia provides the opportunity to investigate three quite distinct cultural groups inhabiting a single, relatively small geographic area.

The initial plan for the Malaysian research was to follow a single sample of Chinese, Malay, and Tamil infants from birth through the first birthday with a variety of assessment and observational procedures. Time considerations ultimately required that we modify that plan, with the result that two separate studies were conducted. That reported here involved the behavioral assessment of a sample of newborns delivered in the public maternity hospital serving the federal capital of Kuala Lumpur. The second study, reported elsewhere (Woodson & da Costa, 1984), was a longitudinal observational investigation of infant-caretaker interaction in families living in a rural area approximately 60 km south of Kuala Lumpur.

Research Questions

The basic reason for performing cross-cultural research is to be able to compare the behavior of newborns from one culture with that of newborns from another culture. Having said this, however, it is important to specify exactly what is to be compared. We believed that three types of comparisons would be required in order to utilize fully the information gathered in Malaysia.

First, the Malaysian sample could be compared to other samples in terms of the amounts or quantities of specific behaviors exhibited by the average newborn. For instance, would Malaysian newborns be more alert or less irritable than those of other cultures? Would they exhibit different levels of motor maturity? Would they show more rapid or slower response decrement? Such comparisons are the stuff of cross-cultural work, and in examining them, the Malaysian study would continue the tradition established in earlier cross-cultural investigations of newborn behavior.

A second way in which the Malaysian sample could be compared to other samples is in terms of the dimensions of individual differences in behavior among newborns. At least in theory, newborns of different cultures could be similar with respect to the amounts of various behaviors yet could differ in terms of the dimensions of variation characteristic of each sample. Hence, individual differences might be pronounced for state control and minimal for response decrement in one sample of newborns while the reverse could be true for another sample. With a few exceptions (deVries & Super, 1978; Horowitz et al., 1973), the cross-cultural literature on newborn behavior had largely failed to consider this type of comparison.

Besides providing insight into the nature of the individual differences that feed into a culture's child-rearing system, this sort of comparison would have important methodological implications. If it was to provide a useful method for documenting the similarities and differences between newborns of different cultures, the BNBAS would have to yield basic dimensions describing individual differences in behavior common to all newborns. Without such a metric, there would be little point in conducting cross-cultural research in this area. This type of comparison would also serve to link the Malaysian research with the large number of reports concerning patterns of individual differences on the BNBAS.

A third type of comparison between the Malaysian sample and other samples would concern the variables associated with individual differences in behavior. For instance, would the relationship between a given perinatal experience and some aspect of newborn behavior be the same in our Malaysian sample as in other samples of newborns? In many ways, this type of comparison would be the most significant to emerge from the research. While those already discussed would be limited to describing central tendencies and patterns of variation in behavior, this third comparison would help to determine whether the mechanisms responsible for behavioral differences among neonates from one culture operate in all cultures.

Thus, the analyses presented in this chapter addressed three basic questions. First, would the average level of performance found among Malaysian newborns on the BNBAS be comparable to that found in other samples of newborns? Second, would the dimensions of behavior along which the Malaysian newborns varied be comparable to those along which other neonates had been found to differ? Third, would the variables associated with differnces in behavior among the Malaysian newborns be comparable to those found to be associated with similar behavioral differences among other groups of newborns?

Methods

Samples

Although directly concerned with the sample of Malaysian newborns examined in the hospital, references are made in this chapter to three groups—the research sample, the survey sample, and the comparison sample.

Malaysian research sample. The sample of newborns studied in Malaysia consisted of 41 Chinese, 37 Malays, and 35 Tamils. The hospital's routine policy was to discharge healthy mothers and newborns not later than 48 hr after delivery, effectively limiting each newborn in the study to a single assessment at an average age of 22 hr with a range of 12 to 36 hr.

Selection criteria were applied to insure that only healthy, low-risk newborns were examined. These criteria included documented antenatal care confirming an uneventful pregnancy free of maternal illness; an unassisted labor of spontaneous onset; a spontaneous vaginal delivery; and no postnatal complications for either mother or newborn. The facts that all neonates were of adequate weight-for-date according to local standards (Cheng, Chew, & Ratnam, 1972) and received an Apgar score at delivery of at least 8 attest to the optimality of the research sample.

Malaysian survey sample. Although basic growth standards were available for Malaysian newborns and infants (Cheng et al., 1973; Dugdale, 1969; Kim & Eng, 1960), little information was available concerning the population served by the hospital in which the research was conducted. In order to provide some idea of how the research sample compared to the population served by this hospital, a survey was conducted by the authors. A day was chosen at random from each of the 12 months during which the research was performed. The hospital records for all live births on each of these days were coded for maternal ethnicity, age, gravidity, economic status, length of labor, drugs administered during labor, mode of delivery, and neonatal gender, length, weight, gestational age by dates, and Apgar score at birth.

A total of 388 such records were coded, an average of 32 live births per day. Of this number, 322, or 83%, were Chinese, Malay, or Tamil neonates born within 2 weeks of the expected date to women from households in which the primary source of income was manual labor, the economic stratum of the research sample. These 322 records thus provided a reference group against which to gauge the representativeness of the research sample.

English comparison sample. To provide perspective on the results of the Malaysian research, data are also reported in this chapter from a study of 72 1-day-old English neonates born in London and examined by the authors (Woodson, Blurton Jones, da Costa-Woodson, Pollock, & Evans, 1979). Although examined by the same individuals with the same assessment procedure, this English sample differed from the Malaysian sample in one very important respect. While the Malaysian sample was restricted to healthy newborns selected after delivery, the English sample was part of a prospective study in which recruitment took place during the seventh month of pregnancy. As a result, the English sample was more heterogeneous than the Malaysian in terms of prenatal and perinatal experience. Forty-six percent of the labors in the English sample involved syntocinon stimulation with amniotomy; 91% of the women were administered obstetric pain-relief medication; 39% of the deliveries were operatively or mechanically assisted; and 23% of the neonates had Apgar scores of less than 8.

Procedures

Behavioral assessment. Each newborn was examined with the Brazelton Neonatal Behavioral Assessment Scale (Brazelton, 1973). One procedural and two scoring modifications were made to the conventional technique. The procedural change involved the use of an observer during the assessment. Using a standard protocol, this individual recorded a running commentary of the assessment's progress, noting the newborn's spontaneous behavior and elicited responses as well as behavioral state at each 15-second mark during the assessment.

The observer was added to the assessment procedure primarily to allow more assessments to be performed during the limited time available for that portion of the Malaysian project. The observation record proved particularly useful in the rapid and accurate assignment of scores to the individual neonate. The observer's presence also allowed the examiner to concentrate more fully on the newborn during the assessment, certain that a detailed account of the assessment would be available upon completion. The observer continued to be utilized druing the subsequent study of English newborns. The authors alternated in the roles of examiner and observer.

The scoring modifications involved the items Response Decrement and Lability of Skin Color. Rather than use each separate decrement score, the highest of the scores was used as a measure of the neonate's performance on Response Decrement. The Lability of Skin Color item was not used because of the multiracial makeup of the Malaysian sample.

Following the behavioral assessment, a clinical examination was performed to assess the neonate's gestational age (Dubowitz, Dubowitz, & Goldberg, 1970).

Sample Characteristics

Before discussing the results obtained in the behavioral assessment, it is appropriate to consider how representative the sample of newborns examined in this research was of Malaysian newborns in general. Certainly in the area surrouding Kuala Lumpur, antenatal care and hospital delivery were the rule rather than the exception. Despite limited resources, the Ministry of Health operated an efficient network of maternal and child health facilities starting with local clinics staffed by a nurse with midwivery training and going through to district hospitals. In concert with traditional midwives, the Ministry of Health nurses monitored the antenatal progress of women in their area and directed those with complications to the district hospital. As a result, a basic antenatal history was available when a woman presented herself at the hospital for delivery. Hence, while perhaps not comparable to those in the less-developed portions of the country, the mothers and newborns examined in this research did appear to be representative of those in the area surrounding the capital.

As seen in Table 1, the research sample was quite similar to deliveries in this hospital in terms of maternal age, gravidity, birthweight and birth length, Apgar score, percentages of male and female newborns, length of labor, and utilization of obstetric pain-relief medication. Because we attempted to examine approximately equal numbers of Chinese, Malay, and Tamil neonates, the research sample was not representative of the hospital population in terms of ethnicity, Malays being underrepresented and Tamils overrepresented. Since the selection criteria limited the research sample to newborns delivered spontaneously from unassisted labor, the research sample also underrepresented pharmacologically assisted labors and nonspontaneous deliveries.

As can be seen in Table 2, the Chinese, Malay, and Tamil groups differed on a number of background demographic, obstetric, and neonatal variables. Age was significantly associated with culture ($F(2,110) = 5.92$, $p < .01$), with Malay mothers the oldest and Tamil mothers the youngest. Since the average

Table 1. Comparisons between Malaysian Research and Hospital Survey Samples

	Research ($n = 113$)		Survey ($n = 322$)	
	M	SD	M	SD
Maternal age	24.5	5.3	26.3	5.7
Gravidity	2.6	2.1	2.9	2.4
Birthweight (kg)	2.92	0.41	3.00	0.48
Birth length (cm)	48.7	1.9	48.8	2.2
Apgar	9.4	0.6	9.3	1.2
Labor (hr)	9.44	5.49	9.93	6.67
	Percentages			
Male	53		53	
Labor analgesia	39		38	
Chinese	36		37	
Malay	32		47	
Tamil	32		16	
Syntocinon stimulation	0		11	
Spontaneous delivery	100		86	

duration of labor generally decreases with age (Friedman, 1967), this difference also may have accounted for the relatively shorter duration of the first stage of labor of Malay women ($F(2,110) = 3.22$, $p < .05$). Malay women were also the least likely to receive analgesia during labor ($\chi^2(2) = 6.05$, $p < .05$), possibly a reflection of their shorter labors. Finally, while not differing from Chinese and

Table 2. Comparisons between Chinese, Malay, and Tamil Portions of Research Sample

	Chinese ($n = 41$)		Malay ($n = 37$)		Tamil ($n = 35$)	
	M	SD	M	SD	M	SD
Maternal age	25.0	5.1	26.3	6.0	22.3	3.9
Gravidity	2.5	1.9	3.2	2.7	2.3	1.6
Labor stage 1 (hr)	9.6	5.6	7.2	4.0	10.1	6.2
Labor stage 2 (min)	29.2	19.4	22.8	15.1	25.6	19.5
Blood pressure (mmHg)[a]	93.1	8.7	89.2	11.0	91.1	9.5
Weeks gestation	39.0	1.8	39.7	1.4	39.3	1.7
Birthweight (kg)	2.96	.39	3.02	.49	2.77	.32
Apgar	9.5	0.6	9.4	0.6	9.4	0.7
	Percentages					
Male	54		50		54	
Labor analgesia	51		25		41	

[a]Expressed as mean arterial pressure (MAP), where $\text{MAP} = \dfrac{2(\text{diastolic}) + \text{systolic}}{3}$.

Malay newborns in assessed gestational age or birth length, Tamil newborns weighed significantly less than their Chinese and Malay counterparts (F(2,110) = 3.73, $p < .05$).

These differences were for the most part sample-specific since, with the exception of that concerning maternal age, none of them emerged from comparable analyses of the survey data. Nevertheless, the fact that the three groups differed on these background measures necessitated special care in the later analyses concerning the correlates of individual differences in newborn behavior.

Results

Reflex Items

Since Geber and Dean's (1957) pioneering work with African newborns, the issue of culturally related differences in the newborn's basic motor responses has received considerable attention (Leiderman, Babu, Kagia, Kraemer, & Leiderman, 1973; Warren, 1972). About neonates of Asian or Oriental descent, Freedman (1971) reported remarkably high rates of weak standing and stepping responses among Navajo Indian neonates. In light of this literature, the results contained in Table 3 are particularly interesting.

In contrast to Freedman's findings, the proportions of newborns exhibiting

Table 3. Percentage of Sample Exhibiting Weak or Atypical Reflex Responses

Reflex	Chinese	Malay	Tamil	English
Plantar grasp	5	0	3	3
Hand grasp	2	2	3	3
Ankle clonus	2	0	0	1
Babinski	0	3	0	1
Standing	15	10	15	17
Stepping	20	18	21	18
Placing	7	5	8	8
Incurvation	9	13	11	10
Crawling	14	15	15	12
Glabella	0	0	0	0
Tonic deviation	2	3	0	1
Nystagmus	0	0	0	0
Tonic neck	2	2	8	4
Moro	5	8	6	9
Rooting	14	8	17	15
Sucking	12	7	15	11
Passive arms	12	5	6	9
Passive legs	2	5	3	4

Table 4.   Mean BNBAS Scores for Chinese, Malay, Tamil, and English Samples

BNBAS Item	Chinese	Malay	Tamil	English
Response decrement	6.00	5.94	5.97	6.55
Orientation inanimate visual	4.54	4.11	4.41	4.56
Orientation inanimate auditory	5.44	5.78	5.41	5.66
Orientation animate visual	5.02	4.78	4.95	4.96
Orientation animate auditory	5.76	5.58	5.84	5.98
Orientation animate visual and auditory	5.56	5.83	5.49	5.09
Alertness	4.29	4.36	4.49	4.45
General tonus	5.85	5.47	5.14	5.63
Motor maturity	4.93	5.25	4.57	5.14
Pull-to-sit	4.66	4.50	4.97	4.95
Cuddliness	4.93	5.11	4.43	4.89
Defensive movements	4.66	4.61	4.30	5.16
Consolability	5.98	6.06	6.81	5.56
Peak of excitement	5.71	5.61	4.86	5.92
Rapidity of buildup	3.68	3.53	3.00	4.86
Irritability	3.02	3.25	2.51	4.23
Tremulousness	4.07	4.69	4.60	5.70
Activity	4.99	5.20	4.87	5.53
Startles	2.83	2.89	2.70	4.00
Lability of states	4.00	4.28	3.51	4.19
Self-quieting activity	5.51	5.56	6.68	5.36
Hand-mouth facility	5.54	5.72	5.51	5.59

weak extensor thrust or primary walking responses in the three groups of Malaysian newborns were comparable to those found in the English sample. Table 3 also shows that the proportions of newborns displaying weak or atypical responses on the other reflex items contained in the behavioral assessment were comparably low for Malaysian and English newborns. As discussed later, the only consistent motoric differences found between newborns of the Malaysian sample and those of the English sample concerned the frequencies of tremor and startle during the behavioral assessment. In general, then, the reflex items contained in the BNBAS provided little basis for discriminating the newborns of the Malaysian sample from those of the English sample.

Behavioral Assessment: Group Differences

Comparisons within the Malaysian sample. Table 4 contains the means of the BNBAS items for the Chinese, Malay, and Tamil samples along with those of the English sample. Inspection of these values reveals few large differences, either within the Malaysian sample or between the Malaysian groups and the English sample. Before discussing those differences that did emerge, it is important to emphasize that a 1-point difference on a BNBAS item is considered adequate for the purposes of reliability—the largest mean difference contained in

Table 4 is 1.86 points. Hence, though they may be significant in statistical terms, the following behavioral differences were subtle indeed.

One-way analyses of variance of the Chinese, Malay, and Tamil groups uncovered only two statistically significant differences, the first on the Peak of Excitement item ($F(2,110) = 3.99$, $\rho < .025$) and the other on the Self-Quieting Activity item ($F(2,110) = 3.46$, $\rho < .05$). Post hoc analyses indicated that the Tamil newborns were responsible for these differences, exhibiting a lower peak state of excitement and more sustained self-quieting than either the Chinese or the Malay infants. Similar but nonsignificant trends were found for other BNBAS items related to crying. Compared to Chinese and Malay newborns, Tamil newborns were more easily consoled, built more slowly to the initial bout of crying, were less irritable during the assessment, and changed state less often.

The average score of the Chinese, Malay, and Tamil groups on the remaining scale items were remarkably comparable. For the Orientation items (i.e., Orientation Inanimate Auditory through Alertness on Table 4), the greatest differences between the group means was 0.37 points, while for those concerning tone and motor activity the greatest differences was 0.68 points, with the group means on the Response Decrement item within 0.06 points of one another.

The results of these preliminary analyses will be considered later in the chapter. At this point suffice it to say that the most pronounced differences between Chinese, Malay, and Tamil newborns concerned items reflecting the latency, frequency, and duration of crying and that these differences were a consequence primarily of the low levels of irritability exhibited by the Tamil newborns. Again, these differences were not of great magnitude, in no instance involving more than 2 points of a 9-point scale.

Comparisons between Malaysian and English samples. The analyses discussed above showed that differences between the Malaysian groups were generally minimal and confined to BNBAS items concerned with crying rather than alertness, motor activity, or response decrement. Differences between the Malaysian groups and the English sample also emerged for that cluster of items concerning newborn crying during the assessment.

Of the four groups examined in one-way analyses of variance, the English newborns had the highest mean scores on Peak of Excitement ($F(3,181) = 5.08$, $\rho < .01$), Rapidity of Buildup ($F(3,181) = 9.25$, $\rho < .01$), and Irritability ($F(3,181) = 9.35$, $\rho < .01$) and the lowest average scores for Consolability ($F(3,181) = 3.16$, $\rho < .05$) and Self-Quieting Activity ($F(3,181) = 3.37$, $\rho < .05$). Hence, the English newborns exhibited a higher peak state of excitement during the assessment, built more rapidly to the initial cry, were more irritable, showed less sustained self-quieting, and were more difficult to console than the newborns examined in Malaysia. As had been the case within the Malaysian sample, the BNBAS differences found in these analyses concerned aspects of crying.

An additional set of significant differences was found in comparing the Chinese, Malay, Tamil, and English newborns. While the groups were comparable on the motor activity and tonus items (i.e., General Tonus, Motor Maturity, Pull-to-Sit, Cuddliness, Defensive Movements, Activity, and Hand-Mouth Facility), significant differences emerged for Tremulousness ($F(3,181) = 4.77$, $p < .01$) and Startles ($F(3,181) = 8.19$, $p < .01$). Thus, compared to the Malaysian newborns, the English newborns were more tremulous and startled more frequently during the assessment.

As the analyses within the Malaysian sample had shown, no differences were found between the English and Malaysian samples on the items related to orientation, alertness, or response decrement.

In summary, even when their differences were statistically significant, the scores of the four groups of newborns on the BNBAS were rather similar. The most consistent set of differences, both within the Malaysian sample and between the Malaysian and English newborns, concerned aspects of crying. In addition, the Malaysian newborns had fewer tremors and startled less than their English counterparts. The remaining BNBAS items failed to distinguish the Chinese, Malay, Tamil, and English newborns from one another.

Behavioral Assessment: Dimensions of Variation

Investigations of the dimensions of individual differences on the BNBAS have generally used the factor-analytic approach (Horowitz et al., 1973, 1977; Lester, Emory, Hoffman, & Eitzman, 1976; Osofsky & O'Connell, 1977; Strauss & Rourke, 1978). These investigations have identified two primary dimensions of variation on the BNBAS, one defined by the orientation and rated alertness items and the other defined by the items concerning crying.

Given the number of BNBAS items to be considered, the relatively small sizes of the Chinese, Malay, and Tamil samples ruled out applying factor analysis to each group. Instead, product-moment correlations were used to identify the patterns of covariation within each group of newborns. As will be shown, these patterns of covariation were comparable between the Chinese, Malay, and Tamil samples. Each group's BNBAS data were accordingly collapsed into a single sample and then subjected to factor analysis for comparison with the English sample.

Comparisons within the Malaysian sample. The product-moment correlations among the BNBAS items that typically define the Alertness and Irritability dimensions are contained in Tables 5 and 6. Inspection of these results clearly indicates strong interrelationships among the items in each cluster.

Whether Chinese, Malay, or Tamil, neonates of the Malaysian sample receiving a high score on the Alertness item performed well on each of the specific Orientation items. Similarly, regardless of culture, Malaysian newborns with a high score for Peak of Excitement were generally irritable during the assessment, built rapidly to the initial cry, showed little effective self-quieting, and were difficult to console.

Extant factor analyses of BNBAS data indicate that the newborn's perfor-

Table 5.   Correlations among Orientation and Alertness Items in Malaysian Sample

		Inanimate auditory	Inanimate visual	Animate auditory	Animate visual	Animate visual and auditory
Alertness	(C)[a]	.55	.50	.52	.77	.70
	(M)	.59	.64	.68	.76	.80
	(T)	.72	.71	.77	.80	.80
Inanimate auditory			.61	.47	.53	.51
			.60	.53	.47	.67
			.64	.74	.59	.75
Inanimate visual				.38	.45	.49
				.49	.51	.57
				.54	.71	.74
Animate auditory					.57	.71
					.66	.64
					.84	.78
Animate visual						.78
						.73
						.84

[a]C = Chinese; M = Malay; T = Tamil

mance on the Alertness dimension is largely independent of that on the Irritability dimension. To determine whether this was the case within each of the Malaysian groups, the average of each set of within-cluster correlation coefficients was computed and compared with that of the between-cluster coefficients. As seen in Table 7, the within-cluster average was substantially higher than the

Table 6.   Correlations among Irritability Items in Malaysian Sample

		Lability of states	Peak of excitement	Rapidity of buildup	Irritability	Self-quieting activity
Consolability	(C)[a]	−.53	−.83	−.61	−.79	.55
	(M)	−.34	−.65	−.56	−.38	.54
	(T)	−.48	−.52	−.38	−.70	.64
Lability of states			.62	.45	.50	−.48
			.65	.52	.60	−.38
			.45	.35	.61	−.41
Peak of excitement				.70	.72	−.64
				.73	.72	−.48
				.49	.68	−.52
Rapidity of buildup					.65	−.54
					.69	−.49
					.51	−.57
Irritability						−.66
						−.52
						−.50

[a]C = Chinese; M = Malay; T = Tamil

Table 7.   Average Within- and Between-Cluster Correlations in Malaysian Sample

	Within Alertness Cluster	Between Clusters	Within Irritability Cluster
Chinese	.57	.26	.67
Malay	.62	.18	.51
Tamil	.72	.14	.51

between-cluster average for each of the Malaysian groups. Hence, regardless of culture, the Malaysian newborn's performance on the items defining the Alertness factor was largely independent of that on the items defining the Irritability factor.

Comparisons between Malaysian and English samples. The analyses highlighted above demonstrated two strong patterns of covariation in the BNBAS data for each Malaysian group, one involving items concerning alert behavior and the other involving items reflecting irritable behavior. The similarity between the results for the Chinese, Malay, and Tamil groups suggested that little information on individual differences would be lost if the groups' BNBAS data were combined into a single sample for subsequent analysis and comparison with the English sample. The Malaysian and English data were therefore subjected to principal-component analyses followed by varimax factor rotation. Tables 8 and 9 contain the item factor loadings for the BNBAS items that defined the two primary dimensions of variation in each sample.

For both Malaysian and English newborns, the dimension accounting for the greatest percentage of variation received its defining loadings from the orientation-related and rated alertness items. The second dimension of variation in each sample was defined by BNBAS items concerned with crying. The magnitude and direction of the loadings of those items defining each dimension of variation were strikingly similar for each sample. As in the preponderance of existing factor analyses of BNBAS data, the primary dimensions of individual differences on the assessment among both Malaysian and English newborns were Alertness and Irritability.

Table 8.   Factor Loadings of BNBAS Items Defining Alertness Factor

BNBAS Item	Malaysian Sample	English Sample
Orientation inanimate visual	.72	.88
Orientation inanimate auditory	.81	.75
Orientation animate visual	.83	.87
Orientation animate auditory	.82	.78
Orientation animate visual and auditory	.88	.85
Alertness	.87	.92
Activity	.43	.62
Percent variation	22.9	26.2

Table 9.   Factor Loadings of BNBAS Items Defining
Irritability Factor

BNBAS Item	Malaysian Sample	English Sample
Lability of states	.59	.41
Consolability	−.78	−.74
Peak of excitement	.88	.86
Rapidity of buildup	.77	.72
Irritability	.82	.73
Self-quieting activity	−.75	−.69
Percent variation	18.1	15.7

Behavioral Assessment: Correlates of Individual Differences

As noted earlier in the chapter, the Chinese, Malay, and Tamil samples differed from one another on several demographic, obstetric, and neonatal variables. The relationships of these factors with culture anticipates a major difficulty in examining the correlates of individual differences in newborn behavior. Given the covariation among these factors, the relationship between any one factor and behavior on the BNBAS may be either masked by or dependent on the influence of a third factor.

An inspection of the interrelationships among the potential correlates of newborn behavior illustrates the degree of this confounding. As noted earlier, culture in the Malaysian sample was significantly related to maternal age, the lengths of the first and second stages of labor, use of obstetric analgesia, and birthweight. Malaysian women who were administered analgesia, in turn, were younger $(F(1,111) = 4.44, p < .05)$, had longer labors $(F(1,111) = 7.50, p < .01)$, and developed higher blood pressure during labor $(F(1,111) = 5.55, p < .01)$ than those who were not administered such medication.

Such covariation is neither unique to the sample studied in Malaysia nor surprising in any sample drawn from a hospital's general population of deliveries (Kraemer, Korner, & Thoman, 1972). Except in those relatively rare circumstances in which the investigator controls obstetric decisions (Kron, Stein, & Goddard, 1966), demographic, obstetric, and neonatal variables should be expected to covary in studies such as this. For instance, younger women generally are in labor longer than older women. Longer labor is more stressful, which could result in a positive association between length of labor and a physiological index of stress such as blood pressure. A longer and more stressful labor should in turn increase the likelihood that pain-relief medication will be administered. In a sample such as that studied in Malaysia, the failure to find some degree of covariation among such variables would in fact be surprising.

Two steps are necessary in order to determine the relationship between a given antecedent variable and newborn behavior in this situation. First, a common dimension of behavioral variation must be identified. Then the effects of covariate factors must be statistically controlled before examining the relationship between a given variable and behavior. In the case of the Malaysian sample, the correlational analyses reported earlier identified two dimensions of variation—Alertness and Irritability—common to Chinese, Malay, and Tamil newborns and thus appropriate for the analysis of the Malaysian sample as a whole. Accordingly, scores for these two factors were computed for each of the Malaysian newborns. Multiple-regression analyses were then performed on each factor score, with gravidity, the durations of the first and second stages of labor, exposure to obstetric analgesia, maximum blood pressure during labor, birthweight, assessed gestational age, gender, and culture serving as independent variables.

The analysis of the scores on the first factor failed to find any significant relationships between the variables listed above and newborn alertness. However, the analysis of the second factor score uncovered a number of significant relationships between the independent variables and newborn irritability, as summarized in Table 10.

A high score on the irritability factor corresponded to a high peak state of excitement, rapid buildup to the initial cry, frequent bouts of crying, poor consolability, and ineffective self-quieting. Malaysian newborns exhibiting this pattern of behavior during the assessment were born following a longer second stage of labor, were exposed to higher maternal blood pressure during labor, tended not to be exposed to obstetric analgesia, and were of greater asssessed gestational age. This irritable pattern of behavior was also more characteristic of Chinese and Malay than of Tamil newborns, reaffirming the trend evident in the earlier analysis of individual BNBAS items.

Straightforward comparison of these findings with those of other studies of

Table 10. Summary of Multiple-Regression Analysis of Irritability Scores in Malaysian Sample

Variable	b[a]
Gravidity	.04
Labor stage 1	−.04
Labor stage 2	.21*
Labor blood pressure	.27**
Labor analgesia	−.30**
Birthweight	−.11
Gestational age	.20*
Gender	.01
Culture	.26*

[a]Standardized regression coefficient.
*$p < .05$.   **$p < .01$.

neonatal behavior are problematic for a variety of reasons. Different investigators pursuing different questions tend to focus on different variables. Consequently, a variable shown to be significant in one study may simply not be reported in other studies, as was initially the case with labor blood pressure in the Malaysian research. Equally problematic is the tendency for samples to differ substantially on variables of interest. For instance, in the English sample used here for comparative purposes, less than 10% of the labors did not involve pharmacological pain relief and nearly half included pharmacological induction or acceleration of labor. In contrast, over half of the Malaysian labors were free of pain-relief medication and all were of spontaneous onset and culminated in unassisted delivery. Differences among investigators in the way they assess newborn behavior also frustrate attempts at comparison between studies. Korner, Gabby, and Kraemer (1980) examined the relationship between maternal antenatal blood pressure and newborn irritability, using monitored activity as their measure of irritability. Similarly, Richards's (1977) study of the influence of obstetric factors on newborn behavior used the neonate's reaction to the cessation of nonnutritive sucking as a measure of irritability.

In light of these considerations, the comparison of the factors associated with irritability in the Malaysian study with those reported in other investigations is made and should be interpreted with caution. Bearing this caveat in mind, several parallels can be noted between the results summarized in Table 10 and those obtained in other investigations.

The Malaysian neonate born after a shorter gestation was less irritable than the neonate of a greater assessed gestational age. In a sample of American neonates examined with the BNBAS, preterm birth was found to be associated with reduced crying and greater consolability, while postterm delivery was associated with increased crying and difficulty in consoling (Field et al., 1978).

A longer second stage of labor was associated with greater irritability among Malaysian newborns. Similarly, Richards (1977) found that English neonates delivered from relatively longer labors were notably restless and fussy, reacting with greater crying when a pacifier was taken from them during a nonnutritive sucking test.

Exposure to higher maternal blood pressure during labor was associated with greater irritability among the Malaysian neonates. Chisholm, who studied Navajo neonates (Chisholm, Woodson, & da Costa-Woodson, 1978), and Korner et al. (1980), who studied American neonates, each found comparable associations between prenatal exposure to elevated maternal blood pressure and greater newborn irritability and/or activity.

Malaysian neonates exposed to obstetric narcotic analgesia during labor received lower scores on the Irritability factor than did those not exposed to such medication. Similarly, Yang, Zweig, Douthitt, and Federman (1976) found decreased crying among that part of a sample of American newborns exposed to narcotic analgesia during labor.

Finally, a significant association was found in the Malaysian sample between culture and irritability, with Malay newborns receiving the highest and Tamil neonates the lowest score on the Irritability factor. Using a forerunner of the BNBAS, Freedman and Freedman (1969) demonstrated differences on the same aspect of behavior between Chinese-American and European-American neonates.

The problems discussed earlier would in all likelihood work against obtaining concordant results from comparisons across different studies. In spite of this, each of the variables associated with differences in irritability among Malaysian neonates could be shown to bear a similar relationship with the same aspect of behavior in other newborn samples.

Discussion

The results of the Malaysian research speak to two sets of issues. The first concerns the BNBAS as a technique for describing and measuring newborn behavior. The second is the perspective on newborn behavior resulting from cross-cultural research.

A basic reason for studying newborn behavior is to understand the processes linking the prenatal and postnatal phases of development. Newborn behavior both reflects the effects of experience prior to birth and provides the newborn with the means to affect the postnatal environment, particularly the caretakers. As such, newborn behavior affords us the opportunity to investigate the basis of continuity across developmental periods.

If we are to take advantage of this opportunity we clearly need a reliable means of describing and measuring those aspects of newborn behavior which are affected by prenatal experience and through which the newborn affects the environment. Despite its faults (Prechtl, 1982), the BNBAS appears to fill this need. The results reported here concur with those of similar analyses in indicating that the BNBAS yields reliable dimensions of individual differences in newborn behavior that primarily concern behavioral state.

The significance of these observations should not be underestimated. If the BNBAS did not reliably identify stable dimensions of variation in newborn behavior, we would lack the metric necessary for documenting both similarities and differences between newborns. At the same time, the fact that the primary dimensions of individual differences on the BNBAS concern behavioral state is significant. As Korner (1972) notes, state is the mediating variable through which the newborn interacts with the environment. Caretakers *may* respond to the subtle parameters measured by techniques more strictly neurological than the BNBAS, but they clearly *do* respond to the state attributes measured by the BNBAS. Observational studies have shown that the range, content, and quality of caretaker-newborn interaction are affected by factors such as the newborn's alertness, irritability, consolability, and state control (Brazelton, 1962; Thoman, 1979). The immediate impact of these behavioral attributes on caretaker-newborn interaction may help to account for their association with subsequent indices of the caretaker-infant relationship (Waters, Vaughn, & Egeland, 1980). The picture of the newborn's state characteristics provided by the BNBAS is therefore of the utmost value.

Given state's pivotal importance, we should take pains to insure that our measures of that variable are the best possible (Sameroff, 1978). While the balance of studies indicate that the primary dimensions of variation on the BNBAS concern state, disagreements have arisen concerning the manner in which to quantify these differences. On the one hand are investigators who use either the BNBAS items themselves or summary measures of behavior empirically derived from analyses of BNBAS data. On the other hand are those who utilize summary ratings of BNBAS performance based on clusters of individual items identified a priori on conceptual grounds (Als, Tronick, Adamson, & Brazelton, 1976). In some instances, as is the case with the Orientation and Alertness items, the two approaches yield quite comparable results. In other instances, however, their yields are not similar. Thus, while the empirical analyses have uniformly failed to find any association between the Response Decrement items and those defining the Irritability factor, the a priori approach places these items together in the Regulation of State cluster.

Unless this treatment of BNBAS data can be shown to be superior in some fashion to the empirical treatment, its use would appear difficult to justify. At the very least, proponents of the a priori approach should explain why and how items presumed to reflect a process underlying and organizing behavior fail to exhibit stable patterns of covariation among themselves. If it is in fact variation in attributes such as alertness and irritability that helps to predict differences in developmental outcome, there seems little to be gained from contaminating that variation with differences among newborns on BNBAS items not empirically related to the Alertness or Irritability dimensions.

In planning and executing the Malaysian research we shared a motivation common to all cross-cultural investigators—to describe characteristics unique to a group of neonates not previously investigated. We left for Malaysia expecting to find differences but returned impressed by similarities. The study was thus to a degree a disappointment. However, this disappointment was more than offset by other realizations about newborn behavior which arose from the experience of conducting such research in another culture.

One such realization was that while newborns of different cultures may be similar to one another in terms of behavior, the consequences of that behavior for development may vary in important ways depending on the newborn's culture. To cite a very simple example, consider the culture-dependent consequences of impaired sucking in the newborn. Since the newborn's ability to nurse helps determine whether or not breast-feeding is established (Sjolin, Hofvander, & Hillervik, 1977), a weak sucking response on the part of the newborn places the burden on the mother to maintain the momentum for breast-feeding. Given readily available substitutes for and social pressures against breast-feeding, all but the most dedicated of mothers will abandon the attempt and turn to formula-feeding. Since breast-feeding confers a degree of protection against ailments such as whooping cough and diphtheria (deMuralt, 1978), the newborn fed on formula is more prone to recurrent infection than is the one who receives pro-longed breast-feeding. This is true even in relatively advantaged societies (Cunningham, 1977) and is a major cause of infant mortality and morbidity in less-developed countries (Morley, 1973). Consequently, the fact that the newborn's sucking response is weak may have vastly different implications depending on the type of environment in which the newborn is to develop. If so, then the finding that a perinatal experience, such as exposure to obstetric analgesia, reduces the newborn's ability to maintain a state adequate to support vigorous sucking merits particular attention against the background of infancy in Malaysia.

Another valuable lesson learned from the Malaysian research was not immediately apparent but was appreciated only with time. It was the importance of focusing on the processes linking prenatal and postnatal observations rather than on the observations themselves. This point was forcefully driven home in our attempt in the subsequent London study to replicate the association found in the Malaysian study between maternal labor blood pressure and newborn irritability. That attempt failed and from that failure we began to appreciate the meaning of the original finding (Woodson et al., 1979). Maternal labor blood pressure could be a significant correlate of newborn irritability in one sample but not in another, not because the initial finding was a fluke but because maternal blood pressure was merely one of a number of variables related to fetal status during labor. When the process that determines fetal intrapartum status began to be examined, what appeared to be a failure to replicate began to fall into place. What was stable and replicable across samples was not a relation between newborn behavior and any one of a number of correlates of fetal status, but instead a process through which a variety of factors capable of affecting fetal status could thereby affect newborn behavior. In the case of the relatively homogeneous and low-risk Malaysian sample, the important perinatal variable happened to be maternal labor blood pressure. In the more heterogeneous London sample, variables such as syntocinon stimulation and the adequacy of fetal growth, whose effects on fetal status outweighed that of blood pressure, had the more decisive influence on fetal status and hence on newborn irritability.

The final lesson derived from the Malaysian research concerned behavioral differences between newborns from different cultures. The question was not whether such differences could be shown to exist—ours and other studies had shown that they did. The question instead concerned the interpretation of such differences. What exactly could be shown in demonstrating behavioral differences between newborns of different cultures?

The analyses of the Malaysian data indicated that in the first instance it may have been demonstrated only that experiential factors vary as a function of culture and that the effects of these factors on newborn behavior are consistent across cultures. This was evident in the Malaysian sample in the relationship of culture with a complex of demographic, obstetric, and neonatal variables related to newborn irritability. The same could be expected in other circumstances involving culturally determined differences in prenatal and perinatal experience. Depending on the research setting, these factors could include strictures applied to the pregnant woman's diet and activity, the location and management of labor, birth rites, and lying-in arrangements.

Ours was not the first cross-cultural report to highlight the contribution of experiential factors to behavioral differences between groups of newborns from different cultures. Freedman (1971) noted the same phenomenon in his comparison of Caucasian-American and Chinese-American neonates and used statistical methods to control for the efects of several demographic and obstetric variables. As in the Malaysian study, Freedman demonstrated behavioral differnces between newborns of differnt cultures that persisted after controlling for a finite set of experiential factors. He was thus confronted with the same question that we faced in the Malaysian research: What did these cultural differences signify?

Freedman proposed that these differences were a consequence of genotypic differences between cultures. Support for that interpretation came from two sources. First, twin studies had provided fairly convincing evidence that genetic factors did affect a range of developmental phenomena (Freedman, 1965; Wilson, 1975). It would thus be surprising if the newborn's behavior did not fall within that range. Second, genetic markers could be used to distinguish members of different cultures from one another. The mapping of blood group, race, and culture onto one another provided a clear illustration of this.

Despite the corroborating evidence, we were and continue to be uncomfortable with Freedman's interpretation. The reason for our concern is quite simple. If experiential factors that differed between cultures were known to affect newborn behavior, how could we be certain that all such factors had been identified and considered in our analyses? The introduction of the experiential variables into the multiple-regression analysis of the Malaysian irritability scores had reduced by nearly 20% the proportion of variation in irritability associated with culture. That analysis clearly did not exhaust the list of culturally determined experiential factors capable of affecting the newborn's behavior.

To attribute cultural differences in newborn behavior to genetic factors on the basis of having excluded what was certainly only a portion of the set of experiential factors capable of influencing newborn behavior thus appeared to us incautious at best. The investigation of genetic influences on newborn behavior should be pursued. However, we doubt seriously that the cross-cultural context provides the appropriate setting for such investigations.

References

Als, H., Tronick, E., Adamson, L., & Brazelton, T. (1976). The behavior of the full-term yet underweight newborn infant. *Developmental Medicine and Child Neurology, 18,* 590–602.

Brazelton, T. (1962). Observations of the neonate. *Journal of the American Academy of Child Psychiatry, 1,* 38–58.

Brazelton, T. (1973). *Neonatal Behavioral Assessment Scale.* London: Spastics International Medical Publications/Heinemann Medical Books.

Brazelton, T., Koslowski, B., & Tronick, E. (1976). Neonatal behavior among urban Zambians and Americans. *Journal of the American Academy of Child Psychiatry, 15,* 97–107.

Brazelton, T., Robey, J., & Collier, G. (1969). Infant development in the Zinacanteco Indians of southern Mexico. *Pediatrics, 44,* 274–290.

Cheng, M., Chew, P., & Ratnam, S. (1972). Birthweight distribution of Singapore Chinese, Malay, and Indian infants from 34 weeks to 42 weeks gestation. *Journal of Obstetrics and Gynaecology of the British Commonwealth, 79,* 149–153.

Chisholm, J., Woodson, R., & da Costa-Woodson, E. (1978). Maternal blood pressure during pregnancy and newborn irritability. *Early Human Development, 2,* 171–178.

Cunningham, A. (1977). Morbidity in breast-fed and artificially fed infants. *Journal of Pediatrics, 90,* 726–729.

deMuralt, G. (1978). Maturation of cellular and humoral immunity. In U. Stave (Ed.), *Perinatal physiology* (2nd ed.). New York: Plenum Medical.

deVries, M., & Super, C. (1978). Contextual influences on the Neonatal Behavioral Assessment Scale and implications for its cross-cultural use. *Monographs of the Society for Research in Child Development, 43 (5–6,* Serial No. 177), 92–101.

Dubowitz, L., Dubowitz, V., & Goldberg, C. (1970). Clinical assessment of gestational age in the newborn. *Journal of Pediatrics, 77,* 1–10.

Dugdale, A. (1969). The weights of Malaysian infants up to one year. *Medical Journal of Malaya, 23,* 244–246.

Field, T., Hallock, N., Ting, C., Dempsey, J., Dabiri, C., & Shuman, H. (1978). A first-year follow-up of high-risk: Formulating a cumulative risk index. *Child Development, 49,* 119–131.

Freedman, D. (1965). An ethological approach to the genetical study of human behavior. In S. Vandenberg (Ed.), *Methods and goals in human behavior genetics.* New York: Academic Press.

Freedman, D. (1971). Genetic influences on development of behavior. In G. Stoelinga & J. van der Werff Ten Bosch (Eds.), *Normal and abnormal development of behavior.* Leiden, The Netherlands: Leiden University Press.

Freedman, D., & Freedman, N. (1969). Behavioural differences between Chinese-American and European-American newborns. *Nature, 224,* 1227.

Friedman, E. (1967). *Labor: Clinical evaluation and management.* New York: Appleton-Century-Crofts.

Geber, M., & Dean, R. (1957). The state of development of newborn African children. *Lancet, 1,* 1216–1219.

Horowitz, F., Aleksandrowicz, M., Ashton, L., Tims, S., McCluskey, K., Culp, R., & Gallas, H. (1973, April). *American and Uruguayan infants: Reliabilities, maternal drug histories, and population differences using the Brazelton Scale.* Paper presented at the biennial meeting of the Society for Research in Child Development, Philadelphia, PA.

Horowitz, F., Ashton, L., Culp, R., Gaddis, E., Levin, S., & Reichmann, B. (1977). The effect of obstetrical medication on the behavior of Israeli newborn infants and some comparisons with Uruguayan and American infants. *Child Development, 48,* 1607–1623.

Kim, C., & Eng., Y. (1960). The development and growth of some Singapore children. *Journal of the Singapore Paediatric Society, 2,* 74–94.

Korner, A. (1972). State as variable, as obstacle, and as mediator of stimulation in infant research. *Merrill-Palmer Quarterly, 18,* 77–94.

Korner, A., Gabby, T., & Kraemer, H. (1980). Relation between prenatal maternal blood pressure and infant irritability. *Early Human Development, 4,* 35–39.

Kraemer, H., Korner, A., & Thoman, E. (1972). Methodological considerations in evaluating the influence of drugs used during labor and delivery on the behavior of the newborn. *Developmental Psychology, 6,* 128–134.

Kron, R., Stein, M., & Goddard, K. (1966). Newborn sucking behavior affected by obstetric sedation. *Pediatrics, 37,* 1012–1016.

Leiderman, H., Babu, B., Kagia, J., Kraemer, H., & Leiderman, G. (1973). African infant precocity and some social influences during the first year. *Nature, 242,* 247–249.

Lester, B., Emory, E., Hoffman, S., & Eitzman, D. (1976). A multivariate study of the effects of high-risk factors on performance on the Brazelton Neonatal Behavioral Assessment Scale. *Child Development, 47,* 515–517.

Morley, D. (1973). *Paediatric priorities in the developing world.* London: Butterworth.

Osofsky, J., & O'Connell, E. (1977). Patterning of newborn behavior in an urban population. *Child Development, 47,* 515-517.

Prechtl, H. (1982). Assessment methods for the newborn infant: A critical evaluation. In P. Stratton (Ed.), *Psychobiology of the human newborn.* New York: Wiley.

Richards, M. (1977). An ecological study of infant development in an urban setting in Britain. In P. Leiderman, S. Tulkin, & A. Rosenfeld (Eds.), *Culture and infancy: Variations in the human experience.* New York: Academic Press.

Sameroff, A. (1978). Summary and conclusions: The future of newborn assessment. In A. Sameroff (Ed.), Organization and stability of newborn behavior: A commentary on the Brazelton Neonatal Behavioral Assessment Scale. *Monographs of the Society for Research in Child Development, 43* (5–6, Serial No. 177), 102–117.

Sjolin, S., Hofvander, Y., & Hillervik, C. (1977). Factors related to early termination of breast feeding. *Acta Paediatrica Scandinavica, 66,* 505–511.

Strauss, M., & Rourke, D. (1978). A multivariate analysis of the Neonatal Behaviorla Assessment Scale in several samples. In A. Sameroff (Ed.), Organization and stability of newborn behavior: A commentary on the Brazelton Neonatal Behavioral Scale. *Monographs of the Society for Research in Child Development, 43* (5–6, Serial No. 177), 81–91.

Thoman, E. (1974). Disruption and asynchrony in early parent-infant interactions. In D. Sawin, R. Hawkins, L. Walker, & J. Penticuff (Eds.), *Exceptional infant IV: Psychosocial risks in infant-environment transactions.* New York: Brunner/Mazel.

Warren, N. (1972). African infant precocity. *Psychological Bulletin, 78,* 353–367.

Waters, E., Vaughn, B., & Egeland, B. (1980). Individual differences in infant-mother attachment relationships at age one: Antecedents in neonatal behavior in an urban, economically disadvantaged sample. *Child Development, 51,* 208–216.

Wilson, R. (1975). Twins: Patterns of cognitive development as measured on the Wechsler preschool and primary scale of intelligence. *Developmental Psychology, 11,* 126–134.

Woodson, R., Blurton Jones, N., da Costa-Woodson, E., Pollock, S., & Evans, M. (1979). Fetal mediators of the relationships between increased pregnancy and labour blood pressure and newborn irritability. *Early Human Development, 3,* 127–139.

Woodson, R., & Da Costa, E. (1984). The influence of the social and physical environment on infant-caretaker interaction. *Developmental Psychology, 20,* 473–476.

Yang, R., Zweig, A., Douthitt, T., & Federman, E. (1976). Successive relationships between maternal attitudes during pregnancy, analgesic medication during labor and delivery, and newborn behavior. *Developmental Psychology, 12,* 6–14.

CHAPTER 12

The Hmong in America: Infant Behavior and Rearing Practices

Sharon Muret-Wagstaff

Department of Pediatrics,
Hennepin County Medical Center,
Minneapolis, Minnesota

Shirley G. Moore

Institute of Child Development,
University of Minnesota,
Minneapolis, Minnesota

> O Chestnut tree, great rooted blossomer,
> Are you the leaf, the blossom or the bole?
> O body swayed to music, O brightening glance,
> How can we know the dancer from the dance?
> —W. B. Yeats, "Among School Children"

Developmentalists, like poets, are intrigued and puzzled by parts and wholes. Cross-cultural researchers have tried to understand individual behaviors, or parts, that covary in one culture by studying them as they separate in another culture. However, the second "separated" variable, like Yeats's dancer, is inevitably tied again to a broader cultural dance.

---

* This research was supported in part by a fellowship to the first author from the University of Minnesota Center for Early Education and Development. Portions of this study were presented at the biennial meeting of the Society for Research in Child Development, Detroit, April 1983.

The authors gratefully acknowledge the help of the staff of the Hennepin County Medical Center; the advice and assistance of Ly Vang, Mary Yang, Song Yang, and Phoua Thao; and the participation of the mothers and babies in this study.

Participants in the present study of newborn behavior and rearing practices were of two distinct cultural groups—Hmong families recently arrived from Laos in Southeast Asia, and their new American neighbors, a group of economically disadvantaged Caucasian families—all living in the inner city in Minneapolis, Minnesota. The families in the first group are among the estimated 60,000 Hmong refugees who arrived in the United States between 1975 and 1981, fleeing their war-torn homeland following the takeover in Vientiane by the Pathet Lao and the ensuing Communist reprisals against the Hmong. More than 10,000 Hmong people now live in the Minneapolis–St. Paul urban area (Olney, 1983; U.S. Department of Health and Human Services, 1982; Yang, 1982).

The Hmong People

The fragmented history of the Hmong people dates back to ancient China where they were known as Miao or Meo. Today they prefer to be called Hmong, meaning "free man." The Hmong lived as a close knit minority group in China, resisting subjugation and finally migrating southward to the isolated mountaintops of Laos nearly 200 years ago. While rich oral legends abound in songs and chants, no written version of their monosyllabic, tonal language is known to have existed until the 1960s or 1970s, when Christian missionaries began to develop a Latinized script. The Hmong have a widely circulated belief that records of their history and legends were intricately embroidered as embellishments on clothing centuries ago, that they might be preserved secretly when other Hmong records were destroyed by their would-be conquerors. The fine needlework of Hmong women today, which has served important ritual and social functions, is a special source of pride. However, any historical notes which may have been locked in the tiny embroidered and appliquéd patterns passed from mother to daughter are now lost to the past (White, n.d.).

Economy

On the ridges of the Laotian mountains where the Hmong lived as migratory slash-and-burn agriculturists before the war years, days were labeled by the waxing and waning of the moon and seasons were named according to appropriate farming activities. Fields were cleared from February until April and planting took place in May. The warm rainy season would last until about September and crops were harvested early in the dry season, lasting from October until March. The chief festival, the New Year, was celebrated in December, in the cold season following harvest. The high altitudes were ideal for cultivation of opium poppies, which gave the Hmong economic strength and independence and allowed them to buy silver, fabric, cooking utensils, shoes, and thread from the Chinese and Laotian opium dealers. Other crops included rice, corn to feed the animals, and other vegetables. Cows, water buffaloes, horses, pigs, and chickens were sometimes raised and traded. Typically, the Hmong household or village was self-sufficient (Center for Applied Linguistics, 1979).

Social Organization

The patrilineal clan system, designated by surname, dominates Hmong social organization in both Laos and America and serves as a primary focus for the culture. Members adhere strictly to clan exogamy, which forbids two people of the same clan to marry one another. Upon marriage, a woman keeps her surname but identifies herself thereafter in every other way as a member of her husband's clan. This system cross-cuts dialect groups, which in Laos are primarily the White, Blue, or Green Hmong. When two persons of the same clan and dialect group meet, (for example, two White Hmong with the surname of Yang) the next order of business is a comparison of genealogies to determine whether or not they are lineage mates, descended from the same known ancestor. Lineage mates can count on one another for help when faced with serious problems, conflicts, or expenses. They refer to one another in terms meaning "my older" or "my younger." The phrase for lineage means "cluster of brothers" or "one ceremonial household" (Barney, 1967; Dunnigan, 1982; Lee, 1981).

The typical Hmong household in Laos includes a man and his wife or wives, his sons and their wives and children, his unmarried daughters, and sometimes other dependent relatives, with as many as 35 people under one roof. Final authority rests with the male head of the household, who is responsible for household property. Upon his death, the property remains with the household and the eldest son takes over. A person who moves out no longer shares in the distribution of household assets. A village may contain from 1 to 40 such households, with a head man who is commonly the eldest male head of household of the dominant clan.

Relations between households and clans are enhanced by marriages. A boy of one clan may become acquainted with a girl of another when one village invites another to share the New Year festivities. Interest heightens through a traditional game in which a ball is tossed back and forth between lines of boys and girls opposite each other, the girls dressed in colorful, meticulously sewn dresses and elaborate silver necklaces. Later, the boy visits the girl's village and secures a go-between, usually an older brother or paternal uncle, to negotiate a marriage with the girl's parents. In one variation, the young man and his male relatives "abduct" the girl, often with her full knowledge and consent. She calls for help, and her mother (never her male relatives) comes and may verbally abuse the boy and hit him with a stick. This is intended to convince the pursuing clan of the girl's value to her own household and clan.

After the "abduction" of the girl to the boy's household, an elaborate wedding takes place days or even months later. During the days of negotiating and feasting back and forth between the bride and groom's homes, pigs and chickens are slaughtered for meals and rituals and a bride price, which the groom's household pays to the bride's family, is agreed upon. Fines are paid to make up for past grievances suffered by the bride's clan at the hands of the groom's clan. The married son often lives in his father's household with his wife and young children until, at about 30 years of age, he establishes his own household nearby. Many sons remain in the father's household for life. Divorce is permitted but it is infrequent and discouraged. Divorce threatens to disrupt relations between clans, and divorce fees are accordingly high.

Polygyny is permitted in Laos. One wife directs the household activities of the other wives. A widow may marry her deceased husband's younger (but not older) brother and remain in the same household (Barney, 1967; Center for Applied Linguistics, 1979; Lee, 1981; U.S. Department of the Army, 1970; Vang, 1982).

The Laotian Hmong house is made entirely of wood such as teak, bamboo, or pine, with a dirt floor, two doors, and no windows. One door serves ordinary purposes and the other has ceremonial functions; the fireplaces are used for cooking and social gatherings; and one wall of the large living area is reserved for a shrine or altar for the spirits. Furnishings include a few wooden benches, a rice pounder, and storage accommodations. Some households have a low bamboo table, but people often squat on the floor around a meal instead, the men eating first. The sleeping area consists of a wooden platform several inches off the ground. Children sleep with their parents or grandparents until they are 6 or 7 years old. Adolescent girls and boys have separate sleeping quarters. Near the houses are granaries on stilts and other buildings for pigs, chickens, horses, and other animals (Lee, 1981).

At "first cock crow" (about 4:00 a.m.) the women rise to start the fire, go to the stream for the day's supply of water, and feed the animals. After the morning meal, all able adults and older children walk 1 to 3 hr by trail to the field to work, with infants on their mothers' backs. Other children under 7 years may accompany the family to the field to help, or they stay at home with grandparents, who are highly respected. Men construct and repair buildings and fences, clear fields, farm, care for livestock, and hunt. Along with farming, women care for children, prepare and serve food, feed animals, carry all water, spin, weave, and sew. Children gather firewood, assist with farming and chores of the same sex parent, and care for younger children. Their work directly affects the welfare of the household and they are expected to be obedient and responsible. By 8 years of age, a Hmong girl is quite competent at domestic chores and taking care of

Photo 1.   Hmong mother and baby. (*Photo copyright: Minneapolis Star and Tribune.*)

babies, often carrying a younger sibling on her back. A few boys are sent away to schools where they learn to read and write in the Laotian language, but girls are rarely formally educated. While children are basically the responsibility of their immediate parents, everyone in the household participates in their informal education, training, and social guidance (Center for Applied Linguistics, 1979; U.S. Department of the Army, 1970). Barney (1967) reports never having seen physical punishment of children.

Chicken, rice, vegetables, and a few fruits are basic to the Hmong diet. Babies are breast-fed for 1 to 4 years, when the next baby is born, after which no milk is consumed. Tea is the primary drink. Malaria, headache, fevers, toothaches, goiter, respiratory illness, parasites, and various intestinal problems were frequent occurrences in Laos. Because people were isolated in the hills without medicine or hospitals, opium was the last resort for problems that were not resolved with the help of a shaman or elderly women herbalists. Seasonal malnutrition before gathering the harvest was not uncommon. Infant mortality was estimated at 30% in 1970 (U.S. Department of the Army, 1970) and, similarly, at 250 per 1,000 live births in a carefully studied Hmong village in Thailand in 1977 (Lee, 1981).

Although Laotian Buddhists and Christian missionaries have had some impact,animism is the prevalent religious perspective and spirits are an integral part of everyday Hmong life. Beliefs and practices vary by region, clan, and lineage. In fact, one way Hmong people determine closeness of family ties is by comparison of details of the rituals of each party's household. The Hmong believe all things in nature are inhabited by spirits. If one worships one's ancestors correctly and does not offend them, the spirits of those ancestors will provide protection from malevolent spirits and bring prosperity.

Each person is believed to have several souls. If the soul, which normally stays with the body, is lost or frightened away, a person becomes ill and the shaman must perform rituals to call it back. A shaman can also divine other causes of illness, cure certain sicknesses, interpret signs and dreams, predict the future, and communicate with the spirit world. Animal sacrifices and other offerings are made to ancestor spirits. A woman and her children belong to the spiritual circle of the husband and his lineage (Barney, 1967; Bliatout, 1982).

Resettlement in the United States

Daily life has changed radically for the Hmong people who sought refuge in the cities of the United States, France, Canada, and Australia (Morin, 1983). Physiologic effects of stress, along with economic and political hardship, erosion of their cultural inventory, guilt at having survived when others have not, grieving for the lost homeland, and anxiety about an uncertain future, have taken their toll on the Hmong, as evidenced by self-reporting of financial, mental/emotional, health-related, and marital difficulties in the U. S. To the dismay of both the Hmong people and Western doctors, over 30 young healthy Hmong male refugees have died suddenly in their sleep without detectable cause since leaving their homeland (Bliatout, 1982). However, families are forging a new stability by undertaking secondary migrations to reestablish kinship ties, eagerly making use of schools and other community resources, and taking creative advantage of new technological devices such as tape recorders for communicating with separated relatives (Scudder & Colson, 1982; Westermeyer, 1983).

Childbirth in Laos and the United States

Traditional Hmong childbirth practices strongly influence Hmong preferences in the U.S., where prenatal care may be delayed, parity is high, short spacing occurs between pregnancies, yet babies are healthy (Ehlinger, 1983). In Laos, during the prenatal period, a woman gathers large quantities of long grass which will serve as her bed during the first few postpartum days of heavy bleeding and will then be burned. The household accumulates extra chickens for her special postpartum diet. In some clans, a silver necklace is fashioned to be placed for good luck around the newborn's neck immediately upon delivery, and before the cord is cut. If silver is not available, white string will do. The husband's parents instruct the couple in the details of childbirth and infant care.

A woman's husband and mother-in-law are her primary birth attendants, although other adults (but not nursing mothers) may be present for prayers and chants. An herbalist, or medicine woman, may administer herbal tea in difficult labors or attempt to alter the baby's intrauterine position manually. At the onset of labor, it is important for the woman to hurry to the home of her husband or of his lineage mates in order to avoid the potential harm of unfriendly spirits.

The woman labors in bed, but moves to a squatting position for the delivery, sometimes using a low stool. Generally, the husband positions himself behind his wife with his arms locked around her chest so that she can lean against him, while the woman's mother-in-law prepares to receive the child. In the U.S., Hmong women continue to prefer the squatting position for delivery (Nelson & Hewitt, 1983; Potter & Whiren, 1982; U.S. Department of the Army, 1970).

American birth attendants have remarked about the particularly relaxed way the Hmong women labor and give birth, dressed in their traditional cotton blouses and long skirts. They do not use American childbirth relaxation techniques, but remain quiet and subdued throughout labor, appearing to experience less anxiety than their American-born counterparts. Progress through labor is marked only by subtle changes in breathing or facial expression. Fathers continue to provide sensitive, soothing physical and emotional support to their wives. Medications are seldom required, and the rate of obstetrical complications is unusually low (Nelson & Hewitt, 1983).

In Laos, on delivery of the child, the father cuts the umbilical cord with two pieces of sharp bamboo or, in more recent years, a boiled knife or scissors. The father or the mother-in-law then washes and wraps the baby. American nurses were surprised to learn that these "natural" mothers did not want to hold their infants until after the babies were bathed (Mullet & Seubert, 1982). Likewise, Hmong women express surprise that Americans want messy babies placed on their abdomens. A birth deformity or a protracted labor may be considered a reflection of the mother's or father's past misdeeds (Potter & Whiren, 1982).

The placenta of a male baby is buried beside the center post of the traditional Hmong house, emphasizing the boy's future position and obligations. The placenta of a female baby is buried beneath the parents' sleeping quarters, where a woman usually gives birth. Following burial of the placenta, the father offers prayers to the spirits on the baby's behalf, and the new mother lies before the hot fire for 3 to 25 days. During the 30-day postpartum period, the Hmong mother's diet is restricted to steaming hot water, boiled chicken, broth, and rice. All water must be boiled and kept hot, whether for drinking or for cleaning (Nelson & Hewitt, 1983; U.S. Department of the Army, 1970).

The baby's naming ceremony takes place at 3 days of age, with the shaman or village elder officiating. Chickens are sacrificed to the spirits, who have led the soul of a dead ancestor into the body of the newborn child. The father invites male heads of households and their families to attend the feast. In the ceremonies, two cooked chickens, a boiled egg, and a candle are used. Strings about 15 cm long are passed around to the men in attendance. The elder first ties a string around the baby's wrist and makes a wish for the child, such as good health, long life, and prosperity. The other men follow in order of their status until the baby has received many strings and wishes. Strings may also be tied around the wrists of the parents and siblings. Men are the first to eat the ceremonial dinner, followed by the children and then the women. The naming ceremony continues to be celebrated in the U.S. and attests to the degree to which children are prized and valued (Potter & Whiren, 1982; U.S. Department of the Army, 1970). At this time, also, the paternal grandmother shaves the baby's head to protect the child from fear of thunder during the next rainy season. A girl's ears are pierced with needle and thread, but no special significance is attached to this act.

The mother returns to the field to work at some time during the first month, depending on her health and the necessity in the work force, with her baby tied to her back so that breast-feeding can proceed at very frequent intervals and entirely on demand. Observers in Laos noted that babies were never left to cry (U.S. Department of the Army, 1970). The elaborately hand-sewn baby carrier is a cotton rectangle, about 40 by 58 cm, which supports the baby's body, with a smaller rectangle sewn at the top to support the neck. The central part of the baby carrier is often intricately figured batik, decorated with bright geometric appliqué, embroidery, and tiny yarn pompoms. Long bright cotton sashes sewn to the corners of the carrier are wrapped around the mother's body to hold the baby securely.

Babies also wear a variety of skullcaps, beautifully decorated with cross-stitching, applique, coins, and beads. One belief holds that head coverings keep babies' spirits from slipping out. Another holds that the hats are worn to fool mischievous spirits into believing the children are flowers. Thus disguised, the children are less apt to have their own more flighty spirits lured away (White, n.d.).

Comparison of Infant Behavior and Rearing Practices

Behavioral differences between infants of different cultures have been attributed to genetically determined characteristics such as temperament (Freedman & Freedman, 1969), to environmental influences (Super, 1976), and to interaction between the two (Keefer, Tronick, Dixon, & Brazelton, 1982). The specific aim of the present investigation was to extend the data pertaining to behavioral similarities and differences between Oriental and Caucasian newborns, both by sampling behavior over time and by collecting concurrent medical and environmental information. The newborns of newly immigrated Hmong women were compared with an American Caucasian sample, and the study was facilitated by the fact that most diverse cultural groups live side by side in the same inner city neighborhood. Medical data were collected, infants were tested five times (on days 1 and 3 in the hospital and days 7, 14, and 28 at home) with the Brazelton Neonatal Behavioral Assessment Scale (BNBAS; Brazelton, 1973); mothers were interviewed; and aspects of maternal caretaking were observed at home.

Methods

Subjects

In all, 21 Hmong and 21 American Caucasian infants and their mothers participated. Criteria for inclusion in the study were singleton birth by spontaneous vaginal delivery; gestation of 38 to 42 weeks, determined by examination; birthweight of 2,500 to 4,000 g of birthweight; normal pediatric examination; no obstetrical or neonatal complications such as sepsis, premature rupture of membranes, or asphyxia; absence of maternal chronic disease; maternal age of 17 years or more; and at least 1 adult other than the mother living in the household. Mean Apgar score at 5 min for each group was 8.9. A sedative or analgesic during labor was administered to 8 Caucasian mothers. Birthweight did not differ significantly between groups (Hmong = 3,181 g, Caucasian = 3,249 g). The study included 9 female and 12 male Hmong infants, and 14 female and 7 male Caucasian infants.

All babies roomed with their mothers. Of the Hmong mothers, 5 combined breast- and bottle-feeding, while the remainder used formula feeding exclusively. Among the Caucasian mothers, 11 breast-fed and 10 used formula. Of these 21, 16 were living with the baby's father, and 12 of these 16 mothers were married. A total of 20 Hmong mothers lived with the baby's father, and 21 were married. Hmong households had greater density ($M = 8.3$ persons) than Caucasian households ($M = 4.9$ persons). A total of 81% of the Hmong and 24% of the Caucasians lived in extended family households. There was at least 1 other child in 18 Hmong and 11 Caucasian homes. Maternal age ranged from 17 to 43 in the Hmong group ($M = 25.5$) and from 18 to 33 in the Caucasian group ($M = 22.9$). In this highly mobile population, more than half the subjects in each group had moved at least once in the preceding year; 6 moved at least once more during the baby's first month.

Hmong mothers represented 9 and fathers represented 12 of the 23 known clans in Laos. Only 1 of the 13 largest Hmong clans was not represented. Participants included both White and Green Hmong. Hmong mothers had been in the United States an average of 17.3 months at the time of delivery, and 7 had lived in at least one other U.S. city.

Procedure

All Hmong and Caucasian mothers who delivered eligible newborns at Hennepin County Medical Center during the 5-month study period were invited to participate. Those Hmong mothers who had difficulty with English listened to a taped description of the project in Hmong by a native speaker. The tape had been translated from English to Hmong by one bilingual Hmong and from Hmong to English independently by another until close agreement with the original English version was obtained. One of the 22 infants admitted was dropped because of maternal anxiety with separation from the infant during the initial examination. A Caucasian mother refused for nonspecific reasons, and 5 others refused for reasons of the "bother" or "problem" of having an outsider come into the home.

In the hospital, the BNBAS, with the pinprick item omitted, was administered in a quiet room with subdued lighting, without the mother present, on days 1 and 3 of life. It was emphasized that the infant "could do his or her best" without distractions, and when the baby had been fed within the preceding 2 hours (a requirement for day 1 and day 3 examinations). Medical data were collected from the chart and the mother was interviewed on day 3. One of three female translators assisted non-English-speaking mothers. The BNBAS was administered at home on days 7, 14, and 28 in the room of the mother's choice when she felt the baby was "ready," often with other family members present. No environmental restrictions were imposed. All BNBAS examinations were conducted within 24 hr of the appointed time.Following the BNBAS, the aroused infant dressed only in a diaper, was handed to the mother, and a dress-and-settle adaptation of Ainsworth's 9-point sensitivity versus insensitivity to the baby's communications scale (Ainsworth, Bell, & Stayson, 1974) was administered. This extension of the scale was based on Sander's (1962) observation that the central issue in mother-child interaction between birth and 2 months involves the degree to which the mother's behavior is specifically appropriate to the baby's state and given cues. The infant's state of arousal was noted according to criteria used by Brazelton (1973), and the mother's behavioral responses were compared to predetermined criteria for sensitive versus insensitive responses to the six possible states. On a few occasions in each sample the mother handed the baby momentarily to another family member. This person's responses to the baby were included, assuming that the mother's choice of an alternative caretaker was dictated by her sensitivity to the baby's needs.

On day 28, 12 observation items from Caldwell and Bradley's (1978) Home Observation for the Measurement of the Environment (HOME) were scored for their presence or absence. These items were chosen according to their relevance to the neonate, and keeping in mind the avoidance of items requiring verbal report or understanding and those biased with regard to the Hmong culture (e.g., presence of books for preliterate society, ownership of uniquely Western baby equipment).

Of the 210 scheduled visits, 7 Hmong and 6 Caucasian BNBAS examinations were missed (6.2%). No subject missed more than 1 of 5 examinations. American Caucasian female observers were generally welcomed in homes in both groups. Hmong siblings and adults alike nearly always watched the BNBAS quietly, smiling at infant displays of positive abilities. Caucasian mothers often watched the exam, while Caucasian siblings were more interested in test materials than in the test or the baby. Normal household routines such as cooking and conversations occurred freely in the presence of observers.

The examiner for the BNBAS and a reliability observer were both trained to reliability of > .85 by the Boston Children's Hospital training group (Brazelton, 1973). Reliability observations were conducted (10 in the Caucasian group and 9 in the Hmong group) throughout the project, sampling from all times of measurement in each group. A 1-point difference on an item was considered an agreement. Mean reliability, calculated by agreements divided by agreements plus disagreements, was .95 with a range of .89 to 1.0. Mean reliability for the 9-point sensitivity scale in the dress-and-settle situation was .90.

Attempts were made to eliminate cultural biases in research materials and tasks through extended discussions with Hmong interpreters and mothers and through pilot interviews and observations, but undoubtedly some remained. For example, the Hmong had no word for *rattle*, and found it odd during the BNBAS that we would make such noise or that we would want to arouse a sleeping baby.

Results

BNBAS. The 25 BNBAS items (excluding the aversive pinprick stimulus, which was not administered) were recoded as described by Lester, Als, and Brazelton (1982) into seven cluster scores for each of the five times of measurement. The Reflexes cluster and the Habituation cluster were not analyzed because of the normalcy of reflex items and to the high frequency of babies who were awake or who awoke quickly at home and could not be scored on habituation-related items. The remaining five behavior clusters were Orientation, Motor Performance, Range of State, Regulation of State, and Autonomic Regulation. A sixth cluster, Irritability, was added as suggested by Kaye (1978) and Crockenberg and Smith (1982). Two-tailed *t*-tests were carried out on parametric data, with paired *t*-tests for matched data, and the chi-square test with Yates correction was used for nonparametric data.

As can be seen from Table 1, Hmong infants, compared to Caucasians, scored substantially more favorably on orientation to visual and auditory stimulus on days 1, 7, 14, and 28. Hmong infants performed less favorably than Caucasians on the Motor Performance cluster on days 1 and 3, and again on day 28, largely reflecting the single item concerning head lag rather than a generalized motor immaturity. Range of State and Autonomic Regulation clusters differed substan-

Table 1.   Behavioral Performance of Hmong ($N = 21$) and Caucasian ($N = 21$) Infants for Brazelton Scale Clusters[a]

Cluster		Day 1 H	Day 1 C	Day 3 H	Day 3 C	Day 7 H	Day 7 C	Day 14 H	Day 14 C	Day 28 H	Day 28 C
Orientation	M	4.1	2.5	4.1	3.1	4.5	3.1	5.8	3.7	6.9	4.6
	SD	1.47	1.14	1.66	1.46	1.83	1.8	1.39	1.8	1.02	1.79
	N	15	18	15	15	18	19	20	18	17	20
	t[b]	3.6172***		1.9842		2.3134*		4.1212***		4.6105***	
Motor Perfor-	M	3.6	4.5	3.6	4.2	3.5	4.0	4.2	4.3	4.3	5.2
mance	SD	.98	.57	.54	.99	.96	.58	.59	.90	1.03	.89
	N	19	20	20	19	20	20	20	19	19	21
	t	3.4224***		2.5443*		1.8933		.6851		2.9958**	
Range of	M	3.9	3.4	3.9	3.4	3.0	3.1	3.0	3.4	2.2	2.9
State	SD	1.03	.85	1.15	1.03	1.34	1.03	1.14	.92	.97	1.04
	N	19	20	20	19	20	20	20	19	19	21
	t	1.5686		1.3779		.1721		1.2768		2.4625*	
Regulation of	M	4.1	3.5	3.5	3.3	3.6	3.9	4.0	3.6	3.8	3.2
State	SD	1.37	1.50	1.40	1.38	1.67	1.71	1.35	1.45	1.23	1.14
	N	19	20	20	19	20	20	21	19	19	21
	t	1.1899		.5657		.4030		.7930		1.5424	
Autonomic	M	6.5	6.5	6.7	6.2	7.1	7.2	7.5	7.3	8.0	7.7
Regulation	SD	.78	.69	.86	1.17	1.01	.75	.75	.90	.17	.51
	N	19	20	20	19	19	20	20	19	19	21
	t	.2208		1.6704		.4242		.9467		2.1165*	
Irritability[c]	M	4.2	5.3	3.7	4.3	2.5	4.1	2.6	4.3	2.1	3.4
	SD	1.52	1.97	1.11	2.10	1.09	2.08	.73	1.84	.53	1.80
	N	19	20	20	19	20	20	20	19	19	21
	t	2.0463*		1.1383		3.1014**		3.9853**		2.8143**	

Note. H = Hmong, C = Caucasian.
[a]Lester, Als, & Brazelton (1982).   [b]Two-tailed t tests.   [c]Kaye (1978); Crockenberg & Smith (1982).
*$p < .05$.   **$p < .01$.   ***$p < .002$.

tially only on day 28, with Hmong babies scoring less optimally on the first cluster and more optimally on the second. (Clustering of items for the Range of State cluster may have masked individual differences in which Hmong babies tended to show low peaks of excitement and few state changes, and Caucasian babies tended to show high peaks of excitement and many state changes, both receiving the same nonoptimal score.) No group differences were found in Regulation of State. Finally, Hmong babies' scores on the Irritability cluster showed them to be less irritable than Caucasian babies on all days except day 3. No sex differences were found on any cluster.

Maternal sensitivity. Scores on the 9-point maternal sensitivity scale administered at each of the three home visits were averaged across time. Mean sensitivity scores were significantly higher in the Hmong group ($M = 8.64$) than in the Caucasian group (M = 5.44), $t(40)$ = 4.4880, p < .01. Hmong maternal sensitivity scores clustered at the high end of the scale, indicating very little variability in the population, compared with Caucasian mothers. To test the relation between maternal sensitivity and cluster scores, an analysis was conducted comparing the babies of high- and low-sensitivity mothers within cultural groups. A judgment was made that the most meaningful split of the sensitivity scale in terms of impact of maternal responsiveness on the infant might occur between scores of 7 (sensitive) and 5 (inconsistently sensitive). Mothers with mean sensitivity scores of 7 or higher formed a high-sensitivity group (N = 12), and the remainder formed a low-sensitivity group (N = 9). Since all Hmong mothers scored in the high-sensitivity-group range, no further analyses were made of this group.

Within the Caucasian group, high versus low sensitivity related to correspondingly high versus low infant orientation abilities on all three home administrations (see Table 2), a pattern similar to that observed between the two cultural groups overall. While all groups improved as expected in their ability to orient to stimuli between days 1 and 28, only the group of infants of low-sensitivity Caucasian mothers declined in group performance between hospital day 3 and initial home exam on day 7 (paired $t(6)$ = 2.9431, p < .05).

Within the Caucasian group, maternal sensitivity also distinguished between more and less irritable babies on days 14 and 28. Infants of high-sensitivity mothers showed less irritability than did those of low-sensitivity mothers (see Table 2).

HOME. Total scores for the 12-item subset of the HOME scored on day 28

Table 2. **Orientation and Irritability Cluster Scores of Caucasian Infants of High (N = 12) and Low (N = 9) Sensitivity Mothers[a,b]**

		Day 1		Day 3		Day 7		Day 14		Day 28	
		High	Low	High	Low	High	Low	High	Low	High	Low
Orientation	M	2.77	1.97	2.85	2.75	4.02	1.91	4.42	2.76	5.49	3.58
	SD	1.12	1.07	1.23	1.14	1.84	1.22	1.48	1.83	1.82	1.08
	N	11	7	8	6	10	8	10	8	11	9
	t[b]	1.5037		.1554		2.7869*		2.1321*		2.7712*	
		High	Low	High	Low	High	Low	High	Low	High	Low
Irritability	M	5.19	5.54	4.12	4.59	3.61	4.78	3.21	5.84	2.64	4.30
	SD	1.84	2.26	2.14	2.17	1.93	2.18	1.50	.96	1.05	2.20
	N	12	8	11	8	11	9	11	8	12	9
	t	.3772		.4658		1.2740		4.3230**		2.2975*	

[a]High sensitivity = $M \geq 7$, low sensitivity = $M < 7$ on the administration of the maternal sensitivity scale.
[b]Two-tailed t tests.
*p < .05.   **p < .01.

showed differences between cultural groups, the Hmong scoring more optimally, $t(39) = 2.8112$, $p < .01$). The two items that differentiated groups most clearly indicated that Hmong mothers were more likely than Caucasian mothers to caress the baby at least once during the visit, $\chi^2(1) = 5.6335$, $p < .05$), and that Hmong mothers tended more than Caucasian mothers to keep the baby within visual range and to look at the baby often ($\chi^2(1) = 11.6129$, $p < .01$).

Maternal interview. Interviews on day 3 were composed of simple demographic questions and four brief open-ended questions. When asked, "Whom do you expect to help you at home?" mothers in both groups listed a variety of relatives and other people. Differences between groups were suggested, however, in mothers' reports of perceptions of problems and preferred coping styles. Among Caucasian mothers, the most difficult problems were judged to be finances (28.6%), family problems (19%), and child-care problems (28.6%). None of these were reported by Hmong mothers, with the exception of child care, which was listed by 2 women as a logistical problem.

Hmong women cited the language barrier (57.1%) as the single most difficult problem they had to face. When asked, "What do you do when things are hard and you feel sad? What helps?" twice as many Hmong (57.1%) as Caucasians (28.6%) reported seeking out another person. For example, 61.9% of the Caucasian women preferred individual or isolated strategies, such as "get my hair done" or "get away by myself" as compared to 14.3% of the Hmong mothers. When Hmong mothers were asked, "What special plans do you have?" their most frequent reply was "go to school" (33%), while the most frequent reply for Caucasians (33%) was "move."

Summary of Results

The most dramatic differences between Hmong and Caucasian infants in this study were the superior scores of the Hmong children on two clusters: Orientation and Irritability. Although the two groups differed on day 28 in Range of State and Autonomic Regulation, differences on these clusters were not present at earlier points in the testing. While the Motor Performance scores of Hmong infants were lower than those of Caucasian infants on days 1, 3, and 28, these differences can be accounted for largely by one measure, head lag, which differentiated strikingly between the groups.

Hmong mothers were, overall, scoring virtually at ceiling on the Ainsworth Maternal Sensitivity Scale. As might be expected, for Caucasian mothers, low maternal sensitivity predicted their infants' low scores for Orientation and suboptimal scores on Irritability. HOME scores indicated that Hmong mothers were more attentive to their babies. While maternal interviews indicated that Caucasian mothers felt more stressed by financial crisis, family problems, and child care demands, they were were less likely than Hmong mothers to turn to others for help.

Discussion

The differences found in this study between the Hmong and Caucasian populations in infant behavior and maternal sensitivity are difficult to disentangle because the behavioral parts covary within their respective cultural wholes. However, patterns of data suggest that something more than genetic differences contributes to optimal infant behavior, and something more than the simple effect of infant behavior on the caregiver engenders maternal sensitivity. Medical data, physiological factors, and cultural context futher complicate the picture. These issues will be discussed below within the context of our data.

Medical/physiological sources of influence. A number of factors relating to health and physiologic status were potential sources of impact on infants and mothers in this study. As nearly as can be determined, the two populations were free of obstetrical and neonatal complications.

Some Caucasian mothers (8) did receive various medications during labor, but no differences could be detected between the behavior of their infants and those of non-medicated Caucasians. However, several other factors may have contributed to differences. For example, no Hmong mothers smoked prenatally while several Caucasian mothers did. Hmong women had lower systolic blood pressures than Caucasian women both prenatally ($t(39) = 4.8610$, $\rho < .01$) and at its peak during labor ($t(32) = 2.7341$, $\rho < .05$). Low ponderal indices (less than 2.3%) were detected in 5 Caucasian and 1 Hmong newborn despite meeting strict pediatric criteria for birth weight, gestation, and good health. The ponderal index is a ratio of body weight (in grams) to the cube of the length (in centimeters), expressed as a percentage, and indicating fetal nourishment. The presence of these babies in the Caucasian group represents more than twice the incidence expected among full-term births in the U.S. (Miller & Hassanein, 1971, 1973). Als, Tronick, Adamson, and Brazelton (1976) found that the most pronounced difference between full-term babies with low ponderal indices and those with normal ponderal indices was the remarkably poor interactive behavior (a composite which included all BNBAS orientation items) of the underweight infants in the first days of life. The presence of the 5 babies with low ponderal indices in this Caucasian sample of 21 may be considered a cautionary signal that this particular socially and economically disadvantaged sample tends toward some risk factor which contributed to the infants' relatively low hospital scores on the Orientation cluster. Congenital but nongenetic factors such as these deserve further investigation.

Maternal Sensitivity: Direction of Effects

It is reasonable to hypothesize that sensitive mothering leads to optimal, or near optimal, infant performance. It is, however, just as possible that optimally performing infants inspire their mothers to display more sensitive mothering. Does the evidence support a baby-to-mother direction of effects? Although evidence is sparse, generally it does not. As noted earlier, infants of highly sensitive mothers in both cultural groups showed superior orientation abilities and reduced irritability. Most interesting to us in regard to possible early influences on baby behavior is that group differences in maternal sensitivity may have been operating even in the first few hospital days (prior to assessment) when all mothers had rooming-in. The maternity staff noted informally a high priority among Hmong mothers for keeping their babies close, warm and dry, frequently fed, and consoled. Weight loss data support these observations. There were no exclusively breast-fed infants in the Hmong sample, so breast-fed Caucasian babies could not be compared across cultures. However, among bottle-fed infants, Hmong babies had lost a 42% smaller proportion of their birthweight than had Caucasian babies by the second day of life ($t(23) = 2.3877$, $\rho < .05$).

It is conceivable, of course, that the Hmong practice of frequent, almost continuous feeding may have accounted for infant behavioral differences. It is interesting to note, however, that differences in weight loss for infants of high- versus low-sensitivity Caucasian mothers were in the same direction as the group effects, though they did not reach statistical significance. High-sensitivity Caucasian mothers may have been helping their babies maintain body weight through demand feeding and other mothering behaviors.It is quite possible that ponderal indices and maternal sensitivity interact as well. In the subset of the 6 infants with low ponderal indices, 2 had low-sensitivity mothers and 4 had high-sensitivity mothers. All but 1 baby scored lower than the mean for his or her respective cultural group on the Orientation cluster of the BNBAS on day 1. However, all 4 babies born to high-sensitivity mothers had Orientation scores higher than the group mean by day 28. A baby of a low-sensitivity mother remained low in the group over time, and 1 baby of a low-sensitivity mother who showed high orientation ability on days 1 and 3 dropped below the group mean on the final three measurements. In the 6 cases cited, maternal sensitivity appeared to be an overriding factor by the end of the first month.

In the case of the Caucasian mothers in this sample, it seems unlikely that low-sensitivity mothers as opposed to high-sensitivity mothers were simply responding to suboptimal infant abilities, since inspection of the Orientation means shows that babies of low-sensitivity mothers actually had begun to improve in the hospital in abilities related to human interaction, but then declined initially at home. Additionally, within the Caucasian sample (see Table 2), irritability differences between babies of high- versus low-sensitivity mothers which were pronounced on days 14 and 28 were indistinguishable during the hospital period.

One might reasonably expect maternal age and previous experience in child rearing to affect sensitivity in mothering. While the Hmong mothers were on the average slightly older and more often multiparous than the Caucasians, these factors did not explain sensitivity differences within the Caucasian group. In fact, young Caucasian primiparae showed a slight, nonsignificant tendency toward greater sensitivity. Also, breast- and bottle-feeding and sex of the infant were divided between high- and low-sensitivity Caucasian mothers exactly in proportion to their distribution in the overall Caucasian group, and hence did not appear to influence sensitivity in caregiving.

While a number of Caucasian mothers attained the same very high sensitivity ratings as the Hmong, observers noted interesting differences in style between Caucasian and Hmong mothers. A Caucasian mother might at times tap the baby's cheek to elicit a smile, while the Hmong mothers were never seen doing this. Caucasian mothers displayed affection with kisses and stroking, while Hmong mothers tended to nuzzle their babies. High-sensitivity Caucasian mothers actively sought vocal face-to-face interaction, alternately stimulating and soothing their babies precisely in tune with the infant's state of arousal. In contrast, high-sensitivity Hmong mothers tended to greet their babies with vocalization and a smile, then wait attentively for subtle changes in the infants' expression or vocalizations, which the mothers almost invariably imitated.

Cultural Context

Researchers have generally attempted to provide identical research settings or insure their comparability when measuring behavior across cultures. Similarly, in the U.S., developmental studies often hold parental education, geographic or ethnic factors, and socioeconomic status constant in order to focus on other variables of interest. The implicit assumption is that educational level and economic circumstances are markers for a host of other factors. These nuisance variables presumably affect behavior in systematic ways. In the present study, cultural differences are complicated by the immigrant status of the Hmong families. The Hmong mothers lived in poverty and, coming from a preliterate society, could not read or write in any language. Their only education to date was an American English course. Yet in all likelihood they are among the most competent and adaptive of their population, given the extraordinary obstacles they have overcome in order to survive and maintain their families. Even simple differences in family solidarity, indicated by household composition, set them apart from their American Caucasian counterparts.

In contrast to the approach holding context constant, deVries and Super (1978) and Zaslow and Rogoff (1981) suggest acknowledging and describing ways in which contexts vary, and evaluating their influence on behavior. Additionally, Whiting (1980) notes the influence of settings assigned by the parent on the child. In the latter part of the present study, when babies were measured at home, the setting in which infant behavior was measured varied by culture-specific circumstances and by the active choice of mothers. On home visits, observers had the impression that, while Hmong households contained more people, Caucasian households often seemed more chaotic and distracting. In 16 Caucasian and 10 Hmong homes we visited, television sets were playing at customary volume in the rooms where the babies were when we entered. Mothers varied widely in their alteration and management of this and other aspects of the setting. The data, while far from conclusive, are at least consistent with the hypothesis that infant behavior varies in part as a function of culturally dictated settings and, within a culture, as a function of settings chosen or altered in accord with the mother's sensitivity to her infant's state and needs.

Cultural factors may have borne directly on neonatal behavior in several ways besides feeding practices during the early hospital period. Health practitioners note that the Hmong women's "culture and life experiences have prepared them [to labor and give birth] in a vastly superior way to the typical American woman" (Nelson & Hewitt, 1983, p. 12). It is conceivable that qualitative differences during birth may have contributed to the observed differences in early neonatal behavior. Finally, as indicated previously, a low ponderal index has been shown to affect neonatal behavior in other research (Als et al., 1976). The fact that 24% of the babies in the present Caucasian sample were discovered to have low ratios of weight to length may indicate borderline nutritional status for the mothers in this group, a common predicament for urban mothers in poverty (Ehlinger, 1983).

Maternal sensitivity and caregiving practices demonstrated in this study are almost certain to have been profoundly influenced by cultural prescriptions and constraints. Motherhood is clearly the role of the Hmong woman in her patrilineal household and society, and she is highly valued for performing well. Sibling caretaking under the watchful eye of mothers and grandmothers is common, with implications for the competence of young girls when they themselves become mothers. LeVine (1977) offers a provocative hypothesis regarding the high level of responsiveness to infants in cultures with high infant mortality rates and severely limited resources for responding to disease. In his analysis, customary caretaking behavior is organized around the goal of survival, although parents may not be fully aware of the adaptive value of the pattern as it has evolved. The infant is kept on or near a caretaker's body day and night, which prevents accidental injuries such as cooking-fire burns or being trampled by livestock, and allows constant monitoring. Crying is attended to quickly. Feeding is frequent and on demand, which increases the signal value of crying for reasons of illness, and prevents dehydration secondary to diarrhea.

Members of the extended family (81% of the Hmong mother-infant pairs lived in this situation), in this sample, provided not only emotional comfort but also direct, culturally distinct information and feedback, as well as assistance related to infant caretaking. Family members not only supported the mother's ministrations but actively soothed, fed, and otherwise cared for babies in the same sensitive fashion as the mothers. Maternal responsiveness to newborn infants' cues among the Hmong showed strong resilience despite stress which seemed at least equal to that of their American counterparts.

From an economic perspective the entire traditional Hmong household in

Laos is invested in its newest member. Children contribute significantly to the family work force. Later, through marriage, they provide the primary linkages to other households and clans, enlarging possibilities for cooperative ventures and material reciprocity. When children reach maturity, they support their elderly parents.

In contrast, many cultural factors appear to work against optimal infant behavior and maternal sensitivity for members of the American Caucasian sample in this study. Societal expectations for modern American women generally preclude feeding babies at the high frequency rate typical for the Hmong. In fact, many Hmong women in the U.S. have switched from breast-feeding, which can be done only by the mother, to bottle feeding, which can be done by baby-sitters, reportedly in response in part to an American institution new to the Hmong women—school (Mullett & Seubert, 1982). They cannot conceive of making their babies wait for a feeding for 4 hours (the typical American feeding interval) or until class ends.

Unlike the Hmong infant, the baby born to an American household is undeniably an economic drain with no expected material returns for the mother or the household. Compared to the Hmong mother, the inner-city American mother has very little support, feedback, or assistance in child rearing. Devices such as infant seats, cribs, playpens, and infant swings, commonly used by mothers in this sample, physically separate the mother from her baby and render many of the baby's subtle cues unavailable to her. An unduly heavy burden is placed on the infant to elicit caretaking, and on the mother to provide it. Finally, it is possible that the generally lower and more variable maternal sensitivity of mothers in the American Caucasian sample is an outcome of the processes, largely unstudied, which increase susceptibility of urban families to depression, emotional disturbance, marital discord, and family breakdown (Rutter, 1981).

As Cole's group has noted, perhaps the clearest lesson of cross-cultural research is that variables of interest to developmental psychologists are rarely, if ever, independent (Laboratory of Comparative Human Cognition, 1979). The interwoven nature of culture, caregiving, and infant behavior demonstrated by studies such as this one should alert researchers and policy makers to the potential domino effects, both wanted and unwanted, of change in any single realm. In particular, the interactive and covarying factors in the environmental context of infant behavior demand systematic investigation.

References

Ainsworth, M. D. S., Bell, S. M., & Stayton, D. J. (1974). Infant-mother attachment and social development: 'Socialization' as a product of reciprocal responsiveness to signals. In M. P. M. Richards (Ed.), *The integration of a child into a social world.* Cambridge, England: Cambridge University Press.

Als, H., Tronick, E., Adamson, L., & Brazelton, T. B. (1976). The behavior of the full-term but underweight newborn infant. *Developmental Medicine and Child Neurology*, *13*, 590–602.

Barney, G. L. (1967). The Meo of Xieng Khouang Province, Laos. In P. Kunstadter (Ed.), *Southeast Asian tribes, minorities, and nations*. Princeton, NJ: Princeton University Press.

Bliatout, B. T. (1982). *Hmong sudden unexpected nocturnal death sydrome: A cultural study*. Portland, OR: Sparkle.

Brazelton, T. B. (1973). *Neonatal behavioral assessment scale*. London: Spastics International Medical Publications/Heinemann Medical Books.

Caldwell, B. M., & Bradley, R. H. (1978). *Home observation for measurement of the environment*. Little Rock: University of Arkansas Press.

Center for Applied Linguistics (1979). *Glimpses of Hmong history and culture* (Indochinese Refugee Education Guides, General Information Series No. 16). Arlington, VA: National Indochinese Clearinghouse, Center for Applied Linguistics.

Crockenberg, S. B., & Smith, P. (1982). Antecedents of mother-infant interaction and infant irritability in the first three months of life. *Infant Behavior and Development*, *5*, 105–119.

deVries, M., & Super, C. M. (1978). Contextual influences on the neonatal behavioral assessment scale and implications for its cross-cultural use. In A. J. Sameroff (Ed.), Organization and stability of newborn behavior: A commentary on the Brazelton Neonatal Behavioral Assessment Scale. *Monographs of the Society for Research in Child Development*, *43* (5–6, Serial No. 177), 92–101.

Dunnigan, T. (1982). Segmentary kinship in an urban society: The Hmong of St. Paul-Minneapolis. *Anthropological Quarterly*, *55*(3), 126–134.

Ehlinger, E. (1983). Unpublished data from the Bureau of Maternal and Child Health, Minneapolis Health Department, Minneapolis, MN.

Freedman, D. G., & Freedman, N. C. (1969). Behavioral differences between Chinese-American and European-American newborns. *Nature*, *224*, 1227.

Kaye, K. (1978). Discriminating among normal infants by multivariate analyses of Brazelton scores: Lumping and smoothing. In A. J. Sameroff (Ed.), Organization and stability of newborn behavior: A commentary on the Brazelton Neonatal Behavioral Assessment Scale. *Monographs of the Society for Research in Child Development*, *43* (5–6, Serial No. 177), 60–80).

Keefer, C. H., Tronick, E., Dixon, S., & Brazelton, T. B. (1982). Specific differences in motor performance between Gusii and American newborns and a modification of the Neonatal Behavioral Assessment Scale. *Child Development*, *53*, 754–759.

Laboratory of Comparative Human Cognition (1979). Cross-cultural psychology's challenges to our ideas of children and development. *American Psycholgist*, *34*, 827–833.

Lee, G. Y. (1981). The effects of development measures on the socio-economy of the White Hmong. Unpublished doctoral dissertation, University of Sydney, Australia.

Lester, B. M., Als, H., & Brazelton, T. B. (1982). Regional obstetric anesthesia and newborn behavior: A re-analysis toward synergistic effects. *Child Development*, *53*, 687–692.

LeVine, R. A. (1977). Child rearing as cultural adaptation. In P. H. Leiderman, S. R. Tulkin, & A. Rosenfeld (Eds.), *Culture and infancy: Variations in the human experience* (pp. 15–280). New York: Academic Press.

Miller, H. C., & Hassanein, K. (1971). Diagnosis of impaired fetal growth in newborn infants. *Pediatrics*, *48*, 511–522.

Miller, H. C., & Hassanein, K. (1973). Fetal malnutrition in white newborn infants: Maternal factors. *Pediatrics*, *52*, 504–512.

Morin, S. P. (1983, February 16). Many Hmong, puzzled by life in U.S., yearn for old days in Laos. *The Wall Street Journal*, pp. 1,18.

Mullett, S. E., & Seubert, S. (1982). A primary nursing project with Southeast Asian maternity clients. In C. N. Uhl & J. Uhl (Eds.), *Proceedings of the Seventh Annual Transcultural Nursing Conference*. Salt Lake City: University of Utah Press, Transcultural Nursing Society.

Nelson, C. C., & Hewitt, M. A. (1983). An Indochinese refugee population in a nurse-midwife service. *The Journal of Nurse-Midwifery*, *28* (5), 9–14.

Olney, D. (1983). The Hmong and their neighbors. *CURA Reporter*, *8*(1), 8–14. Minneapolis: University of Minnesota, Center for Urban and Regional Affairs.

Potter, G. S., & Whiren, A. (1982). Traditional Hmong birth customs: A historical study. In B. T. Downing & D. P. Olney (Eds.), *The Hmong in the West*. Minneapolis: University of Minnesota, Center for Urban and Regional Affairs.

Rutter, M. (1981). The city and the child. *American Journal of Orthopsychiatry*, *52*, 610–625.

Sander, L. W. (1962). Issues in early mother-child interaction. *Journal of the America Academy of Child Psychiatry*, *1*, 141–166.

Scudder, T., & Colson, E. (1982). From welfare to development: A conceptual framework for the analysis of dislocated people. In A. Hansen & A. Oliver-Smith (Eds.), *Involuntary migration and resettlement*. Boulder, CO: Westview.

Super, C. (1976). Environmental effects on motor development: The case of "African infant precocity." *Developmental Medicine and Child Neurology*, *18*, 561–567.

U.S. Department of the Army (1970). *Minority Groups in Thailand* (Department of the Army PAM No. 550-107). Washington, DC: U.S. Government Printing Office.

U.S. Department of Health and Human Services (1982). *Report to the Congress: Refugee Resettlement Program*. Washington, DC: U.S. Government Printing Office.

Vang, K. N. (1982). Hmong marriage customs: A current assessment. In B. T. Downing & D. P. Olney (Eds.), *The Hmong in the West*. Minneapolis: University of Minnesota, Center for Urban and Regional Affairs.

Westermeyer, J. (1983). Hmong refugees in Minnesota: Characteristics and self perceptions. *Minnesota Medicine*, *66*, 431–439.

White, V. (n.d.). *pa ndau: The needlework of the Hmong*. (Unpublished manuscript.) (Available from Virginia White, 23 Sixth Street, Cheney, WA 99004.)

Whiting, B. (1980). Culture and social behavior: A model for the development of social behavior. *Ethos*, *8*, 95–116.

Yang, D. (1982). Why did the Hmong leave Laos? In B. T. Downing & D. P. Olney (Eds.), *The Hmong in the West*. Minneapolis: University of Minnesota, Center for Urban and Regional Affairs.

Zaslow, M., & Rogoff, B. (1981). The cross-cultural study of early interaction: Implications from research on culture and cognition. In T. M. Field, A. M. Sostek, P. Vietze, & P. H. Leiderman (Eds.), *Culture and early interactions*. Hillsdale, NJ: Erlbaum.

CHAPTER 13

Biology, Culture, and the Development of Temperament: A Navajo Example*

James S. Chisholm

Department of Anthropology
University of New Mexico
Albuquerque, New Mexico

It has long been apparent to infancy researchers that no one discipline has a unique command of the methods and concepts needed to construct comprehensive models of early development. In recent years it also has become apparent that the construction of such models would benefit from the contribution of anthropology, a discipline most practiced in describing and measuring cultural differences and their influence on development.

But to speak of "the" anthropological contribution is to credit the discipline with a kind of unity it may only now be developing. Historically, the greatest disunity in anthropology has been along the lines of the familiar nature–culture problem. New developments in both anthropology and evolutionary biology, however, are suggesting ways around this counterproductive dichotomy.

A good case in point is in the study of behavioral styles of Navajo infants, children, and adults, whom developmental psychologists, anthropologists, and psychiatrists uniformly have characterized as quiet, shy, and withdrawn. These behavioral styles have been atttributed commonly to such cultural influences as use of the cradleboard, but more recently they also have been attributed to genetic factors in the form of an "Oriental temperament" among the Navajo. My purpose in this chapter is to outline recent advances in an evolutionary biological

* The research on which this chapter is based was supported by a grant from the Harry Frank Guggenheim Foundation to Nick Blurton Jones of the Institute of Child Health, University of London, and by a grant from the National Science Foundation. My thanks to Nick and to these organizations for their support and encouragement, and to V. K. Burbank for comments on an earlier draft.

approach to development and culture and thereby to suggest why certain cultural influences—but not the cradleboard—are more likely to influence the development of these behavioral styles.

An Evolutionary Approach to Development and Culture

Among many evolutionary biologists and biologically minded developmental psychologists there is the growing conviction that developmental plasticity may be especially characteristic of humans and may be biologically adaptive in the phylogenetic sense. Developmental plasticity is defined as the genotypical capacity to develop the optimum phenotype in a wide variety of developmental environments. This growing conviction has a number of roots. One is the increasing evidence in developmental psychology that early experience is likely to affect later behavior only under the most stable environmental circumstances (e.g., Bateson, 1976, 1982; Chisholm, 1983; Dunn, 1976; Kagan, 1980, 1981; Kagan, Kearsley, & Zelazo, 1980; Sameroff, 1975; Sameroff & Chandler, 1975).

Another source of this growing conviction about natural selection for developmental plasticity has been the recent interest among evolutionary biologists in the evolution of ontogenetic patterns. This interest has stemmed from research in comparative zoology and behavioral ecology that shows broad similarities in the ontogeny of species, according to two different modes of natural selection: r- and K-selection (MacArthur & Wilson, 1967; Pianka, 1970; Wilson, 1975). The concepts of r- and K-selection, along with the related evolutionary concept of life-history tactics (Gadgill & Bossert, 1970; Horn, 1978; Stearns, 1976), and a dissatisfaction with evolutionary explanations of behavior formulated only in terms of the genotype, have led to exciting new approaches in the study of the evolutionary significance of ontogenetic patterns (e.g., Bateson, 1982; Gould, 1977, 1982; Plotkin & Odling-Smee, 1979, 1981).

These are the concepts that seem destined to be most useful in sorting out those aspects of the social-cultural environment that make a difference in development. Before exploring these concepts, however, it will be useful to describe first a concept of adaptation that provides the most basic evolutionary biological rationale for expecting natural selection for developmental plasticity.

Slobodkin and Rapoport (1974) suggest that the genotypical basis for an ontogenetic capacity to develop the optimum phenotype in a variety of developmental environments is the result of natural selection for increasingly numerous, complex, sophisticated, and finely tuned "environmental tracking mechanisms." Environmental tracking is the process whereby natural selection produces the virtually universal "good fit" between organism and environment. Slobodkin and Rapoport argue that in the long run there will tend to be natural selection for better environmental tracking because organisms with more and more sophisticated environmental tracking mechanisms will have more ways of responding to the environment and thus will be more "adaptable."

Behavior itself is a good example of an environmental tracking device. Behavioral responses to the environment have been selected for because they provide a high degree of response flexibility that protects or conserves the slower and more costly potential response capacity latent in the gene pool. Slobodkin and Rapoport suggest that increasingly sophisticated environmental tracking mechanisms are selected for because such sophistication or complexity provides what they term "an optimal strategy of evolution" (Slobodkin & Rapoport, 1974). The essence of this strategy is that responses to the environment are more or less appropriately scaled to the impact and scope of the environmental perturbation; the quickest and least costly responses are made first, and if the perturbation to which they are the response is short, of little impact, or unique, and if the responses are successful in alleviating the stresses associated with the perturbation, then the organism's capacity to respond successfully or adaptively to future perturbations is not compromised.

If the initial response is not successful, because the perturbation is more severe and/or longer-lasting, then these quick and low-cost responses may be called into play more frequently and may trigger deeper, slower, and potentially more costly response mechanisms. In the long run, plasticity, flexibility, and adaptability in behavioral responses will tend to be favored by natural selection because they tend to protect or conserve the latent adaptability of the slower, deeper, and most costly physiological, demographic, and population genetic adaptive mechanisms. These latter reactions are ultimately the least flexible ways of responding to the environment, because they depend for their adaptive potential on mutation or recombination producing just the right set of new alleles for selection to act on.

This evolutionary trend toward greater response flexibility enables organisms to track short-term environmental changes phenotypically while reserving genotypical response capacity for responding to long-term environmental changes. There thus will tend to be natural selection for what Waddington (1968) called an "essential indeterminancy" in the ontogenetic effect of the genotype on the phenotype—because the genotype will be altered only when the phenotypical responses (perhaps especially the behavioral ones) at each higher level in the response hierarchy have been shown to be at least minimally effective. This short-term or immediate plasticity not only gives natural selection more time to weed out the truly unfit (as opposed to the simply unlucky), but also focuses selection pressure on those parts of the phenotype that bear a more direct relation to information carried in the DNA.

It is worth pointing out that culture itself has long been considered the human environmental tracking device par excellence (i.e., the relative success of human responses to environmental perturbations depends more—or at least more immediately—on information stored in the minds of members of a culture than on information stored in the DNA). Indeed, one important conceptualization of culture is that of an information storage device (Goodenough, 1981). This metaphor allows us to conceive better how the behavioral plasticity that makes many kinds of learning possible also makes culture itself and the learning of culture possible; the genotypical capacity to develop the optimum phenotype in a variety of natural and social-cultural environments has been especially favored during hominid evolution because it resulted in a most sophisticated environmental tracking mechanism: culture (cf. Durham, 1979).

Closely related to this abstract conceptualization of natural selection for behavioral plasticity are the more concrete concepts of life-history tactics and the ontogenetic patterns associated with r- and K-selection. The major impetus for the relatively new wing of evolutionary biology concerned with life-history tactics has been the realization that while most evolutionary models are based on how many copies of one's genes are passed into the next generation, little account has been taken of the fact that the organism first had to survive, and then grow and learn, before it could successfully reproduce (see, e.g., Gadgill & Bossert, 1970). Thus, natural selection could not be expected to maximize reproductive potential at the expense of simple survival and ontogenetic preparation for reproduction. Therefore, in any given environment, there should be measurable trade-offs between adaptations for survival, growth and development and learning, and reproductive rate.

The concepts of r- and K-selection describe what some of these trade-offs are and how they are likely to have been selected. In r- and K-selection are represented opposite ends of a continuum of natural selection. In unpredictable environments, or environments where some predictable major perturbation has a periodicity greater than the life span of the individuals, there are often catastrophic mortality rates in which large numbers of individuals die not so much because they are unfit, but because they are unlucky. Mortality is not directed; the difference between survival and mortality does not depend on within-population differences in genotypes or phenotypes.

When selection is thus so undirected it is also unfocused, and cannot work to produce a more efficient phenotype. Instead, it can only work to produce a reproductive strategy based on transmitting as many copies of parental genes as possible into the next generation as quickly as possible. The evolutionary payoff here is obvious: Individuals able to reproduce more rapidly and/or in greater numbers are disproportionately represented in future generations by virtue of their head start in filling available niche space. This is the essence of the r-strategy. The essence of the K-strategy, however, is to ensure that at least some copies of parental genes make it into the next generation, even if the total number is not high. This is an adaptation to the high levels of intraspecific competition that characterize populations at carrying capacity in more constant or predictable environments. Because there is no evolutionary payoff in having large numbers of offspring (for this would increase the already high rates of intraspecific competition and endanger the survival of any offspring at all), the selection pressures in K-type environments are for increased efficiency in the exploitation of scarce resources.

A valid quick conceptualization of K-selection is natural selection for "fewer and better offspring." "Better" is usually interpreted as increased efficiency in the exploitation of resources, but another interpretation is that at least a major aspect of "better" includes more sophisticated, complex, and finely tuned environmental tracking mechanisms. This is because with a more constant and predictable environment, high intraspecific competition, and more directed mortality, natural selection is less random and individuals are likely to be selected against as a result of some function inefficiency in the way they respond to their sociocultural and physical environments.

Selection for more efficient responses to the environment, for more complex and finely tuned environmental tracking mechanisms, seems to be achieved in K-selection primarily through selection for retarded development. This may have been accomplished through the favoring of regulator genes delaying the switching on of structural genes that code for the production of endocrine substances that determine the onset, rate, and period of physical growth and development processes and sexual maturation processes (cf. Gould, 1977, 1982; King & Wilson, 1975). Retarded development would tend to maintain or increase reproductive success because with a long period of infant or juvenile dependency and delayed sexual maturity, individuals become more efficient in exploiting resources and more reproductively competitive by virtue of having more time to learn about their environments (in this case, especially their social-cultural environments) before they themselves reproduce. An increased capacity for learning constitutes not only the most adaptively significant and phenotypically plastic environmental tracking device known, but also the very basis of culture.

Individuals who develop slowly not only have more time to learn about the environments in which they will lay their reproductive potential on the line, but also are likely to be better able to learn. By retarding the rate of somatic development (and/or extending its period), neural structures are given more time to differentiate. Growth is not a unidimensional increase in size, but also includes development, differentiation, and an increase in organizational complexity. Because organisms with retarded somatic development develop for longer periods, morphological, neurological, endocrine, and (ultimately) behavioral organization can proceed farther in descendant forms than they did in ancestral forms. This increase in organizational complexity by itself tends to increase adaptive potential (behavioral-developmental plasticity). The organism is presented to its developmental environment for longer periods of time in succeeding generations in a physiological-neuroendocrine state that is initially more plastic, more sensitive, or more responsive to environmental influences. This may be the epitome of environmental tracking: the evolution of neuroendocrinological epigenetic rules specifying (in the absence of pathology) that, at least within limits, the individual's behavior should come to be determined more immediately or proximally by the individual's environment.

This evolutionary view of culture as an environmental tracking mechanism accounts for the empirical findings in developmental psychology that early experience seems to affect later behavior only when the developmental environment is most stable. Natural selection among the hominids has resulted in ontogenetic patterns in which the developing individual's behavior is progressively more immediately influenced by the content of his or her culture. Thus, major differences in developmental patterns should be attributable to the most enduring, widespread, and constant aspects of the content of an individual's culture.

This general prediction can be refined by adding that significant differences in developmental outcome should be attributable to the most enduring, widespread, and constant aspects of the content of culture which the developing individual cannot substantially affect by his or her own behavior. One reason why early experience may often have no effect on later behavior is that the early experience has the immediate effect of engendering a response in the child that actually prevents the early experience from having any maladaptive long-term consequences.

We already know that infants can affect the behavior of their caretakers (Bell, 1968; Lewis & Rosenblum, 1974), and we have begun to incorporate these effects into our developmental models (e.g., the transactional model of Sameroff, 1975; Sameroff & Chandler, 1975). This kind of influence from the infant on the developmental environment suggests that Waddington's (1975) notion of "canalization" may be more than a simple metaphor. An evolutionary view of development predicts, as Sameroff and Chandler put it, that

> The human organism appears to have been programmed by the course of evolution to produce normal developmental outcomes under all but the most adverse of circumstances. Any understanding of deviances in outcome must be seen in the light of this self-righting and self-organizing tendency which appears to move children toward normality in the face of pressure toward deviation. (Sameroff & Chandler, 1975, p. 71)

While we have only a rudimentary grasp of the mechanisms whereby infants may "move toward normality," the concepts of life-history tactics suggest that these mechanisms will begin to operate when "pressure toward deviation" begins to affect the infant's chances for ultimate reproductive success (i.e., his or her survival, growth and development, and learning).

Even more refinement in our expectations about early cultural influences on development can be introduced by observing that not only should these cultural influences be enduring, widespread, constant, and unaffected by infant or child behavior, they also should constitute an integral part of the means whereby members of a culture adapt to what have been the most enduring, widespread, and constant environmental pressures over a time span longer than the lives of most individual members of the culture. That is, if culture constitutes the paramount human environmental tracking mechanism, and if learning culture is the paramount human developmental task, then developmental outcome should be affected most by those aspects of culture most intimately related to successful environmental adaptations by adult members of the culture.

Reasoning from this evolutionary approach to development and culture, I now will proceed with an example of how it may be used to interpret empirical data on infant development, focusing on the development of individual behavioral styles reported to be common among the Navajo. Before presenting these data, however, it is necessary first to provide an overview of the cultural context of Navajo infancy.

The Navajo

The Navajo (who refer to themselves in Navajo as the *Dine* and in English as members of the Navajo Nation) number about 160,000 people living on the 18 million acres of the Navajo reservation in portions of Arizona, New Mexico, and Utah. The Navajo reservation is a place of great but harsh beauty, where the terrain is difficult, the soil is poor, rainfall is sparse, and where today there is rampant unemployment (in some communities it approaches 75%). The few jobs that are available are typically many miles from home, as are the schools, and many Navajos spend several hours a day on the reservation's inadequate roads. In the rural areas, where most Navajos still live, electricity and running water are rare. In the rural areas, most families still maintain herds of sheep, and the demands of sheep herding dictate daily life now as much as they did 100 years ago.

The Navajo are an Athapaskan-speaking people who are thought to have entered the Southwest perhaps only 600 years ago, after leaving northern Canada. They entered the Southwest with an economy and social organization that had long been based on hunting and gathering. There were no chiefs and no political organization above the level of rather loosely organized bands, but the common language and an extensive clan system cross-cut membership in the scattered bands.

After their entry into the Southwest, the Navajo continued their basic hunter-gatherer adaptation. The Navajo borrowed many aspects of Pueblo culture, including the techniques of agriculture. Because of erratic and sparse rainfall, however, Navajo agriculture was never extensive, and they continued to fill a hunter-gatherer niche, practicing agriculture only intermittently, when seasonal movements and rainfall permitted. With the coming of the Spaniards, who brought horses and sheep, in the mid-1500s, the Navajo soon became accomplished pastoralists. With the reservation's spotty rainfall and inadequate grazing lands, however, flocks were kept small and typically were herded long distances for feed and water. Neither the adoption of agriculture nor pastoralism entailed major reworking of Navajo social organization, as the primary units of Navajo hunter-gatherer social organization did not have to change much and were even "preadapted" for farming and herding in an area of limited and widely scattered resources.

While the Navajo did borrow much from the Pueblo culture, there was also considerable raiding and theft between the two peoples. When the Spanish entered the Southwest the material rewards of raids against enemies increased dramatically. There were, however, retaliatory raids against the Navajo, during which the Spanish took slaves. Allied with the Spanish, and on their own, the Utes and Paiutes also engaged in raids on the Navajo. Finally, with the coming of the Mexicans in 1821, and the Americans in 1848, the enemies of the Navajo continued to grow, and raiding often turned into outright warfare. In 1864 the situation came to a head with Kit Carson's infamous scorched-earth campaign against the Navajo, during which they suffered complete military defeat, and all but a few hundred were imprisoned off their traditional lands for four years. During this imprisonment the Navajo suffered disease, malnutrition, persecution, and most had their first experience with federal Indian policy. Thus, for as many as 600 years the Navajo lived with the threat—or promise—of a raid, or outright war, never very far away.

After their release from prison camp in 1868, when the reservation was established, the Navajo entered a period of struggle, restarting their economy and learning to live under the bureaucratic paternalism of the federal government. In the early reservation years there was isolated fighting between Navajo bands and Anglo settlers at the edges of the reservation.

From the Navajo point of view, if relations with the larger Anglo society surrounding them have since then no longer been warlike, they have been characteristically confusing, often precarious, and marked by insensitivity on the part of the Anglos. The Navajo have had to adjust to the erratic and often contradictory policies of the federal government. They also have had to deal with unscrupulous traders, businessmen, Bureau of Indian Affairs officials, and the uncertainties of an impersonal national economy and welfare programs. And for over 100 years the Navajo have had their children (often forcibly) removed to BIA- and missionary-run schools where they often were punished for speaking Navajo and usually allowed to go home only during the summer. During the 1930s the federal stock-reduction program on the reservation was perceived as disastrous meddling by Washington bureaucrats, and it is still a source of strong feelings today.

More recently, many Navajos are dismayed by what they see as simply more imperialism on the part of coal and oil companies that are digging and drilling, with woefully inadequate recompense, on many parts of the reservation that have sacred significance. Many Navajos today also are dismayed by the apparent insensitivity and bungling of Congress that has resulted in the failure to resolve the decades-old territorial dispute with the neighboring Hopi tribe. Finally, the state of the national economy in the early 1980s has not been kind to the Navajo, and there are severe unemployment problems compounded by reductions in social service programs. And even today, racial prejudice is not unknown.

Except for a handful of small urban centers, the Navajo reservation is characterized by very low population density. In the vast majority of the reservation's rural areas, sheep herding continues as the primary subsistence activity. Poor grazing conditions, the rough terrain, and widely scattered water holes or wells all dictate that people must reside in well-dispersed clusters. The traditional Navajo homesite is the camp. Typically a camp consists of three or four separate hogans or houses in a cluster, and the residents of a camp constitute a matrilineal extended family. There is, however, considerable variation in the type and size of camps across the reservation. While matrilineal extended family camps may be the most common over all, in some locales other types are more common, and in some areas the majority of camps are not extended family camps at all, but isolated nuclear family camps consisting of a single family living in one hogan. The local-area variability in residence patterns has been attributed to ecological and economic causes, according not only to the results of empirical research (e.g., Aberle, 1961; Chisholm, 1981a, 1983; Levy, 1962; Witherspoon, 1970), but also to what Navajo people say themselves (Reynolds, 1979).

The effects of these economic-ecological factors on the environment of Navajo infancy are clearly seen in Navajo infants' opportunities for social interaction. In many isolated nuclear-family camps, children have only their parents and siblings to interact with and are likely to have little or no contact with strangers until they are a few years old. In the larger extended family camps, children typically have not only more playmates, of a wider age range, but also more caretakers and the opportunity for meeting more strangers. Mothers in extended-family camps also have a good deal more help with child care from older children in the camp as well as from other adults.

The Cradleboard

Any description of the environment of Navajo infancy would be incomplete without an account of the cradleboard and its use, especially because of its frequently supposed contribution to Navajo temperamental styles. The cradleboard is still in widespread use in many parts of the reservation. Recent descriptions, compared to early accounts (e.g., Leighton & Kluckhorn, 1948; Mason, 1888), and the recollections of elderly Navajo, suggest there have been only relatively minor changes in the way it has been used.

Infants are placed on the cradleboard within the first week of life and the average age of last use is just over 10 months (with a very wide range of variability). In the first 3 months of life, infants are on the cradleboard 15–18 hr a day (most of which time they are asleep), and each succeeding quarter they spend approximately 3 hr less each day within its confines. The cradleboard is confining. The swaddling effect of the bindings used to hold the child to the board reduces afferent proprioceptive stimulation to the central reticular formation of the brainstem (Lipton, Steinschneider, & Richmond, 1965), with the result that infants on the cradleboard are consistently in lower states than those not confined (Chisholm, 1983; Chisholm & Richards, 1978).

The state-reducing effect of the cradleboard is one of the main reasons for its use. The cradleboard makes child care easier. Observational data and mothers' reports showed that infants slept longer and with fewer startles when on the cradleboard, and that the cradleboard provided a handy means of "caching" the infant nearby while the mother went about her domestic chores; indeed, spot-observation data revealed that infants on the cradleboard were significantly more likely to be within arm's reach than infants not on the board (Chisholm, 1983).

Another function of the cradleboard, at least before the introduction of modern diapers, was to hold in place the shredded bark of the desert cliffrose that was used as an absorbent material between the infant's legs. In many respects, the cradleboard should be thought of as the functional equivalent of diapers. In Navajo, the word for cradleboard, 'awééts'aal, translates literally as "baby [his] diaper." J. W. M. Whiting (1981), in a cross-cultural survey of cradleboard use, notes a worldwide distribution pattern that correlates nicely with environmental factors, suggesting that the diaper function of the cradleboard may be widespread.

In sum, cradleboard use among the Navajo is primarily functional. Because mothers are able to influence infant state by placing an infant on the cradleboard (or taking the infant off), they have another way of achieving at least short-term "goodness of fit" between the infant's state and their own activities. In addition to its diaper function, the cradleboard also provides a measure of protection for the infant, promotes mother-infant proximity by making travel away from home easier, and because of its motor-restraint function, reduces the frequency of those occasions when the mother must interfere with her child's activities (but there is no evidence of cradleboard effects on motor development; see Chisholm, 1983). Taken together, these cradleboard functions seem to have been successful adaptations by the Navajo to the demands of child care in a hunting-gathering society where movement is great, social organization is fluid, women's labor is vital, and the environment is harsh.

But because of its state-reducing effect on the infant, the cradleboard has an effect on the infant's behavior and thus also on the behavior of the infant's social partners. In addition to promoting sleep, the cradleboard makes mothers and infants less mutually responsive, and their interactions, if not shorter, are less intense (Chisholm, 1983).

This reduced intensity, and especially this reduced response contingency, might, according to a strict interpretation of attachment theory, satisfy the conditions for anxious or insecure attachment among the Navajo, with all the long-term sequelae that condition may entail. Psychoanalytic interpretations of the effects of the cradleboard (e.g., the "swaddling hypothesis" of Gorer; see Gorer, 1949; Gorer & Rickman, 1949) also have suggested long-term effects. And Anglo-American folk wisdom has held too that use of the cradleboard is the main reason why Navajo people do not act like Anglo-Americans. Each of these assertions about the long-term effects of the cradleboard has been supported, as it were, by the strikingly consistent reports of Anglo-American anthropologists, psychologists, and psychiatrists about Navajo behavioral/temperamental styles. From an etic, or non-Navajo, point of view, many Navajo people seem especially quiet, shy, withdrawn, or even to be suffering, as Kluckhohn put it, from "morbid melancholia" and "endemic uneasiness" (Kluckhohn, 1947a, 1947b; 1985).

Similar accounts have emphasized excessive amounts of fear, anxiety, depression, and shame among the Navajo (e.g., Kluckhohn, 1944; Kluckhohn & Leighton, 1946/1974; Leighton & Kluckhohn, 1948; Leighton & Leighton, 1942; Schoenfeld & Miller, 1973). Specific "evidence" for these interpretations typically includes reference to the Navajo custom of gaze aversion. For example:

> Unlike middle-class whites, the direct open-faced look in the eyes was avoided by Navajos. In fact Navajos froze up when looked at directly. Even when shaking hands they held one in the peripheral field of the eyes, letting the message of the other person's warmth and pleasure at seeing a friend seep through a long-clasped, but delicately held hand. I ultimately learned that to look directly at a Navajo was to display anger. (Hall, 1969, p. 379)

This brief introduction to the Navajo provides a background for the following examination of the behavior of Navajo infants. My purpose in the following section is to review arguments about the existence of a genetically determined "Oriental temperament" among the Navajo, and to suggest that for good evolutionary biological reasons "typical" Navajo behavioral/temperamental styles are more likely a result of cultural beliefs and values about appropriate behavior than of either use of the cradleboard or this "Oriental temperament."

Navajo Infant Behavior

Both Navajo and Anglo-Indian Health Service pediatric personnel have long taken it for granted that newborn Navajo infants are quieter and generally easier to work with than newborn Anglo infants. Using an earlier version (Freedman &

Brazelton, 1971) of the Brazelton Neonatal Behavioral Assessment Scale (here-after, BNBAS; Brazelton, 1973), Freedman (1971, 1974a, 1974b, 1976) was the first to provide an empirical and detailed description of the behavior of newborn Navajo infants. His studies showed that Navajo newborns indeed were consistently quieter and less irritable than Anglo-American newborns, and that Navajo newborns clustered with Chinese and Japanese newborns while the white American infants stood by themselves. The Navajo, Chinese, and Japanese infants differed from the Anglo-American infants most dramatically on the test items assessing "temperament, which seemed to tap excitability/imperturbability" (1971, p. 220). The "Oriental gene pool" infants differed from the Caucasian infants in being less irritable, slower to reach a crying state, less labile in state, better at self-quieting, and more easily consoled if they did become excited.

My own research with the BNBAS on Navajo newborns replicated Freedman's results in all important respects. In the comparison between Navajo and Anglo-American infants' performance on the BNBAS, the Navajo infants showed significantly less irritability, more self-quieting, lower peak of excitement, less rapid buildup, and lower lability of states (see Table 1). Moreover, principal-component analyses showed that these BNBAS test items formed a significant dimension of both within- and between-group differences (Chisholm, 1983).

Because older Navajo children and Navajo adults are so often characterized as quiet, shy, and withdrawn, and because newborn Navajo infants are also thus characterized, one explanation of the adult behavior styles might be that they are the expression of an "Oriental temperament" that is continuously manifest throughout the life cycle. Freedman's evidence of similar BNBAS performance by Navajo, Chinese, and Japanese infants is highly suggestive, especially since we also know that these peoples are genetically more similar to each other than any of them are to Caucasian populations. We also know that there are other ways in which members of the "Oriental gene pool" differ from Caucasians. Wolff's (1977) data on greater vasomotor responsivity to small amounts of alcohol among Asian and American Indian peoples is suggestive of group differences in autonomic nervous system functioning.

Similarly, Kagan and his associates (Kagan et al., 1980), noting a "disposition toward inhibition" in the behavioral/temperamental styles of Chinese children in Boston, suggest that peak levels of autonomic arousal in these children, while not higher than in a Caucasian comparison group, may persist longer. Working with Asian and Caucasian adults, Lazarus and others (Lazarus, Tomita, Opton, & Kodama, 1966) and Crider and others (Crider, Shapiro, & Tursky, 1966) also report that the Asian groups maintained high levels of ANS activity (electrodermal activity) longer than Caucasians did.

Any simple genetic explanation for Navajo-Anglo differences in neonatal behavior, however, is almost certain to be inadequate. In my own research with the BNBAS, levels of Navajo neonatal irritability were highly correlated with maternal blood pressure during the second trimester of pregnancy (Chisholm,

Table 1.   Navajo and Anglo Brazelton Scale Scores

Brazelton Scale Item	Days 1–3					Days 4–10				
	Navajo (n = 23)		Anglo (n = 10)			Navajo (n = 18)		Anglo (n = 15)		
	M	SD	M	SD	p <[a]	M	SD	M	SD	p <[a]
Response decrement										
To light	7.8	1.3	6.3	2.0	.05	8.6	.7	7.5	1.4	.05
To rattle	8.3	1.1	7.9	1.6		7.8	1.6	7.5	1.7	
To bell	9.1	.6	9.3	1.2		8.5	1.0	8.1	2.0	
Orientation										
Inanimate visual	4.5	1.3	5.3	1.2		5.9	1.1	5.1	1.4	
Inanimate auditory	5.4	.9	6.3	.5	.001	6.2	1.1	5.6	1.0	
Animate visual	5.0	1.7	5.3	1.0		6.2	1.1	5.8	1.8	
Animate auditory	5.5	1.2	6.1	.6		6.1	.9	5.7	1.3	
Animate visual and auditory	5.5	1.6	6.2	1.4		6.4	1.1	6.1	1.5	
Alertness	5.0	2.0	5.2	1.8		6.3	1.5	5.5	1.6	
General tonus	5.5	.7	5.7	1.2		5.7	.9	6.3	.5	.02
Motor maturity	5.0	1.5	4.8	1.5		6.1	1.1	5.7	1.3	
Pull-to-sit	5.3	1.8	6.2	1.7		5.1	1.3	6.0	1.5	
Cuddliness	5.2	1.4	5.1	.8		5.2	2.0	4.9	1.0	
Defensive movements	5.9	1.7	5.3	1.9		6.9	1.1	5.7	1.3	
Consolability	7.0	1.7	6.6	2.2		8.1	2.0	6.6	1.6	.001
Peak of excitement	5.4	1.1	6.3	1.1	.05	4.9	1.3	6.9	1.0	.001
Rapidity of buildup	3.4	1.8	5.4	1.9	.01	2.3	1.7	4.9	1.6	.001
Irritability	4.1	1.8	5.7	1.9	.05	3.4	1.8	5.8	1.2	.001
Activity	4.7	1.0	5.2	1.0		5.2	.9	5.5	.7	
Tremulousness	3.6	1.7	5.3	2.2	.05	2.4	1.3	3.3	1.8	
Startles	3.2	1.1	4.9	2.5		2.4	1.0	4.4	2.1	.01
Lability										
Of skin color	5.4	1.4	5.1	1.5		4.4	1.6	5.2	1.3	
Of states	2.7	.8	6.0	1.7	.001	2.3	1.0	4.7	2.1	.001
Self-quieting activity	6.9	1.1	4.6	2.1	.01	7.0	1.8	1.7	1.8	.001
Hand-mouth facility	7.5	2.0	5.9	1.5	.02	6.4	2.0	5.3	2.8	
Smiles	.5	1.0	.0	.0		1.3	1.3	.6	1.6	

Note. From *Navajo Infancy: An Ethological Study of Child Development* (p. 128) by J. S. Chisholm, 1983, Hawthorne, NY: Aldine. Copyright 1983 by J. S. Chisholm. Reprinted by permission.
[a]All tests of significance are two-tailed *t*-tests.

1983; Chisholm, Woodson, & da Costa-Woodson, 1978). In more recent studies, maternal blood pressure during the middle trimester also proved to be a better predictor of neonatal irritability than did racial/ethnic differences and other correlates of irritability (Chisholm, 1981b; cf. Korner, Gabby, & Kraemer, 1980). The point is that epigenesis begins at conception, not birth, and that even if there is a significant genetic component to levels of newborn irritability, the expression of the genes involved may vary according to the prenatal developmental environment (cf. Chisholm & Heath, 1987).

In any event, while the behavioral physiological approaches to temperamental differences discussed above are more useful than the impressionistic descriptions of child and adult behaviors that are supposed to be evidence for continuity in temperamental style, there seem to be no longitudinal studies of the relevant physiological measures. But even if there were, the question would concern what produced or maintained the continuity. Kagan et al. (1980), for example, while recognizing the likelihood of a "disposition" toward wariness and inhibition among the Chinese children they studied, noted also that conditions of child-rearing in the Chinese homes tended to maintain these behavioral styles.

Caudill and his colleagues (Caudill, 1972; Caudill & Weinstein, 1969) reached the same conclusions. The Japanese infants they studied in Japan were similar to the Japanese, Chinese, and Navajo infants that Freedman observed: They cried less than Anglo infants, vocalized less, and were less motorically active. This dimension of differences also persisted, Caudill and others argue, because Japanese mothers interacted with their infants in such a way as to maintain the infants' behavior. And working with mothers and infants of recent Japanese descent in the United States, Caudill and Frost (1973) showed that both mothers and infants showed behavior patterns more similar to those of American mothers and infants than to Japanese mothers and infants in Japan. The consensus in developmental psychology seems to be that developmental continuity consists of more than a correlation between two measures at two times, even if they are physiological ones; it must still be demonstrated what factors served to maintain the correlation.

One such factor might be use of the cradleboard. Freedman (1974a) has suggested that because of their greater quietness and lesser irritability, Navajo infants may be more accepting of the cradleboard than more irritable infants and thus may predispose Navajo parents to use the cradleboard. This kind of reasoning is attractive (i.e., the notion that infants may influence the caretaking behavior of parents or their own developmental environment). There is, however, no evidence that Navajo parents use the cradleboard because their children have low levels of irritability.

The amount of cradleboard use varies greatly across the reservation (and there even seems to be no correlation with degree of acculturation). Moreover, observations and parental reports indicate that Navajo infants regularly cry when first placed on the cradleboard, and that Navajo parents simply expect this and put up with it, just as Anglo parents typically put up with their infants' cries when put into their cribs for a nap. Finally, the hypothesis that newborn temperament may "select" the cultural practice of swaddling or use of the cradleboard receives no support from the fact that these practices correlate better with climatic factors than with racial/ethnic factors (Whiting, 1981).

Thus, even if Navajo newborns should be "predisposed" to accept the cradleboard, this is not an explanation for Navajo use of the cradleboard. Nor can any effects of cradleboard use on the infant be attributed to newborn Navajo temperament through its effects on hypothetical parental "predispositions" to use the cradleboard with quiet and nonirritable infants.

There is, in any case, no evidence that the cradleboard has any long-term effects on behavior, and thus no evidence that the cradleboard can somehow help to maintain newborn temperament in such a way that it becomes manifest in adult Navajos as quietness, shyness, and reserve. Factor analysis of Navajo mother-infant interaction behaviors in the first year of life revealed a cradleboard factor, but one which accounted for only 6% of the total variance and which was nonsignificant.

Multiple-regression analyses, with the cradleboard entered as one of many predictor variables and mother-infant interaction variables entered as dependent variables, showed that the cradleboard was a reliable predictor of only a tiny fraction of these interactive behaviors, and that these were hardly surprising (e.g., after infants begin locomotion, being on the cradleboard predicts low levels of locomotion). Finally, using as dependent variables those mother and infant behaviors on which the Navajo sample differed most from an Anglo-American comparison group, another series of multiple-regression analyses showed that use of the cradleboard accounted for virtually none of the Navajo–Anglo group differences in patterns of mother-infant interaction (Chisholm, 1983).

The conclusion is that use of the cradleboard is not related to either within- or between-group differences in patterns of mother-infant interaction and that the observed effects of the cradleboard are transient in the extreme, holding only while the infant is actually on the cradleboard. The reason, I have suggested, that the cradleboard has no long-term developmental effects is that such effects would, according to all theory, be detrimental (e.g., for motor development, the attachment process, developmental psychodynamics, or aspects of early cognitive development) (Chisholm, 1983). In other words, I suspect that it is not so much that our various theories are wrong (e.g., one need not be surprised to learn that constant cradleboard use for the entire first year affected motor development), but that as Bateson (1976) and others have argued, developmental control mechanisms may really exist, and infants may have been, as Sameroff and Chandler put it, "programmed by the course of evolution to produce normal developmental outcome under all but the most adverse of circumstances" (1975, p. 71).

In the case of the cradleboard, there seem to be three candidates for such developmental control mechanisms. First, infants consistently cry before they are removed from the cradleboard, and it is reasonable to suppose that they cry thus "in order" to be removed. Second, after release from the cradleboard there is almost invariably a bout of especially intense and affectionate mother-infant interaction which is likely due at least in part to the infant, and which may function as an interactive behavioral correlate of the "catch-up growth" described by Prader, Tanner, and von Harnack (1963). Third, although not apparently because of any infant behavior, infants on the cradleboard were observed to be in significantly closer proximity to their mother than infants not on the cradleboard, and this increased proximity may function as an alternate to the kinds of mother-infant interaction that are immediately affected by the cradleboard and which the attachment theorists have emphasized so much (Chisholm, 1983).

Thus, if the behavioral/temperamental styles of older Navajo children and adults really are developmentally related to neonatal temperament patterns, the cradleboard is not a good candidate for explaining how they are maintained. Are there any other candidates for this maintenance function? One possibility is the effect of the early social organization of infancy (i.e., the Navajo infant's opportunity for social interaction with others as it is affected by family size, household density, and residence patterns). These factors have been implicated in a number of cross-cultural developmental studies.

Whiting and Whiting (1975), for example, report in their summary analyses of the six-cultures study that a major determinant of child behavior was the "status of the target," that is, the age/sex/kinship identity of the person with whom the child was interacting. More recently, B. B. Whiting (1980) has argued that knowing the age/sex/kinship identities of potential interactors in the social setting which occupy most of a child's time will allow one to predict accurately the characteristic patterns of interpersonal behavior. But in addition to the age/sex/kinship identities of potential interactors, the simple number of potential interactors may be expected to affect the nature of early interactions—not only because the number is likely to covary with the age/sex/kinship distribution, but also because the number clearly affects the child's opportunity for any interaction at all.

In a study of the Logoli of Kenya, for example, Munroe and Munroe (1971) found that in large households infants were held significantly more often than in small ones, and that in large households caretakers responded more quickly to infant cries. They also showed an inverse relationship between measures of mother-infant attachment and household size. Munroe and Munroe (1980) also have shown a correlation between multifamily household structure and permissiveness in parental socialization styles, as has Seymour (1983). Leiderman and Leiderman (1977) make similar kinds of arguments about the effects of polymatric versus monomatric households among the Kikuyu of East Africa.

Family size and household density among the Navajo, reflected in the differences between extended-family camps and nuclear-family camps, emerged as the most powerful predictor not only of individual differences in patterns of mother-infant interaction within the Navajo sample, but also between the Navajo sample and an Anglo-American comparison group. For example, children in extended-family camps, where there were 1.6 more peers (age 0–3 years), 2.9 more potential child caretakers or playmates (age 3–12 years), and another 3.6 teen-aged or adult caretakers, were observed to be away from home significantly more often than nuclear-family camp children, outside their homes more often (if within the camp), less likely to be in the company of their mothers, but more likely to be held or carried by their mothers if their mothers were present, and more often in the company of large numbers of other people than nuclear-family camp children.

The nuclear-family camp children, perhaps as a result of their lesser experi-ence with large numbers of other people, especially strangers, showed more fear of strangers than the extended-family camp children and showed it earlier. The Navajo extended-family camp children, compared to Anglo children living in nuclear families in Flagstaff, Arizona, resembled the Anglo nuclear-family chil-dren more than the Navajo nuclear-family children did. Mother-infant interaction in Navajo nuclear families, for example, was characterized by the lowest levels of mutual gazing, mother talking to child, mother approaching or leaving child, child vocalizations, child vocalizing and looking at mother, child approaching and leaving mother, and the shortest average duration of mother-infant interac-tive exchanges. On all these measures Navajo extended-family mothers and infants ranked second, and Anglo nuclear-family mothers and infants ranked highest.

Conversely, this consistent rank-ordering was precisely reversed on a measure of the frequency with which others present during mother-infant interaction directed behaviors toward the infant; during interaction in Navajo nuclear fam-ilies this was highest, it was intermediate in Navajo extended families, and lowest in Anglo nuclear families. Multiple-regression analyses also showed that this measure was the best single predictor of individual differences in patterns of mother-infant interaction among the Navajo and the best predictor of Navajo-Anglo group differences in mother-infant interaction.

These data constitute good support for the arguments of the Whitings, the Munroes, and others that variability in the number and age/sex/kinship identities of infants' potential social partners have systematic effects on the style of interac-tive behaviors seen. The fact that the Navajo and Anglo nuclear families were at opposite ends of this distribution suggests that abstract social structural variables (e.g., residence classifications) may not always serve as adequate indirect mea-sures of infants' social opportunity, especially for cross-cultural comparisons. However, in conjunction with other factors that affect the child's opportunity for social interaction, such as mothers' work loads and daily routines, the long-term importance of interactive opportunity for the development of interactive behav-ioral styles is likely to be great.

There may be an evolutionary biological rationale for such expectations about the long-term effects of differences in children's opportunities for social interac-tion. Since there is no way that a child can affect the number of potential interactors or their age/sex/kinship identity, the behavioral styles learned in interaction with these others should have lasting effects, as the Whitings and others have argued and as the data reported here also suggest. Because the cradleboard has one effect of reducing the mother-infant mutual responsivenes that seems to be so crucial for the attachment process, and because the infant can respond to these short-term cradleboard effects in a way that may prevent any deleterious long-term sequelae, we should not expect the cradleboard to have long-term effects.

Differences in children's opportunities for social interaction, however, may represent simple alternative developmental pathways, and the child's sensitivity to these differences simply makes it possible for children to be socialized to fit the enormous variety of adult behavior patterns. The sensitivity of infants to different patterns of early cosocialization would mean that they could develop normally almost regardless of the developmental environment created by the vagaries of human ecology, economy, history, and all the other determinants of cultural diversity.

In addition to the role that Navajo patterns of early social opportunity may play in maintaining (or entraining) quiet and nonintrusive temperamental styles, there is another dimension of Navajo culture, especially widespread and pervasive, that also seems likely to help maintain these early temperamental styles. As mentioned before, from an outside observer's perspective Navajo people often seem quiet, shy, withdrawn, and even anxious or depressed, and these impressions are often used to support the notion of some genetic or constitutional basis for an "Oriental temperament" among the Navajo. Notwithstanding the possibility that Navajo newborn temperament may make it easier for infants to learn adult behavior styles (although this has not been demonstrated), it is instructive to learn that these behavioral styles have cultural meaning and are specifially taught, and that from an emic, or Navajo observer's, perspective a quiet, nonintrusive behavioral style is considered appropriate and good. Moreover, the argument can be made that this behavioral style constitutes a successful response to some of the most pervasive and enduring problems facing the Navajo for several centuries.

Understanding Navajo "temperament" from an emic perspective is perhaps best achieved through analysis of the Navajo concepts *nila* ("it's up to you") and *t'áá bee bóholníih* ("it's up to him to decide"). The essential meaning of these expressions is that one should not impose one's will on others, that one cannot make unilateral decisions that are binding on others, that the individual in inviolable, and that everyone is his or her own boss. As Lamphere (1977, p. 41) explains, "The phrase *t'áá bee bóholníih* combines Navajo emphasis on both autonomy and consensus, and it entails egalitarian rather than hierarchical authority relations." For most non-Navajo Americans, cooperation and autonomy are two aspects of human social behavior that are in potential conflict.

Lamphere argues that the concept *t'áá bee bóholníih* actually fuses the high value that Navajos place on both cooperation and autonomy. She suggests that for the Navajo there is no inherent conflict between a high valuation of mutual cooperation and interdependence and an equally high valuation of individual autonomy. Potential conflicts of interest can be circumvented by striving for consensus, for while it is always up to the individual, each individual's autonomy is preserved through individual valuation of cooperation and consensus. To put it another way, cooperation and interdependence are simply and fundamentally good and necessary, but the individual has exclusive rights over the use and disposal of his or her property, time, and action.

Thus, gaze aversion, silence, and "delicate" handshakes are not evidence for fear, shyness, or anxiety as much as they are signs of respect for the other individual. This interpretation, based on an assessment of Navajo cultural values about appropriate behavior, gains additional support from Basso's (1970, 1979) research among the Western Apache, another Southern Athapaskan tribe and near neighbors of the Navajo. According to Basso, and in my own experience, the Navajo are "strikingly similar" to the Western Apache in the manners listed below (Basso, 1970). The special value of Basso's descriptions of Western Apache cultural values about appropriate behavior is that these descriptions are derived from what amount to a series of ethnic jokes about white Americans, told by Apaches, and the resulting contrast between Apache beliefs and values about appropriate behavior and those of white Americans makes the Apache (and similar Navajo) values especially clear. The most prominent value that emerges from Basso's analysis is that of respect for the inviolability of the individual. For example:

they are forcefully struck by the speech of Anglo-Americans, which is regularly described as being too fast, too loud, and too "tense". . .

[quoting an Apache] "Whitemen make lots of noise. With some who talk like that—loud and tight—it sounds too much like they mad at you. With some, you just can't be sure about it, so you just got to be careful about it, so you just got to be careful with them all the time."

[quoting another Apache] "Even if it's something little—like they want you to close the door—even for something like that, some Whitemen talk like they bossing you around. It's like shooting rabbits with a .30-.30."

To insist that [a] visitor come inside, to command him, is to overrule his right to do as he chooses, thereby implying that he is a person of little account whose wishes can be safely ignored. "When you talk to people like this," one of my consultants said, "you run over them. You make them feel small." To avoid such displays of disrespect, Apaches either refrain from issuing directives or construct them in ways so circumlocutional and oblique that they typically carry the force of observations rather than [orders].

Backslapping and vigorous handshaking are regarded as direct and unwarranted encroachments upon the private territory of the self. . . Prolonged eye contact, especially at close quarters, is typically interpreted as an act of aggression, a display of challenge and defiance. . . By Apache standards, Whitemen are entirely too probing with their eyes and hands, a distasteful tendency that Apaches take to be indicative of a weakly developed capacity for self-restraint and an insolent disregard for the physical integrity of others. As one of my consultants put it: "Whitemen touch each other like they were dogs." (Basso, 1979, pp. 51–60)

The road to cooperation and interdependence must therefore be through the individual's recognition of the inviolability of other individuals. The inviolability and inherent dignity of the individual are recognized, in part, by not imposing on others through loud or fast speech, tense speech, too many questions, commands, or invasion of personal space. Silence, gaze aversion, and a disinclination to touch others may be evidence for shyness, shame, or even anxiety and depression among Anglo-Americans, but among the Navajo they are more likely to be evidence of an individual's ability to act in terms of cultural beliefs and values about interdependence and autonomy.

It is probably impossible to demonstrate a causal relationship between a people's past and details of their present-day behavior and values, but as outlined previously, the material facts of Navajo life and history have been such that it cannot be surprising that they value cooperation, interdependence, and individual autonomy. For 500 years the Navajo have lived under constant, widespread, and often severe ecological, economic, and military/political pressures. Balancing a mixed hunting-gathering-herding-farming-raiding economy in an arid, empty, and difficult terrain demanded that each person or family had the right to exploit whatever scattered and intermittent resources were available, whenever and wherever they appeared.

The right of the individual to freedom of action would have been one way of ensuring the most effective harvesting of such resources. The high valuation of individual autonomy and of interdependence and consensus thus might have provided individual Navajos with an emotional and even philosophical basis for the more or less constant movement, dissolution, and alliance of social groups of varying sizes, and for the sharing and redistribution of goods and services in spite of fluid and shifting patterns of social organization.

Even more, given the Navajos' long history of raiding and warfare with their neighbors, and especially their devastating military defeat and imprisonment by the U.S. Army, and the subsequent century of (from the Navajo point of view) less than friendly relations with Washington and a fair amount of racial/ethnic prejudice directed against them, it is perhaps all to easy to understand why Anglo ethnographers and others have so frequently observed that the Navajo suffer from a "high degree of tension," "morbid melancholia," and "endemic uneasiness." What they have described, from their outside observer's point of view, may only be the behavioral manifestation of Navajo beliefs and values about appropriate behavior toward strangers, to outsiders, and perhaps especially to Anglos, who have been the historical source of much Navajo tension and unease.

From the Navajo point of view, it is not only the interpersonal behavior of Anglos that often seems to reflect a disregard for the dignity and autonomy of the individual, but also the history of Navajo-Anglo group relations that does so. In a historical sense, maintaining a certain level of wariness and reserve around Anglos has probably been appropriate and adaptive behavior. As LeVine has expressed:

> cultural evolution within human populations also produces standardized strategies of survival for infants and childrn, strategies reflecting environmental pressures from a more recent past, encoded in customs rather than genes and transmitted socially rather than biologically. (LeVine, 1977, p. 16)

Determining what the limits of developmental plasticity may be is, of course, our major research problem, but it might be easier to do this if we begin with the notion that adaptation begins with the individual's immediate responses to the environment. To adapt is to evolve, to develop, or to learn ways of responding to the environment that make it easier to respond to the environment in the future. The genes most often associated with this happy state of affairs seem to have been most frequent among hominids, who have evolved the genetic capacity for culture. But to the extent that culture is adaptive, then it is the content of culture, not our genetic capacity for it, that is most immediately adaptive. This is because humans track their environments through the content of culture—not the capacity for culture.

References

Aberle, D. F. (1961). In D. M. Schneider & K. Gough (Eds.), *Matrilineal kinship*. Berkeley: University of California Press.

Basso, K. (1970). To give up on words: Silence in Western Apache culture. *Southwestern J. Anthropology, 26(2)*, 213–230.

Basso, K. (1979). *Portraits of the "whiteman": Linguistic play and cultural symbols among the Western Apache*. New York: Cambridge University Press.

Bateson, P. P. G. (1976). Rules and reciprocity in behavioral development. In P. P. G. Bateson & R. A. Hinde (Eds.), *Growing points in ethology*. Cambridge: Cambridge University Press.

Bell, R. Q. (1968). A reinterpretation of the direction of effects in studies of socialization. *Psych. Review, 75*, 81–95.

Brazelton, T. B. (1973). *Neonatal Behavioral Assessment Scale*. London: Spastics International Medical Publications/Heinemann Medical Books.

Caudill, W. (1972). Tiny dramas: Vocal communication between mother and infant in Japanese and American families. In W. P. Lebra (Ed.), *Mental health research in Asia and the Pacific: Vol. 2. Transcultural research in mental health*. Honolulu: University of Hawaii Press.

Caudill, W., & Frost, L. A. (1973). A comparison of maternal care and infant behavior in

Japanese-American, American, and Japanese families. In W. P. Lebra (Ed.), *Mental health research in Asia and the Pacific: Vol. 3. Youth, socialization, and mental health.* Honolulu: University of Hawaii Press.

Caudill, W., & Weinstein, H. (1969). Maternal care and child rearing in Japan and the United States: An interim report. Psychiatry, 32, 12–43.

Chisholm, J. S. (1981a). Residence patterns and the environment of mother-infant interaction among the Navajo. In T. Field, A. Sostek, P. Vietze, & P. H. Leiderman (Eds.), *Culture and early interactions.* Hillsdale, NJ: Erlbaum.

Chisholm, J. S. (1981b). Prenatal influences on Aboriginal–White Australian differences in neonatal irritablity. *Ethology and Sociobiology, 2,* 67–73.

Chisholm, J. S. (1983). *Navajo infancy: An ethological study of child development.* Hawthorne, NY: Aldine.

Chisholm, J. S., & Heath, G. (1987). Evolution and pregnancy: A biosocial view of prenatal influences. In C. Super (Ed.), *The role of culture in developmental disorder.* New York: Academic Press.

Chisholm, J. S., Woodson, R. H., & da Costa-Woodson, E. (1978). Maternal blood pressure in pregnancy and newborn irritability. *Early Human Development, 2(2),* 171–178.

Crider, A., Shapiro, D., & Tursky, B. (1966). Reinforcement of spontaneous electrodermal activity. *J. Comparative and Physiol. Psychl., 61,* 20–27.

Dunn, J. (1976). How far do early differences in mother-infant relations affect later development? In P. P. G. Bateson & R. A. Hinde (Eds.), *Growing points in ethology.* Cambridge: Cambridge University Press.

Durham, W. (1979). Toward a coevolutionary theory of human biology and culture. In N. Chagnon & W. Irons (Eds.), *Evolutionary biology and human social behavior: An anthropological perspective.* North Scituate, MA: Duxbury Press.

Freedman, D. G. (1971). Genetic influences on the development of behavior. In G. B. Stoelinga & J. J. van der Werff ten Bosch (Eds.), Normal and abnormal development of behavior. Leiden, The Netherlands: Leiden University Press.

Freedman, D. G. (1974a). Cradleboard and temperament: Cause or effect? Paper presented at the annual meeting of the American Association for the Advancement of Science, San Francisco.

Freedman, D. G. (1974b). *Human infancy: An evolutionary perspective.* Hillsdale, NJ: Erlbaum.

Freedman, D. G. (1976). Infancy, biology, and culture. In L. Lipsitt (Ed.), *Developmental psychobiology.* Hillsdale, NJ: Erlbaum.

Freedman, D. G., & Brazelton, T. B. (1971). The Cambridge Neonatal Scales. In G. B. Stoelinga & J. J. van der Werff ten Bosch (Eds.), *Normal and abnormal development of behavior.* Leiden, The Netherlands: Leiden University Press.

Gadgill, M., & Bossert, W. H. (1970). Life historical consequences of natural selection. *American Naturalist, 104,* 1–24.

Goodenough, W. (1981). *Culture, language, and society* (2nd ed.). Menlo Park, CA: Benjamin Cummings.

Gorer, G. (1949). Some aspects of the psychology of the people of Great Russia. *American Slavic and East European Review, 8,* 155–160.

Gorer, G., & Rickman, J. (1949). *The People of Great Russia.* London: Cresset.

Gould, S. J. (1977). *Ontogeny and phylogeny*. Cambridge, MA: Harvard University Press.

Gould, S. J. (1982). Change in developmental timing as a mechanism of macroevolution. In J. T. Bonner (Ed.), *Evolution and development*. New York: Springer-Verlag.

Hall, E. T. (1969, March). Listening behavior: Some cultural differences. *Phi Delta Kappan*.

Horn, H. (1978). Optimal tactics of reproduction and life history. In J. R. Krebs & L. B. Davies (Ed.), *Behavioral ecology*. Oxford: Blackwell Scientific Publishers.

Kagan, J. (1980). Perspectives on continuity. In O. G. Brim & J. Kagan (Eds.), *Constancy and change in human development*. Cambridge, MA: Harvard University Press.

Kagan, J. (1981). Universals in human development. In R. H. Munroe, R. L. Munroe, & B. B. Whiting (Eds.), *Handbook of cross-cultural human development*. New York: Garland.

Kagan, J., Kearsley, R. B., & Zelazo, P. R. (1980). *Infancy: Its place in human development*. Cambridge, MA: Harvard University Press.

King, M. C., & Wilson, A. C. (1975). Evolution at two levels in humans and chimpanzees. *Science, 188,* 107–116.

Kluckhohn, C. (1944). *Navaho witchcraft*. New York: Beacon-Free Press.

Kluckhohn, C. (1947). Some aspects of Navaho infancy and early childhood. *Psychoanalysis and the Social Sciences, 1,* 37–86.

Kluckhohn, C., & Leighton, D. (1974). *The Navaho* (rev. ed.). Cambridge, MA: Harvard University Press. (Original ed. published 1946)

Korner, A., Gabby, T., & Kraemer, H. C. (1980). Relation between prenatal maternal blood pressure and infant irritability. *Early Human Development,* 4(1), 788–791.

Lamphere, L. (1977). *To run after them*. Tucson: University of Arizona Press.

Lazarus, R. S., Tomita, M., Opton, E. M., & Kodama, M. (1966). A cross-cultural study of stress-reaction patterns in Japan. *J. Pers. and Social Psych., 5,* 622–633.

Leiderman, P. H., & Leiderman, G. C. (1977). Economic change and infant care in an East African agricultural community. In P. H. Leiderman, S. R. Tulkin, & A. Rosenfeld (Eds.), *Culture and infancy: Variations in the human experience*. New York: Academic Press.

Leighton, D., & Kluckhohn, C. (1948). *Children of the people*.Cambridge, MA: Harvard University Press.

Leighton, D., & Leighton, A. (1942). Some types of uneasiness and fear in a Navaho community. *American Anthropologist, 44,* 194–209.

LeVine, R. A. (1977). Child rearing as cultural adaptation. In P. H. Leiderman, S. R. Tulkin, & A. Rosenfeld (Eds.), *Culture and infancy: Variations in the human experience*. New York: Academic Press.

Levy, J. E. (1962). Community organization among the western Navajo. *American Anthropologist, 65,* 781–801.

Lewis, M., & Rosenblum, L. (Eds.). (1974). *The effect of the infant on its caregiver*. New York: Wiley.

Lipton, E., Steinschneider, A., & Richmond, J. (1965). Swaddling: A child care practice: Historical, cultural, and experimental observations. *Pediatrics, 35,* 519–567.

MacArthur, R. H., & Wilson, E. O. (1967). *The theory of island biogeography*. Princeton, NJ: Princeton University Press.

Mason, O. T. (1888). Cradles of the American aborigines. *U.S. National Museum Annual Report 1886–1887, Part 2*, 161–212.

Munroe, R. H., & Munroe, R. L. (1971). Household density and infant care in an East African society. *J. Social Psych., 83*, 3–13.

Pianka, E. R. (1970). On r- and K-selection. American Naturalist, 104, 592–597.

Plotkin, H. C., & Odling-Smee, F. J. (1981). A multiple-level model of evolution and its implications for sociobiology. *Behavioral and Brain Sciences, 4*, 225–268.

Prader, A., Tanner, J., & von Harnack, G. (1963). Catch-up growth following illness or starvation. *J. Pediatrics, 62*, 646–659.

Reynolds, T. R. (1979). *Residential ideology and practice among the Sheep Springs Navajo*. Unpublished doctoral dissertation, Department of Anthropology, University of British Columbia, Vancouver, Canada.

Sameroff, A. (1975). Early influences on development: Fact or fancy? *Merrill-Palmer Quarterly, 21*(4), 267–294.

Sameroff, A., & Chandler, M. J. (1975). Reproductive risk and the continuum of caretaking casualty. In F. D. Horowitz, E. M. Hetherington, S. Scarr-Salapatek, & G. M. Siegel (Eds.), *Review of child development research* (Vol. 4). Chicago: University of Chicago Press.

Schoenfeld, L. S., & Miller, S. I. (1973). The Navajo Indians: A descriptive study of the psychiatric population. *Internat. J. Social Psychiatry, 19*(1,2), 31–37.

Seymour, S. (1983). Household structure and status and expressions of affect in India. *Ethos, 11*, 263–277.

Slobodkin, L., & Rapoport, A. (1974). An optimal strategy of evolution. *Quar. Rev. Biol., 49*, 181–200.

Stearns, S. C. (1976). Life-history tactics: A review of the data. *Quar. Rev. Biol., 51*, 3–47.

Waddington, C. H. (1968). The theory of evolution today. In A. Koestler & J. Smythies (Eds.), *Beyond reductionism*. New York: Macmillan.

Waddington, C. H. (1975). *The evolution of an evolutionist*. Edinburgh, Scotland: Edinburgh University Press.

Whiting, B. B. (1980). Culture and social behavior: A model for the development of social behavior. *Ethos, 8*, 95–116.

Whiting, B. B., & Whiting, J. W. M. (1975). *Children of six cultures*. Cambridge, MA: Harvard University Press.

Whiting, J. W. M. (1981). Environmental constraints on infant care practices. In R. H. Munroe, R. L. Munroe, & B. B. Whiting (Eds.), *Handbook of cross-cultural human development*. New York: Garland.

Wilson, E. O. (1975). *Sociobiology: The new synthesis*. Cambridge, MA: Harvard University Press.

Witherspoon, G. (1970). A new look at Navajo social organization. *American Anthropologist, 72*, 55–66.

Wolff, P. H. (1977). Biological variations and cultural diversity: An exploratory study. In P. H. Leiderman, S. R. Tulkin, & A. Rosenfeld (Eds.), *Culture and infancy: Variations in the human experience*. New York: Academic Press.

Part IV

AFTERWORD

CHAPTER 14

Culture and Newborn Behavior: Uses of the NBAS in Different Cultural Settings

T. Berry Brazelton

*Children's Hospital Medical Center,
Boston, MA*

Since its publication as a National Spastics Foundation monograph in 1973, the Neonatal Behavioral Assessment Scale (NBAS) has been increasingly utilized to assess the remarkable, complex behavior of the human newborn. Its use in the United States has already resulted in more than 150 published monographs. Studies with the NBAS can be classified under six headings:

1. Studies of high-risk infants, especially premature or small-for-gestational age infants who were deprived in utero;
2. Studies on the effects of perinatal influences, such as obstetric medication, hyperbilirubinemia, and phototherapy;
3. Studies on the effects of intrauterine variables, such as maternal undernutrition and maternal addiction;
4. Studies of prediction from neonatal behavior to future outcome;
5. Uses of the NBAS as a form of intervention with parents of babies at risk;
6. Cross-cultural comparisons of newborn behavior.

This last type of study provides us with a unique opportunity to evaluate genetic differences and the influence of environmental variables on these differences. For example, the neonate's behavior cannot be considered genotypic, inasmuch as it is already influenced by intrauterine conditions. If it were possible to control adequately for such a variable as maternal malnutrition, it probably would become apparent that the same degree of undernutrition would influence African and Asian neonates in significantly different ways. The differences in outcomes in behavior as assessed in the neonatal period would lead us to a better understanding of the differences in genetic endowment. But each intrauterine variable would have to be well understood as it influenced the genetic programs of the developing fetus. The behaviors that were minimally influenced would highlight the processes of genetic adaptation over the centuries in each genetic line, and would likely form the universal bases for behavior in that genotype. The more easily influenced or changed behaviors would not be those necessary for survival but, rather, the more recently acquired behaviors (such as orientation behaviors or complex motor actions), and might be those that were influential in establishing individual differences within the group. At birth, groups of behaviors would not only point to differences in prediction for the baby's capacity for survival and for immediate adaptation to his extrauterine environment, but would also help us establish the behaviors that predict the future outcome. In each culture, the kind of universal behaviors with which parents are presented would be likely to set minimal expectations for their parenting. The more individuated behaviors would be likely to establish the range of individual differences for parental behavior within each culture.

Hence, an evaluation of the neonatal behaviors within each culture offers us a wide range of opportunity for examining the expectations of that culture for effective child-rearing practices. The normal or "average" infants offer us one window, or baseline. The extreme variants give us a chance to understand the adaptations that must be available to nurture that culture's at-risk infants, for example, the infanticide of less-than-optimal !Kung babies (Konner, 1977) and, at the other extreme, the opportunities for variability of nurturing with the more gifted babies. The way that significant intrauterine variables influence genetically endowed neonatal behaviors, then, becomes our first window into a culture's expectations for its children. Assessment of intrauterine conditions should be a major effort in any cross-cultural study. The intrauterine variables are not simply additive in their effects but are likely to be synergistic. Hence, genotype as it interacts with prenatal variables becomes a first, but complex, set of evaluations, if one is to look at cross-cultural differences among neonates.

Assessment of the baby for signs of maturity or immaturity becomes a powerful window into the experience of the fetus. A baby who is mature in such assessments as provided by Dubowitz (Dubowitz, Dubowitz, & Goldberg, 1970) but who is dysmature in appearance and/or behavior is pointing to placental insufficiency of significant duration. In the U.S. we are beginning to understand the effect of this nutritional deprivation on cellular replication (DNA), on RNA storage within cells, and on neurophysiological interconnections as they affect the future neonate's behavior. Further, we are gaining insight into how such deprivation predicts to parental difficulties in organizing these babies over time. The chapters by Saco-Pollitt, Walsh Escarce, Garcia Coll, and others present examples of such powerful intrauterine nutritional deprivation. The neonatal behavior of the babies in these studies can be seen as a window back into the uterus.

It is critical in newborn evaluation to assess the physical signs of maturity, and of dysmaturity (or small-for-gestational-age characteristics as represented by the ponderal index—a length-to-weight ratio outlined by Miller and Hassanein (1973) for a U.S. sample). If newborns are short and immature for their gestational age, they are likely to represent a more prolonged kind of chronic intrauterine depletion. Their short growth reflects the degree of deprivation, as do their immature-for-age characteristics. These babies' behaviors might be expected to be adaptive to survival but not rich in complexity, or they might be expected to predict to optimal outcomes for their future. Hence, a careful assessment of gestational age, of signs of intrauterine stress, and of maturity equivalent to the duration of gestation could be coupled with the neonate's behavior to represent the earliest expression of an interaction between genetic endowment and environmental influences.

The opportunity to see the neonate's behavior as a reflection of differences in genetic and environmental influences gives us more than a picture of the wide range of neonatal capacities. It also provides us with a base for understanding the predictions from neonatal to later development. If we can see the neonate's behavior as dynamic, changing in response to his or her initial adjustment to labor, delivery, and the new environment, we can begin to visualize through these changes the behavioral systems that will predict to the neonate's future. If we can assess accurately the environmental influences as represented by child-rearing practices in each culture, we can estimate their value in helping the neonate recover from birth and the stresses of achieving a new homeostasis. Then the neonate's behavior, as it changes from day to day and from week to week in the newborn period, becomes a second, powerful reflection of the nature-nurture equation. Each culture will give us a better opportunity to visualize this change and to evaluate the ingredients—both from the baby and from the environment.

We are convinced from our own work that one assessment amounts to only no more than a screening technique. Certainly one exam should be able to rule in or out neurological integrity and/or congenital defects. And as is suggested in the chapters of, for example, Fricker and his colleagues, Saco-Pollitt, Walsh Escarce, and Garcia Coll, it may reflect the variations between normal and at-risk behaviors in a particular culture. But a more powerful window into the endowment of each baby would be offered by several successive exams. Administration of exams and the way babies organize themselves become a way of estimating how the earliest experiences influence the genetic organization of babies.

The most powerful window into genetic differences will be offered by comparing the "recovery" of the baby over the first few days of life, and the changes in behaviors in the first month, from one set of environmental factors and one genotype to another (see, for example, the chapters by Landers and Muret-Wagstaff and Moore). After reading these chapters, I am more convinced than ever that we need a comparison of "recovery curves" in each culture. This will mean that two or three exams in the neonatal period must become a requirement for all studies, and that we explore new statistical techniques for evaluating change among the four systems that we can evaluate—state, autonomic, motor, and attention—as a dynamic window that is likely to vary systematically from one culture to another. Then, cross-cultural comparisons will yield an even better window into the intrauterine influences on differences in gene pools and the way these differences, as reflected by neonatal behavior, react with extrauterine influences to predict to babies' future.

It seems obvious, then, that the newborn is not simply a product of nature but is already affected by the interaction between nature and nurture. The neonate's progress over the first month will reflect the effects of the early environment. We are struck with how early the neonate's behavior reflects differences in handling (see Landers, Muret-Wagstaff and Moore). Rather than use the NBAS to try simply to compare genotypic behaviors across cultures, I would rather suggest that this instrument might be seen as a first window into the phenotypic behavior of this culture. The variability of the newborn's behavior could then give us a window into the range of individual differences among neonates available to this particular culture. The parental responses, as well as the child-rearing practices, could be seen as being shaped by or adapted to the kind of babies parents have. For when the culture respects its babies' behavior, it is likely that the practices will be shaped to the kind of babies the parents produce. The outcome over time then becomes a way of visualizing the interaction between the newborn's potential and the culture's expectations.

We strongly recommend, therefore, (a) careful reliability checks of examiners before a study, as well as repeated checks along the way; (b) repeated observations of the baby over the first few weeks of life; (c) careful collection of prenatal influences; (d) use of ponderal index, gestational age, dysmaturity, and neurological assessments, as well as the NBAS; (e) use of the data with the concepts of systems within the baby (or clusters; see Lester, Als, & Brazelton, 1982) as they change over time; (f) careful observations of the earliest perinatal influences or child-rearing expectations within each culture. If all studies can be performed with equivalent standards and equivalent reliability, we can utilize a large data base within which to make comparisons from one culture to another.

We have learned a great deal from reliability training of field workers who use the NBAS in other cultures. After reliability of over 90% is established on babies before a study is instituted, we have tested workers after their return from a year or more of study. Of course, they have slipped in certain ways. We now expect slippage in observers who are sensitive to different groups of babies and who tend to establish a new mean for these babies' behavior. Their slippage will conform to child-rearing expectations as expressed by parents who watch them. Hence, when the parents return we ask the examiners to demonstrate babies to us, before they examine too many Caucasian babies or before they observe our examination procedures again. As they perform the exam, we make notes about new differences in their exam. These, then, become our best window into the cross-cultural differences to which they are conforming. As we go over these often very subtle differences, we can see which ones are due to differences in the behaviors of neonates they have examined, and which changes in the exam have been made to conform to parental expectations (see deVries & Super, 1978). Instead of error, slippage then becomes a subtle window into cross-cultural differences.

The opportunity to publish so many excellent studies from other countries has led us to try to evaluate what we have learned from each of these chapters. My comments will not do justice to each study, but I shall try to use them to highlight both what we did learn and how we might build on them to improve our models for future cross-cultural studies on infancy.

The Saco-Pollitt study of the effect of altitude on size and morbidity of neonates in the high Andes in Peru is an excellent example of controlling for one prenatal variable such as altitude and relative hypoxia. Nutrition, socioeconomic status (SES), and other known variables were seen as added in responsibility to altitude for the deficits in size and significantly decreased neonatal behavior. The high-altitude group, with similar SES, nutrition, and other variables, were compared to a lower-SES sample in Lima. If these variables were used as synergistic to each other rather than additive, one might perhaps be better able to predict which fetuses may be most at risk for depressed behavior in the neonatal period. Using multivariate analysis, could one predict which children would have sensorimotor or learning disabilities? Could we develop a formula for analyzing changes in scores, in order to enhance our ability to predict to future well-being?

We also need to agree upon a correlation matrix that can be useful in comparing small groups of babies across cultures. In this case, the three factors that were formed by the correlation coefficients, and which explained a total of 61% of the variance, were quite similar to the four factors derived in an earlier study (see Als, Tronick, Lester, & Brazelton, 1979). We have since formulated a 7-factor scoring, derived by a combination of empirical and clinical scoring, which seems to be more sensitive to prenatal and perinatal factors (Lester et al., 1982). We need to collect and collate data from a large combined sample in order to test the value of different statistical techniques. Such a large sample could then be used as a base for comparing data around the world. In this case, while we do not know what the comparative effect of being Peruvian might be, these data could be used to establish a base of lower-SES babies for comparison with lower-SES babies elsewhere. Saco-Pollitt's ideas about how these babies' condition at birth shapes the child-rearing practices of the high-altitude culture is an interesting one and deserves attention in other cultural settings.

The study by Fricker, Hindermann, and Bruppoeher was striking because of its assessment of 1,123 children. With such a large number, statistical manipulations of data become possible and questions of importance to all of us can be tested. The questions of optimal time of day for the exam, of its relation to last feeding, of which initial state is optimal for starting the exam, of sex differences, and of the effect of interexaminer differences in reliability are all examined. The fact that it reveals that examiners need to maintain frequent reliability checks does not surprise us, but the data show how easily examiner bias can enter into such an interactive exam. We now feel that examiner reliability needs to be checked every fifth baby—and more in the handling of the baby than in the scoring. If one cannot wait for a baby to be in these preferred states, perhaps the early maneuvers to rouse the baby must be more vigorous and the concept of best performance utilized in order to bring the baby up to optimum before the exam is brought to a close. Otherwise, it would be difficult to know whether the behavior was just state-related or whether the baby was organically depressed.

In this study, if we had two or three exams on each baby, rather than one single exam, the opportunity to examine the effects of the prenatal and perinatal variables would be significantly enhanced. Although there were significant effects from tobacco, coffee consumption, and prenatal medications, our understanding of these might have been enhanced by multivariate analyses in which other prenatal and perinatal variables were used as synergistic. The fact that there are significant effects of single prenatal and perinatal variables makes us eager to use a multivariate model to reexamine the data for subtle but important effects of less significant variables when they are utilized singly. This study is an extremely valuable one in pointing to examiner variables that influence the scores in such an epidemiological study, as well as in underscoring the importance of timing the exam for optimal outcomes. This indicates the fragility of data that can be collected from an instrument that is so sensitive.

The Nepalese study of a high-risk population (1.5–2% infant mortality, 10 times as high as in the U.S.) by Walsh Escarce demonstrates the importance of intrauterine influences such as undernutrition in setting the stage for future infant mortality and morbidity. The ponderal index at birth did not help to differentiate the behaviors of these babies, and one wonders whether there are more appropriate ways of assessing intrauterine deprivation across cultures. If there is chronic undernutrition, the length-weight ratio does not reflect deprivation, as both length and weight are affected equally by prolonged malnutrition and depression of DNA replication over the 9 months of gestation. These babies can be seen to make adaptive adjustments to their intrauterine conditions. Their motor and autonomic responses were excellent and the orientation responses were adequate. These scores were significantly better than they were in comparative U.S. samples. This might represent a difference in the way intrauterine influences affect genetic endowment or adaptation over years of poverty in other cultures. It might be seen as an example of a culture's adaptation over generations to poor nutrition, in that the small mothers produce significantly smaller offspring, but the necessary ingredients for the fetus's adaptation is provided by the otherwise inadequate-appearing diet.

Dr. Escarce's description of the beliefs and practices of handling the new baby seem to bear out the observation that the culture reinforces the motor and autonomic stability of the baby by massage and the rituals surrounding the baby's earliest experiences. Relative motor advancement seems to result (see also Landers's chapter).

Winn, Morelli, and Tronick report on a study of 19 newborns among the African pygmies. The Efe were observed to pass their new babies from one adult to another, with 3.7 to 5.3 different caregivers handling the baby over a 2-hr observation period. Meanwhile, on the NBAS the infants were unusually fussy and difficult to console. It seemed as if the practice of repeatedly sharing small babies was an adaptation to the kind of baby with which the culture was presented. Although the baby spent more time with the mother than with anyone else, the extended adult group seemed to take an equal role in helping these fussy babies quiet down—many adults nursing and handling them. Thus, Bowlby's ideas of a single initial attachment of the child to the mother were adapted in this culture to the kind of fussy baby with which the mother was presented. The cultural goal seemed to be to create quiet, consolable babies. The lack of apparent relationship of newborn measures in the NBAS as predicting to the kind of caregiving newborns received seemed to represent a failure in the NBAS as an assessment. There are two possible interpretations for this finding from which we can profit. The NBAS is an interactive scale, and it measures the baby's responses within an actively responding caregiver relationship. As the newborn responds to a sensitive observer, he or she is no longer the fussy, inconsolable individual that might have been the case without the individualized attention of the observer. The sensitive caregiver smoothed out the baby's behavior. Were the multiple caregivers concentrating on the baby and responding in an actively consoling way, or were they just "holding" the infant? The other explanation could be that multiple handling could in itself create fussy babies. At any rate, this study points to the important fact that the NBAS is only a first step toward establishing an assessment of babies. When the scores of the NBAS do not completely describe the sample under observation, one should add a set of scores that are sensitive to the differences in the observed group. In this case, an additional set of scores added to lability of states or to consolability might have helped to differentiate among these babies and to predict to their frequent handling.

This study raises the important question of whether babies lead the cultural practices that attempt to help them adapt, or whether the cultural practices shape babies' behaviors in the first few days and weeks of life.

Garcia Coll's chapter cites a previously published study of neonatal behavior using the NBAS in a group of teenage mothers in Puerto Rico. In this group it is the norm to have an unwed pregnancy in midadolescence. The high-risk factors of hypertension, anemia, nutritional adequacy, and cephalopelvic disproportion with prolonged labor lead to small-for-gestational age (SGA) babies who are relatively shorter and lighter than the norms for Puerto Rican neonates. Although SES and maternal education influence the outcome of the neonates, a major predictive factor in the newborn's behavior and physical outcome involves whether the maternal grandmother backs up her daughter's pregnancy. If so, the medical and social variables are influenced toward a better outcome for the neonate. In this study, the babies in Puerto Rico were better off than a comparable lower-SES group in Providence. This is an excellent example of using the neonate's behavior as assessed by the NBAS as an outcome measure for studying the variables in pregnancy that lead to good and bad outcomes for the newborn. In Garcia Coll's study, the neonate's behavior, Cohler's Maternal Attitude Scale, as well as Crockenberg's child-rearing observations (in press) demonstrated a more positive outcome for babies of adolescents in a supported environment. If we really want to influence and improve the outcome of babies and their teenage mothers in any culture, Dr. Garcia Coll points out that we need to educate young women, improve their role choices, and offer them the equivalent of their own mother's support. These point to salient variables toward improvement of conditions for women in our own culture.

The study of black American infants by Rosser, Randolph, and Gaiter represents a study of a subculture in the U.S. that has long been needed. In order to establish norms for the black culture and to better support early child-rearing practices for young black mothers, it is critical to have a normative base of behaviors in the neonates from this group. Designed and carried out by black observers, this study presented the opportunity to collect and understand the mother's expectations for their babies, their perceptions of the infants' abilities, and their own goals as parents. Observations in the neonatal period and in longitudinal follow-up bear out these reported goals. The powerful effect of socioeconomic status in setting the stage in utero for the outcome of the babies' behavior is again replicated. A comparison of middle- and lower-SES babies revealed the ranges of behaviors in each group of 40 neonates and can serve as a baseline group for future studies. In both groups of black infants, motor competence was observed as being significantly higher than that of Caucasians at 2 days. The only difference between higher- and lower-SES groups was in the Autonomic Stability cluster in the higher-SES group when prenatal and obstetrical risk factors were controlled. Mother-infant interactions among the two groups were not significantly different. In this study, as in others mentioned previously, I would wish for a multivariate use of prenatal and perinatal variables to compare to the NBAS measures. Also, an analysis of the two NBAS exams at 3 and 30 days of life with a concept of recovery over time might yield a more productive way of looking at the variability of neonatal responses as they are compared to prenatal and perinatal variables. Certainly, those babies who were excellent in motor and orientation responses seemed better equipped to shape their mothers' behaviors at 1 month. These robustly interactive infants were more exciting to mothers and fulfilled their hopes and expectations for early motor development. A within-group comparison of the higher- and lower-scoring babies might yield a predictive score to their 3-year-old performance. This score would confirm the transactional model—that optimal neonatal performance reinforces optimal parental responsiveness and leads ultimately to a better outcome. In a subculture such as that of U.S. blacks, it would be important to understand the interactive forces that lead to optimal outcome. If the baby's behavior in the neonatal period can be seen as a source of strength for future maternal expectations, the opportunity for early intervention with parents of depressed infants could be addressed with more conviction.

Landers's elegantly designed study in southern India is a fine example of the value of multiple exams in the neonatal period. One question Dr. Landers addresses—the influence of intrauterine undernutrition on babies' growth, as measured in this group of poor people in India—shows that we cannot answer it by our present techniques. The use of the ponderal index ratio of height to weight may not reflect the same incidence of placental deprivation in that culture that it does in the U.S. For example, 45% of Indian newborns would be below the ratio of 2.3, or the U.S. 10th percentile. In the U.S., this would represent a deprived group of babies. And yet, in India as well as in Nepal, the neonates apparently were well proportioned, were responsible on the NBAS, and showed no real evidence of the kind of vulnerability one would expect to see in deprived newborns in the U.S. There needs to be a normative study in each culture in which such variables can be evaluated against a normal range for that particular genotype. In the Landers study, the fetus may well have been protected by an adequate intake of fish protein for a small race, in spite of what appeared to be a low-calorie diet for Caucasian needs. The question of the effects of intrauterine undernutrition on infant growth was highlighted and made clearer by her careful use of many prenatal variables that might have influenced the neonates' behavior.

The opportunity to follow neonatal behaviors as closely as this over the first month is a rare one; it provides us with many questions, if not answers. The fact that habituation and orientation were good in these babies and improved very little over time may indicate how well equipped they were for the early demands of their environment. These behaviors seemed to be least affected by early environmental influences. By contrast, motor development, which is highly prized by this marginally poor Indian culture, was reinforced early by the vigorous massage and oil bathing that was performed. These babies improved significantly in motor, autonomic, and reflex behavior over the first 30 days. To me, this represents an instance of how early the newborn reflects environmental practices that are adaptive for him or her. Regulation of state decreased over time and may represent a warning that the baby was being subtly overloaded in another area by all of this stimulation. Landers postulates that environmental factors are already influencing the baby's skill development by days 5–10.

Landers's chapter points again to the difficultiers in controlling for the variables of timing and performance of the NBAS on home visits—such as (a) being closely observed by persons from other cultures who have values we may not be aware of, and (b) trying to find the baby in an appropriate state for examination.

This is an excellent example of an in-depth study of infants which so far has followed the babies only into later infancy. The opportunity to evaluate the many maternal and intrauterine variables, to examine immediate perinatal practices against the curves of recovery in neonatal behavior, is a rare one. It gives us a depth of understanding to evaluate the adaptiveness of early child-rearing practices as they affect neonatal behavior in such a culture. The babies' motor "precocity" at 3 months on the Bayley exam (129 average) appears to be a reflection of the early emphasis on motor stimulation. Whether this will persist into later childhood and how these early influences predict to future competence will need to be tested with longer-term outcome studies on these same children. This study presents an instance of the optimal use of such an exam as the NBAS in another culture.

The Portuguese study of early contact between mother and baby and of rooming-in changed the practices of newborn nurseries all over Portugal. With the publication of this study by a leading pediatrician, many nurseries in Portugal have changed to the practice of rooming-in. Gomes Pedro's use of the NBAS as an outcome measure to prove the value to the baby of such attention as the presence of the mother presents an excellent example of being able to change medical practice with a research study.

The improvement in consolability, motor maturity, and orientation in the experimental rooming-in group already by day 3 demonstrate how the early environment can improve babies' behavior. By day 28, the continuing improvement in all these behaviors in the baby are reflected in significant gains on the part of the mother in affectionate behaviors, in consoling, and in attention. The fact that the third NBAS exam was performed in front of the mother was not accounted for as an intervention, but it should have been. The combination of early extended contact, of rooming-in, and of NBAS demonstration in the newborn period were defined by this excellent study. The opportunity to have three NBAS exams for evaluating both early environmental influences and outcome effects on the increasing organization in the neonatal period are well outlined by this study. The future use of the recovery curves as Gomes Pedro used them in the two groups studied will become a baseline for comparison of Portuguese babies to other genetic groups.

Hawthorne Amick's study used the baby's behavior in the NBAS to reflect the deleterious effects of present nursery care practices on the neonate. In her clinical research, she was successful in sensitizing the special care nursery to the effects on the baby and, indirectly, on the mother-infant relationship. Although her chapter is not explicit on how she utilized the baby's behavior to influence change, her efforts were rewarded. Increasingly, the NBAS is being used in clinical settings as a means of sensitizing parents to the competencies of their individual infants, thereby enhancing the parent-infant relationship.

Auerbach and her colleagues point out the many genetic and cultural influences of the behavior of the different genotypes in Israeli babies. Origin of the mothers (Eastern or Western), as well as their level of education, became the most significant variables that influence the outcome of these babies. In this report, a shortened verison of the NBAS-K was utilized only once, between 3 and 4 weeks of age, and in the parents' home with a parent present. Many items (pinprick, undress, reflexes) were omitted, so these data will not be comparable to other genetic groups of infants. However, within-group comparisons on this one exam showed improved alertness, motor maturity, and smiling in babies of higher-educated Eastern mothers. Eastern babies were more alert and self-quieted more than Western babies. High-education infants from homes in both Eastern and Western groups had improved motor maturity and quality of alertness. These differences are not considered of real importance and the authors point to the overall similarities in neonatal behavior as being more significant than the differences. They emphasize that differences cannot be overemphasized as being due to genetic differences. In such a small group, the differences, though significant, cannot be generalized to answer an important question.

The most interesting aspect of this chapter is the presentation of the concept of a mapping sentence, making explicit the interrelationships of intrauterine variables, perinatal variables, child-rearing practices, and mother-infant observations, especially in view of their relationship to the infant's performance (NBAS-K). This is done in an attempt to bring single items into appropriate clusters for analysis in relation to other prenatal, perinatal, and cultural variables.

The Auerbach et al. chapter reemphasizes the importance of collecting enough data in the neonatal period—both in numbers of subjects and in repeated measures in the neonatal period—to be able to assess the many variables that influence the neonate's behavior. Genetic endowment is a baseline variable only. Of course, the universals in neonatal behavior are more significant across genotypes than are variations. The intrauterine variables must be seen as interacting with genetic endowment; their influence is limited by genetic responsiveness. The problem becomes that of constructing a "map" or a systems approach that can encompass the relatively influential and those noninfluential variables affecting each genotype. To expect these to be reflected in markedly different neonatal behavior would be absurd. Yet to ignore even subtle variations would mean to miss the opportunity to evaluate such intrauterine and genetic influences. The complex influences of early environmental practices add even more complexity. We do not yet know which parent-infant practices are influential in producing change in the neonate. We feel that certain adaptive behaviors (autonomic, reflex behaviors, etc.) are less likely to be influenced by environmental change over the neonatal period and reflect inner stability, whereas orientation, habituation, and range of state may be highly correlated with experience in the newborn period. We need more comparable data both across cultures and within our own to begin to understand the complexity of organization and responsiveness which the neonate presents, as reflected by the NBAS.

Also, we need to improve our analytic techniques as well as our observational ones, rather than to give up our questions on the basis of null results. The Auerbach et al. study does not prove or disprove genetic differences, nor the intrauterine effects of lower SES, or of maternal education, although there are significant differences that do suggest that all three could be profitably studied in an Israeli group. In order to do that more effectively, several complete exams (NBAS plus NBAS-K) over time, a more complete data set of intrauterine and perinatal influences, as well as a more complete observation of early environmental caregiving practices, would be necessary. If I were to make statements about relative genetic and environmental variables in Israel, the NBAS observations would need to be complete and repeated in the newborn period so they could be compared to other cultural groups and to other prenatal and perinatal influences. The suggestion for mapping sentences for all groups is a valid attempt to lead us to a better approach to analysis of complex data.

Woodson and de Costa have studied 113 neonates of three cultures in Malayasia—the Chinese, Malay, and Tamil newborns. Although this study suffers in certain ways—one exam only, unequal amounts of maternal analgesia and anesthesia among the groups, having used the four a priori dimensions (Als et al., 1979) as outcome summary variables—it does point to some subtle differences among the groups of babies. Woodson and de Costa point to the problem of deciding what is a real difference in scores of single items when there is a 1-point difference allowed in reliability training. Their differences ranged from 1–1.8 points among the groups. We have felt that differences that are significant should not be ignored, regardless of the degree of score differences. These authors indicate a behavioral difference that has been observed in many babies by reliable observers, and a difference that might be even more significant in a larger sample. In this study, the same factors turned up differentiating the groups as have been found in many other studies—handling of state, orientation, and consolability. The comparative English group were even more different from the Malaysian groups; this adds to the reliance and credibility of the group differences. The a priori dimensions have not proven to be as sensitive as the more recent seven clusters described in Brazelton, Nugent, & Lester (1986). It would be interesting to reanalyze these data with the more sensitive clusters to see whether they brought out even more differentiation. If one accounts for prenatal variables such as minor differences in maternal blood pressure (presumably a reflection of maternal well-being) and in maternal analgesia, the neonatal differences are still seen to be significant among the Malaysian cultures. Woodson and de Costa do not set store by these minor but significant differences in newborn behaviors as differentiating among genotypic behaviors. We would agree that such subtle differences could be due to many other intrauterine and perinatal factors as well as the ones they have studied. Their study brings out the importance of establishing a set of universally accepted variables that could be collected in all studies in order to account for as many of these as possible. Then the neonate's behavioral differences as reflected by repeated exams over the initial adjustment period might give us a better idea of the subtle but real differences from one culture to another. In Malaysia, as anywhere else, it would be likely that neonatal differences might shape the responses of parents to their babies, and it would be an opportunity to define the relative contribution of genotypic and phenotypic differences in the baby toward influencing cultural practices among three such subcultures in the same country.

Muret-Wagstaff and Moore have studied a displaced Laotian culture, the Hmong, as they try to integrate themselves into an American culture. This people's strong cultural values have been assailed by war and suffering, by displacement to an entirely alien culture, and now by their attempts to adapt to a new culture in the U.S. Muret-Wagstaff and Moore studied Hmong and American Caucasian infants and their mothers living in inner-city Minneapolis. They used the NBAS on five occasions (days 1, 3, 7, 14, 28), the last three at home with parents observing. Only a minimum of observations was missed. This points to the observer's success in completing the exam if he or she is determined. Often the conditions for the exam at home were not optimal unless the observer waited for the baby to sleep. The Hmong tendency to administer frequent feedings made this even more difficult.

This was a richly conceived and executed study. The comparisons between Hmong and U.S. babies in seven clusters showed the Hmong as quieter motorically, less irritable, and more measured on state range, as well as higher on orientation to visual and auditory items. These constellations are ones we have found in Japan as well, and they seem to be characteristic of an Oriental genotype. In this study, their persistence for 28 days is of great interest and, since they are correlated with a higher degree of maternal sensitivity in the Hmong mothers, it may well reflect the mothers' sensitivity and respect for their babies' behaviors. The Caucasian mothers who were high in sensitivity to their babies reinforced them for improvement in performance over time, as did the Hmong mothers. This study is a fine example of a method for evaluating the relative range of genetic differences between the babies of two cultural groups. In order to clarify these differences, however, a multivariate analysis of the known prenatal factors (medication, smoking, diet, etc.) in the two groups would have been of value. Recovery curves to evaluate the changes in data sets over the five exams would heighten the differences between the two groups and would contribute to our understanding of the effect of the early child-rearing practices that were so different in the two groups. Last, one must be impressed with the strength of the Hmong culture and their respect for infancy. This value of the new mother cushions the baby for optimal development, as well as the parent for her job of early attachment. Muret-Wagstaff and Moore's description of this culture in transition provides a solid baseline for future studies of these Hmong babies as they integrate themselves into our culture.

Chisholm's chapter uses his study of Navajo Indian babies in the southwestern United States to raise many philosophical questions about the interaction between genetic endowment and the influence of the environment on shaping the outcome. He, as others, addresses the influence of the baby on the environment, although as a long-term adaptation to the stronger cultural forces that dominate adult behavior. In an unpredictable environment, the strategy for survival or short-term goals for the baby are uppermost (R-strategy). Hence, the phenotype of the baby is valued for its survival value. Individual differences are neither valued highly nor fostered in child-rearing practices. In a more sophisticated, predictable environment, attention is paid to reproducing valued parental genetic differences. Individuality of the baby is likely to be prized. Adaptive learning and educational techniques are utilized. (This is labeled a K-strategy.) Child-rearing practices reflect the stability and flexibility of outcomes that can be adaptive within the culture. The adaptations of the cultural group to fit the infant's characteristics are taken more seriously in this latter K-strategy. Using the NBAS with this group of Navajos, Chisholm found differences in their arousal patterns, in their adaptations to restraints, and in consolability, which he likened to the Oriental genotype found in other studies. The custom of using the cradleboard to restrain babies and to help them adapt to the mobility of their mothers seemed appropriate for these quiet, consolable babies. The practices seemed to be designed to shape them toward the accepted behaviors of quiet, respectful adults—gaze aversion, silence, respect for personal space, and individual autonomy. Navajo babies seemed to represent phenotypic adaptations in the uterus which are then reinforced to adapt to the demands of a besieged society, which the Navajos are. In turn, the earliest child-rearing practices reinforce and enhance the babies' temperamental capacities for survival in a demanding, unpredictable environment in which individuality is at risk and adaptation for survival is based on the group's ability for achieving short-term goals.

In all these excellent studies, the focus has been on the newborn baby's behavior as an outcome of a combination of the genetic endowment and the intrauterine influences that have already shaped it at birth. Our own model is that there are subtle but important differences in the way genotypic endowment is influenced by such intrauterine influences as diet, infection, drugs, placental insufficiency, and short-term and long-term insults that affect cellular replication (DNA) and cellular manufacture (RNA). Hence a detailed observation of the neonate for dysgenetic defects, for signs of immaturity relative to gestational age, for signs of inadequate stores of fat, and inadequate cellular contents, as represented by the ponderal index, as well as for stage of maturity (Dubowitz or Lubchenco) needs to be added to the behavioral profile of the newborn (NBAS) in order to assess intrauterine experience as that has shaped the genotype. Then, repeated assessments over the period of the neonatal adjustment will present us with a window into the coping patterns of neonates in each culture. As we link environmental observations of parent-infant interaction to these neonatal assessments, we can begin to get a better idea of the interaction of nature and nurture. The strategies with which neonates cope with their new environemnts may well predict to their later adaptations within their cultures. The opportunity to see neonates across many cultures and to begin to sort out the variables necessary to understand the variability of human behavior: This embodies the excitement of this book.

References

Als, H., Tronick, E., Lester, B. M., Brazelton, T. B. (1979). Specific neonatal measures: The Brazelton Neonatal Behavioral Assessment Scale. In J. D. Osofsky (Ed.), *The handbook of infant development* (pp. 188-215). New York: Wiley.

Brazelton, T. B., Nugent, J. K., & Lester, B. M. (1986). The Neonatal Behavioral Assessment Scale. In J. D. Osofsky (Ed.), *The handbook of infant development*. New York: Wiley.

Brazelton, T. B.; Nugent, J. K.; Lester, B. M. The Newborn Behavioral Assessment Scale. In J. Dsofsky (Ed.) *The Handbook of Infant Development*. New York: Wiley, 1987.

Crockenberg, S. (in press). Support for adolescent mothers during the post-natal period: Theory and research. In Z. Boukydis (Ed.), *Research on support for parents and infants in the post-natal period.*

deVries, M. & Super, C. (1978). Contextual influences on the Neonatal Behavioral Assessment Scale and implications for its cross-cultural use. In A. Sameroff (Ed.), Organization and stability of newborn behavior: A commentary on the Brazelton Neonatal Behavioral Assessment Scale. *Monographs of the Society for Research in Child Development, 43* (Serial No. 177), 92-101.

Dubowitz, L., Dubowitz, V., & Goldberg, C. (1970). Clinical assessment of gestational age in the newborn infant. *Journal of Pediatrics, 77,* 1-10.

Konner, M. (1977). Infancy among the Kalahari Desert San. In P. H. Leiderman, S. R. Tulkin, & A. Rosenfeld (Eds.), *Culture and infancy: Variations in the human experience.* New York: Academic.

Lester, B. M., Als, H., & Brazelton, B. (1982). Regional obstetric anesthesia and newborn behavior: A reanalysis towards synergistic effects. *Child Development, 53,* 687-692.

Miller, H.C., & Hassanein, K. (1973). Fetal malnutrition in white newborn infants: Maternal factors. *Pediatrics, 52.*

Author Index

Subject Index

A

Abortion, Puerto Rico, 117
Adoption, Puerto Rico, 117
Ainsworth Maternal Sensitivity Scale, 330–332
Anesthesia during Labor, *see* Labor and Delivery
Anthropometry Measures
 Nepal, 78, 80
 Peru, 14, 16
 South India, 177, 181–182, 197–199
 Switzerland, 29, 37
Anxiety and Stress with Premature Infant (Maternal), 240–242, 260–264
Apgar Scores
 Black American, 139
 Caucasian American, 327
 Hmong American, 327
 Malaysia, 300–301
 Nepal, 77–78
 Peru, 12
 Portugal, 225
 Switzerland, 29, 36
Attachment, mother–infant, 215–223

B

Bayley Scales of Infant Development, 50, 145, 170, 177–178, 197, 199–201, 277, 376
Birthweight of Newborn
 Efe (Zaire), 90–91, 95–96, 99–100, 103–105
 Great Britain, 237–239, 244–245, 258–259, 264
 Nepal, 65–67, 80
 Peru (Andes), 6–8, 14, 16, 20
 Peru (Lima), 16
 Peru (Puno), 20

 South India, 180–182, 191, 193–195, 197–200
Blood Pressure
 Hmong American mothers, prenatal and during labor, 333
 Malaysian mother during labor, 308, 313
 Malaysian newborn, 309–310
 Navajo mothers during pregnancy, 352–353
Bonding
 mother–infant
  Great Britain, 238–242, 263
  Portugal, 212, 214, 216–217
  South India, 173–174
Brazelton Neonatal Behavioral Assessment Scale (BNBAS), *see* Neonatal Behavioral Assessment Scale (NBAS)
Brunet–Lezine Infant Test, 277

C

Caesarean Delivery, *see* Labor and Delivery
Caretaking, Efe (Zaire)
 behavioral definitions of caretaking measures, 99
 birthweight and caretaking, 99–100
 group demography and caretaking, 100, 104
 relationship between infant fussiness at older ages and caretaking, 100–103
 relationship between newborn arousal, reactivity, and caretaking, 100–101
Cerro de Pasco, Peru, 10–12
Child-Rearing, *see* Cultural Beliefs and Child-Rearing Practices
Cohler's Maternal Attitude Scale, 123–125, 374
Communication of Infant, 223
Conception
 attitudes and beliefs, Nepal, 71
Continuous Care and Constant Contact Model, 89

393